THE EU AND THE WTO

The EU and the WTO
Legal and Constitutional Issues

Edited by
GRÁINNE DE BÚRCA
and
JOANNE SCOTT

·HART·
PUBLISHING

OXFORD – PORTLAND OREGON
2001

Hart Publishing
Oxford and Portland, Oregon

Published in North America (US and Canada) by
Hart Publishing
c/o International Specialized Book Services
5804 NE Hassalo Street
Portland, Oregon
97213-3644
USA

Distributed in the Netherlands, Belgium and Luxembourg by
Intersentia, Churchillaan 108
B2900 Schoten
Antwerpen
Belgium

First published 2001, reprinted 2002

Hart Publishing is a specialist legal publisher based in Oxford, England.
To order further copies of this book or to request a list of other
publications please write to:

Hart Publishing, Salter's Boatyard, Folly Bridge,
Abingdon Road, Oxford OX1 4LB
Telephone: +44 (0)1865 245533 or Fax: +44 (0)1865 794882
e-mail: mail@hartpub.co.uk
WEBSITE: http//www.hartpub.co.uk

British Library Cataloguing in Publication Data
Data Available
ISBN 1–84113–199–7

Typeset by Hope Services (Abingdon) Ltd.
Printed and bound in Great Britain by
Biddles Ltd, www.biddles.co.uk

Preface

THIS BOOK, which originates in a workshop held at the European University Institute in May 2000, seeks to address some of the complex issues arising in the context of the interaction between two powerful economic systems, the World Trade Organisation and the European Union. The growing anti-globalisation protest movements tend to present these two entities as similar or even identical phenomena: specifically, as the creations of unaccountable policy elites which are collectively undermining the traditional functions of the state in the name of free trade. Despite the undoubted political and rhetorical force of such depictions, they tend to ignore significant differences between the EU and the WTO in terms of their authority, scope, structure, impact, and modes of legitimation. They are two similar and related entities which are nonetheless quite different in key respects.

The essays in this volume attempt to explore and elucidate some of the legal and constitutional complexities of the relationship between the EU and the WTO, focusing particularly on the impact of the latter and its relevance for the former. The effect of WTO norms is evident across a broad range of European economic and social policy fields, affecting regulatory and distributive policies alike. The book does not purport to be in any way exhaustive or even to cover the key fields in this respect. Instead a number of significant areas have been selected to exemplify the scope and intensity of impact, including EC single market law, external trade, structural and cohesion funding, cultural policy, social policy, and aspects of public health and environmental policy. Secondly, various parts of the book seek specifically to examine the points of intersection—political, judicial and quasi-judicial—between the EU and the WTO which serve to mediate the relationship between their legal orders. And thirdly, most of the essays in the volume explore in one way or another the normative dimension of the relationship between the EU and the WTO. A number of the essays do so directly by investigating (and disagreeing over) the political and legal foundations of the WTO and the nature of its claims—often based on one of the twin discourses of constitutionalism and human rights—to legitimacy.

We are grateful to the Research Council of the EUI for financial support, to Susan Garvin for invaluable administrative assistance and to all who were present at the workshop for their participation and contributions.

GRÁINNE DE BÚRCA
JOANNE SCOTT

Contents

List of Contributors

Armin von Bogdandy is Professor of public law, European law, international economic law, and philosophy of law at Johann Wolfgang Goethe-Universität, Frankfurt am Main, and judge at the OECD nuclear energy tribunal.

Gráinne de Búrca is Professor of Law at the European University Institute in Florence.

Thomas Cottier is Professor of European and International Economic Law, University of Berne, and Director of the World Trade Institute.

Marise Cremona is Professor of European Commercial Law, and Deputy Director of the Centre for Commercial Law Studies, Queen Mary, University of London.

Piet Eeckhout is Professor of European Law and Director, Centre of European Law, King's College, London, and Visiting Professor at the College of Europe, Bruges.

Christophe Germann is attorney at law, DES (Geneva) and research fellow, World Trade Institute, Berne, Switzerland.

Peter Holmes is Jean Monnet Reader in the Economics of European Integration at the School of European Studies and Sussex European Institute, University of Sussex, and also teaches at the College of Europe, Bruges.

Robert Howse is Professor of Law the University of Michigan Law School.

Tilman Makatsch is a Doctoral Candidate at Johann Wolfgang Goethe-Universität, Frankfurt am Main.

Steve Peers is Reader in Law at the University of Essex.

Ernst-Ulrich Petersmann is Professor of International and European law in the Robert Schuman Centre of the European University Institute, Florence.

Miguel Poiares Maduro is Professor in the Faculdade de Direito da Universidade Nova de Lisboa, Co-Director of the Academy of International Trade Law (Macau) and external Professor at the Instituto Ortega y Gasset (Madrid) and the College of Europe (Natolin).

Joanne Scott is University Lecturer in European Law and Fellow of Clare College, Cambridge.

Elisabeth Tuerk is a Staff Attorney at CIEL's European office in Geneva, Switzerland.

Neil Walker is Professor of Law at the European University Institute, Florence.

Bruno de Witte is Professor of law in the Robert Schuman Centre of the European University Institute (on leave from the University of Maastricht).

1

The Impact of the WTO on EU Decision-making

GRÁINNE DE BÚRCA and JOANNE SCOTT

INTRODUCTION

EU LAWYERS HAVE long been used to reflecting on the fundamental ways in which the legal systems and governance of its component states have been affected by their membership of the European Union. In more recent times, however, and in particular since the conclusion of the Uruguay round and the signing of the World Trade Organisation Agreements in 1994, lawyers have been confronting an ever more complex set of questions concerning the relationship between the norms of the different systems and the impact of the strengthened system of international trade law, not only on the states individually but also on the EU and its institutions. There are numerous aspects to the question of how, in substantive and procedural terms, the process of political and legal decision-making in the European Union is affected by the EC's membership of the WTO. Most obviously, there are a number of hotly debated legal issues, which are addressed elsewhere in this book,[1] dealing with the exact legal status and effect of WTO norms within the European legal order. Secondly, there are sector-specific questions concerning how particular EC policies are affected by the provisions of the relevant agreements. Thirdly, there is a need to examine the extent to which and the way in which the EU institutions and organs seek to integrate the substantive obligations contained in the various agreements into their political and legislative processes. A fourth and significant dimension which is not often explored concerns the likely impact, not of the actual provisions of the WTO Agreements, but of the general principles and due process norms being developed by the dispute settlement bodies, not only on the adjudicative methods of the Court of Justice, but also more generally in the interpretation of provisions of the EC Treaties and EC law, in particular when the scrutiny of trade restrictions arises.

---

[1] See in particular the chapters by Armin Von Bogdandy and Tilman Makatsch, "Collision, Coexistence or Co-operation? Prospects for the Relationship between WTO Law and European Union Law" and Steve Peers, "Fundamental Right or Political Whim? WTO Law and the European Court of Justice" pp. 111 and 131.

This chapter concentrates primarily on the third and fourth categories outlined above, and it is divided into three parts. The first part considers briefly some of the points of comparison and contrast between the EU and the WTO, and the relevance of these similarities and differences for the interpretation and effect of the respective norms of each system. The second part takes two case studies in order to examine in more concrete detail some of the ways in which WTO norms and provisions are likely to influence and be integrated into the EC decision-making processes. The first of these examines the recently proposed amendment to the EC Cosmetics Directive and the second the ramifications of a pending legal challenge to a recent regulation on aircraft noise. The final part of the chapter considers the general principles and procedural norms evolving and being developed at WTO level, and at how these are likely to be relevant for the ECJ and EC decision-making bodies more generally.

PART ONE

The EU and the WTO share a number of obvious features: both are organisations established primarily to promote trade between states. They are also distinctively different in many respects: the WTO is a very broad multilateral organisation while the EU is a geographically limited regional entity. Further, even in the early stages when it was primarily a common market, the EEC has always been a more closely integrated collection of states than the GATT or the WTO. Nonetheless, the EEC's common market was modelled partly on the GATT, and many of the EC Treaty provisions clearly reflect this. Interesting comparisons can be drawn between the similar EC and GATT rules on matters such as internal taxation, discriminatory and non-discriminatory trade restrictions.[2] It might be expected that given the EC's experience in dealing internally with many of these same issues, such as the removal of discriminatory barriers to trade and of disproportionate regulatory restrictions between states, it would be well equipped to respond to such issues arising in the context of a multilateral trade organisation of which it is a member.

However, the situation is rather different where it is not a case of the EC enforcing the rules of the internal market against one of its own Member States, but instead the EC confronting a WTO-based challenge to one of its own regulatory measures. This is not only because of the tighter supranational legal and constitutional framework of the EC as compared with the looser international legal nature of the WTO and its agreements, but also because of the development of the EU into an entity which, in the scope of its aims and its policies, is much more than a trade organisation. Whatever the significance of the developments which emerged from the Uruguay round, with the move from GATT

---

[2] See J.H.H. Weiler, "The Constitution of the Common Market", in P. Craig and G. de Búrca, *The Evolution of EU Law* (Oxford: OUP, 1999).

1947 to GATT 1994 and the establishment of the WTO, it remains a fundamentally different entity from the European Union. Its aims and objectives, its political institutions, its dispute resolution bodies, its instruments, although sharing common features, are profoundly different in key respects from those of the EU. Two fundamental differences between the EC/EU and the WTO—in the legal-institutional dimension and the policy-substantive dimension—lie at the heart of many of the tensions created by the application of the rules and norms of the latter to the former. These are the dimensions which need to be borne in mind when examining the impact of the WTO on EC decision-making. Yet at the same time, a degree of convergence can be seen, and at the very least some degree of mutual influence between the two systems, in particular as the WTO Appellate Body, with its rather more juridical nature than the previous GATT panels, begins to develop its jurisprudence through the disputes coming before it.

The EEC began life, along with the other two Communities, primarily as a common market; an area which, although going beyond a free trade zone having established fairly strong legal and political institutions to achieve its goals, was not at the time the kind of ambitious political and constitutional entity which it undoubtedly is today. It has since that time expanded the scope of its policies from those such as trade, agriculture and competition to a whole range of others including environmental, consumer and social policy. Secondly, its institutions have also evolved, with an increasingly evident desire for greater constitutional legitimacy to underpin the extent and nature of its powers and functions. Despite the argument that its key or core priorities remain those of the promotion of trade, the multiple aspirations and tasks of the EU as a closely integrated regional organisation are unquestionable. Its role and functions are wide and general and the balance sought between the imperative of free trade and its many other policy goals is complex. Even if the EU's identity as a "polity" continues to be contested, the WTO, despite the institutional and substantive changes brought about by the Marrakesh agreements, falls well short of being described as such. It is an international organisation which shares many of the core aims and tasks set for itself by the EEC—primarily those of promoting trade and raising the standard of living—albeit not on a regional but on a worldwide basis, and it currently lacks both the aims and the instruments to become a more general organ of world governance. To use the terminology familiar in the EC context, its methods and instruments are those of negative rather than positive economic integration (if integration is not too loaded or too strong a word for the establishment between states of a high level of open trade and market access).

At the same time, it is true to say that the very success of the WTO in establishing a rule-of-law-based system for promoting multilateral trade/commerce has led to arguments for its development of more democratic institutions and more positive instruments, partly to build on the success of a co-operative international organisation which has allowed for the peaceful resolution of disputes between states, but more particularly in order to build respect for other values and policies more strongly into its framework. The centrality and strength of the most favoured nation (MFN), non-discrimination and other rules on trade effectively consign all other important policies—not only those such as environmental, health, social and cultural policies, but even the position of developing countries—to the status of exceptions which must be argued for within relatively strict constraints, rather than important competing or even co-equal policies in their own right.[3]

Nevertheless, while there may be no parallel at WTO level to the mixture of negative rules and positive policies seen in the EC's combination of Treaty-based trade-restriction prohibitions on the one hand and legislative harmonisation/co-ordination measures on the other, there is nonetheless a strong emphasis on the need to agree and to develop positive international standards through acceptable and legitimate processes as one crucial way of addressing the tension between the goals of trade liberalisation and legitimate regulation. The WTO does not have its own standard-setting processes and its own political institutions for developing such norms, but other international bodies such as the WHO, ISO, the Codex Alimentarius and the OECD are indicated as sources of guidelines and norms for Member States.[4]

It is interesting to observe how the EC, long used to grappling within its own borders with the problem of how to reconcile free trade provisions with national regulatory interests,[5] has responded when it has found itself in the position of the member whose regulatory policies—such as those on beef hormones, eco-labelling or aircraft noise—are open to challenge for compatibility with the rules of the trade organisation. This may be an analogy which has its limits, but it is not inapt to compare the response of the ECJ, in confronting the rules of this international organisation which are potentially in conflict with the rules and policies of the EC, with that of various national constitutional courts to the conflicts which have arisen between fundamental national norms and EC law. In denying the direct effect of the GATT and insisting on the effectiveness of its provisions within the EC legal order only in so far as the institutions of that order have expressed or implied that it should have such effect, the ECJ's response is not dissimilar in certain ways to the assertion of various national

---

[3] Even the new commitment to sustainable development in the preamble to the WTO agreement does not amount to any kind of environmental integration clause like that inserted into the EC Treaty, and the status of environmental issues continues to be that of an exception which must be positively argued for under the GATT, SPS (Application of Sanitary and Phytosanitary Measures) and TBT (Technical Barriers to Trade) agreements.

[4] Quite apart from the many legitimacy concerns and other objections to the way in which international standardisation comes about, the various difficulties encountered in trying to reach agreement on international standards frequently results in the postponement of and hindrance to the attempts by individual members in the meantime to adopt legitimate non-trade policies, such as, for example, the EC leg-hold trap Regulation 3254/91 [1991] OJ L308/1, and the long saga of its bringing into force and application.

[5] These are exemplified particularly clearly in disputes arising before the ECJ under provisions such as Arts. 28 and 30 of the EC Treaty.

courts that EC law does not take effect unconditionally and supremely within the national legal order, but must always be channelled through national constitutional provisions, which will themselves limit its applicability where it comes into potential conflict with basic norms of the national order. In each case there is an apparent desire on the part of the judicial authority on the one hand to respect the legal obligations of membership of the organisation—in the case of national courts by acknowledging the *prima facie* requirement to give primacy to EC law, albeit in their own way, and in the case of the ECJ by acknowledging the binding nature of WTO law—but equally an intention to impose limits on the way in which those obligations take effect, so as to protect the integrity of aspects of their own legal order and the perceived distinctiveness of the values and norms constituting their political order.

This judicial response is not of course open to the political institutions, to whom the direct effectiveness or otherwise of the WTO agreements has less immediate relevance.[6] A fundamental, if rather obvious, point to emphasise is that whatever controversy there may be over the exact legal status of WTO law within the EC legal order, there is no question about the binding nature of the former. The EC, as a signatory and party along with its Member States to the WTO, clearly accepts that the obligations contained in the WTO agreements are legally binding upon it. How those obligations are to be given effect may be a matter of dispute, but their binding nature is not, and it is primarily the political institutions which must give effect to WTO law. If an EC action or measure is found to conflict with the provisions of the GATT, for example, it is up to the Commission and the other institutions to find a solution which is compliant.

The European Commission found itself in relation to the beef hormones dispute, for example, in the position *vis-à-vis* the WTO bodies which various EC Member States have found themselves in *vis-à-vis* the EC, being sanctioned for introducing a public health and consumer protection policy which was apparently not sufficiently supported by scientific evidence. Whereas the ECJ had rejected a challenge to the ban on hormones in beef in the earlier *FEDESA* case,[7] the Appellate Body of the WTO reached a different conclusion in response to the complaints brought by Canada and the USA in finding that the measure was

---

[6] See e.g. the integration of WTO considerations into the preparatory stages on the decision-making process in the Commission's proposed amendment to Council Directive 76/769/EEC relating to restrictions on the marketing and use of dangerous substances: COM(99)620: "In order to be WTO consistent, restrictions on some azo dyes need to be well justified by health risk to the consumers". See more generally the WTO consciousness which infuses the Commission's recent Communication on the Precautionary Principle: COM(2000)1 final, and also its 18th Annual Report to the Parliament on the EC's anti-dumping and anti-subsidy activities: COM(2000)440. For other examples see the proposal for a regulation on foodstuffs hygiene: COM(2000)438, [2000] OJ C365/43, and in particular point 28 of the recitals concerning compliance with obligations in the WTO SPS Agreement.; also the proposed amendment to Article 19 of Directive 85/611 on collective investment in transferable securities (including non-European funds), COM(2000)329 [1985] OJ C311/302 which the explanatory memorandum deems necessary in order not to 'run counter to WTO commitments".

[7] Case 160/88 *FEDESA* v. *Council* [1988] ECR 6399.

not based upon an assessment of risk.[8] This dispute, and the difference between the balance struck, the method for striking the balance and indeed the result reached in the respective adjudicative tribunals of the EU and the WTO, raises obvious questions about the likelihood of the Appellate Body's approach influencing the ECJ's methods of interpretation and approach to judicial review. It does not necessarily raise the question whether the ECJ would or should treat WTO provisions as being directly or indirectly effective within the EC legal order. Rather the question is whether, when confronting a similar set of questions about the justifiability of a ban on hormone-treated beef in the context of the EC Treaty's prohibition on trade restrictions with its exception for legitimate public health measures, the ECJ might adapt its approach so as to make more likely a congruence between the two. However, as suggested above, this is not a one-dimensional legal question whether the ECJ as an adjudicative body should be influenced by or should adopt the reasoning of the Appellate Body in relation to a similarly structured set of legal provisions governing trade. It is a more complex question precisely because the values which underpin the assessment made by the Appellate Body and the ECJ respectively are likely to reflect both the institutional differences (for example in terms of the possible reasons for judicial deference to the lawmaking bodies) and the substantive normative differences (for example, in terms of the particular balance struck at EU level between trade liberalisation and public health/consumer concerns) between those two organisations.

PART TWO: TWO CASE STUDIES

We will now look briefly at two topical case studies, each of which exemplifies different aspects of the way in which WTO norms and provisions may affect EC decision-making, and at different stages of the decision-making process.

Case Study One: The Cosmetics Directive

Our first case study examines the attempt by the Commission, in drafting the latest proposed amendment to Council Directive 76/768,[9] to ensure that the measure is WTO-compliant, indeed arguably over-compliant.

---

[8] See J. Scott, "Of Kith and Kine (and Crustaceans): Trade and Environment in the EU and WTO" in J.H.H. Weiler (ed.), *The EU, NAFTA and the WTO: Towards a Common Law of International Trade* (Oxford: OUP, 2000) , S. Pardo Quintillán, "Free Trade, Public Health Protection and Consumer Information in the European and WTO Context" (1999) 33 *Journal of World Trade* 147 and R. Howse, "Democracy, Science and Free Trade: Risk Regulation on Trial at the WTO" (2000) 98 *Mich.LR* 2329.

[9] [1976] OJ L262/169. The Directive has so far been amended 25 times. For a consolidated version see: *http://europa.eu.int/eur-lex/en/lif/reg/en_register_133016.html*.

Council Directive 76/768 set out to approximate Member States' laws relating to the marketing and sale of cosmetics. Amongst other things it requires Member States to prohibit the marketing of cosmetics which contain any of the substances listed in the various annexes to the Directive.[10] Article 4(1) of the Directive also provided for a ban on the marketing of cosmetics containing ingredients or combinations of ingredients tested on animals.[11] The original date for the coming into force of the ban was after 1 January 1998, but this was postponed until after 30 June 2000 by the Commission.[12] The basis for this postponement was the insufficiency of progress in developing satisfactory methods to replace animal testing which are scientifically validated as offering an equivalent level of protection for the consumer. By March 2000, at the time of the Commission's proposals for an amendment to the basic Directive, only three alternative methods had been validated, of which two are available.[13] For this reason the Commission proposed a further postponement pending adoption and transposition of its additional far-reaching proposals for amendment of the Directive, amounting to a substantial modification of the original Directive.

The Commission explains in the explanatory memorandum to its proposal that the two overriding objectives of the proposed amendment are consumer safety and the reduction and the eventual elimination of animal suffering.[14] It also highlights the WTO as a restrictive context within which these aims have to be pursued: "However, for any measures to be effective and enforceable it is also necessary to take account of the constraints arising from compliance with international trade rules, in particular those of the WTO".[15] Four more precise objectives are then set out in the memorandum. The first is to introduce a definitive prohibition on the performance of experiments on animals for finished cosmetic products in the territory of the Member States of the EU. The second is to replace the previously envisaged ban on the marketing of substances containing ingredients tested on animals by a combination of the proposed prohibition on the *performance* of such experiments, and a requirement making mandatory the use of validated alternative methods, when they become available, for testing chemicals used in cosmetics. The third aim is to revise the Directive so as to make it WTO-compliant. One stage in this process seems to be again to

[10] It was one of the Commission's Directives adapting these annexes to technical progress which formed the subject matter of the well known case of Case 212/91, *Angelopharm GmbH* v. *Freie Hansestadt Hamburg* [1994] ECR I–0171, in which the ECJ held that the listing of substances in the Annexes should have been justified by a report from the Scientific Committee on Cosmetic Products and Non-food Products.

[11] This was introduced by Council Directive 93/35 [1993] OJ L151/32.

[12] See Commission Directive 97/18 [1997] OJ L114/43.

[13] These relate to the assessment of skin corrosivity and to the assessment of phototoxicity. See COM(2000)189 final, p. 2. At the stage of writing, the proposal is wending its way slowly through the legislative processes of the Community, with a common position not expected from the Council until summer 2001. In the meantime, on 3rd April 2001 following strong lobbying by animal welfare interest groups, the European Parliament on its first reading of the proposal rejected the Commission's view and reinstated the ban, arguing that it could be justified under the WTO.

[14] COM(2000)189 final, p. 2.

[15] *Ibid.*, p. 3.

postpone the entry into force of the ban on the marketing of cosmetics containing ingredients tested on animals, and which would have applied to all products including those from third countries, and not just those originating within the EU. At the same time the Commission has declared its intention to seek the mutual recognition, in co-operation with third countries, of test data from *in vitro/in vivo* studies. The fourth and final aim is said to be the improvement of information provided to the consumer, to allow the use, subject to EC guidelines, of claims indicating that animal testing has not been performed. The bottom line of the proposed amendment is expressed by the Commission in the following terms:

> "To take account of the need to comply with international law, the proposed amendment prohibits the performance of tests on animals on the territory of the Member States for the purpose of complying with Directive 76/768/EEC, but not the marketing of products which have been tested on animals. This represents an advancement for animal protection in the European Union. Moreover, the prohibition in its revised form cannot be challenged under WTO rules".[16]

This sentiment has been reflected in answers which the Commission has given to Members of the European Parliament on this subject.[17] The main concern expressed by the Commission in its current proposal in relation to the compatibility of the ban envisaged in the earlier Article 4(1)(i) of the Directive with WTO rules is that it is likely to contravene Article III.4 of the GATT, as constituting discriminatory treatment between like products originating within the EU and those originating outside. According to the Commission, since "the test method does not have any physical effect on the product, discrimination on this basis could be considered to be contrary to WTO rules".[18] The assumption here is that products physically constituted in the same way remain 'alike' regardless of differences in their method of production or harvesting. Consequently differ-

---

[16] *Supra* n. 14, p. 4.

[17] See, for example, Written Question E–0949/98 by Mark Watts (PSE) to the Commission (30 March 1998) on the subject of animal protection in GATT/WTO. The answer was given by Sir Leon Brittan on behalf of the Commission (7 May 1998) in the following terms:

"It is correct that the Community's obligations under the World Trade Organisation (WTO) agreement are among the elements which must be taken into account when developing any policies which may affect trade, including those mentioned by the Honourable Member. However, as the Honourable Member indicates the General agreement on tariffs and trade (GATT)/WTO does not prevent the introduction of measures which are considered to be necessary for the protection of animals on the territory of the Community.

It is the Commission's view that it cannot unilaterally impose the Community's welfare-based production standards on third countries. For example, WTO rules do not permit the Community to prohibit imports of cosmetic products on the sole ground that they have been tested on animals, even if the Community imposes such an animal-testing ban for marketing of Community products. Rather than proceeding to an import ban of such products, the Community should focus on the creation of multilateral standards for animal welfare. The Community should first try to convince its trading partners to modify their policies in the direction it thinks appropriate. Consumers in Europe should, moreover, be in a position to make an informed choice about the animal welfare aspects of the products they buy, for example through labelling schemes."

[18] *Supra* n. 14, p. 3.

ences in treatment predicated upon differences in production or harvesting techniques will represent discriminatory treatment under the GATT. Thus, to prohibit the importation of cosmetics from third countries which have been tested on animals while permitting the marketing and sale of EC-originating cosmetics which are alike, other than for the fact they were not tested on animals, would be unlawful under Article III.4. It was this kind of reasoning which underpinned the panel reports in the (in)famous *Tuna/Dolphin* "cases".[19]

The Commission goes on to say that it is "doubtful whether Article XX of the GATT could provide sufficient justification of this measure",[20] the implication being that it is unlikely that the measures in question could be justified as being necessary to protect animal life or health pursuant to Article XX(b).

This seems a cautious analysis on the Commission's part. Had it been committed to introducing a general ban on products which have been tested on animals, it could have pursued this more convincingly. It is, after all, far from settled that such a ban would contravene GATT (or other WTO agreements such as the Agreement on Technical Barriers to Trade) as the European Parliament's recent reinstatement of the ban during the co-decision procedure indeed suggests. As regards the conclusion that non-animal tested and animal-tested products are necessarily "like products" within the meaning of Article III.4, it should be pointed out that the panel reports in the *Tuna/Dolphin* "cases" were never adopted, and that this issue has not been addressed by the more recently established Appellate Body. The case for treating certain process-based product bans of this kind as capable of being compliant with GATT, Article III has recently been made—both on doctrinal/jurisprudential grounds and on policy grounds—by Howse and Regan.[21] In the subsequent Shrimps/Turtles "case" brought against the USA in relation to a process ban on "turtle-unfriendly shrimp", no attempt was made to argue the "like" product point under GATT, Article III, and the case instead focussed upon the scope of the Article XX exceptions and the "chapeau" thereof.[22]

Equally, in the case of an EU cosmetics ban, there seems to be no clear reason to conclude at the outset that, even if Article III did catch the ban in the first instance, it is "very doubtful" that it could be saved under the GATT, Article XX(b) exception, concerning the protection of the life and health of humans, animals and plants. The requirements of Article XX(b) and of the "chapeau" of Article XX do not seem insurmountable in a case such as this, and the EU's

---

[19] *United States Restrictions on Imports of Tuna* (1992) 30 ILM 1598 (*Tuna/Dolphin* I), (1994) 33 ILM 839 (*Tuna/Dolphin* II).

[20] *Supra* n. 14, pp. 3–4.

[21] R. Howse and D. Regan, "The Product/Process Distinction: An Illusory Basis for Disciplining 'Unilateralism' in Trade Policy" (2000) 11 *EJIL* 249.

[22] *United States—Import prohibition of certain shrimp and shrimp products (http://www.wto.org/english/tratop_e/dispu_e/distab_e.htm) Shrimp/Turtle* was concerned with Art. XX(g) on the conservation of natural resources. But the outcome of the case focused upon the manner in which the trade-restrictive measures had been applied and their compatibility with the 'chapeau' of Art. XX which must be respected regardless of which of the exceptions is invoked.

behaviour would not seem comparable to the impugned behaviour of the United States in *Tuna/Dolphin* or *Shrimp/Turtle*. Two points in particular point in the EU's favour. First, the ban would be on a "batch by batch" basis and not a country-wide basis. That is to say that only cosmetic products tested on animals would be prohibited, regardless of the overall regulatory policy of the exporting state. Market access to the EU would not be contingent upon a change of policy on the part of the government/legislature of the state of export, but merely upon the practices of the manufacturer in question. Secondly, the EC's position could be strengthened by the fact that it has been working on the development of alternative methods of scientific testing, in particular through the European Centre for the Validation of Alternative Methods and the application of those methods by the Scientific Committee on Cosmetic Products and Non-food Products, and apparently "stepping up negotiations within the OECD" to have these accepted at on a more global scale.[23] The circumstances are not necessarily comparable to those condemned in Shrimp/Turtle, where the USA was held to have failed to negotiate adequately with the various countries involved, or to pursue more actively the attempt to agree international standards—behaviour which resulted ultimately in the non-fulfilment of the requirements of the "chapeau" to Article XX.[24] The EU's apparent efforts to develop internationally acceptable alternatives to testing on animals, in addition to the fact that the coming into force of the ban was postponed pending the development of such methods, provides further evidence of caution before resorting to what the Appellate Body has called a "heavy weapon" of international trade.

There are a number of possible explanations for the Commission's retreat from a general ban in the EU on cosmetic products tested on animals. It is certainly possible that the Commission genuinely considers that such a ban could not be WTO-compliant, and has been influenced in contrast to the Parliament, to take a cautious view of the possibility for legally maintaining a process-based restriction on trade under those agreements. In this case the fear of the WTO may loom larger than the WTO itself. In view of the context of the EU's proposed ban, and the more nuanced approach of the Appellate Body in Shrimp/Turtle, where it focuses upon the circumstances of application of specific measures rather than drawing crude distinctions between entire categories of measures which may or may not be allowed, it is not improbable that the EU could apply such a ban in a manner which is WTO-compliant. At the very least the EU has a strongly arguable case. In this respect it is interesting to note that the EU has on its books other examples of import bans which would be less readily justifiable before the WTO dispute settlement bodies. To take just one example, Council Directive 91/629[25] provides that animals coming from outside the EU must be accompanied by a certificate issued

---

[23] See the Opinion of the Economic and Social Committee on the Commission's proposal, CES(2000)998, [2000] OJ C367/1 at para. 2.6.

[24] *Ibid.*, para. 166. For a full discussion of this, and more generally the due process requirements which are said to underpin the chapeau, see Part Three below.

[25] Laying down minimum standards for the protection of calves [1991] OJ L340/28.

by the competent authority of that country, certifying that they have received treatment at least equivalent to that granted to animals of Community origin as provided for by the Directive.[26] Thus, veal calves which have been raised in conditions which are not certified to be equivalent to those of the EU may not be imported into the EU; this regardless of whether the standard which has been breached could be said to be such as to impinge upon the quality of the product itself, or merely upon the "quality" of the circumstances in which it is produced or reared. It is, however, perhaps significant from the point of view of the GATT/WTO that this equivalence is demanded only in the case of live calves being imported into the EU, and not in the case of dead calves (i.e. veal) being imported into the EU. In view of this and other examples, and their dubious but uncertain legality, and in view of the fact that the Community finds itself on both sides of the process/product distinction debate,[27] it could be that ambiguity serves the Community well. It may be reluctant to seek clarification of the parameters of Articles III and XX in this respect for fear of the repercussions that might ensue beyond the sphere of animal testing in the cosmetics industry. On the other hand, attesting perhaps more to the fragmented or at least imperfectly co-ordinated institutional nature of the Commission rather than to a deliberate strategy of ambiguity or contradictoriness on the issue, the Commission's communication to the Council and Parliament on "Integrating environment and sustainable development into economic and development co-operation policy" indicates a bolder approach to the product/process distinction and, by implication, to the possible WTO-compatibility of a measure such as the cosmetics ban or related labelling requirements.[28]

One thing that is clear is that whatever the final outcome in terms of the construction of the relevant GATT norms, in the case of the cosmetics ban, this further (indefinite) delay, accompanied by a statement of intention to initiate bilateral talks with third countries on the mutual recognition of tests establishing alternative measures, would represent an additional important element in terms of likely WTO compatibility. Only time will tell, but it is not impossible that the Commission is preparing the ground for an eventual ban more carefully, in the light of the lessons of the Shrimp/Turtle dispute.

On the other hand, since there is room for argument on the legal point, it may be that the Commission's latest proposal reflects its own policy preferences (or at least the policy preferences of some of its directorates general), and that just

---

[26] Art. 8.

[27] It is interesting to n. that the EC intervened in the tuna/dolphin dispute in favour of the position of the complaining parties, against the United States.

[28] In this Communication the Commission declares that the EC is seeking in the course of the next WTO Round to "clarify", amongst other things, "the relationship between WTO rules and Non-Product Related Process and Production Methods requirements", including in the context of eco-labelling schemes. According to the Commission "the Round should reach a clear understanding that, subject to the necessary safeguards, there is scope within WTO rules to use market based, non-discriminatory, non-protectionist instruments to achieve environmental objectives and to allow consumers to make informed choices". See COM(2000)264, para. 4.2.1.

as Member States often point to the constraints imposed by EC membership to justify an unpopular measure adopted at home, the Commission may choose to do so *vis-à-vis* the WTO. This is particularly relevant in view of the European Parliament's strong and vocal preference—most recently evident in its amendment of the Commission's proposal—for the adoption of a ban on cosmetics tested on animals.

Perhaps most interesting, however, is the possibility suggested by this case study that the effect of the WTO on EC decision-making will not always be obvious or clear-cut. The question of the direct applicability or effectiveness of GATT norms within EC law on the one hand, and the nature of the response of the EC to a ruling of a panel or the Appellate Body against it on the other, are very clear instances of the impact of the WTO on EC decision-making. But the more indirect forms of impact, whereby some of the general and ambiguous norms in the WTO agreements, and the complex or inconclusive decisions of the dispute resolution bodies, are interpreted and applied by the EC political institutions in their formulation of legislative measures, are equally significant. It is very likely that those institutions will, as is arguably true of the Commission in its proposal to amend the Cosmetics Directive, add their own gloss or dimension to the rules within that interpretative process, which may lead, if not necessarily to over-compliance, at least to results which do not seem to flow inexorably from the text or jurisprudence of the WTO.

Case Study Two: The Regulation on Civil Subsonic Jet Aeroplanes

The second case study focuses upon a different stage of the decision-making process; not a pre-legislative attempt to "WTO-proof" the legislative measure, nor an *ex post facto* response to a finding of violation by the WTO dispute settlement bodies, but a challenge to an EC Regulation brought by a private party before a national court in the UK.[29] The challenge was brought by Omega Air Ltd., a company trading in aircraft, to Council Regulation 925/1999 on re-certified civil subsonic jet aeroplanes,[30] and the English High Court has referred a number of questions to the European Court under Article 234 TEC.[31]

In simplified terms, the Regulation provides that re-certified civil subsonic jet aeroplanes could no longer be registered or operated within the EU after a certain date.[32] Effectively, planes of this kind which meet the noise standards of

---

[29] Case C-27/00, R v. *Secretary of State for the Environment, ex parte Omega Air Ltd*, QBD, 25 November 1999.

[30] [1999] OJ L262/23.

[31] A preliminary reference in Case C–122/00 has also been made in similar terms by the Irish High Court from legal proceedings brought by Omega concerning the same Regulation, and a direct action Case T–165/99 was also initiated by it before the CFI. On 7 March 2000, the CFI ordered that the direct action be stayed pending the outcome of the preliminary reference proceedings before the ECJ.

[32] The Regulation had not yet entered into force, and although technically speaking the High Court was being asked to give a declaration about the legal effectiveness of the Regulation in the UK, the main aim of the action brought by Omega was to obtain a reference to the ECJ seeking a declaration of its invalidity.

Chapter 2 of the Chicago Convention on International Civil Aviation, but not the higher standards of Chapter 3 of that Convention, would no longer be permitted to be registered or operated in the EU. However, certain planes of this kind which, although not initially compliant with Chapter 3 standards, were subsequently modified to meet those standards would not be covered by the prohibition. According to Article 2 of the Regulation, "civil subsonic jet aeroplanes which have been modified to meet Chapter 3 standards by being completely re-engined with engines having a bypass ratio of three or more" would not be covered by the prohibition. Much of Omega's fleet of aeroplanes had been re-engined with a bypass ratio of less than three, and therefore would be caught by the Regulation. However, Omega's claim was that despite the lower bypass ratio, the re-engined aircraft nonetheless met the noise standards established by Chapter 3 of the Chicago Convention.[33]

The English High Court identified three grounds of invalidity of the Regulation, these being reflected in the question referred:

"Is Article 2(2) of Council Regulation (EC) No 925/1999 invalid insofar as it defines 'recertificated civil subsonic jet aeroplanes' so that re-engined aeroplanes 'with engines having a by-pass ratio of three or more' are not subject to prohibitions imposed by the Regulation but aeroplanes wholly re-engined with engines having a by-pass ratio of less than three are subject to prohibitions, having regard in particular to:

   (i)   the duty to give reasons under Article 253 of the EC Treaty;
   (ii) the general principle of proportionality;
   (iii) such rights as private parties may derive from the General Agreement on Tariffs and Trade and/or the Agreement on Technical Barriers to Trade?"

The third ground for invalidity concerned Article 2 of the Agreement on Technical Barriers to Trade (TBT) which provides, amongst other things, that WTO members must ensure that technical regulations are not adopted or applied with the aim or effect of creating unnecessary obstacles to international trade. The Article provides also that such regulations should not be maintained if the objectives can be addressed in a less trade-restrictive manner, and further that where relevant international standards exist, members must use them as a basis for technical regulations, and that such regulations are, where appropriate, to be based on product requirements based on performance rather than design. The use of bypass ratio (BPR) as a criterion of noise is a design feature rather than a performance standard, as indicated in Article 2 TBT, and the accepted "international standards", as included in the Chicago Convention, were expressed in terms of decibel levels rather than BPR.

---

[33] The primary aim of the EC Regulation, as set out in the preamble, was indeed to reduce noise emissions from aeroplanes. It is noteworthy that the Council did not include, in the preamble or recitals to the Regulation, the suggestion made by the Economic and Social Committee in its opinion on the measure, that the aim of the Regulation in prohibiting re-engined aircraft of the kind in question was not only that of reducing noise pollution, but also the likelihood that the use of new aircraft would increase passenger safety and public safety in general. See [1998] OJ C284.

Significantly, Omega did not pursue this third head of invalidity in its submissions to the European Court. This is stated to be due to the judgment of the European Court in *Portugal* v. *Council*,[34] albeit that Omega observes that were the European Court to take a different position in the future regarding to the status of the WTO Agreement (or specifically the TBT Agreement) in Community law, then Omega will rely on such a ground. Crucially, however, Omega contends that the TBT Agreement remains highly relevant to the first two grounds of invalidity.[35]

On the issue of reasoning Omega points to the failure in the Regulation to give reasons why a by-pass ratio criterion is used, and why this by-pass ratio was set at three. They argue that recourse to such criteria is arbitrary and unjustifiable, and incapable of rational justification, and that the criteria are not on any reasonable view relevant to achieving the declared objectives of the Regulation. In submitting that it was incumbent on the Community institutions to put forward reasons in respect of these criteria, Omega points to a number of factors. These include the fact that the Regulation departs from internationally agreed noise certification criteria under the Chicago Convention, and that they impose design (not performance) standards, allegedly in contravention of the TBT Agreement. Omega asserts that in the case of a departure from the accepted norm, it is necessary to have "a particularly thorough and convincing statement of reasons".[36] This reflects its further contention that, "at least in the normal case", EC law requires the Community to adopt internationally recognised standards where they are available, and that it similarly imposes a requirement that technical standards be set by reference to performance and not design criteria, and hence that the TBT Agreement merely reflects Community law in this latter respect. On the issue of reasoning, Omega's arguments were resoundingly accepted by the High Court, which held that the Regulation "appears to be wholly defective in its reasons".[37]

The High Court's own provisional conclusion on the adequacy of the reasons was clearly directly influenced by the provisions of the TBT Agreement, in the

[34] Case C–149/96 [1999] ECR I–8395 para. 47: "the WTO agreements are not in principle among the rules in the light of which the Court is to review the legality of measures adopted by the Community institutions".

[35] Omega further sets out submissions that the Regulation is in breach of the general principle of non-discrimination, and nn. that although the High Court rejected those submissions in making the reference, Omega draws them to the Court's attention so that the Court may consider them of its own motion. In addition this issue has been referred to the ECJ by the Irish High Court in the parallel Case C–122/00, and Omega will be making full submissions on the issue to the ECJ in those proceedings.

[36] Here they are drawing upon Advocate General Capotorti in Case 158/80, *Rewe-Handelsgesellschaft Nord GmbH* v. *Hauptzollamt Kiel* (Butterboats) [1981] ECR 1805. They also point to the judgment of the Court in this case, observing that three features were cited by the Court there in explaining why the Regulation concerned was invalid; the Regulation was a departure from the rules of the Common Customs Tariff, no reasons were given for that departure, and there was a contradiction in the recitals themselves. Omega argues that the same or similar features are present in the case at hand, including departure from the Chicago Convention and the TBT Agreement.

[37] *Supra* n. 29.

sense that the need for the EC legislature to give more satisfactory reasons to explain the use of BPR as a criterion for determining acceptable noise levels seems to have been based precisely on the failure to follow the indications in Article 2 of the TBT. The move from the use of decibel level, which had been used in international agreements and established in the Chicago Convention on International Civil Aviation, to the use of BPR therefore needed explanation, and in the English court's view had not adequately been explained. The implication of this part of the judgment is that whether or not the provisions of the TBT are directly effective, their existence imposes a procedural obligation on the EC institutions to provide an adequate explanation for the departure from the norms or guidelines laid down therein. This is evident from the judgment, where the national judge began by accepting the respondent's presentation of the jurisprudence of the ECJ concerning the degree of specificity required when reasons are being given for the adoption of a regulation—i.e. that where a regulation is concerned, the reasons may be confined to indicating the general objectives and the general situation which led to its adoption, and that it is not necessary to require a specific statement of reasons for each of the technical choices made by the institution, and yet he goes on later to conclude that the Regulation is defective in its reasoning for not explaining why a BPR standard was used.

Another interesting feature of the case is the fact that whereas the judge rejected the attempt to make the standards in the Chicago Convention relevant by means of an argument based on Article 307 EC,[38] he clearly treated them as being of indirect relevance via the combination of the provisions of the TBT Agreement on the one hand, and the Community requirement of giving reasons on the other hand:

> "It is the Chicago Convention and the International Civil Aviation Organisation ICAO which have set international standards based on decibel measurement. . . ".

The judgment then set out the relevant provisions of Article 2 of the TBT, including the stipulation that members shall use relevant international standards as a basis for technical regulations, and continued:

> "I am quite satisfied that the relevant international standards are the Chicago Convention. It seems to me that if it is decided to move from the decibel related method to a BPR method, some sort of explanation is required . . . the Regulation seems to be wholly inadequate in its reasons".[39]

---

[38] Art. 307 EC effectively declares that the obligations deriving from agreements concluded before the date of accession to the EC between one or more Member States and one or more third country are not to be affected by the provisions of the EC Treaty. This Art. has not given rise to much success before the ECJ when it has been invoked to establish the priority of the provisions of certain international agreements over EC law, including in the infamous banana litigation, and after the judge in this case dismissed it, it did not form part of the questions referred to the ECJ under Art. 234.

[39] *Supra* n. 29.

While this clearly falls short of giving effect either to the aircraft noise standards contained in the Chicago Convention or to the provisions of the TBT agreement on technical regulations, the imposition, through the reasoning requirement, of an obligation on the EC institutions to explain why the standards established in the main international agreement on aircraft noise have not been used, when the TBT agreement by which the Community is bound actually specifies that appropriate international standards of this kind should be used, clearly makes the provisions of both agreements highly relevant for the Community's decision-making process, in particular if the English court's approach is followed by the ECJ.[40]

Omega's arguments in respect of breach of the general principle of proportionality are not entirely dissimilar to those outlined above in respect of the reasoning requirement. Their fundamental contention is that there is no rational relationship between the means deployed by the Regulation and the main aim which it pursues; namely the control of noise emissions at Community airports. They argue moreover in favour of a stricter standard of proportionality review in a case such as this where the Community has departed from internationally agreed standards and from the terms of the TBT Agreement. Thus, the TBT Agreement, although acknowledged not to be of direct effect nor to constitute a standard against which the European Court will assess the legality of Community acts, is invoked as a means of increasing the rigour with which established grounds of review will be applied, and of constraining the degree of discretion which these permit the Community institutions. In the event that the European Court accepts Omega's arguments, and indeed the conclusions of the English High Court, it will be apparent that an absence of direct effect on the part of the WTO Agreement should not necessarily be equated with an absence of relevance or effect within the European and national courts. Particularly important in this respect, as noted above, is the manner in which substantive obligations which inhere in the WTO package may be translated by courts and transformed into procedural requirements; notably but perhaps not only a duty to give reasons. It is with this issue of procedural requirements and the WTO Agreements that this next section is concerned.

PART THREE: ORIGINS AND IMPACT OF PROCEDURAL DUE PROCESS NORMS
DERIVING FROM GATT/WTO

This part of the chapter considers the decision of the Appellate Body (AB) in the Shrimp/Turtle dispute,[41] and considers the way in which procedural due process

---

[40] The rash of cases before the CFI and the ECJ in recent years which use a strong requirement of reasoning as a means of integrating other potentially more controversial norms into EC decision-making procedures (such as the principle of transparency and access to documents, before that was actually enshrined in the EC Treaty—see, e.g., Case T–105/95, WWF v. Commission [1993] ECR I–5721 and Case T–105/95, Svenska Journalistforbundet v. Council (Swedish Journalists case) [1998] ECR II–2289, which suggests that it is quite likely to do so.

[41] Supra n. 22.

norms were invoked by it in condemning the manner in which the relevant US import restrictions had been applied. The intention is to examine both how these norms were developed within the specific doctrinal context of the GATT agreement, and what their relevance is likely to be for the EC decision-making process.

Put briefly, the *Shrimp/Turtle* case concerned US prohibitions on the importation of shrimp or shrimp products from countries which had not been certified pursuant to so-called Section 609 which forms part of the domestic public law of the USA. This provided that certification was to be granted to countries with a fishing environment which did not pose a threat to the incidental taking of sea turtles in the course of shrimp harvesting, and hence in which there was no risk, or only a negligible risk, that sea turtles would be harmed by shrimp trawling. It provided further that certification could be granted to harvesting nations which provided documentary evidence of the adoption of a regulatory programme governing the incidental taking of sea turtles in the course of shrimp trawling that was comparable to the US programme, and where the average rate of incidental taking of sea turtles by their vessels was comparable to that of the USA.

The AB accepted that the above regime was of a kind which is capable of falling within the GATT, Article XX(g), exception. It related to the conservation of exhaustible natural resources, and was made effective in conjunction with restrictions on domestic production or consumption.[42] Nonetheless, the AB went on to find that the manner in which the measures had been applied was such as to render them incompatible with the "chapeau" of Article XX. This requires that such measures not be applied in a manner which would constitute a means of arbitrary or unjustified discrimination between countries where the same conditions prevail, or a disguised restriction on trade. A wide range of factors contributed to its findings in this respect including, for example:

—the failure of the USA to engage in serious across-the-board negotiations with third countries, with a view to concluding bilateral or multilateral agreements. Thus the measures were applied in a manner which was unilateral and non-consensual;

—the rigidity with which officials made certification determinations, and the existence of little or no flexibility regardless of how appropriate the US model harvesting programme was for the conditions prevailing in the exporting state;

—the failure of the USA to respect standards of basic fairness and due process in the application of Section 609. Particularly important in this respect were the absence of any opportunity for the applicant to be heard or to

---

[42] This of course presupposes that the measures in question were contrary to GATT in another respect. The panel report found the measures to be contrary to GATT, Art. XI, and this finding (though contentious, especially as regards its relationship with GATT, Art. III) was not appealed by the USA.

respond to arguments before a certification decision was adopted, the failure to render a formal reasoned decision and to notify the party of it, the absence of any procedure for appeal or review of a decision to deny certification, and overall the "singularly informal and casual" nature of the procedure, making it impossible for applicants to know whether Section 609 was being applied in a manner which is fair and just.

This chapter will turn first to a preliminary issue in respect of the AB's findings in this respect. This relates to the link between the procedural defects identified by the AB and the concepts of unjustified and arbitrary discrimination which underpin the Article XX "chapeau".

The AB findings are somewhat ambivalent as regards the role played by the concept of unjustified or arbitrary discrimination. Its language is such on occasion as to suggest the emergence of standards for the application of import restrictions which operate independently of any discrimination threshold. Thus, the AB speaks of the principle of good faith, and the requirement which flows from this that the right to invoke GATT exceptions be exercised "reasonably".[43] Elsewhere, it speaks of abuse or misuse of the provisional justification made available by Article XX(g), observing that a measure may amount to such "not only where the detailed operating provisions of the measure prescribe the arbitrary or unjustifiable activity, but also where a measure, otherwise fair and just on its face, is actually applied in an arbitrary and unjustifiable manner".[44] It is self-evident that measures may be applied in a manner which is arbitrary or unjustified, or indeed in a manner which is not reasonable, while not giving rise to discrimination which is arbitrary or unjustified. There is a clear difference between measures which are arbitrary and/or unjustifiable, and those which discriminate arbitrarily and/or unjustifiably.[45]

---

[43] Para. 158.

[44] Para. 160.

[45] At para. 150 the AB states that, as decided in the US Gasoline case, the nature and quality of the "discrimination" referred to in the "chapeau" to Art. XX "is different from the discrimination in the treatment of products which was already found to be inconsistent with one of the substantive obligations of the GATT 1994, such as Art I, III or XI", because "the provisions of the chapeau cannot logically refer to the same standard by which a violation of a substantive rule has been determined to have occurred". It is arguable, however, that a different interpretation of the phrase in the "chapeau" to Art. XX is possible. Why is it illogical for the "discrimination" therein to refer to the discrimination which established the breach of one of the other GATT norms? An equally plausible interpretation is that Art. XX exists precisely to exempt measures which have been found to discriminate, but that the scope of the exemption is exhausted where the discrimination in question becomes arbitrary and unjustifiable. Thus only a reasonable, proportionate, necessary etc. degree of discrimination will remain within the bounds of Art. XX. The terms "arbitrary" and "unjustifiable" are sufficiently broad and open to encompass exactly the sorts of procedural standards of fairness and rationality which the AB goes on to require of the USA in this case. And if it were accepted that the discrimination referred to in the "chapeau" simply refers to the nature of the measure which has already been found to breach one of the other substantive GATT provisions, then the focus on the limits of the exception need not be on differential treatment as such, but rather on the excessive or unnecessary or arbitrary nature of the way in which the respondent Member has chosen to act. Of course, if the GATT over the years since its original drafting—and just like the EC Treaty before it—has gradually been "bent" to address not only *de jure* and *de facto* discrimination, but also

Elsewhere, however, the AB is more careful to assert the existence of a link between the behaviour in question and the (unjustifiably or arbitrarily) discriminatory outcome. Hence the AB cites differing treatment as regards "phase-in" periods for compliance, and technology transfer efforts, as factors contributing to a finding of unjustifiable discrimination. The rigid and unbending standards according to which the possibility of certification is assessed are conceived as discriminatory because they imply the same treatment for countries characterised by diverse conditions, and do "not allow for any inquiry into the appropriateness of the regulatory program for the conditions prevailing in those exporting countries".[46] Also important to the assessment of the AB is the failure of the USA to engage in "serious, across-the-board negotiations" before instituting the regime in question. This "failure to have prior consistent recourse to diplomacy . . . produces discriminatory impacts on countries . . . with which no international agreements are reached or even seriously attempted".[47] The fact that the United States negotiated seriously with some, but not with all other Members is found to be discriminatory in effect and unjustifiable.[48] Finally the AB, in focussing upon the lack of basic fairness and due process accorded to those whose applications for certification are rejected, concludes that these countries are (arbitrarily) discriminated against *vis-à-vis* those Members which are granted certification.[49]

It is clear that there is a tension inherent in the AB report. It shifts somewhat uneasily between recourse to standards which are not predicated upon an assessment of comparative treatment—basic fairness, just treatment, reasonableness—to notions of discrimination which by definition require a comparative perspective. In so far as the AB, straining to remain within a certain interpretation of the text of the Article XX "chapeau", focuses upon a different kind of discrimination from that inherent in the breach of the substantive GATT Article,[50] this emerges at times as a less than adequate or convincing peg upon which to hang its various wide-ranging due process concerns. Not only is it not always clear what the factual basis of the discriminatory conduct is (notably as regards the comparison between the fairness and due process treatment of those whose applications are successful and those whose are not), but in normative terms one is left with the feeling that in many respects it is not the discrimination as conceived by the AB which renders the US behaviour objectionable, but the behaviour itself.

---

obstacles to trade which seem genuinely non-discriminatory in nature (Weiler (1999), *supra* n.2), then the focus on "discrimination" in the "chapeau" to Art. XX would indeed have to relate to the manner in which one of the non-trade-based regulatory policies in paras. (a)–(j) was being pursued or applied, unless the AB chose to focus instead on the notion of a "diguised restriction" on trade.

[46] Para. 165.
[47] Para. 167.
[48] Para. 172.
[49] Para. 181.
[50] See *supra* n. 45 for discussion.

Thus, for example, the failure of the United States to negotiate seriously with some of the parties concerned is surely objectionable in and of itself, rather than on the basis that it did pursue serious and effective negotiations with some parties. Had the USA treated all WTO members with the same high-handed disrespect, negotiating with none rather than some, its behaviour would, if anything, have been worse rather than better. The various international law instruments which the AB cites in order to highlight the importance attached to multilateral solutions to environmental problems, especially where the resources in question are situated outside the territory of the importing states, are not predicated upon the logic of discrimination, but upon the need for international co-operation and consensus. Even-handedness in respect of a failure to negotiate would not in any sense mitigate the wrong-doing. Similarly, had the USA denied basic due process to all applicants, including those who were by chance successful (and in certain respects this does indeed seem to have been the case in the Shrimp/Turtle dispute), thus pursuing an entirely consistent, though fundamentally procedurally flawed, approach, few would argue that this ought to attenuate, as opposed to exacerbate, the legal position of the USA.

It is interesting to observe in this respect that the AB notes that GATT, Article X.3, bears upon the matter at hand. This lays down certain due process requirements relating to the uniformity, impartiality and reasonableness with which the relevant measures are to be administered, and to judicial, arbitral or administrative review and correction of the administrative action concerned. This is conceived of by the AB as establishing minimum standards for transparency and procedural fairness, and although the AB does not purport to apply this provision specifically in the context of the case at hand it notes that:

> "Inasmuch as there are due process requirements generally for measures that are otherwise imposed in compliance with WTO obligations, it is only reasonable that rigorous compliance with the fundamental requirements of due process should be required in the application and administration of a measure which purports to be an exception to the treaty obligations of the Member imposing the measure and which effectively results in a suspension *pro hac vice* of the treaty rights of other Members".[51]

This, like the previous arguments, militates strongly in the direction of an approach to standards of procedural fairness and due process which goes beyond the non-discrimination premise. After all, as noted, Article X.3 is predicated, *inter alia*, upon the concept of reasonableness which operates without reference to considerations of discrimination.

What is clear, then, is that procedural factors played an important, perhaps crucial, role in the AB's report. The failure of the United States to engage in serious, comprehensive, negotiations emerges as one such factor, alongside a more general conception of procedural fairness and due process. What is less clear

---

[51] Para. 182.

is the basis upon which they did so, and in particular the issue of whether their relevance was confined to contributing to a finding of unlawful discrimination within the meaning of the Article XX "chapeau", or whether they might be regarded as having assumed an independent life of their own. As noted above, the AB's report is somewhat ambivalent in this respect. Moreover, in so far as it does posit a link between procedural deficiencies and discrimination, due partly to its conviction that the reference to discrimination in the "chapeau" must be something different and separate from the discrimination inherent in the breach of the substantive GATT obligation,[52] its reasoning is at times somewhat strained, particularly as regards basic fairness and due process considerations. Yet, whatever the specific intention of the AB in this report, and regardless of the AB's not always entirely convincing insistence that it is through the lens of discrimination that such procedural values find expression in GATT Article XX, the report serves to highlight the broader issue of the proper place of process considerations in assessing the legality of member restrictions on trade. This is a debate with important implications for the EU—which can be illustrated, for example, if we apply it to the context of the Cosmetics Directive discussed above, and to the need for the EC to pursue in a fair and comprehensive way the search for consensus on scientifically validated alternatives to animal testing before introducing a ban—and also for the premises and legitimacy of the evolving WTO system. The relevance of the debate for the aircraft noise case is also clear. There, in the context of a legal system which denies the WTO direct effect, it is proposed that the WTO, and the internationally agreed standards to which general reference is made in the WTO and on which derogations are often required to be based, enter that same legal system by means of a procedural route, especially in the guise of the reasoning requirements.

Before turning to consider these issues more generally, a preliminary observation may be made. The AB does not offer a convincing basis in law for the specific values which it emphasises. In terms of the duty to negotiate, it points to the "very policy objective" of the measure in question, and to a range of international environmental instruments which offer sustenance in this respect in view of the factual background of the case at hand.[53] More generally, in construing the Article XX "chapeau", the AB invokes the principle of good faith, one expression of which it considers the "chapeau" to constitute. It notes that this principle is both a principle of law and a general principle of international law, and that it conceives its task as being to interpret the "chapeau", "seeking additional interpretative guidance, as appropriate, from the general principles

---

[52] *Supra* n. 45.

[53] Para. 168. Two of these instruments, the Rio Declaration on Environment and Development and Agenda 21, are referred to in the Decision on Trade and Environment which provided for the establishment of the WTO Committee on Trade and Environment. In addition, the WTO members in the Report of the Committee on Trade and Environment themselves state a preference for multilateral solutions to environmental problems of a transboundary or global nature, namely solutions based on international co-operation and consensus.

of international law".[54] It offers, in a footnote, some suggestions for further reading on this general principle, including references to cases before the International Court, and a specific quotation from an academic work on this subject. This quotation is suitably vague, equating *bona fide* with "appropriate and necessary" and "fair and equitable".[55] Thus, almost from nowhere the AB is articulating a range of standards, in this case procedural standards, compliance with which is to be regarded as a prerequisite for lawful derogation from a GATT obligation. It remains uncertain to what extent these standards remain specific to the circumstances of the case at hand, and to what extent they may be generalisable to additional categories of cases.

It is thus clear that there is considerable uncertainty about the origin and scope of the due process norms invoked by the AB in the Shrimp/Turtle ruling. It is this very flexibility which renders the development potentially so important. Such is the malleable nature of the concepts employed (basic fairness and due process, for example) that the creative potential which underpins them is vast. One only need look to the jurisprudence of the US Supreme Court, and other transnational regimes such as the European Convention on Human Rights (ECHR), and to witness their expansion of the scope and application of due process and procedural constraints, to appreciate the degree of authority that this development implies for the AB in its interpretative role.

It is interesting to observe, as does Marise Cremona in her chapter in this book, that a parallel development has to some extent taken place in the EU.[56] The European Court in developing general principles of Community law has looked both to process and to substance. Thus, for example, it has developed general principles pertaining to the protection of legitimate expectations, legal certainty, and to the concept of a fair hearing and rights of the defence. The duty to give reasons is already inherent in the EC Treaty in so far as it concerns Community institutions, but has been construed by the European Court as binding also on the Member States when they are acting within the scope of Community law. Not only have these general principles been developed on a legal basis which is textually insecure, as in the WTO example, but there are similarities too in terms of their scope of application. Thus, the general principles are binding not only upon the Community's own institutions, but also upon the Member States when they act to implement Community law or, significantly for our purposes, to derogate from one of the fundamental freedoms guaranteed by the Treaty. Thus, where a Member State seeks to depart from the principle of free movement, in the name of one or other societal interest recog-

---

[54] Para. 158. Cf. *Classification of Certain Computer Equipment* where the AB rejected the panel's conclusions that interpreting the meaning of a tariff concession in the light of the "legitimate expectations" of the exporting members is consistent with the principle of good faith interpretation under Art. 31 of the Vienna Convention.

[55] See n. 156. The work which it cites is B. Cheng, *General Principles of Law as Applied by International Courts and Tribunals* (London: Stevens and Sons Ltd. 1953).

[56] M. Cremona, " Neutrality or Discrimination? The WTO, the EU and External Trade" p. 151.

nised by Community law, it may do so only in a manner which is consistent with the general principles of Community law. And in fact the proportionality test, encompassing notions of rational connection, necessity and non-arbitrariness, was developed in a number of early ECJ cases in relation to the EC Treaty's version of the Article XX chapeau, i.e. the provision in Article 30 (ex Article 36) that the exceptional measures permitted by that provision "shall not, however, constitute a means of arbitrary discrimination or a disguised restriction on trade between Member States".[57]

That said, although it is clear that parallel developments have taken shape in the EU and WTO in this respect, important differences have already emerged in the nature of the norms which are deemed to underpin attempts to derogate from rules in one or other of the two systems. Thus, for example, while the concept of legitimate expectations is one of the most important and most often invoked general principles of Community law,[58] the AB has shown a marked reluctance thus far to accord it a role in the interpretation and application of the WTO Agreement. Thus, for example, in *EC Classification of Certain Computer Equipment* the panel invoked the concept of (substantive) legitimate expectations in assessing whether the EC, in classifying LAN equipment as telecommunications equipment rather than ADP machines, had acted inconsistently with GATT Article II.1 by according LAN equipment treatment less favourable than that laid down in a tariff concession. The United States argued, on the basis of the negotiating history and the actual tariff treatment accorded to LAN equipment during the relevant negotiations that it reasonably expected the EC to treatment this equipment as ADP machines. The panel accepted that legitimate expectations are a "vital element in the interpretation of Article II and tariff schedules". While accepting that the circumstances of the conclusion of a treaty may be a supplementary means of interpretation of that treaty,[59] and that the subsequent classification practice of the EC is a relevant factor, the AB on the contrary found that the (subjective) legitimate expectations of an exporting member are not relevant in assessing whether a violation of Article II.1 has occurred. It did so on the basis of its interpretation of the GATT and of the Vienna Convention, observing that:

> "The purpose of treaty interpretation under Article 31 of the *Vienna Convention* is to ascertain the *common* intentions of the parties. These *common* intentions cannot be

[57] It is true that in the EC context, however, the limits on unilateral action by Member States deriving from procedural requirements of negotiation and consultation with the Commission and with other Member States are more often than not specifically imposed by secondary legislation which aims to harmonise the rules in the sector in question, rather than being developed through the kind of reasoning seen in AB shrimp report: see e.g. Case 28/84, *Commission* v. *Germany* [1985] ECR 3097 on Germany's attempted import ban on feeding-stuffs for calves containing certain additives.

[58] T. Tridimas, *General Principles of Community Law* (Oxford: OUP, 1999) and S. Schønberg *Legitimate Expectations in Administrative Law* (Oxford: OUP, 2000).

[59] Pursuant to Art. 32 of the Vienna Convention.

ascertained on the basis of the subjective and unilaterally determined "expectations" of *one* of the parties to a treaty".[60]

That differences in approach will emerge is in a sense inevitable given the very different conceptual basis of the EC development relative to that in the WTO. Many of the procedural norms in question arise in the context of the European Court's jurisprudence on the protection of fundamental human rights; a conceptual basis which thus far is lacking in the AB, and which took shape in the EU in very particular circumstances concerned with reinforcing the supremacy of Community law. Without engaging here in a detailed analysis of the different process norms protected in the two legal orders under discussion, it is nonetheless important to highlight the legal issues which arise in the EU as a result of differences in conception in this respect.

If we are not entirely misconceived in our reading of the GATT/WTO there appear to be a number of situations in which these procedural-type norms developed by the AB would be of relevance before the European Court, if the European Court is to play a role in ensuring the GATT/WTO compatibility of Community law and/or national law.

First, and most obviously, in the assessment of the legality of Community measures restricting third country trade.

Secondly, in the context of the Community's common import regulation,[61] and specifically Article 19(2) thereof. This provides, or is construed as providing, specific authorisation to the Member States in the context of the operation of the common commercial policy for the maintenance of such national measures which are necessary to ensure protection of one of the societal interests laid down. The list of such interests is identical to that in Article 30, though the final sentence to Article 30 is not replicated in the context of the common import regulation. It has been argued that "for reasons of consistency", "mandatory requirements in the meaning of the *Cassis de Dijon* case law should be added" to this list;[62] thus here the European Court is placed in the position of assessing the legality of Member State restrictions on third country trade. It does so on the basis of the Common Imports Regulation which is, in turn, closely related to the

---

[60] *Supra*, n. 54, *European Communities—Classification of Certain Computer Equipment*, para. 84. It is interesting that the AB equated legitimate expectations with a purely subjective conception of what the USA had come to expect on the basis of the tariff schedule and negotiations, whereas the USA in its arguments talks of the reasonable (connoting an objective assessment) expectations of the partners (plural) of the member which made the concession. Generally, though, the scepticism of the AB as regards the notion of legitimate expectations is indicated by its propensity to place the term in inverted commas whenever reference is made to it.

[61] Council Regulation 519/94 on common rules for imports from certain third countries [1994] OJ L67/89.

[62] P. Demaret, "Environmental Policy and Commercial Policy: The Emergence of Trade-Related Environmental Measures (TREMs) in the External Relations of the European Community" in M. Maresceau, *The European Community's Commercial Policy after 1992: the Legal Dimension* (The Hague: Martinus Nijhoff, 1993) p. 337. If consistency is indeed to be achieved then this would imply that attempts to apply this regulation in a manner which is consistent with GATT/WTO will spill over to Arts. 28–30 TEC.

EC Treaty free movement rules and to its internal market objectives.[63] In construing the Common Imports Regulation (and by implication the free movement rules more generally, if these two regimes are not to diverge) the European Court must, from a WTO perspective, do so in a manner which is WTO-compliant.

Thirdly, in the application of Articles 28–30 TEC. In so far as a Member State restriction on intra-Community trade applies to all goods in free circulation, it will also restrict the entry of third country goods. Any derogation from the principle of free movement within the internal market must be GATT/WTO-compliant in so far as it relates to third country goods. As the notion of a customs union demands, the same rules are in practice applied to all goods in free circulation regardless of their origin.[64] Thus if the Article 30 derogation is not to be applied in such a way as to breach GATT/WTO norms it will have to be read in a manner which is consistent with the obligations this imposes, including the due process obligations articulated in the Shrimp/Turtle ruling. Of course this point takes us well beyond the single issue of the nature of the Community's general principles and the question whether these might be anticipated to evolve in the light of developments in the WTO. It raises the much broader issue of the capacity of WTO law to "spillover" to the Community's legal order, not merely in respect of its formulation of external trade policy, but in respect of its single market objectives. It does, however, serve to highlight that in so far as such spillover does occur, it may be anticipated to be wide-ranging

---

[63] See, e.g., the recital in the preamble to Regulation 519/94: "Whereas completion of the common commercial policy as it pertains to rules for imports is a necessary complement to the completion of the internal market and is the only means of ensuring that the rules applying to the Community's trade with third countries correctly reflect the integration of the markets".

[64] This is not intended to suggest that GATT Art. XXIV would serve to justify the Community sanctioned national restrictions in such a situation; though this issue does raise interesting questions about the scope of Art. XXIV. Even if Art. XXIV can justify measures which are inconsistent with Arts. III or XI of the GATT (in other words these are conceived as falling within the phrase "certain other [as well as MFN] GATT provisions" in *Turkey—Restrictions on Imports of Textiles and Clothing Products*—it would be necessary to demonstrate that the formation of that customs union would be prevented if it were not allowed to introduce the measure at stake; the measure in question being the application of Art. 30 or mandatory requirements in such a way as would imply a breach of GATT rules in so far as it is being applied to third country goods in free circulation. The customs union in question (the Community internal market) is not dependant in its operation upon Art. 30 etc. being applied in a way which is not consistent with parallel GATT exceptions. On the contrary, it is open to the Community either to interpret these provisions in the light of its GATT obligations or to introduce harmonising legislation at Community level which is such to pre-empt Member State recourse to Art. 30. This latter possibility is assisted by virtue of the European Court's insistence (see Case C–1/96, *Compassion in World Farming*, [1998] ECR I–1251) that even minimum harmonisation measures may be 'exhaustive' in nature and operate to pre-empt recourse to Art. 30, though doubts remain whether this would be so in the context of, for example, measures predicated upon Art. 175 TEC which by definition allow Member States to adopt more stringent measures subject to compliance with the Treaty. But whichever, if either, of these two routes comes to be preferred (WTO friendly interpretation or pre-emptive harmonisation) will have enormous constitutional significance in the EU, in terms of the role and approach of the European Court, the relationship between negative and positive integration measures in the EU, and the regulatory autonomy of Member States.

and to affect Community norms with a relevance well beyond the free movement sphere. This is an issue which arises also in the case studies outlined above.

Leaving aside for the time being the specific question of the implications of the Shrimp/Turtle report for the EU, it is necessary to consider more generally the issues raised by the due process dimension of this report for the international trading order. The report of the AB is politically astute. The subject matter of the dispute is sensitive and pertains to environmental protection, and in this respect was viewed very much as a "test case". The US measures are of a kind which are particularly controversial. Not only do they seek to promote the protection of resources (sometimes) situated outside of their territory, but more importantly they seek to do so on the basis of country-based (rather than batch-by-batch based) trade restrictions pertaining to compliance with production process standards. The AB was in a difficult position. And yet it succeeded through recourse to the "chapeau", and to the distinction between the nature of national restrictions and the circumstances of their application, to walk a fine line between the demands of the environmentalists and those of the free trade lobby. Nonetheless, though expedient in the case at hand, the approach adopted by the AB raises a number of problems.

Most obviously the creativity of the AB, in formulating due process requirements on a textual basis which is, at best, rather weak, gives rise to important questions concerning the legitimacy of its decision-making role.[65] This is exacerbated by the very considerable uncertainty surrounding both the legal basis and the content of its findings. Moreover, it is not at all clear how constructive a development this due process turn will prove to be more generally in distinguishing legitimate from illegitimate measures in the context of GATT rules and exceptions. It was at its most effective in the Shrimp/Turtle dispute, accompanied as it was by the element of surprise. The USA had not taken steps to wrap up its measures in the colours of due process, because it had not anticipated its legal obligation to do so.[66] In future, with states on their "due process" guard, clear-cut cases of due process abuses are less likely to arise. In so far, therefore, as the decision of the AB might be seen as having served "basic fairness" and procedural due process in the conduct of trade relations, that should be con-

---

[65] For an excellent discussion of this see R. Howse, 'Adjudicative Legitimacy and Treaty Interpretation in International Trade Law: The Early Years of WTO Jurisprudence' in J.H.H. Weiler, *supra* n. 8 above. Another view we offer is that the AB could have mounted a more convincing argument in favour of these developments through recourse, not to the concept of discrimination, but to the notion of a disguised restriction on trade also included in the Art. XX "chapeau". After all many of the elements of the AB's due process norms are transparency related and so could be justified as necessary to make a proper assessment of whether the measures in question were applied in such a way as to be a disguised restriction on trade. Equally, within the concept of a disguised restriction one might be able to introduce the idea of least restrictive means, and in this way ground the duty to negotiate aspect of the AB's findings. Further, the possibility of giving a different interpretation to the notion and significance of "discrimination" in the "chapeau" is suggested *supra* at n. 45.

[66] Though perhaps at least in respect of the duty to negotiate it ought to have done so, not least in the light of the Panel's findings in the Tuna/Dolphin II report.

ceived as a positive development, especially in so far as the duty to negotiate serves to prevent such disputes from arising in the future. However, absent the element of surprise it is not at all clear that procedural norms can succeed in serving as a workable or effective "bright line" according to which the legality of measures may be assessed.[67] On the other hand, the requirement of giving reasons to explain why internationally agreed standards were not followed in cases like the Omega hushkits dispute above may serve as a more effective means of revealing protectionist motives or other unconvincing explanations for trade restraint.

There are those who assert a potentially important role for procedural-type rules in this respect. Thus, in the context of Articles 28–30 TEC, Maduro argues that "the Court of Justice should not second-guess national regulatory choices, but should instead ensure that there is no under-representation of the interests of nationals of other Member States in the national political process".[68] One can see elements of this too in the thinking of Van Gerven AG in *Gourmetterie van den Burg*, a case before the European Court which is not entirely dissimilar in terms of the issues it raises to the Shrimp/Turtle dispute.[69] The Advocate General, in assessing the proportionality of the measure at hand, observes that it was adopted on the basis of a unilateral appraisal of the interests involved, and without taking into account interests which may warrant or justify the prohibited activity in question.

In this sense, the kind of procedural values highlighted by the AB in the Shrimp/Turtle report may be viewed as operating to promote more "inclusive"[70] political processes, whereby "outsiders" in national or other terms may secure access to previously closed sites of political authority within states. Thus, in that regulatory choices (and many other kinds of decisions) adopted within a single state have important consequences outside the territory of that state, the state no longer represents the uniquely appropriate site for democratic decision-making.[71] In the same way as the capacity of state-based government for effective rule may be diminished by virtue of a disjunction between the levels at which political and economic power operate, so too democracy may be undermined where the demos is territorially defined on the basis of pre-existing allegiances, rather than on the basis of actual interdependence, physical and economic.

---

[67] This is a phrase used by Howse and Regan, *supra* n. 20, where they talk of "bright-line rules desinged to avoid the need for context-sensitive judgment".

[68] M. Maduro Poiares, *We, the Court: The ECJ and the European Economic Constitution* (Oxford: Hart Publishing, 1998) p. 173.

[69] Case C–169/89, [1990] ECR I–2143.

[70] See also R. Howse and K. Nicolaidis, "Legitimacy and Global Governance: Why Constitutionalizing the WTO is a Step too Far?" (unpublished manuscript, 2000).

[71] See also the chapter by Miguel Maduro in this volume, "Is there any Such Thing as Free or Fair Trade? A Constitutional Analysis of the Impact of International Trade on the European Social Model".

Thus, it may be argued that the WTO, through the constitution of due process requirements, promotes transnational political engagement which may serve to attenuate the gap between atomistic political community and multiple, overlapping communities defined by inter-dependence rather than splendid isolation. In so far as these due process requirements seek to promote the audibility of the voices not merely of "foreign" governments, but also of individual traders (for example exporters of shrimp refused certification under Section 609), there has been a tendency to view the emerging democracy according to deliberative rather than representative models and, in keeping with such models, to lay emphasis upon the open-ended and adaptable nature of actors' preferences and the value of experimentation and mutual learning in the adjustment of such preferences.[72] In this sense the challenge for the WTO would be to ensure that states (and the EU itself) do more than cynically construct the trappings of due process, and that they listen, explain, respond and, where appropriate, revise. It is for this reason that the previously mentioned "element of surprise" is all-important, and that the due process standards according to which members will be assessed capture the 'essence' of the deliberative ideal; an essence which depends in part upon its very elusiveness, and upon its capacity to resist translation into fixed rules which may routinely and cynically be applied.

There is of course a strange irony inherent in what is being described above. The Appellate Body, against a backdrop of radical value pluralism, is adopting a "lighter" touch in terms of substantive review. In addition, however, it is scrutinising and evaluating the decision-making processes underpinning the contested measures adopted within the Member States. In invoking exceptions to the GATT the Appellate Body insists that certain procedural standards be complied with; this notwithstanding the procedural deficiencies which underpin the functioning of the WTO, including the activities of its Appellate Body.[73] Yet this is perhaps an irony which we can enjoy. In the first place, as Walker also observes, hypocrisy may have a civilising effect. The EU, for many years, endorsed a form of human rights conditionality *vis-à-vis* its own members and its trading partners the standards underpinning which were not binding upon itself. The hypocrisy did not go unobserved and over time the EU accepted that it too was bound to comply with the relevant standards of protection. Equally, it is by no means uncommon that a non-state polity (notably the EU) challenges us to look more closely and more critically at the functioning of the state, thus inducing a form of critical reflexivity. Talk of subsidiarity in the EU focussed

---

[72] J. Cohen and C. Sabel, "Directly-Deliberative Polyarchy" (1997) 3 *ELJ* 313; O. Gerstenberg and C. Sabel, "Directly Deliberative Polyarchy: an Institutional Ideal for Europe?" in C. Joerges and R. Dehousse (eds.), *Good Governance and Administration in Europe's Integrated Market* (Oxford: OUP, forthcoming 2001).

[73] As Neil Walker observes in his chapter below, there are those who argue that the coherent theme of the Seattle protests was procedural, "an outcry against the general exclusion of civil society from all but the very margins of the WTO framework": Walker, p. 32 below, and n. 6.

attention upon the premises underpinning the distribution of authority within the Member States, and in particular the place of sub-state authorities therein. Talk of transparency in the EU served to highlight the secretive nature of many government functions within the Member States. Talk of comitology reminded us to study more closely, and more critically, the functioning of committees at the national level. Bad practices at a level of governance susceptible to criticism due to its disassociation from the state with its traditionally "thick", territorially bounded legitimacy, have served to induce a self-consciousness about the premises underpinning the exercise of power even at a level (within the state) where traditionally such premises lay beyond the critical gaze.

The irony of the WTO preaching due process and basic fairness to the Member States aside, it is readily apparent that there is something interesting and important happening here. At the same time as one non-state polity—the EU—is looking increasingly to procedural techniques as a means of circumscribing Member State autonomy in governance,[74] against a backdrop of growing substantive flexibility, another (the WTO) is looking to procedural techniques to define the scope of residual Member State autonomy in a framework of market integration. Thus in the context of both "negative" and "positive" integration, the non-state polity is using procedural techniques both to guide Member State intervention in the market, and similarly to define the limits to that intervention. Particularly important in this respect are rules pertaining to participation, consultation and "due process" concerns. Against a backdrop of radical value pluralism, in integrating markets, such procedural techniques are increasingly deployed in the management of transnational markets. They do not represent a panacea. Nonetheless they offer one way of assessing the legality of Member State restraints on trade, and the additional prospect that their application may serve to enhance the quality of decision making within states and within the EU, in particular by enhancing the audibility of voices from outside the territory of the state concerned.

CONCLUDING COMMENTS

This chapter has sought to trace the ways in which WTO norms—both the provisions of its constituent treaties and more generally the principles and procedural norms being developed by its dispute settlement bodies—are increasingly affecting and being taken into account in EU governance, including by its legislative and judicial bodies. The ways in which Member States and EU institutional actors consider themselves bound to observe the provisions of WTO agreements, and the standards and norms to which those instruments refer, are

---

[74] See, e.g., the chapters by C. Barnard and J. Scott in G. de Burca and J. Scott, *Constitutional Change in the EU: From Uniformity to Flexibilty?* (Oxford: Hart Publishing, 2000), and the growing interest in the "open method of co-ordination" with its emphasis upon bench-marking and experimentation, first deployed in the context of the EU employment strategy.

more complex and subtle than the debates on direct effect and justiciability can capture. The reciprocal influence of the processes taking place in the context of the WTO, in particular encouragement for the multilateral negotiation and development of internationally agreed standards and for practices of dialogue and consultation before the adoption of trade-restrictive action, may provide some (albeit slight) cause for optimism in the face of fears about the growth of a free trade leviathan which increasingly restricts the policy choices not only of individual states, but also of the European Union itself.

2

The EU and the WTO: Constitutionalism in a New Key

NEIL WALKER

INTRODUCTION

MERELY TO CONTEMPLATE conceiving of the EU and the WTO in constitutional terms, which is a first aim of this contribution, invites formidable analytical and normative objections. The endeavour of imagining and presenting the European Union as a constitutional entity has long been both contested as a conceptual possibility and controversial as a political project. Indeed, as the idea of a specifically European Union constitutionalism has gained ground amongst some constituencies,[1] including key legal actors within the Union itself,[2] and as it has insinuated itself into the wider political debate,[3] the opposition of many other groups and commentators has become correspondingly more vociferous and determined.[4] Moreover, even within and between those constituencies who might accept as broadly coherent and legitimate a European constitutional discourse, there are profound and perhaps intractable differences about what this might mean in more concrete terms.[5] The debate about the constitutionalisation of the WTO has gained momentum only more recently, and,

[1] The literature is now vast. For an overview of recent strands of debate, see C. Joerges, Y. Meny and J.H.H. Weiler (eds.), *What Kind of Constitution for What Kind of Polity? Responses to Joschka Fischer* (Florence, Robert Schuman Centre, 2000).

[2] In particular, the ECJ in a famous line of cases. See e.g Case 294/83, *Parti Ecologiste "Les Verts* v. *European Parliament* [1986] ECR 1339; Opinion 1/91 *Re the EEA Agreement (No.1)* [1991] ECR 6079.

[3] See, e.g., the influential speech by German Foreign Minister Joschka Fischer in May 2000: "From Confederacy to Federation: Thoughts on the Finality of European Integration", reproduced in Joerges *et al. supra* n.1, 19; the new Treaty of Nice has established a clear if limited constituional agenda for the next Intergovernmental Conference: *Declaration on the Future of the Union included in the Final Act of the Conference*, Annex IV of the text of the Treaty of Nice, SN 533/00, 12 December 2000.

[4] See, e.g., C. Koenig, "Ist die Europaische Union Verfassungsfahig?" [1998] *Die ffentliche Verwaltung* 268. Telling of the strength of the constitutionalising momentum, however, is the fact that even organs and interests traditonally opposed to the development of autonomous political capacity for the European Union have begun to accept the basic terms of the constitutional agenda, if only as a way of limiting the EU's power; see, e.g., *The Economist*, 28 October 2000.

[5] For example, the Eurosceptic *Economist* (n.4 *supra*) has a very different constitutional vision from the pro-integrationist German foreign minister Fischer (n.3 *supra*).

although now well and truly joined within the academic community,[6] does not, at least as yet, figure so prominently in the self-understanding of key actors within the WTO framework. In its own terms, however, it appears no more hospitable to the type of broadly persuasive conceptual and normative grounding which is sought. If anything, indeed, the more modest status of and momentum behind constitutional discourse in relation to the WTO suggest an even more arduous course for such an endeavour.

Moreover, to contemplate *the relationship between* the EU and the WTO in similarly constitutional terms, as I shall also attempt to do in a preliminary fashion, invites the same objections as above and some additional ones. It invites the same objections in that, before we can begin to think of constitutions and constitutionalism in a relational mode, we must first be able to imagine the *entities to be related* as constitutional entities. It invites additional objections in that in any case constitutional discourse has traditionally been viewed as "entity-bound", however controversial the definition of a qualifying entity, rather than as something which can speak coherently and legitimately to the relationship between entities.

At root, the conceptual and the normative objections have to do with the resilience of the state, and indeed of the "states system",[7] as an analytical and ideological template for thinking about constitutionalism. My aim in this chapter is to argue that there is a way of at least addressing, though not of course resolving to general satisfaction, these conceptual and normative objections, and that there is a value in so doing; that we can find a less conceptually loaded and normatively compromised language in which to conceive of the EU and WTO in constitutional terms; and that such a language may indeed pay certain explanatory dividends in terms of our understanding of the relationship between these two entities, and even, if more tentatively, offer some assistance in the normative project of reimagining these relations in more legitimate terms. In brief, this argument involves breaking the statist frame within which, despite a growing literature self-consciously committed to overcoming this limitation,[8] we still tend to view constitutions and constitutionalism. More constructively, it involves developing constitutional analysis in a pluralist fashion through three related moves, each of which explores constitutionalism as relevant to, indeed constitutive of, all polities—state or non-state, mature or emergent, consoli-

---

[6] See, e.g., R. Howse and K. Nicolaidis, "Legitimacy and Global Governance: Why Constitution-alizing the WTO is a Step Too Far," in P. Sauve and A. Subramanian (eds.), *Efficiency, Equity, Legitimacy and Governance: The Multilateral Trading System at the Millenium* (Washington, DC, Brookings Institution Press, forthcoming); T. Cottier, *Limits to International Trade: the Constitutional Challenge* (2000) paper to ASIL Conference; J. Jackson, *The World Trade Organisation: Constitution and Jurisprudence* (London, RIIA, 1998); E-U. Petersmann, "The WTO Constituion and Human Rights" (2000) 3 *Journal of International Econmic Law* 19; C. Schmidt (present volume).

[7] See, e.g., R. Falk, *Predatory Globalization: A Critique* (Cambridge, Polity, 1999) ch.2.

[8] See, e.g., D. M. Curtin, *Postnational Democracy* (Utrecht, Universiteit Utrecht, 1997); J. Shaw, "Postnational Constituionalism in the European Union" (1999) 6 *European Journal of Public Policy* 579.

dated or contested. First, constitutionalism and constitutionalisation are conceived of not in black-and-white, all-or-nothing terms but as a question of nuance and gradation. There is no unitary template in terms of which constitutional status is either achieved or not achieved, but rather a set of loosely and variously coupled factors which serve both as *criteria* in terms of which forms of constitutionalism can be distinguished and as *indices* in terms of which degrees of constitutionalisation can be measured. Secondly, the variable constitutional profile of different polities in terms of the applicability of these abstract criteria is in turn informed by the *variable structural position* of different types of polity within the global configuration of authority. Thirdly, to return to the ancillary purpose of the chapter, constitutionalism in a plural order is *necessarily* conceived of not only as an internal property of polities but as a medium through which they interconnect—as a characteristic of the relationship between sites of authority as well as an internal characteristic of these authoritative sites.

CONSTITUTIONAL PLURALISM

Let us begin, then, by looking briefly at the resilient influence of the statist frame of reference, and how this has affected how we look at—or in some cases refuse to look at—entities such as the EU and the WTO in constitutional terms. As already noted, the reasons for this resilience are both conceptual and normative. Although these are closely connected, the flow of the following argument is better served if we deal with the conceptual objections first and return to the normative objections only towards the end of the chapter.

In their analysis of the development of the European polity, Shaw and Wiener describe how the "often invisible touch of stateness"[9] affects—infects even—our understanding and evaluation of non-state entities. For example, many of the supposed normative shortcomings of non-state entities, "including deficits of democracy, legitimacy, accountability, equality and security" are measured against statist standards (real or imagined) and defined in terms of a statist template. This tendency should not surprise us. After all, the vocabulary with which we seek to make sense of political entities, including all the key values listed above, has undergone centuries of development and refinement within the context of the state. And what is true of these individual terms may be even more resoundingly true of a portmanteau idea such as constitutionalism, which seeks to provide an organising framework of practical reasoning for the application and balancing of particular political values.

---

[9] J. Shaw and A. Wiener, "The Paradox of the European Polity" in M. Green Cowles and M. Smith (eds.), *State of the European Union 5: Risks, Reform, Resistance and Revival* (Oxford, OUP, 2000).

In crude terms, we might respond in four ways to the profound "problems of translation"[10] this historical legacy causes for the assessment of non-state polities. First, we could ignore the problems of translation, allowing the touch of stateness to do its invisible work, a ghostly template for all discussion about the proper ordering of the public domain. Secondly, we could deny or minimise them, assuming the work of translation and recontextalisation of abstract concepts to be essentially unproblematic. Thirdly, we could succumb to them, viewing the work of translation to be so difficult and risk-laden as to be impossible or at least ill-advised, and advocating instead the development of an entirely new normative language. Fourthly, and in my view most appropriately, we could, in full acknowledgment of the difficulties and risks involved, engage with the problems of translation.

Let us begin this engagement, then, by suggesting a broader conceptual framework for understanding the nature and limits of constitutional discourse, one which is not state-bound. The notions of constitution and constitutionalism, however else we may dispute their meaning, are unarguably bound up with, indeed provide the normative vocabulary for, the mutual articulation of law and politics.[11] More specifically, as already suggested, constitutional law and discourse have typically been concerned not just with the articulation of law and politics in general, but with their mutual articulation within a particular polity. Indeed, constitutional law seeks to elaborate the normative order in terms of which that polity is identified and regulated *qua* polity. Constitutional law and discourse, thus, should be understood not, or not just, as an external map of the polity, but as one of the polity's key defining and constitutive features. This is not to argue in Kelsenian terms for a purely legal-constitutional understanding of polity formation and development, but rather to posit the mutual constitution of law and politics in a dynamic and ongoing process. Politics—in the grounded sense of the affairs of a polity—cannot be conceived of without a legal setting and framework. Yet on the other hand, law—and constitutional law *a fortiori*—always supposes some prior political setting. In this process of mutual constitution and containment, therefore, constitutional law is recursively involved in both the *presentation* and the *representation* of the polity—both seeking to reflect the prior political state and in that process simultaneously translating and redefining that prior political state in legal-constitutional terms.[12]

Two important points flow from this analysis. In the first place, constitutional law is clearly an internal and intrinsic characteristic of a polity. There can be no polity without a constitutional discourse, just as there can be no constitu-

---

[10] J.H.H. Weiler, *The Constitution of Europe: "Do the New Clothes Have an Emperor?" And Other Essays on European Integration* (Cambridge, CUP, 1999) 270.

[11] I am deeply indebted to the work of Bert van Roermund and Hans Lindahl for this section of the argument: see, e.g., H. Lindahl and B. van Roermund, "Law without a State? On Representing the Common Market" in Z. Bankowski and D. Scott (eds.), *The European Union and its Order; The Legal Theory of European Integration* (Oxford, Blackwell, 2000) 1.

[12] See, e.g., H. Lindahl, "Sovereignty and Symbolization" (1997) 28 *Rechtstheorie* 3, drawing upon the work of Ernst Cassirer.

tional discourse without a polity as its object of analysis and representation. Secondly, as the idea of a polity, or political community, is simply that of a setting for the practice of politics, it is not bound to or exhausted by the idea of the modern national state (indeed, as a matter of etymology, it derives from the city-state, or *polis*, of archaic and classical Greece). In turn, therefore, we must recognise constitutional law, or some functionally equivalent label, as necessary to and constitutive of the legal normative order of contemporary non-state and post-state polities just as it is necessary to and constitutive of the legal normative order of state polities.

But, to restate the problem of translation in terms of this new analytical framework, how do we begin to fill out this broad and inclusive definition of constitutional discourse in a manner which both lends substance to the general idea and yet is sensitive to the huge variation in form and intensity of actually existing constitutional discourses and polity-settings? This requires us to specify a number of factors in terms of which constitutional discourse does its presentational and representational work on behalf of a polity, each of which factors, as already intimated, serves as a criterion in terms of which we can map the distinguishing constitutional features of that polity and provides an index to measure the trajectory and intensity of its constitutionalisation process. What are these factors? First, there is the development of an explicit constitutional discourse—the emergence of a constitutional self-consciousness on the part of those associated with the polity with respect to that polity. Secondly, there is the claim to foundational legal authority, or sovereignty. Thirdly, there is development of jurisdictional scope—the delineation of a sphere of competence. Fourthly, there is the claim to interpretive autonomy—to the entitlement of an organ internal to the polity to construe the meaning and extent of these competences. Fifthly, there is the constitution and regulation of an institutional structure to govern the polity. Sixthly, there is the specification of the conditions and incidents of membership of or association with the polity—the criteria and rights and obligations of citizenship, broadly defined. Seventhly, and closely related to the sixth factor, there are the terms of representation of the membership—the mechanisms, democratic or otherwise, by which their voices are heard and taken into account.

In due course we will seek to justify and to explore these seven indices of constitutionalism—discursive maturity, authority, jurisdiction, interpretive autonomy, institutional capacity, citizenship and representation—both generally and in relation to our two sites of the EU and the WTO. In order to locate this discussion in a contemporary pluralist context, however, we must first say something about the structural position of these two non-state polities within the changing global configuration of legal authority.

Elsewhere, I have begun to develop a framework for understanding structural variation within this ever more complex global configuration.[13] Very briefly,

---

[13] N. Walker, "Flexibility within a Metaconstitutional Frame: Reflections on the Future of Legal Authority in Europe" in G. de Búrca and J. Scott (eds.), *The European Constitution: Between*

this approach argues that as the states system which gradually and unevenly developed after the 1648 Peace of Westphalia[14] begins to buckle under the pressure of globalisation of capital investment, culture, travel, communication media, and of political movements and forms,[15] so too the legal configuration appropriate to that passing order changes. The Westphalian order was basically supported by two complementary frameworks of law—primarily constitutional law, in that original context the law governing the internal order of sovereign states, and secondly and parasitically international law, the law governing the relations between sovereign states. Notwithstanding this duality, this was basically a one-dimensional order of legal authority, in the sense that no serious claims to sovereignty or ultimate legal authority were made other than by or on behalf of the state. In the post-Westphalian legal order, by contrast, we see the growth of polities which are not states but which overlap and rival states in terms of legal and political authority—paradigmatically the currently most mature non-state polity—the EU—but also entities growing in or around the EU in its current moment of "flexibility" such as Schengen and the Eurozone, other regional economic organisations such as the North Atlantic Free Trade Association, the global economic organisation of the WTO itself, and other powerful regional and global organisations without a primarily economic mandate such as the Council of Europe and the UN. Within this new multi-dimensional configuration of authority,[16] classical intra-state constitutional law and inter-state international law are no longer adequate to fill the normative space of cosmopolitan public law.

A fruitful way to characterise this developing post-Westphalian order, it may be argued, is as an interplay between state constitutional sites and constitutionalism on the one hand, and non-state *metaconstitutional* sites on the other. The "meta" prefix, as with meta-ethics and metaphysics, denotes a secondary discourse—in two different senses in the instant case. Metaconstitutional discourse is secondary, first, in the sense that its ultimate historical source and formative influence are the constitutional discourse of the state. That is to say metaconstitutional rules have their origins in the decisions and actions of constitutional states, and this "state pedigree" continues to exert a (more or less) remote influence over the legal-normative character of the non-state site. But metaconstitutional discourse is also secondary in a quite different sense; that its rules, being

Uniformity and Flexibility (Oxford, Hart, 2000) 9; N. Walker, "Beyond the Unitary Conception of the United Kingdom Constitution?" [2000] *Public Law* 384: N. Walker, *Policing in a Changing Constitutional Order* (London, Sweet & Maxwell, 2000) ch.10.

[14] See e.g., D. Held, "The Transformation of Political Community: Rethinking Democracy in the Context of Globalization" in I. Shapiro and C. Hacker-Cordon (eds.), *Democracy's Edges* (Cambridge, CUP, 1999) 84.

[15] For stimulating discussion of the effect of globalisation on patterns of legal and political authority, see Special Issue of *Political Studies*, "Sovereignty at the Millennium", R. Jackson (ed.) (1999) XLVII, 423–604.

[16] N. Walker, "Sovereignty and Differentiated Integration in the European Union" (1998) 4 *ELJ* 355.

about the same subject matter—the constitution and regulation of polities or putative polities—as state constitutional rules, typically come to claim not only a normative authority independent of and irreducible to the historical state source (the counterclaims of state sources notwithstanding), but even a deeper or higher normative authority than state constitutional rules or other "lower" metaconstitutional rules. Indeed, metaconstitutional rules typically purport to authorise, instruct, influence, supplement or supplant these other rules.

The language of metaconstitutionalism presents a way of recognising a number of different dynamics within the emerging post-Westphalian order. More emphatically than some forms of "postnational" constitutionalism,[17] it acknowledges the resilient importance of the constitutional state, as the entity to which much metaconstitutional discourse is ultimately directed, but also, if paradoxically, the entity from which it is ultimately derived. At the same time, it also acknowledges the depth, breadth and durability of the challenge to the authority of the constitutional state, as evident in the claims of normative superiority, or at least the absence of normative deference, implicit in the discourse emanating from the growing range of metaconstitutional sites. Moreover, to focus on the problems of translation set out above, it acknowledges both the continuities and discontinuities between the public law discourses of the state and the non-state sphere. It indicates an internal relationship between the two discourses, metaconstitutionalism seeking to address at various levels of remove the problems of polity formation and regulation originating within and still much centred around state constitutionalism. Yet in rejecting the language of state constitutionalism *simpliciter*, it implies that the discourse of the non-state public law domain is ultimately of a somewhat different order—requires a different key—from the discourse of the state public law domain. Finally, the language of metaconstitutionalism is explicitly relational, capturing the complexly-layered character of the new post-Westphalia pluralism. That is to say, metaconstitutional sites are defined in relational terms rather than as isolated monads. Unlike the modern state, they do not pretend to be self-contained, comprehensive polities, exhausting the political identities, energies and aspirations of their members or associates. Indeed, it is artificial even to conceive of such sites as having separate internal and external dimensions, since their very identity and *raison d'être* as polities or putative polities rest at least in some measure on their orientation towards other sites.

---

[17] See n.8 *supra*. Some forms of postnational constitutionalism, or constitutional pluralism, for example the work of Francis Snyder (see, e.g., "Governing Economic Globalization: Global Legal Pluralism and European Law" (1999) 5 *ELJ* 334) would extend the analysis of post-national sites further to include not only political sites but also sites that are "market-based, being generated by economic actors as part of economic processes" (372). While this type of approach can be highly fruitful, it is not pursued here as, on my view, economic as opposed to political sites do not provide generative contexts for constitutional discourse, which is my immediate concern. Economic and other private actors remain highly relevant to my analysis, but in terms of their relationship to political sites rather than as primary locations on the governance map.

This conceptual framework may yield important insights about the implications of the relationship between the EU and the WTO for the post-Westphalian
order, but only if it can rise to a challenge posed by that same relationship. The
EU–WTO relationship challenges our conceptual framework in the sense that it
presents its limiting case. Significantly, the EU–WTO relationship is situated at
the "meta-meta" level; in other words, it constitutes a relationship between
meta sites, each of which is the product of earlier relations—international agreements—between state sites. It is, therefore, in terms of our conceptual scheme,
at the highest level of abstraction from the historically foundational constitutional state sites. It is also, then, a very different type of relationship from the
classical one-dimensional bilateral or multilateral international relationship
between state constitutional orders, or even to the relationship between state
sites and meta-sites. Yet it remains connected to state constitutionalism in two
important senses. First, the two meta-sites, and the relationship between these
sites, are linked to state constitutionalism through an unbroken historical chain,
however attenuated. Secondly, in the new multi-dimensional configuration of
authority it is in any case artificial to examine particular dyadic relations in
isolation, especially relations between meta-sites, which by their very nature
disrupt and overlap the mutually exclusive jurisdictional compartments of the
order of states. The EU–WTO relationship, therefore, cannot be bracketed off
from the wider complex of which it is a part. In particular, many of the legal
events and relationships through which the EU and WTO are connected are also
events and relationships which closely involve states, and/or state-based private
actors. Thus states, and state constitutionalism, remain directly implicated in
the overall flow of EU–WTO relations.

THE EU AND THE WTO IN CONSTITUTIONAL PERSPECTIVE

Armed with this conception of the distinctive structural position of the EU and
WTO within the new global configuration, let us now return to the seven criteria or indices of constitutionalism in order to build a constitutional profile of
each. First, there is the existence of a self-conscious discourse of constitutionalism. As we have seen, and as we shall explore further below, both the EU and
the WTO attract extensive and vigorous debate about whether and how they
may be conceived in constitutional terms. But why should the mere existence of
a relevant domain of constitutional discourse and debate be taken seriously as a
constitutional benchmark, particularly as vigorous debate reflects equally vigorous disagreement about the proper content of constitutionalism, and even of
the legitimacy of such a discourse? Is there not at least a whiff of solipsism, of
wish self-fulfillment on the part of one particular and partial perspective or set
of perspectives, in the inclusion of this criterion?

The answer to this possible objection is twofold. In the first place, recall the
proposition that constitutional law and politics are mutually constitutive.

Constitutional law and discourse are no mere reflection of a prior political order, but are recursively implicated in the elaboration of that order. Just as there can be no constitutional discourse in the absence of a referent polity, so there can be no polity in the absence of a referent constitutional discourse. To put it another way, the polity cannot be a polity in the absence of its constitutional imagination as a polity, and it is precisely that "discourse of conceptualization and imagination"[18] which has the capacity to invest the authoritative claims, the institutions and the principles associated with the putative polity with polity-affirming, and thus constitutional, status. In this intensely reflexive process, constitutionalism is not, or not simply, about observing appropriate types of data "out there [in the] constitutional landscape", but is necessarily itself a constitutive process. Of course, the relevant discourse of imagination may be more or less successful in convincing key audiences, both the putative governors and the putative governed, of the authenticity of this or that type, or indeed any claim to constitutional status on behalf of a polity, but this is merely to reiterate the point that constitutionalism and constitutionalisation are best conceived of as matters of degree and intensity.

In the second place, the discourse of constitutional conceptualisation and imagination also has profound consequences for the content of the various "constitutional" claims, institutions and principles whose articulation is relevant to the other criteria and indices of constitutionalism. This is of course trivially and generally true in the sense that no constitutional order is static, but is in a continuous process of reconceptualisation and reimagination. But it is also true in the more subtle and specific sense that a (more or less) successful process of imaginative transformation towards constitutional status itself has the potential to change the texture of the relevant claims, institutions and principles in significant ways. For the claim to constitutional status, and so to "polity-hood", is always an assertion of a *right* to self-government, and so also necessarily involves an acknowledgment of the *demands* of responsible self-government with all that that entails in terms of crafting a legitimate normative order.

Let us then move on to the other factors which invest constitutional discourse with particular content. What of sovereignty and authority? Perhaps even more so than the discourse of constitutionalism itself, the idea of sovereignty is traditionally bound up with the world order of states and requires careful conceptual refinement for its relevance to non-state political orders to be vindicated. In essence, sovereignty consists of a *plausible claim to ultimate authority* made on behalf of a particular polity.[19] This has both subjective and objective dimensions. Subjectively, there has to be common assertion or acceptance by the key officials of the polity in question—in particular its judges—that it is a sovereign polity. Objectively, there must be evidence of a high level of general obedience to the framework of laws which are valid in accordance with the system's

---

[18] Weiler, *supra* n.10, 223.
[19] Walker, *supra* n.16, 356–360.

ultimate criteria of validity. Sovereignty also has closely related internal and external aspects. Internal sovereignty involves the claim that fundamental authority over the internal ordering of the polity is located within that polity, while external sovereignty involves the claim that fundamental authority to represent the polity in its external relations rests with the polity itself.

In its traditional statist version, the claim to sovereignty or ultimate authority implies both autonomy and exclusivity; autonomy, because a derivative or dependent authority is by definition not ultimate; exclusivity, because a world order of states is generally[20] one of discrete and mutually exclusive territorial jurisdictions. Within the symmetrical logic of such an order, a non-exclusive authority is typically a dependent one, in the sense that any other authority claim made over the jurisdiction can be made only by a rival state, which if plausible and effective, as in the tradition of Western imperialism, then becomes an extension of the exclusive claim to authority of that rival state, so defeating or debasing the indigenous claim.[21] In other words the mutual exclusivity of comprehensive territorial jurisdictions in the one-dimensional global map implies a corresponding mutual exclusivity of effective claims to sovereignty.

In the emerging post-Westphalian order, on the other hand, *it becomes possible to conceive of autonomy without exclusivity*—to imagine ultimate authority, or sovereignty, in non-exclusive terms. This is because of the emergence of polities whose posited boundaries are not, or not merely, territorial but also functional. That is to say, claims to ultimate legal authority are no longer limited to (state) claims to comprehensive jurisdiction over a particular territory, but now also embrace functionally limited claims, whether such claims are also territorially limited, as in the EU, or global, as in the WTO. Crucially, the development of functionally limited claims is self-reinforcing to the extent that it allows of the possibility of overlap without subsumption. To be sure, the boundaries between different polities are still deeply contested. Indeed, in a configuration in which overlap and intersection become the norm, these boundary disputes, as we shall see, become more systematic.[22] Yet even so, the advent of functionally limited polities means that the assertion of authority around a disputed boundary does not necessarily impugn the integrity of the other polity *qua* polity. So, for example, to the extent that the claim to sovereignty of the European Union over a range of competences previously within the exclusive jurisdiction of the 15 Member States is plausible and effective, this does not seriously question the continuing sovereignty of the 15 Member States as regards their remaining areas of territorial jurisdiction.[23]

[20] The condominium, an arrangement in which sovereignty is jointly exercised over two or more states, provides an exception to this rule. Historically, condominia have existed from the Sudan to the New Hebrides.

[21] See e.g. R. Jackson, "Sovereignty in World Politics: A Glance at the Conceptual and Historical Landscape" (1999) 47 *Political Studies* 431.

[22] Walker, *supra* n.16, 375–378.

[23] To the extent that such questioning does take place, it tends to derive from a confusion between sovereignty and interpretive autonomy and a consequential exaggeration of the significance

If we accept that in the post-Westphalian order the Gordian knot tying autonomy to territorial exclusivity within the definition of sovereignty has been sev-
ered, and that autonomy alone becomes a sufficient basis for sovereignty, that
does not of course mean that every bare claim to autonomy should be accepted
as evidence of sovereign authority. Such claims must still be plausible in the subjective and objective senses set out above. In these terms, the EU clearly has a
stronger claim to sovereignty than the WTO. The doctrines of supremacy and
direct effect developed by the Court of Justice in the 1960s are deeply embedded
within the normative structure of the polity, accepted by all the main institutional actors and, crucially, by the Member States themselves. For many of the
key institutional actors of the EU, as for many expert observers, this implies the
arrogation of sovereignty within limited spheres, although, to varying degrees
and with various nuances, the states, and their constitutional courts, would
question or qualify this with counterclaims of sovereignty in the last instance
over the terms and limits of this transfer, including a backstop authority to
recover the transferred powers.[24] What is clear, nevertheless, is that so potent is
the EU challenge to traditional state sovereignty that only a radical pluralism
can make sense of the co-existence of the two sets of claims. That is to say, both
sets of sovereign claims are valid and unimpeachable in their own terms, each
claiming the allegiance of key actors. Equally, and turning to the objective
dimension of plausibility, on account of a sophisticated set of inter-systemic
bridging mechanisms centred around the preliminary reference procedure, each
is equally capable of providing a persuasive normative pedigree for and claiming a high level of compliance with regard to the considerable settled corpus of
law drafted, applied and enforced within the sphere of competence of EU law.[25]
So plausible are these rival claims, indeed, that there appears to be no trans-systemic point of view from which we can definitively resolve the areas of tension
between the two sets of claims in favour of one or the other.[26]

In the case of the WTO, there is no equivalent normative momentum towards
autonomy and sovereignty. No doctrine of supremacy has been articulated by
WTO institutions. Nor have they yet claimed the benefit of a general doctrine
of direct effect of WTO norms within other legal orders, and to the extent that
qualifications to this self-limitation have been contemplated under certain
conditions,[27] even these mooted exceptions have been received warily in the

---

of the ECJ's power to determine the boundaries of its own jurisdiction. See text accompanying nn.
33–35 below.

[24] See e.g., B. De Witte, "Sovereignty and European Integration: The Weight of Legal Tradition"
in A-M. Slaughter, A. Stone Sweet and J.H.H. Weiler (eds.), *The European Court and National
Courts: Doctrine and Jurisprudence: Legal Change in its Social Context* (Oxford, Hart, 1998) 276.

[25] See, e.g., Walker, *supra* n.16. 375–378; S. Weatherill, *Law and Integration in the European
Union* (Oxford, Clarendon, 1995) chs. 4–5.

[26] See, e.g., N. MacCormick, *Questioning Sovereignty: Law State and Practical Reasoning*
(Oxford, OUP, 1999) esp. ch. 7.

[27] See in particular *United States—Section 301–310 of the Trade Act of 1974*, Report of the Panel,
1999.

context and from the perspective of the other legal orders in question—EU and state.[28] Thus the doctrinal supports for the sort of independently effective legal framework that sovereignty would demand, even with its post-Westphalian refinements, appear to be missing or at least highly deficient. And indeed, as regards the subjective aspect of plausibility, as already noted the idea of sovereignty seems marginal to or absent from the constitutional understanding of the key institutional players of the WTO system. Some influential actors and commentators, on the other hand, have been prepared at least to contemplate the WTO in terms of sovereignty, although even here the claims are either couched in negative terms—as a way of dramatising and thus deterring a future dystopia,[29] or, if more soberly assessed, are typically partial and heavily qualified.[30] The latter type of claim tends to emphasise gradual shifts in the objective dimension of plausibility; the way in which WTO norms, over half a century of the GATT and increasingly under the extended normative and strengthened institutional framework of the Uruguay Round Agreements, have come, albeit slowly and unevenly, to play a more decisive and less negotiable role in the balancing of key values within the world trading system.

What this suggests is that, within the more fragmented, fluid and contested configuration of authority of a multi-dimensional order, sovereignty too, like the other indices of constitutionalism, becomes more amenable to understanding as a graduated and tenuous property of normative order. While mutual exclusivity remained intrinsic to our definition of sovereignty, a more absolutist, black-and-white mode of analysis and understanding was appropriate, with relatively discrete areas of contestation which themselves tend to be approached and resolved in zero-sum terms and within a limited time-frame. Under the new conditions, sovereignty may be viewed as a emergent and precarious characteristic of many post-state polities within a longer, open-ended time frame, as we have seen of the EU and as we are now witnessing of the WTO. In turn, to what extent and in what ways these sovereignty claims become more or less grounded depends upon the other graduated indices of constitutionalism, to which we now turn.

---

[28] See in particular, on direct effect with regard to Community acts, Case C–149/96, *Portugal* v. *Council*, Judgment of 23 November 1999; commented on by A. Rosas, (2000) 37 *CMLRev.* 797. The ECJ has been more willing to require Member States to respect GATT Agreements: Case 53/96 *Hermes* [1998] ECR I–3603; Case C–61/94 *Commission* v. *Germany*[1996] ECR I–4021. See, more generally, Von Bogdandy and Makatsch (present volume); A.P van Kappel and W. Heusel (eds.), *Free World Trade and the European Union: The Reconciliation of Interests and the Review of the Understanding on Dispute Settlement in the Framework of the World Trade Organisation* (Cologne, Bundesanzeiger, 2000); J.H.J. Bourgeois, "The European Court of Justice and the WTO: Problems and Challenges" in J.H.H. Weiler (ed.), *The EU, the WTO and the NAFTA: Towards a Common Law of International Trade* (Oxford, OUP, 2000) 71.

[29] See, e.g., J.H. Jackson, *The Jurisprudence of GATT and the WTO: Insights on Treaty Law and Economic Relations* (Cambridge, CUP, 2000) ch.19; see also text at n.69.

[30] See, e.g., Howse and Nicolaidis, *supra* n. 6; M. Farrell, *The EU and WTO Regulatory Frameworks: Complementarity or Competition?* (London, Kogan Page, 199) 44.

The third criterion of constitutionalism and index of constitutionalisation, then, is jurisdictional scope. If polities within a multi-dimensional order can be functionally delimited, we have to ask what these limitations are. On the one hand, functional extent is patently a matter of degree, and so fits easily into our understanding of constitutionalism and constitutionalisation as also questions of degree. On the other hand, our sense of an entity as an identifiable polity seems to require a minimum threshold of multi-functionality. The practice of politics, and of government, as generic activities, as opposed to the pursuit of a single policy or a discrete regulatory goal, implies the co-ordination of a number of spheres of activity and the treatment of their mutual ramifications through consideration, negotiating and balancing of the multiple public goods and private interests involved. The history of the expanding competence of the EU from its origins as an organisation to promote regional trade through a common market and, also, if more abstractly, to consolidate post-war peace in Western Europe is too well known to require even a brief synopsis.[31] Suffice it to say that in considerably widening and deepening its sphere of competence, both through extended economic integration in areas such as competition, agriculture and monetary policy and beyond that into social and environmental policy, it manifestly supplies a distinct level of governance. The remit of the WTO is clearly more modest, but it too increasingly conforms to a multi-functional template. Even the original GATT 1947, restricted to the liberalisation of trade in goods, involved a complex balancing of values and interests. Each of its four fundamental working principles—non-discrimination, reciprocity, market access and fair competition—is open-textured, and their iterative interpretation and conciliation have required a complex balance between liberalisation on the one hand and a wide range of national and regional policy interests and the diversity of other public goods these interests articulate or are claimed to articulate on the other.[32] Like the European Union, moreover, the complex and many-tentacled ramifications of free trade have led to a gradual "spillover" of explicit competence into other sectors, including the Uruguay Round Agreements on Trade in Services (GATS) and Trade-related Aspects of Intellectual Property Rights (TRIPS) and extension into other broad policy areas such as competition, investment, agriculture and environmental policy. For reasons discussed below, it would be foolish to draw the developmental analogy with the EU too closely, but the expanding jurisdiction of GATT, too, increasingly fits a model of multi-functional governance.

A similar analysis can be made of our next two criteria. Interpretive autonomy,[33] on the surface straightforward, is on closer examination a tenaciously elusive idea, one which has given rise to a great deal of confusion and which has caused the idea of interpretive autonomy on the part of non-state polities to be

---

[31] See, e.g., Weiler, *supra* n. 10, ch. 2.
[32] Farrell, *supra* n. 30 ch. 1.
[33] T. Schilling, "The Autonomy of the Community Legal Order: An Analysis of Possible Foundations" (1996) 17 *Harvard International Law Journal* 389, 389–390.

falsely challenged or denied. Like so many of the difficulties with charting the post-Westphalian order, these confusions flow from an obdurate reliance upon the paradigm of state constitutionalism in contexts to which it is increasingly inappropriate. Two confusions in particular need to be addressed. In the first place, there is a confusion of meaning—or at least, a tendency to overstate the mutual dependency—between interpretive autonomy, or the power to be ultimate arbiter of disputes about the meaning of the polity's governing constitutional text, including disputes over its jurisdictional reach, on the one hand (i.e. "judicial *Kompetenz-Kompetenz*"), and an open-ended capacity on the part of a polity to determine the extent of its legislative competence on the other (i.e. "legislative *Kompetenz-Kompetenz*").[34] In the context of the Westphalian one-dimensional order of sovereign states, where legislative *Kompetenz-Kompetenz* is the constitutional norm, the interpretive and adjudicative setting of the Supreme or Constitutional Court is typically where this open-ended jurisdictional authority is articulated, applied and affirmed. In these circumstances, the two capacities are closely linked, although still conceptually distinct. Where, on the other hand, a polity is functionally limited by its constituent text, then those who exercise interpretive autonomy on behalf of the polity must equally be subject to these functional limits. In other words, interpretive autonomy is always the dependent variable, tied to the jurisdictional claims of the constituent text of the polity in question. To the extent that these claims are functionally limited, so too is the power of interpretive autonomy. To be sure, such interpretive power may be applied in a controversially extensive manner, may even on some views be abused, but an interpretation of a functionally limited text, however expansive, remains an act circumscribed by an acknowledgment of boundaries within the terms set by a particular interpretive community, rather than a licence to expand jurisdiction indefinitely. Interpretive autonomy, therefore, cannot slip the functional leash, and need not on that ground be excluded as indeterminately open-ended from the constitutional profile of a functionally determinate post-state polity.

A second confusion mirrors that which attends the transformation in the meaning of sovereignty. If ultimate authority in the post-Westphalian order is consistent with autonomy rather than exclusivity, so too the power of ultimate arbitration and interpretation need not be exclusive. Interpretive autonomy means precisely that. It does not necessarily mean that from an external point of view "only the institutions of that particular order are competent to interpret the constitutional and legal rules of that order",[35] but merely that this can be plausibly asserted from a internal point of view. In a configuration of overlapping and

---

[34] T. Schilling, "The Autonomy of the Community Legal Order: An Analysis of Possible Foundations" (1996) 17 *Harvard International Law Journal* 389, 389–390 and T. Schilling, "Rejoinder: The Autonomy of the Community Legal Order" (1996) *Harvard Jean Monnet Working Paper Series*; responding to Joseph Weiler's reply to Schilling's earlier article; Weiler, *supra* n. 10, ch. 9.

[35] Schilling, *supra* n. 33, 389–390.

rival polities—in a landscape of contested boundaries—the supreme judicial authorities of these rival orders will each claim the right to police these contested boundaries in terms of the normative pedigree of their own order and by reference to the rules of adjudication associated with that normative pedigree. In other words, on a pluralist reading the assertion of rival plausible claims to have the last judicial word on an overlapping or disputed question of competence, provided these claims are plausibly made, confirms rather than denies the interpretive autonomy of both the polities or putative polities in question.

For all that it does not imply legislative omnicompetence or unrivalled powers of adjudication, interpretive autonomy remains a powerful index of constitutional maturity. Interpretive autonomy has long been claimed by the European Court of Justice on behalf of the European legal order, giving rise to a series of high-profile constitutional collisions with national constitutional courts staking rival claims.[36] The interpretive autonomy of the global trade regulator on the other hand, has only been plausibly claimed more recently, again with the institution of the WTO in the Uruguay Round. Under the GATT system, the authority of the dispute settlement process was diluted by a number of factors, including procedural delay and uncertainty (in particular the absence of a right to a panel and the lack of firm time-limits); lack of legal rigour, clarity and cohesion in the rulings of panels; uncertainty over adoption of rulings, given the consensus rule and the effective power of veto of losing parties; and delay in and incomplete compliance with panel rulings.[37] The WTO dispute settlement system represents a significant strengthening of interpretive autonomy at all these vulnerable points. In particular, complainants are now entitled to dispute settlement through the Dispute Settlement Body (DSB), and to the automatic adoption of rulings as legally binding between the parties. The establishment of a standing Appellate Body to review the legal reasoning of panels, moreover, provides key institutional support for a shift from diplomacy and inter-state bargaining to "juridification"[38] of the dispute settlement process and of the governing normative order. Yet key aspects of the regulatory system which makes interpretive autonomy such a salient feature of the EU polity remain absent. These include, notably, the inability of either non-governmental parties[39] or, indeed, the WTO itself, notwithstanding the central role played by its Trade Policy Review Mechanism (TPRM) as a monitor of the compliance of states' trade polices with WTO norms, to bring and enforce complaints against government parties. In sum, while the abolition of the consent rule at the points

---

[36] See in particular *Brunner* v. *The European Union Treaty* [1994] 1 CMLR 57.

[37] See, e.g., M.J. Trebilcock and R. Howse, *The Regulation of International Trade* (2nd edn., London and New York: Routledge, 1999) 54–58.

[38] J.H.H. Weiler, "The Rule of Lawyers and the Ethos of Diplomats: Reflections on the Internal and External Legitimacy of WTO Dispute Settlement" (2000) *Harvard Jean Monnet Working Paper Series* 2.

[39] Although the Appellate Body has now made it clear that non-govermental actors can at least present *amicus* briefs; *United States—Import Prohibitions of Certain shrimps and Shrimp Products, Report of the Appellate Body* WT/DS58/AB/R, 12 October 1998.

of application and acceptance means that the WTO now passes the basic threshold test of interpretive autonomy, the institutionalisation of this principle, while greatly boosted by the advent of the Appellate Body, remains significantly less than that achieved within the EU framework.

As regards institutional capacity, the EU clearly has considerable depth and breadth of structures, functions and resources and a significant level of general policy and decisional autonomy. It has well-developed and well-resourced structures across the classical range of polity-governing functions. Legislative and executive functions are complexly shared between Parliament, Council and Commission, and at lower level within the Comitoly system[40]; and judicial functions are largely divided between the Court of Justice and the Court of First Instance. The decisional autonomy of the EU is secured not only by the constitutional authority and resources of the dedicated *communautaire* institutions, the Commission, Court and, increasingly, the European Parliament, but also by the secular trend away from the intergovernmental premise of unanimity and towards majority voting in the Council.[41]

In contrast, "the WTO is still a far cry away from the full constitutional paraphernalia of the EU",[42] although the Uruguay Round has undoubtedly brought significant advances. The very creation of the WTO as an international organisation, as a separate legal entity in international law rather than the mere agreement among contracting parties which was GATT 47, signals an enhanced institutional capacity. The development of a judicial capacity within the DSB has already been referred to. Within the broader governance structure, the main executive body is the biennial Ministerial Conference. Beneath it are the General Council, which has overall supervisory authority on a continuous basis, conducting work on behalf of the Ministerial Council, retaining overall responsibility for the discharge of the functions of the DSB and, in its capacity as Trade Policy Review Body, overseeing regular reviews under the TPRM of the trade policies of each WTO member. There are also specific Councils for each of the three Annex 1 Agreements on goods, services and intellectual property rights respectively, and a number of other committees dealing with detailed areas of the WTO's work agenda. The overall structure is serviced by the Geneva-based Secretariat, headed by the Secretary General.

Quite apart from the lesser effectiveness of its adjudicatory organs, there are at least four ways in which the institutional capacity of the WTO suffers in comparison with that of the EU. In the first place, for all its institutional reforms, the Uruguay Round, despite proposals on the table which would have filled this "constitutional gap", chose not to create an autonomous legislative capacity for

---

[40] See, e.g., C. Joerges and E. Vos (eds.), *EU Committees: Social Regulation, Law and Politics* (Oxford, Hart, 1999).

[41] See, e.g., Weiler, *supra* n. 10, ch. 2.

[42] J.H.H. Weiler, "Epilogue: towards a Common Law of International Trade" in J.H.H. Weiler (ed.), *The EU, the WTO and NAFTA: Towards a Common Law of International Trade* (Oxford, OUP, 2000) 201, at 202.

the new organisation. The means of law-making were instead to remain inter-state bargaining in successive rounds of negotiations. In the second place, in the case of the key executive institution which is recognised by the Agreement, the Ministerial Conference, the voting protocols retain a stronger intergovernmental flavour than they do in the EU Council of Ministers. Consensus remains the norm, although in the absence of consensus some consequential votes, as they do in the Council of Ministers, require a special majority rather than unanimity to pass. Tellingly, however, unlike the Council of Ministers, the one-nation, one-vote rule is retained for the Ministerial Conference, a procedural legacy of the GATT 47's original role as an aggregator rather than a transformer of national voices and interests. Thirdly, the WTO secretariat, its permanent organ and as such most likely to articulate a distinctive WTO ethos, is thinly resourced. Its administrative budget and staffing levels are considerably less than those of the other global sites of economic governance, including the World Bank and the IMF—the other Bretton Woods institutions. The comparison with the European Commission, moreover, is particularly invidious, the WTO Secretariat boasting only 3 per cent of the budget and 2.5 per cent of the staffing levels of the larger entity.[43] Finally, exacerbating these structural limitations, it is arguable that the institutional capacity of the WTO is depleted by the absence or paucity of effective sources of social legitimacy, in particular the lack of a mandate responsive to a diversity of interests and of adequate foundations of democratic accountability and participation.[44]

This last objection points us directly to the last two items on our constitutional inventory—citizenship and representation, which are so closely related that they will be considered together. Within modern constitutional discourse citizenship, like many of the key concepts and mechanisms that we have addressed, has tended to become bound to the state.[45] In that respect, Janoski's otherwise helpfully expansive definition of citizenship as "passive and active membership of individuals in a *nation-state* with certain universalistic rights and obligations at a specified level of equality" (emphasis added)[46] is typically circumscribed. Yet history once more instructs us that the notion of citizenship pre-dates the modern state, supplying one of the "classical ideals"[47] of ancient Athenian and Roman civilisation. And in the EU context, the language of non-state citizenship has again achieved sufficient currency in the post-Westphalian

[43] J.L. Mortensen, "The Institutional Requirements of the WTO in an Era of Globalisation: Imperfections in the Global Economic Polity" (2000) 6 *ELJ* 176, 197–198.

[44] *Ibid.*, 200.

[45] Z. Bankowski and E. Christolodoulis, "Citizenship Bound and Citizenship Unbound" in K. Hutchings and R. Danreuther (eds.), *Cosmopolitan Citizenship* (Basingstoke, Macmillan, 1999).

[46] T. Janoski, *Citizenship and Civil Society: A Framework of Rights and Obligations in Liberal, Traditioal and Social Democratic Regimes* (Cambridge, CUP, 1999) 9.

[47] J.G.A. Pocock, "The Ideal of Citizenship since Classical Times" in G. Shafir (ed.), *The Citizenship Debates: A Reader* (Minneapolis, Minn., and London, University of Minnesota Press, 1998) 31.

age to be promoted, since Maastricht, as an explicit legal status of Union membership under which are grouped a number of specific provisions.[48]

Although this heading describes a rather meagre catalogue of political and mobility rights, if we free ourselves from a rigid legal formalism,[49] we can move beyond the self-understanding of the treaties in our treatment of citizenship in at least two ways. First, we can impute to many of the other substantive provisions of European law a citizenship-constitutive quality. Even in textual terms, the self-proclaimed incidents of European citizenship by no means exhaust the entitlements of citizenship as commonly understood. To return to Janoski's influential scheme, these are generally taken to include certain universal entitlements *re* the polity in both the classical sphere of negative freedoms and in the sphere of political voice and participation, as well as an equality of basic social entitlement sufficient to provide a minimum threshold of well-being and the wherewithal to enjoy and exploit these liberal and political rights. On this wider view the European Union provides a developed infrastructure of entitlements to the "market citizen"[50] around the four freedoms and a more muted recognition of the wider catalogue of classical first-generation rights through its acknowledgment of the Council of Europe's European Convention on Human Rights (ECHR) as a constitutional source.[51] It also supplies a range of political rights centred on direct representation in the European Parliament, and—notwithstanding the continuing absence of significant resources for and mechanisms of redistribution at the European level—a growing range of social rights in employment, and, increasingly, in matters of discrimination more generally.[52] In this broader context of citizenship rights, the growing yet still uneasy and uneven commitment of the EU to an expansive conception of constitutional citizenship is perhaps typified in the freshly minted Charter of Fundamental Rights in the European Union—unprecedented in non-state polities for its breadth and depth of rights coverage yet its edge blunted by its merely declaratory status.[53]

Nevertheless, grand documentary statements apart, if, as some authors have sought to do, we extend our sense of citizenship even further and treat it not only as an abstract status of passive belonging to a polity but also as concrete practice of active engagement with a polity, and thus as generally bound up with the level and quality of representation within the polity, then the EU increasingly presents itself as a sufficient source of authoritative and allocative resources to provide a general site of political struggle—one which is in an

---

[48] Arts. 17–22 EC Treaty.

[49] J. Shaw, "The Problem of Membership in European Union Citizenship" in Bankowski and Scott (eds.), *supra* n. 11, 65.

[50] M. Everson, "The Legacy of the Market Citizen" in J. Shaw and G. More (eds.), *New Legal Dynamics of European Union* (Oxford, OUP, 1995) 73.

[51] Art. 6 TEU.

[52] Art. 13 EC Treaty.

[53] See, e.g., B. De Witte, "The Legal Status of the Charter: Vital Question or Non-Issue?", *Maastricht Journal of European and Comparative Law* (forthcoming, 2001).

increasingly strong sense "constitutive of both individual and group identity"[54] for many Europeans.

This is not to ignore the voluminous and pertinent critique of the Union's democratic deficit.[55] The democratic enpowerment of the European Parliament has been slow, grudging and incomplete, the resulting variability in its capacities and procedures imposing further costs in terms of public understanding. Formal powers aside, the Parliament's remoteness, its lack of political cohesion, its low media visibility, its lack of voter interest and the consequential weakness of its electoral mandate further diminish its representative capacity. Underlying much of this, there is the famous "no demos" thesis,[56] the idea that the absence of a prior European political identity sufficiently grounded in ethnic or cultural homogeneity, still allegedly the exclusive preserve of the Member States, makes the very idea of an active European democracy a false conceit of social engineering.

Yet for all that it points to the genuine problems of a new political community pulling itself up by its own bootstraps, the no demos critique is surely overstated, its essentialist premise unsustainable.[57] To recall an earlier proposition, from a broad constitutional perspective law and politics are most aptly conceived of as mutually constitutive and mutually contained, thus challenging the presumption of the coherence, still less of the necessity, of an *a priori* political community. And, as noted, it is precisely the point of the new generation of citizenship studies, and the new generation of citizenship practice to which these studies refer, that the decision-making and adjudicatory fora of the European political space allow scope, however variable and circumscribed, for the construction and development of new transnational identities, not just amongst powerful producer interests but also for new social movements in areas as diverse as labour, environmental and sexual politics.[58]

In comparison, citizenship and democracy within the WTO register only very weakly. As we have seen, non-state actors cannot enforce rights of market access before the WTO's own DSB, nor is there any constitutional guarantee of their protection before national or European courts. To be sure, this state of affairs has been the subject of remorseless and resourceful opposition by constitutionalists of an economic libertarian persuasion. Indeed, perhaps the most articulate exponent of this position, Ernst-Ulrich Petersmann, has couched the agenda of this movement in the explicit language of citizenship and human rights.[59] Yet it is an agenda which has been effectively resisted thus far, not least because, given the limited jurisdiction and paltry democratic credentials of the

---

[54] Shaw, *supra* n. 49, 89.

[55] See, e.g., Weiler, *supra* n. 10, ch. 8.

[56] Associated in particular with the decision of the Bundesverfassungsgericht in *Brunner* (*supra* n. 36).

[57] See, e.g., Weiler, *supra* n. 10, chs. 7 and 10.

[58] See, e.g., Shaw, *supra* n. 49.

[59] For example, Petersmann, *supra* n. 6 at 24: "As in EC law, 'we the citizens' must become the main subjects and beneficiaries of WTO rules".

WTO, a charter of economic rights would artificially privilege one set of interests over others in what is essentially a controversial exercise of balancing, and would do so in a context in which the capacity for democratic representation and reassertion of countervailing interests is marginal.[60]

What of that broader democratic picture? In the absence of a directly representative assembly, representation within the WTO depends upon indirect representation either through national channels, or within the network of existing WTO institutions and processes. Yet, as regards the first possibility, the poverty of internal consultation and deliberation over national negotiating positions is notorious.[61] As regards the second, the WTO Agreement's acknowledgment of a general policy of co-operation and consultation with NGOs sets an important general precedent,[62] but the continuing absence of institutionalised representation for NGOs within the various policy committees and monitoring mechanisms of the WTO remains marked, as does the limited commitment to the WTO to transparency and information access.[63] Arguably, indeed, the more coherent theme of the Seattle protests was not substantive—different protesters often espousing different and contradictory positions on the balance and relationship between national protectionism, market access and the transnational development of non-trade values—but procedural, an outcry against the general exclusion of civil society from all but the very margins of the WTO framework.[64]

THE CHALLENGE OF CONSTITUTIONAL SCEPTICISM

The above analysis reveal a picture of the WTO as only a very modestly constitutionalised entity, and so also as a very incomplete polity, both in the absolute terms of the criteria and indices set out and in comparison to the European Union. Indeed, there is no single criterion or index in relation to which the constitutional credentials of the WTO are as developed as those of the EU. On the other hand, in some areas, the outlines of WTO constitutionalism and constitutionalisation are becoming well-defined, and in all areas there is some movement on the graph. Clearly, interpretive autonomy is the area of greatest development, with all that this implies in terms of judicialisation and subscription to rule of law values of certainty, predictability and consistent and coherent reasoning. There are also significant developments in the depth and maturity of constitutional discourse, in jurisdictional scope and in institutional capacity. There is much less so in the areas of citizenship and democracy, although even

---

[60] See, further, Howse and Nicolaidis, *supra* n. 6.

[61] Mortensen, *supra* n. 43, 200.

[62] Art. V:2, Marrakesh Agreement; see G. Marceau and P.N. Pedersen, "Is the WTO Open and Transparent?" (1999) 33 *Journal of World Trade Law* 5.

[63] See, e.g., Marceau and Pedersen, *supra* n. 62; J.A. Scholte, R. O'Brien and M. Williams, "The WTO and Civil Society" (1999) 33 *Journal of World Trade Law* 107.

[64] See, e.g., P. Legrain, "Against Globophobia", *Prospect*, May 2000, 30.

here, the vigour of the emerging constitutional discourse allied to developing institutional capacity and judicialisation has created some momentum for change. Finally, the notion of WTO sovereignty is very thinly grounded, although if, as I have argued, sovereignty too may be viewed as an emergent and variable phenomenon, developments in the various other constitutional dimensions will also find an echo here.

If we can assume that this type of approach begins to address the problems of translation which lie at the core of the conceptual objection to the treatment of non-state entities in constitutional terms, in order to pursue its possible advantages in a more applied sense we must first engage with the remaining objection to non-state constitutionalism. This second objection, which concerns the normative implications of the constitutional perspective, has recently been clearly and incisively articulated with regard to the WTO by Howse and Nicolaidis.[65]

Howse and Nicolaidis identify two streams within the constitutionalising tendency in WTO discourse. On the one hand, there is the economic libertarian position, discussed above. On the other hand, more recently there has emerged a range of positions committed in various degrees to a broader model of political constitutionalism.[66] Indeed, this new wave responds to some of the criticisms levelled at the narrower model by calling for the development, in a manner analogous to, although typically more modest than, the earlier development of the EU, of an explicit level of neo-federal governance at the WTO level with powers of positive integration in flanking areas of social policy to provide a more vigorous counterbalance to the organisation's constitutive mandate of market liberalisation. While they acknowledge the marked differences between the two approaches, the bottom line of Howse and Nicolaidis's objection to both models is the same; namely that "their [constitutionalising] trajectory pre-supposes the very conditions of legitimacy that they want to create". Each model in its very distinctive way offers solutions to the global regulation of trade which are controversial both in terms of the institutional design and process they envisage and the substantive outcomes they seek, yet each model seeks to privilege and defend its controversial solutions by couching them in the self-dignifying language of constitutionalism. For Howse and Nicolaidis, however, this strategy cannot succeed, or at least should not be allowed to do so: "For constitutionalization cannot itself create, *ex nihilo* as it were, the conditions of constitutional legitimacy: rather, legitimate constitutionalism depends on those conditions, both conceptually and temporally". To pretend otherwise is viewed as wishful thinking at best, and at worse as a cynical attempt by the proponents of WTO constitutionalism to claim for their preferred model a legitimate authority which it is yet to earn.

---

[65] *Supra* n. 6.

[66] See, e.g., Cottier, Schmidt and Jackson, *supra* n. 6; see also A. Tita, "Globalization: A New Political and Economic Space Requiring Supranational Governance" (1998) 32 *Journal of World Trade Law* 47.

This represents a powerful objection[67] to the expansive use of constitutional discourse in non-state settings, but one that I think can be answered through a series of linked points. To begin with, just as Howse and Nicolaidis interrogate the motives of the advocates of WTO constitutionalism, so we are entitled to ask the same questions of those engaged in "constitutional denial".[68] Who stands to gain from denying constitutional status to the WTO and why? This takes us to the very heart of the political/normative critique of non-state constitutionalism. As regards the EU, the most vehement if seldom the most considered arguments against conferring constitutional status tend to come from those whose interests are bound up with *other* constitutional or proto-constitutional entities, in particular, the Member States themselves. Similarly with regard to the WTO, the most bitter and most powerful campaigns against constitutionalisation have been fought by or on behalf of state constitutional actors, as in the "Great Sovereignty Debate"[69] of 1994 which attended the ratification of the WTO agreement by the United States, and which engaged many mercantilist sections of the national political establishment. The crux of the matter is that there is indeed a cynically self-serving dimension in some of the arguments for constitutionalising the WTO, or at least the arguments on the table are capable of being exploited in that way. Yet, while Howse and Nicolaidis themselves are clearly exempt from such a charge, precisely the same accusation could be made with regard to some of those in the denial camp. Constitutional discourse has a strong and pervasive ideological currency. The claim to constitutional status provides a kind of institutional "symbolic capital"[70] within global power politics to those entities which can successfully make it, and likewise penalises those which are denied it. Recognition of this ideological dimension does not of course provide us with a positive argument in favour of constitutional expansionism, but does at least alert us to the fact that the net effect of denial, and sometimes even the motivation for denial, is not or not only to strike out a constitutional claim as unwarranted in terms of some disinterested standard. An equally pertinent prospect of successful denial in the densely relational multi-dimensional configuration of authority that marks the emerging post-Westphalian age is to increase the relative advantage accruing to rival polities in overlapping domains, the nature and extent of whose own claims to constitutional status may be every bit as ideologically motivated and contestable as those they seek to deny.

Yet two wrongs do not make a right, and to demonstrate that the ideological objection cuts both ways is not to neutralise it. We still need to answer Howse

---

[67] Although not a comprehensive objection, as the authors are prepared to concede the legitimacy of non-state constitutional discourse in the exceptional case of the EU.

[68] N. Walker, "European Constitutionalism and European Integration" [1996] *Public Law* 266, 278.

[69] See J. Jackson, *supra* n. 29, ch. 19.

[70] A term borrowed (with some conceptual license) from P. Bourdieu, *Language and Symbolic Power* (Cambridge, Polity, 1991); see also R. Cotterrell, "Some Aspects of the Communication of Constitutional Authority" in D. Nelken (ed.), *Law as Communication* (Aldershot, Dartmouth, 1997) 129.

and Nicolaidis's fundamental objection that a constitutionalising discourse in the absence of developed constitutional structures and the preconditions of constitutional legitimacy is an empty vessel, and so a sham. To do so, we draw upon some of the arguments developed earlier in the essay to suggest that the sceptics' own position is based upon an inappropriately absolutist and essentialist conception of constitutionalism, and also to suggest that the ideological dimension of constitutionalism, for all its dangers and dark side, can also be viewed in a more positive light.

The sceptical argument is inappropriately absolutist in that in concluding that the WTO, at best only immaturely and emergently constitutional in character, does not as such warrant constitutional status, it presupposes that there is a single threshold point of qualification which allows us to draw a bright line between those entities that can properly claim constitutional credentials and those that cannot. Yet, as I have tried to demonstrate, constitutionalism and constitutionalisation are multi-faceted phenomena, and while the various contributing factors are complexly connected, it is quite possible for a constitutional profile to be well developed in one or more areas— in the WTO's case, interpretive autonomy, judicialisation and the rule of law—but underdeveloped in others—again in the WTO's case, citizenship and representation. Against this multi-factorial backdrop, we can only retain a single threshold test in one of two ways. First, we might insist upon constitutional maturity as regards all factors. But this would make it very difficult to explain, or to legitimate, constitutionalisation as a gradual process, and so very hard to take seriously in constitutional terms not only the tentative steps of a body such as the WTO, but the entire emergent history of the much more developed EU. Secondly, and here the spectre of essentialism looms large, a single threshold test might not insist on maturity across the board, but instead might privilege one factor or set of factors and the legitimacy they confer over others. But it is difficult to imagine how this hierarchy of values and priorities might be established in such a contested area without resorting to precisely the kind of assertively ideological approach—the myopic declaration of the one best, or only, constitutional way—that Howse and Nicolaidis reject.

But there is more to be said for a graduated approach than simply to point to the methodological difficulties of establishing an alternative approach based upon firm conceptual boundaries. Crucially, the absolutism and essentialism implicit in Howse's and Nicolaidis's approach also ignores or underplays the constitutive role and "responsibilising" potential of constitutional discourse and imagination in the development of a polity. And here it is vital to note that in the final analysis the ideological dimension of constitutional politics—its role in the strategic assertion of institutional power and of the interests served by that power—is not the enemy of a normative discourse of responsible self-government but rather its necessary accompaniment, and, indeed, a central part of its generative context. The idea of constitutionalism is linked in a powerful and resilient chain of signification to a whole series of polity-constitutive values, such as democracy, the separation of powers and the rule of law. Those who wish, from whatever motive or combination of motives, to make a plausible claim to constitutional status, must at least *be seen to* take these values seriously, which in turn imposes real constraints and has real consequences for what they propose and enact. To put this point in perhaps unduly cynical terms, just as hypocrisy can have civilising effects,[71] the invocation of constitutionalism tends to structure the ensuing debate between those who would claim, challenge or counterclaim its associated symbolic power (and, in turn, tends to inform the institutional consequences of that debate) in ways which may escape the self-interested intentions of the original protagonists. Paradoxically, constitutionalism may indeed be invoked as a way of closing down debate in favour of a particular institutional balance and value cluster, as in the narrow constitutional vision of the economic liberals, but in practice, as the instant case of constitutional discourse about the WTO aptly demonstrates, the scarcity of and competition over constitutonalism's symbolic capital and the diverse set of values it is capable of signifying often has precisely the opposite effect, opening up a richer and more productive normative debate.[72]

THE RELATIONAL DIMENSION

The beneficial consequences of developing debate over the normative order of the new multi-dimensional configuration in constitutional and in metaconstitutional terms may be tracked further by considering briefly the dimension of relations between non-state polities in general and the EU and the WTO in particular. It was argued earlier that one of the defining features of the emerging pluralist order was precisely its thickly overlapping texture. The network of relations cannot be understood without considering the sites of authority—the nodes of power—which lend shape to the network but, conversely, the sites of authority cannot be understood without considering the network of relations which connect them. Absent the comprehensive jurisdiction of the Westphalian state, the various post-Westphalian state and non-state polities have "partial governance projects" that are closely connected. The juxtaposition and interpenetration of normative concerns; the overlap of citizenries—of *demoi*, of pressure groups, and of key officials or forms of official interest representation, the intersection of jurisdictions; all of these factors bear testimony to the salience of the relational dimension.[73] In turn, this thick web of connections allows and demands a substantial flow of relational politics, which may be conducted in more or less competitive or co-operative vein,[74] and with greater or

---

[71] J. Elster, "Introduction" in J. Elster (ed.) Deliberate Democracy (Cambridge, CUP, 1997) pp.1–18, n. 14.
[72] Thus many of the broader models of political constitutionalism in the literature have been developed in direct response to the restricted constituionalism of the economic libertarians.
[73] Walker, *supra* n. 13, "Flexibility Within a Metaconstituional Frame", pp. 25–30.
[74] Farrell, *supra* n. 30.

less concern for the development of norms which are adequate not only to internal systemic interests and legitimacy concerns and the "partial governance projects" which map the boundaries of systemic jurisdiction, but also to trans-systemic interests and legitimacy concerns and the imagined possibility of more "holistic governance projects" which the transcending of particular jurisdictions permits.

These connections, and the profound questions they pose for the relationship between the parts and the whole, abound in the context of the "meta-meta" relation between the EU and WTO. Normatively, there is much scope for both competition and complementarity between the two polities. As a regional trading organisation, the European Union contravenes the general WTO principle of non-discrimination by imposing a common external tariff on non-members while abolishing tariffs on intra-Community trade. And while this exception to the Most Favoured Nation rule is conceded to regional arrangements under Article XX1V GATT, the terms and conditions of the resulting compromise, clarified but also sharpened by the Uruguay Round's interpretive "Understanding", sustains a considerable area of tension. On the other hand, in many ways the EU provides a role model of trade liberalisation, a miniature template to which the global organisation might aspire and from which it might learn in policy areas as diverse as competition, agriculture and the environment.[75] In terms of citizen representation, the EU and in some respects also each of its Member States are members of the WTO,[76] creating three levels of overlapping *demoi* and intermeshing civil societies. Institutionally, the position of the European Union as a powerful economic bloc, in combination with its developed network of preferential trading agreements with non-member countries, allows the EU considerable scope to exercise its cohesive and influential power within the voting system of the WTO organs to its own advantage.[77] Jurisdictionally, the juridification of the WTO and the sharpening of its judicial and supervisory teeth has increased and intensified the possibilities of engagement between the two systems in areas where their competences overlap and their interests may be in tension. This can be seen, for example, in the WTO's new dispute settlement procedures, where the EU has been the second most active litigant behind the United States, and where issues as central to the EU's policy profile as its Common Agricultural Policy, the Lomé Agreement, the banana regime, and its growing number of preferential agreements with third parties have come under scrutiny; in the frequency with which EU agreements have been investigated by the WTO's new Committee on Regional Trade Agreements[78]; and, of course, in the growing intensity of the pressure upon the ECJ to ascribe direct effect to WTO norms.[79]

---

[75] *Ibid.*, chs. 3–4.
[76] Opinion 1/94 *Re the Uruguay Round Treaties* [1994] ECR I–5267.
[77] Farrell, *supra* n. 30, 8.
[78] *Ibid.*, 21–22.
[79] See references at n. 28.

The detailed substantive and procedural implications of many of these points of connection provide the subject-matter of a number of chapters in this volume, and it is not my intention here to repeat or pursue these various and complex lines of inquiry. My aim instead is the more modest one of exhorting that all such issues should be discussed in constitutional terms, albeit in the new key set by the rather different structural imperatives of relations involving meta-sites. In terms of the arguments set out above, this should not be a surprising or controversial conclusion, but one which is dictated by the very logic of that approach. After all, the constitutional values which were central to the hermetically sealed holistic governance projects of the Westphalian state—representation, legal order and certainty, social belonging, separation of powers and diffusion of authority etc.—remain equally relevant to the trans-systemic re-imagination of a more holistic frame of governance in the post-Westphalian age, even if the institutional context is more plural and its point of departure more partial. It is arguable, moreover, that the constitutionalisation of the relational dimension is no mere secondary consequence of the extension of constitutional discourse to the non-state political domain. Rather, it provides perhaps the most pressing justification for and most obvious beneficiary of that extension.

It is worth remarking that in the context of another key vector in the new multi-dimensional configuration of authority—namely that which connects the EU to its Member States, the constitutional character of the relationship is typically taken for granted not only by those who concede the constitutional status of both parties, but even by those statist interests which would not readily accept such an attribution to the EU. The explanation is simple. If constitutionalism, as suggested, is in outline about the development of a normative model of responsible self-government, then in a closely intersecting global order, it would be artificial not to extend the ambit of responsibility to those adjacent domains of governance which closely impact upon the partial governance projects of the home domain. A responsible attitude to those adjacent domains becomes part and parcel of responsible self-government and, correspondingly, constitutionalism in a relational mode becomes a natural extension of internal constitutionalism.

Of course, as already noted, in the context of EU–Member State relations, since the former is the linear descendant of the latter within the metaconstitutional family tree, there are a number of clearly established bridging mechanisms between the two systems, which means that constitutional relations for the most part follow an authoritatively established and reasonably settled pattern.[80] The relationship between the WTO and the EU, by contrast, is not one of linear descent, but a "meta-meta" relation between two entities which grew separately out of the state system. Accordingly, their framework of mutual recognition and engagement is less settled, less easily identifiable within a recognisably constitutional groove. Yet, provided the basic constitutional status of both—or, indeed, following the logic and precedent of the statist position *vis-à-*

---

[80] See references at n. 25.

vis the EU, of *either*[81]—of the parties is acknowledged; and provided, as is undoubtedly the case, the EU and the WTO—as in the Member State–EU relation, can each be conceived of as engaged in partial governance projects in relation to which the other and adjacent polity site has a crucially complementary role, this more precarious interface is no argument against conceiving of that relation in terms of constitutional discourse also. If anything, the unsettled and underdeveloped normative context lends an even greater urgency to that task.

A wide range of "legitimacy challenges"[82] have been posed to the WTO in its current state of legal and political development, not least in respect of its relations with the EU. The most promising conceptualisations and treatments of these challenges are those which grasp that, in the absence of hegemonic global institutions, the most legitimate site-specific solutions to governance problems are ones which reflexively acknowledge the limitations of their own legitimacy and the partiality of their own systemic perspective, and which seek, in their relational politics, to work within these limitations to recognise and address these governance problems from a more holistic trans-systemic perspective. One of the most incisive attempts to treat the "whole" from the perspective of the "part" in this way, indeed, is to be found in the work of Howse and Nicolaidis itself. Their plea for the WTO, its DSB in particular, to display "institutional sensitivity" in its treatment of the legal interests of democratic states in view of its own lack of democratic legitimacy, yet to utilise its strong adjudicatory presence to develop procedural norms of greater "political inclusiveness" in global trade politics generally, provides an object lesson in how to set about optimising the legitimate use of a partial polity's limited authoritative resources in a system-transcending way. My message to them and to other constitutional sceptics is that, far from being the enemy of that kind of responsible relational politics—although some who are attracted by the symbolic power of constitutional discourse might well be considered as such—the tradition of constitutionalism remains the best-stocked normative reservoir from which it may draw and the most persuasive medium in which it may be articulated.

---

[81] If, e.g., as appears to be Howse's and Nicolaidis's position, the constitutional status of the EU is in principle acccepted, but not that of the WTO (see n. 67), a comprehensively constitutional approach to the EU alone would in any case embrace EU–WTO relations.

[82] Howse and Nicolaidis, *supra* n. 6. See also Scott and De Búrca in the present volume.

3

The WTO and the EU: Some Constitutional Comparisons

PETER HOLMES

INTRODUCTION

THE MAIN PURPOSE of this chapter is to compare the institutional arrangements of the EU and the WTO in order to analyse the different ways in which these arrangements affect economic policy. Part 2 tries to explain why the issues in this book are of interest to economists as well as to lawyers. Part 3 contrasts the institutional "constitutions" of the EU and the WTO. It argues that despite some interesting parallels the two systems are fundamentally different. Part 4 compares the substantive "Constitution of the Common Market Place",[1] with that prevailing under the WTO, looking in particular at non-discrimination versus mutual recognition and harmonisation. It argues that there is an important interplay between the technical mechanisms for addressing trade barriers and the broader "constitutional" issues. In particular if any sort of mutual recognition or harmonisation of norms is to be adopted, attention needs to be paid to the accountability of the bodies setting standards, an issue that has been highly controversial in the EU but which is just emerging in the WTO. Part 5 looks at the implications of the differences in the two systems for dispute settlement and offers some tentative thoughts on the comparison with the early years of the ECJ. In particular it shows how the incompleteness of the WTO system leads to an over-reliance on the dispute settlement mechanism. Part 6 offers the conclusion that the EU remains *sui generis* and any attempts to transpose its experience to the global system are likely to be fraught with problems.

The chapter does not directly address the technical issues of the status of WTO law within the EU legal order, but by comparing the "constitutions" of the EU and the WTO it argues that that these are so different that we should be very sceptical about arguments that the WTO should be "constitutionalised". In

---

[1] J.H.H. Weiler, "The Constititution of the Common Market Place" in P. Craig and G. de Búrca (eds.), *The Evolution of European Law* (Oxford, OUP, 1999) at 349–76.

this, the chapter supports the recent work of Howse and Nicolaidis[2] rather than the thesis of Petersmann.[3]

"CONSTITUTIONS" AND ECONOMIC POLICY MAKING

The notion of a "constitution" is used very differently by different disciplines and intellectual traditions. This chapter will attempt to avoid the technical debates about what a constitution is. For present purposes I will use the term in two senses. In the introductory section I shall attempt to explain why the issues here are of interest to economists, who have a tradition of using the terms "constitution" and "constitutionalisation" to cover almost any arrangement that pre-commits economic policy to a fixed set of rules rather than leaving the government free to adopt any economic policies it wishes. The subsequent sections will focus on the ways in which, in this sense, the EU and the WTO commit their member governments to certain policies. In this part the term "constitution" will be used rather narrowly in the sense that John Jackson uses the term in his book, *The WTO: Constitution and Jurisprudence*, to refer to the institutions and workings of the WTO. In fact if we do accept that the basic rules of the WTO can be called its constitution then it is in fact a theme of this chapter that we can characterise the WTO as largely consisting of its constitution and the jurisprudence of its dispute settlement system, i.e. lacking in capacity to make secondary legislation. At the same time Weiler has referred to the evolution of the overall architecture of the system in his "The Constitution of the Common Market Place".[4]

The present chapter will adopt the simple economic notion of "constitutionalisation" as any institutional arrangement that seeks to ensure that decision-making obeys a set of pre-agreed rules. Economists see constitutions as devices for pre-commitment of economic policy. This is typically a way to handle the "time inconsistency" problem. The government may make promises to act in a certain way in order, for example, to get firms to commit to certain investments. Once the investments have occurred, there is an incentive to renege on the promises so, anticipating this, the firms will not invest. The government is better off if it can tie its own hands (for example by having a constitutional rule that retrospective changes in tax laws are unconstitutional).

An interesting framework for this has been provided by Dixit[5] who observes in a section tellingly entitled "Constitutions are incomplete contracts" that

[2] R. Howse and K. Nicolaidis, "Legitimacy and Global Governance: Why Constitutionalizing the WTO is a Step too Far" in P. Sauve and A. Subramanian (eds.), *Efficiency, Equity, Legitimacy and Governance: The Multilateral Trading System at the Millennium* (Washington, DC, Brooking Institute Press, forthcoming).

[3] U. Petersmann, "The Transformation of the World Trading System through the 1994 Agreement Establishing the World Trade Organization" (1995) 6 *European Journal of International Law* xx at http://www.ejil.org/journal/vol6/no2/art1.html.

[4] Weiler, *supra* n. 1.

[5] A. Dixit, *The Making of Economic Policy, a Transactions Cost Analysis* (Oxford, OUP, 1993).

constitutional arrangements do two things. First they lay down a set of rules for the conduct of economic policy that constrains the freedom of decision-makers. Secondly, recognising that they cannot possibly anticipate every possible contingency, they lay down procedures for settling disputes when cases arise that are not covered by the rules laid down initially. These include both voting rules and decision-making procedures on the one hand, and on the other hand legitimated judicial or other arbitration procedures. Because the rules for conduct are incomplete contracts, the dispute settlement component is crucial.

Brennan and Hamlin say "constitutional economics is the application of the methods and analytical techniques of modern economics to the study of the basic rules under which social orders may operate".[6] The term "basic rules" is used quite broadly in this context, but it would clearly cover the WTO agreements and the basic legal framework of the EU/EC. The key point is that there are certain rules of the game which cannot easily be changed and economic actors can assume that they will be binding on all parties. Brennan and Hamlin identify three reasons, all of them highly applicable to trade policy, why states might wish to bind themselves to rules that they cannot easily escape or change:

(1) the prisoner's dilemma—the isolation paradox where we would individually prefer to act opportunistically while others obey the rules—but on balance we all gain if everyone is constrained: for example we would like to be protectionist, but accept world-wide free trade as better than losing others' markets;

(2) the assurance paradox—we have no desire to break the rules so long as others obey—and so here weaker rules or conventions, or merely assuring information on others' behaviour, may be adequate. Global free trade is our first choice but if others refuse, we wish to be able to retaliate;

(3) we desire rules/institutions to ensure that individually as a trading partner we can pre-commit ourselves to be seen as trustworthy even if others are not. We may actually prefer to be one of the few parties with a reputation for obeying the treaties, as we know we can attract more investment.

All of these are reasons why individuals or countries should sign binding agreements to accept rules that constrain freedom of choice. The macroeconomics literature is full of examples where policy-makers can gain by tying their hands in macro policy in order to gain credibility. This, of course, is a central element in the European Monetary Union (EMU) process. The literature on trade policy reform contains many references to the need for credibility, but it is perhaps surprising that while there has been a consensus among economists for 200 years that free trade is desirable, the advocates of explicitly adopting

---

[6] G. Brennan and A. Hamlin "Constitutional Economics" in P. Newman (ed.), *New Palgrave Dictionary of Economics and the Law* (London, Macmillan, 1998).

constitutional rules to commit to free trade, whilst not wholly absent, are nowhere near as vocal as the advocates of (quasi-)constitutional rules limiting budget deficits or monetary expansion, even though the theoretical case for the latter types of policy is actually more debatable.

Dixit[7] also makes the very fundamental point that Constitutions are not agreed behind a veil of ignorance. He points out that is it naïve to assume people do not know the consequences of their decisions. On the other hand actors may well guess wrong and he suggests that the "constitution" of the original GATT may well have been built based on mistaken assumptions about the development of the world economy.[8] It is already clear that this is the case for the WTO, as Jackson observes.[9] If Weiler's "do and hearken", analysis is correct[10] this applies to the EU too. Indeed this process appears to repeat itself, suggesting, as North does, that any dynamic analysis of institutions should be from an imperfect information evolutionary perspective rather than assuming "rational expectations".[11]

In this chapter therefore we will look at the ways in which member states of the EU and the WTO have tied their hands in matters of trade policy and have tried to extend this tying to cover domestic policies that may affect trade.

Reasons for tying one's hands in trade policy can be defended from a number of perspectives:

(1) mercantilism: if you remove trade barriers, others will too;
(2) liberalism: if you tell your own producers that others have liberalised you can more easily persuade them to accept uncongenial liberalisation at home;
(3) predictability: even imperfect but predictable rules may reduce the risk premium on investment.

Petersmann has argued strongly that democratic governments will not bind themselves adequately enough and should be put under some form of constitutional constraint to do so. He says:

> To date, most national constitutions appear not to have dealt effectively with their task to protect the "domestic policy constitution" from being undermined by abuses of "foreign policy" powers, for instance by import restrictions which tax and restrict domestic citizens and redistribute income ("protection rents") among domestic groups in a welfare-reducing manner.[12]

and

---

[7] Dixit, *supra* n. 5.

[8] *Ibid.*

[9] J. H. Jackson, *The WTO: Constitution and Jurisprudence* (London, Pinter/RIIA, 1998).

[10] J. Weiler, *The Constitution of Europe* (Cambridge, CUP, 1999).

[11] D. North, *Institutions Institutional Change and Economic Performance* (Cambridge, CUP, 1990).

[12] Petersmann, *supra* n. 3.

Separation and limitation of powers and other constitutional restraints on decision-making processes are therefore no less needed at the level of international organizations than at the state level . . . From such a constitutional perspective . . . the WTO dispute settlement system and the various guarantees in WTO law of access to domestic courts discretely enhance "separation of powers" between international and domestic rule-making, administrations and (quasi)judicial dispute settlement mechanisms.[13]

However Howse and Nicolaidis have recently assembled a major critique of this approach. They argue:

First, even in its own terms, the approach under-estimates the conditions under which such constitutionalism as hands-tying can be made legitimate in the WTO context . . . Clearly, what Petersmann characterizes as the pre-commitment of a public interest-motivated government to tie its own hands in the future in dealing with interest groups, is really a commitment to tie the hands of its political opponents, and the groups they represent, should they win a democratic victory in the future.[14]

In this chapter we will somewhat skip over the question of how far the conditions referred to above by Howse and Nicolaidis are actually met in the EU; the theme of the argument is that they are far less well met in the WTO. Moreover we shall argue that the heart of the problem lies in an excessive reliance on the WTO dispute settlement mechanism to resolve what are rather fundamental political problems about how far "domestic" policies must be adapted to the needs of global market access. As trade liberalisation proceeds we find more and more "domestic" rules being captured in the net, or at least coming under attack from other parties. We need rules about rules that distinguish "legitimate" from "illegitimate" consumer protection rules.

It is however an incomplete contract, and whilst the EU has a developed political context surrounding the purely legal dimension of its DSM, the ECJ, the WTO does not. The EU has jurisdiction over a wide range of subjects. Thus within the legal system, the courts are mandated to give full weight to considerations other than trade liberalisation *per se*.[15] And the EU has a political mechanism for rewriting or reinterpreting its contract, which includes the European Council and Intergovernmental Conferences. The WTO has a legal DSM mechanism that has to interpret its "constitution" in a predictable way. But these texts are often ambiguous, intentionally so sometimes. Formally speaking, only the General Council (GC) or the Ministerial Conference (MC) have the right to "interpret"[16] the agreements; however the Appellate Body (AB) must do so if it is to take decisions, and has read into the WTO Agreements its right to apply the Vienna Convention on the Law of Treaties. The fiction, however, can

---

[13] *Ibid.*

[14] Howse and Nicolaidis, *supra* n. 2.

[15] See Art. 30 of the EU Treaty.

[16] See Art. XI.2 of the Marrakech Final Act. "The Ministerial Conference and the General Council shall have the exclusive authority to adopt interpretations of this Agreement and the Multilateral Trade Agreements".

be preserved that the final decision in dispute settlement cases is the General Council acting as the Dispute Settlement Body, because the panels and the AB in principle only make recommendations to the GC. Of course in reality the panels and the AB are able to make the decisions because of the rule that the DSB must accept their recommendation unless there is a consensus against.

The WTO lacks a political mechanism for completing the contract, and for entirely understandable reasons it also moved sharply away from the GATT practice of power and diplomacy as the basis for settling disputes.

The EU has to a large extent succeeded in doing this, but the question remains open how far the existence of a form of legal constitution is primarily a cause or an effect of what Weiler refers to as the "acceptability of the EU regime".[17] If the latter effect is important the WTO will need to concentrate more on making its system work better and finding out how to make an evolutionary path from partial to nearly complete compliance within a rule-based system.

A COMPARISON OF THE "CONSTITUTIONS" OF THE WTO AND THE EU

As we noted above Petersmann has criticised the use of foreign policy powers to affect citizens' rights in the market place. He added:

> In globally integrated economies, "domestic" and "foreign" policies are often no longer separable, and citizens value the "transnational" exercise of their liberties no less than purely domestic activities. National constitutions remain therefore incomplete without effective constitutional constraints on foreign policy powers.[18]

Meanwhile Siedentop remarks that the EU and the WTO have something in common in that, he argues, in both entities the member governments use the traditional executive prerogatives of the state designed for making foreign policy in order to make agreements about "trade" matters that increasingly impinge[19] (as we shall discuss in part 4) on domestic regulations.

An argument can be made however that this parallel is somewhat inexact in a number of ways. The most striking is that the EU system distinguishes very sharply between Treaty changes, which are decided in the classical way that foreign policy is made, with most of the internal processes of the EU's decision-making suspended, and more routine legislative action.

Whilst, as critics frequently point out, the Council of Ministers meets in secret, it is at least the case that draft legislation is published, circulated and debated in the European Parliament, and in some national parliaments, and the Amsterdam Treaty provides for greater transparency.[20] Treaty changes on the other hand are negotiated in private and rarely offered to the public or parliaments until the final take-it-or-leave it ratification stage.

---

[17] Weiler, *supra* n. 9.
[18] Petersmann, *supra* n. 3.
[19] L. Siedentop, *Law Democracy in Europe* (London, Penguin, 2000) 117.
[20] Pinder, quoted in Howse and Nicolaidis, *supra* n. 2.

It is quite clear that if there is a democratic deficit at the EU level, it is even more apparent in the WTO. Decision-making at the WTO corresponds only to the EU in its Treaty-change mode. Whilst the EU Treaties empower the Council of Ministers to make decisions *qua* Council, with some legislative power in the hands of the European Parliament and even the Commission (where there is direct Treaty power or delegated power conferred by legislation), the key feature of the WTO is that all its core rules are in the form of treaties. There are a number of matters where the General Council is empowered to act in the intervals between ministerial meetings, but major decisions, for example to modify one of the agreements in a significant way, must be undertaken by the ministerial meetings.

In principle the General Council can act with less than total unanimity of all members. Hoekman and Kostecki point out that where "Consensus" is called for it means no dissent among those present,[21] but there are other provisions for two-thirds or three-quarters majorities. But as the Seattle disaster revealed one of the *lacunae* in the "constitution" of the WTO is that it lacks the basic rules about rules, who gets to be in closed meetings, who sees the agenda in advance and so on.

The following table tries to summarise the position. The key point is that there is no accountable political element in the WTO. The General Council's voting rules are not really usable. Developing countries object to the disproportionate *de facto* weight of the USA, Japan and the EU, whose representatives say they account for most trade, while the USA in particular would not dream of accepting a voting system in which very populous undemocratic countries could out vote the US and its allies.

The WTO has treaty law negotiated by diplomats. Not only have national political actors rarely been involved in the discussion of new WTO agreements before they are agreed, but many of the parties who then have to sign are not involved in the discussions until the last minute.

The law of the WTO also shares another rather significant characteristic of diplomatic negotiations that has potential for causing trouble. The texts may be deliberately ambiguous to secure agreement (also of course possible in the EU as with the definition of "subsidiarity"). It is not unknown for parties to sign a deal which can be triumphantly taken home so that each partner can present the wording as a victory for its diplomacy, everyone intending that what was actually meant would be decided in a second round of discussions.

Before the WTO, the developing countries could accept their exclusion from decision-making in the GATT "club" because they had a double opt-out. Additional agreements were plurilateral and hence voluntary, while dispute settlement was *de facto* not binding.[22] The trouble is that now the principle of the

---

[21] B.M. Hoekman and M.M. Kostecki, *The Political Economy of the World Trading System* (Oxford, OUP, 1995).

[22] Jackson (*supra* n. 8) argues that adopted panel reports should have been considered as binding as today—it is just that there are fewer of them. Moreover it has been observed that a small state

Table 1: The EU and the WTO: An Institutional Comparison

	EU	WTO	Parallels and Differences
Executive	Commission?	No	WTO has no executive body
Secretariat	Council Secretariat	WTO Secretariat	WTO Secretariat has no *right* to set the agenda
Legislature	Council of Ministers and European Parliament (occasionally Commission e.g. Article 86 (ex 90))	General Council (GC) can make some decisions; normally ministerial meetings have to act.	EU can use QMV sometimes. WTO normally requires consensus—all big players have *de facto* veto
Constituent assembly	IGCs	Ministerial meetings	Both need unanimity but EU more scope for deals.
Court	ECJ (CFI). ECJ is final independent court with formal power to interpret EC Law.	Appellate Body (Panels) Appellate Body interprets *de facto*.	Formally ECJ is aboveCouncil of Ministers. WTO GC has right to overturn AB rulings, but de *facto* AB is final.
Opt outs?	All *acquis* should be accepted by all members, except for exceptionally agreed opt-outs.	Single undertaking (except for plurilateral agreements); new members negotiate schedules ("*acquis*") on entry.	GATT allowed plurilateral agreements; WTO tries to avoid.Precise commitment schedules differ by member:
Nature of rules	Treaty and secondary laws	Treaty rules[23]	WTO cannot really make secondary law

could not necessarily ignore a GATT panel under the old system. A trade diplomat from a small country has observed that they *did* have to comply.

[23] The role of *Codex Alimentarius* standards under SPS agreement is exceptional.

single undertaking means everyone must accept all the WTO *acquis*.[24] *And* that the rules are intended to bind. Jackson argues that the implications for sovereignty were simply not taken in board by the member states when they signed the Uruguay Round.[25]

Weiler argues:

> From interviews with many delegations I have conducted it is clear that, as mentioned above, they saw the logic of the Appellate body as a kind of Super-Panel to give a losing party another bite at the cherry, given that the losing party could not longer block adoption of the panel. It is equally clear to me that they did not fully understand the judicial let alone constitutional nature of the Appellate Body. And yet the Appellate Body is a court in all but name. And it has even a constitutional dimension.[26]

Indeed the member states created one particularly strange anomaly: as noted above, they formally denied the Appellate Body the right to interpret the rules of the Treaty, giving that power to the General Council, but in reality unless it is unanimous the GC has to accept decisions of the Appellate Body. The Appellate Body can thus in effect pre-empt much of the work of the rest of the WTO (for example, deciding if a preferential agreement violates Article XXIV).[27]

By contrast the European Court of Justice was explicitly given the right to interpret EC law. Its doctrine of supremacy and direct effect of EC law proved somewhat controversial, but in Weiler's term it was very quickly "accepted". The EU has evolved in a complex and structured way. The delicate balance between inter-governmentalism, supra-nationalism and judicial activism is set in a context of 50 years of some form of legitimacy, and the balance between trade and non-trade objectives is not left to the ECJ alone.

But, as we shall see, the attempt to bring about genuine free trade by looking beyond border measures alone inevitably creates a serious interface problem between domestic and trade issues, an interface that in the early years the Member States viewed with equanimity as they felt they were in control of the process. Weiler argues that they were not. But at least the EU was their baby, as the WTO is not.

---

[24] But the *FISC* case showed that the Appellate Body has considerable leeway in deciding what decisions of the GATT signatories and of the WTO are legally binding (*United States—Tax Treatment for "Foreign Sales Corporations"*, WTO Appellate Body WT/D5108/AB/R 24 February 2000 especially para. 108.

[25] *Supra* n. 8.

[26] J.H.H. Weiler, "The Rule of Lawyers and the Ethos of Diplomats-Reflections on the Internal and External Legitimacy of WTO Dispute Settlement", Harvard University. Jean Monnet Working Paper 9–2000.

[27] *Ibid*. Weiler writes "[d]e Jure the DSU leaves the final interpretation of the Agreements in the hands of the General Council and Ministerial Conference. *De facto*, unless the Organisation is to break the hallowed principle of consensus, that power has shifted to the Appellate Body".

THE CONSTITUTION OF THE MARKET PLACE

Can we Really Compare the EU and the WTO?

In the above I sought to conduct such a comparison and, hence, this may be the wrong point to ask this question, but though we are used to the fact that the EU is a different animal, it is worth reminding ourselves that GATT itself is a form of preferential trading agreement for goods. It provides for reduced and bound tariffs between members while members are free to treat non-members as they wish. Within the GATT and the WTO there are a number of closer trading arrangements such as the EU, just as for a long time within the original EEC there were closer trading arrangements such as BENELUX within which the Belgium-Luxembourg Economic Union (BLEU) was nested. We can compare the EU and GATT/WTO in the same way that we can make comparisons with and between other bigger or smaller regional groupings such as NAFTA and Mercosur.

In the previous section we looked at the decision-making processes of the EU and the WTO. The next step is to consider the content of the agreements. As we look at different types of trading arrangements we do, in fact, need to look not only at whether they extend to the removal of *all* tariffs, but how far beyond the border they extend, and what is the nature of the dispute settlement system. (In passing we might note that a "customs union" with no common budget such as EU–Turkey or Mercosur is really a free trade area with similar external tariffs.)

The crucial issue for present purposes is how different trading arrangements deal with *non-border* measures and whether there is a binding dispute settlement mechanism that will ensure domestic laws are sufficiently compatible to avoid regulatory barriers, i.e. how much "deep integration" there is. The traditional hierarchy of preferential trade agreement, free trade area, customs union is potentially misleading when the real barriers are regulatory. Thus the European Economic Area, ostensibly a free trade area, could be said to represent deeper integration than some so-called Customs Unions, where only tariff barriers are removed. Moreover, the degree to which a trading arrangement impinges on national sovereignty has much less to do with how completely it removes all tariffs than with its ability to touch domestic policies that could affect trade.

Liberalisation versus Regulatory Sovereignty?[28]

Divergent national regulations can and do pose barriers to trade. While regulations constituting disguised protectionism may be eliminated, as quantitative

---

[28]   This section draws very heavily on P. Holmes and A. Young "European Lessons for Multilateral Economic Integration: A Cautionary Tale" in Z. Drabek (ed.), *Globalization under Threat: The Stability of Trade Policy and International Agreements* (Cheltenham, Edward Elgar, forthcoming).

restrictions (QRs) have been, most regulations serve legitimate and necessary purposes even if they also affect trade. Consequently, they cannot simply be swept aside. Squaring the circle by replacing divergent national rules with common rules, as even the EU has discovered, is fiendishly complicated and time-consuming, at best; and at the multilateral level probably impossible. It is fraught with the risk of accusations of eradication of cultural diversity. In the absence of common multilateral regulations, how can the tension between liberalising trade and addressing market failures be satisfactorily addressed?

The basic ways to resolve these problems in trade are:

—national treatment (non-discrimination),
—mutual recognition (possible when some initial approximation of norms exists),
—harmonisation.

Traditionally the GATT was based on the general principles of non-discrimination in Articles I–III, while the EU for many years sought to use harmonisation, but eventually under the influence of the ECJ moved more towards the principle of mutual recognition. However the WTO and the EU have taken some steps towards each other in recent years. Weiler[29] notes that the ECJ has become more willing in some cases to accept non-uniform national rules that are not inherently discriminatory even if there is a potential impact on trade, while the WTO has introduced a form of harmonisation or at least mutual recognition in the SPS agreement, which requires members to accept plant and animal products that conform to *Codex Alimentarius* standards unless they can show a good reason why their own stricter standards may be safer (see below on beef hormones).[30]

These different approaches are discussed in detail by Trachtman [31] and Nicolaidis[32] who argues that some form of mutual recognition is generally economically superior. It frees consumers to buy what they want, while leaving governments free to choose what production norms they want. But, as Nicolaidis concedes and Gatsios and Holmes also point out, unconditional mutual recognition is a non-starter.[33] Mutual recognition must either be part of some voluntary bilateral deal in which you choose to accept products only from countries whose standards are already broadly equivalent to your own, or you agree some form of basic minimum as part of a more general approach, as under the EU's "new approach" or the SPS agreement.

---

[29] Weiler, *supra* n. 1.

[30] The Uruguay Round TBT Agreement incorporates similar aspirations but appears to be less constraining.

[31] J. Trachtman, "Trade and . . . Problems, Cost-Benefit Analysis and Subsidiarity", Harvard University, Jean Monnet Working Paper 1–97.

[32] K. Nicolaidis, "Mutual Recognition of Regulatory Regimes: Some Lessons and Prospects", Harvard University, Jean Monnet Working Paper 7–97.

[33] K. Gatsios and P. Holmes, "Regulatory Competition", in P. Newman (ed.), *New Palgrave Dictionary of Economics and the Law* (London, Macmillan, 1998).

Table 2: The Implications of Different Trading Rules for National Sovereignty

	Meaning	EU	WTO	Governance
Most favoured nation	Don't discriminate *between* foreigners	—	Key principle of GATT	Minimal constraints on autonomy *after WTO entry* and bindings agreed
National treatment	Treat foreign and home firms equally even if national rules distinct	Some aspects of services and Investment;	Art. III covers facial and non-facial discrimination; TBT; GATS subject to commitments	Big but unpredictable impact if binding Dispute Settlement can determine what is *de facto* discriminatory
Mutual recognition	Equivalence assumed (but subject to challenge)	Pure MR limited in EU	Some unclear obligations in TBT	Potentially very constraining if binding DS; no say in others' norms.
EU new approach: MR + minima	Agreed minimum requirement + reference to standards	Toys directive	SPS where *Codex* rules exist	Agreement on minima needed. EU QMV; *Codex Alimentarius* simple majority!
Harmonisation/ approximation	Everyone has same/similar rules	"old approach" cars and "Euro sausage" myths	TRIPs Telecoms reference paper	Requires "legislative" capacity. Explicit agreement on detail needed; EU: QMV; WTO consensus

Every different approach has institutional or constitutional implications, if it is actually to be effective. But the problem is that to guarantee that regulatory barriers do not impede trade we need either some form of quasi-legislative body that can decide common rules or at least ones that all consider satisfactory, or else a tribunal to decide *ex post* which divergent national rules are in fact discriminatory or impede market access.

To harmonise standards requires a body that is authorised to set standards for everyone. It is for this reason that the GATT did not move down this route and why the issue of majority voting versus unanimity in harmonisation was such a sensitive political issue in the EU. The fact that the *Codex Alimentarius* has been given the right by the SPS agreement to set norms which have a significant legal effect for all WTO members by simple majority voting appears somewhat anomalous, though the Appellate Body acknowledged in *Hormones* that these standards are not binding on the states.[34]

We noted above that mutual recognition of any kind either requires that the parties involved already have common enough preferences to accept each other's standards, or else they have a mechanism for agreeing common standards. Nicolaidis, strongly argues that mutual recognition should be the dominant mode of trade regulation:

> Contrary to the traditional view that MR should be turned to as a "residual" option if policed national treatment is not enough and full harmonization not feasible, commercial diplomacy should adopt mutual recognition as the core paradigm for dealing with regulatory barriers to trade.[35]

She adds however:

> Indeed, if mutual recognition falls short of a supranational transfer of power it constitutes a transnational transfer of power that may with time come to be seen as much of an infringement on sovereignty.[36]

She also points out that:

> European citizens may have applauded the abandonment of the "Euro-breads" plans of the 1970s, but under MR, Italians no more have a say in how to define "pasta", Germans "beer" and the French "dairy products.[37]

But if we are concerned with sovereignty the mere adoption of a non-discrimination requirement also causes problems. National treatment, *if it is to have teeth*, has strong implications too, which we are only just waking up to. If there is to be binding dispute settlement there does not need to be a body to lay down international norms *ex ante* but there needs to be a dispute settlement body with the power to decide *ex post* what is an allowable measure.

No trading system can avoid facing up to some sort of "constitutional" choice about who is to decide what domestic but trade-affecting rules are acceptable.

Trachtman suggests that one should look for an efficiency criterion:

> Thus, in circumstances of low "legislative" transaction costs, a narrow NTR rule (National Treatment) would be sufficient, referring the more difficult decisions to political decision-making. On the other hand, in circumstances of high political transaction costs, it may become more attractive to accept trade-off decisions made by courts, suggesting a LTRAT (Least Trade-Restrictive Alternative Tests), BT (Balancing Tests), CBA (Cost-Benefit Analysis) or CCBA (Comparative Cost-Benefit Analysis) rule.[38]

---

[34] Appellate Body Report, *European Communities—Measures Concerning Meat and Meat Products (Hormones)*, WT/D526/48, 13 February 1998, (hereinafter *Hormones*).

[35] Nicolaidis, *supra* n. 31, para 16.

[36] Nicolaidis, *supra* n. 31, para 33.

[37] Nicolaidis, *supra* n. 31, para 35.

[38] Trachtman, *supra* n. 30, 65.

The problem is surely that when political transaction costs are high the difficulties of internationally acceptable courts are also likely to be high: when achieving a result through negotiation is likely to be time-consuming and costly these are precisely the circumstances when the decisions of allegedly expert tribunals are also most likely to be contested.

Economic Integration in the EU and the WTO[39]

Progress on trade liberalisation within the EU has been possible though difficult only because the approach acknowledges and respects the member governments' prerogative to pursue legitimate public policy objectives, even at the expense of interfering with the four freedoms.[40] The result is that although the EU system is predicated on liberalising inter-state economic exchange, it accepts legitimate national restrictions.

The Treaty of Rome established the core principles of non-discrimination and the free circulation of goods, services, capital and people, albeit crucially within certain bounds. Significantly, however, national rules, at least in part because they addressed valid public policy objectives, could not simply be swept away by the application of treaty principles. Consequently, secondary legislation, which introduced a degree of regulatory approximation, had to be adopted in a number of areas.

The central role played by the European Court of Justice (ECJ) lies in interpreting the provisions of the treaties and subsequent secondary legislation. In particular, the ECJ is charged (at least implicitly) with assessing whether national rules that impede the four freedoms do so within the acceptable limits set by the treaties. Acceptance by governments of negative judgments, particularly in the light until recently of no coercive powers, hinges upon the legitimacy of the ECJ. As we shall argue, the WTO is in a more delicate position where the Appellate Body has to go straight from a Treaty to a binding interpretation even though it is unclear whether WTO members really thought they had invested the Appellate Body with such powers.

The inability of the Treaty alone to deliver economic integration was, in many respects, most evident with respect to goods, although there were also particular problems with transport services. Following the creation of the Customs Union in 1968, it became evident that TBTs were the most significant remaining obstacles to free trade. Most of these rules, however, safeguarded legitimate public policy objectives and so could not simply be swept aside. The Commission's initial response was to seek to agree detailed common rules to

---

[39] This section draws very heavily on Holmes and Young *supra* n. 28.
[40] A.R. Young and H. Wallace, *Regulatory Politics in the European Union: Balancing Civic and Private Interests?* (Manchester, Manchester University Press 2000).

eliminate the awkward national differences that impeded trade. This proved extremely cumbersome, slow and unsatisfactory.[41]

In the early 1980s the EU changed tack. The Commission, building upon the ECJ's *Dassonville* and *Cassis de Dijon* judgments, advanced two core innovations—the mutual recognition principle and the new approach to harmonisation—which paved the way for the Single European Market programme (SEM).[42] The mutual recognition principle assumes that although the Member States' rules may differ in substance, unless proved otherwise, they should be considered to be equivalent in effect. Consequently, the default scenario is for the member governments to accept products legally on sale in other Member States.

The mutual recognition principle, particularly the assumption of equivalence, has been tested numerous times. Significantly, the ECJ has not required governments to provide conclusive proof that a product would harm human health before it can exercise its prerogative under Article 30 (ex Article 36) EC. This was illustrated in the *Eyssen*[43] case, in which the Dutch government's ban on the preservative nisin in processed cheese was challenged as an unfair trade barrier. Although existing scientific evidence on the health risk of nisin was equivocal, the ECJ took the view that a government is entitled to protect its public from substances, the safety of which is subject to scientific doubt. In other words, application of the precautionary principle is sufficient to justify action under Article 30 EC in respect of public health and environmental issues.[44] Weatherill and Beaumont also point out that in the *Cassis de Dijon* case the Court also widened the scope for allowing certain domestic measures that may appear to be violations of Article 30, and which seek to pursue legitimate social aims, but not ones which would be exempted under Article 36.[45] Thus, the Court in *Cassis* extended the sweeping scope of Dassonville to cover virtually any national measure capable of affecting trade, but it felt necessary to add extra escape clauses, "the mandatory requirements". Weatherill and Beaumont argue that the sweeping deregulatory momentum given by this necessitated a parallel legislative revisiting of the issue (which was followed by the Commission in its new approach[46]).

Finally, even when common EU product standards have been adopted, it is possible, under certain circumstances and with the prior approval of the

---

[41] A. Dashwood, "Hastening Slowly: The Communities' Path towards Harmonisation" in H. Wallace and C. Webb (eds.), *Policy-making in the European Community* (2nd ed., Chichester, John Wiley & Sons, 1983).

[42] H. Wallace and A.R. Young, "The Single Market: A New Approach to Policy?" in H. Wallace and W. Wallace (eds.), *Policy Making in the European Union* (3rd ed., Oxford, OUP, 1996).

[43] Case 53/80, *Officier van Justitie* v. *Koninklijke Kaasfabriek Eyssen BV* [1981] ECR 409.

[44] C. Joerges, K.-H. Ladeur and E. Vos, *Integrating Scientific Expertise into Regulatory Decision-Making: National Traditions and European Innovations* (Baden-Baden, Nomos, 1997).

[45] S. Weatherill and P. Beaumont, *EC Law* (London, Penguin, 1993).

[46] *Ibid.* See also P. Craig and G. de Búrca (eds.), *The Evolution of European Law* (Oxford, OUP, 1999) ch. 14.

Commission, for member governments to continue to apply, or sometime to introduce, more stringent national standards under Article 95(4)–(6) EC (ex Article 100a(4)). This provision was included in order to address the Danish and German governments' concern that single market rules adopted under qualified majority voting, with them in the minority, might force them to accept products that they consider unsafe or environmentally harmful. This was underlined by Denmark's (not legally binding) Declaration in the Single European Act to the effect that:

> in cases where a Member State is of the opinion that measures adopted under Article 100a [single market measures] do not safeguard higher requirements concerning the working environment, the protection of the environment or the needs referred to in Article 36, the provisions of Article 100a(4) guarantee that the Member State in question can apply national provisions.

According to the Commission, governments have invoked Article 100a(4) most often in the chemical sector.[47] It is the most likely basis, for example, of the Danish government's recent announced bans on phthalates and lead compounds.[48] Such restrictions are disputed. As far as we know, however, the only legal challenge to have been concluded was the French government's challenge to the Commission's approval of Germany's ban on PCPs. The ECJ, in 1994, overturned the Commission's approval of the ban on procedural grounds.

The Treaty of Amsterdam substantially modified Article 100a(4). These changes require the member government to notify the Commission of the reasons for maintaining the provision, but also permit Member States, with the permission of the Commission, to *introduce* national provisions based on new scientific evidence after the adoption of common measures.

Historically, the General Agreement on Tariffs and Trade (GATT) sought to freeze ("bind") and periodically reduce tariff barriers and to replace quantitative restrictions (QRs) with tariffs, which were then subject to reduction. The notion of a QR under the GATT was much less sweeping than the Treaty of Rome's inclusion of "measures having equivalent effect", though Weiler implied that Article XI could be very widely cast.[49] In addition, the 1947 GATT had no provisions for harmonising laws in order to ensure free trade.

Starting with the 1979 Tokyo Round agreement, however, the multilateral system began to impose disciplines on national regulations that impeded trade—TBTs. This was challenging as the GATT—with several members from the then Socialist bloc—even more than the EU, had to recognise diversity of policy and market structures. Nonetheless, its members sought above all to ensure that whatever systemic diversity existed did not have discriminatory effects on trade. Thus it is not surprising that prior to the WTO, free traders (for

---

[47] Commission, "The single Market in 1995–Report from the Commission to the Council and the European Parliament," COM(96)51, 20 February 1996.

[48] *The Guardian*, 3 May 1999.

[49] Weiler, *supra* n. 1.

example Low[50]) argued that not only were GATT disciplines too weakly defined, they were also too laxly enforced.

The Uruguay Round made major changes to the rules on trade in goods sweeping the main additional agreements (but not that on government procurement) along with the GATT itself under the umbrella of the WTO and its tougher dispute settlement understanding, under which a WTO member can no longer veto the adoption as WTO law of a decision against it. The combination of new restraints on standards and technical barriers and binding dispute settlement makes the parallels (and intersections) between multilateral and EU approaches to trade in goods particularly intriguing.

In a nutshell, the Uruguay Round agreement on technical standards is based on the Tokyo Round code. Both stress the procedural elements of standard-setting, emphasise non-discrimination, and insist that *unnecessary* obstacles to trade must not be created. The 1994 code (Article 2) goes a bit further in saying that international standards shall be used where they exist, unless they are ineffective to pursue "legitimate" ends, though these are not exhaustively defined. It adds that in any departure from international norms, scientific evidence must be "among the relevant considerations". The 1994 code (Article 2.7) also says that member states shall "give positive consideration" to mutual recognition of others' norms that achieve the same effect.

Our argument here is that all these highly technical points create deep constitutional issues, and that the WTO can be seen as a somewhat problematic extrapolation of the EU's experience that harmonisation was impossible and national treatment inadequate, without a full enough consideration of the governance implications.

DISPUTE SETTLEMENT

What we have argued above is that one of the most striking features of the WTO is that because its key texts are treaties negotiated under pressure by diplomats and because it lacks an effective secondary legislative or executive function the WTO relies disproportionately on its dispute settlement system. Inevitably the disputes often involve not so much trade measures as such, but "domestic measures" deemed to be infringing in some way upon WTO commitments.

No one would deny that the most successful part of the new WTO is the working of the Dispute Settlement Mechanism. The Appellate Body is acknowledged by everyone to be doing a remarkably professional job. The question is simply: is it doing too much—and is it doing more than was expected? In this section we will briefly show how the transition from the GATT to the WTO

---

[50] P. Low, *Trading Free* (New York: Twentieth Century, 1993). Low is not untypical in writing, "[s]eriously buffeted by multiple challenges to its authority and integrity the [GATT] system has proven less and less capable of mediating trade relations among countries".

has forced the WTO dispute settlement body to enter the realm of policing *domestic* law.

The WTO DSB has to decide on the basis of the somewhat vague terms of the basic texts what domestic measures which may affect trade are nevertheless legitimate under the rules.

There is a basic problem with decision theory here. Statisticians distinguish the risk of falsely accepting a true hypothesis and falsely rejecting a true one. The fundamental theorem of statistical decision theory is that with a given amount of information you cannot reduce one of these risks without increasing the other.

As the beef case shows, we cannot avoid this "type I and type II" error problem. Only where there is a genuine congruence of preference above all can we really expect everyone to be bound to the same set of rules, or even rules about rules. In particular where we have a domestic measure that purports to be about reducing risk for consumers we may find parties facing each other who have very different views on how far free trade goals should be traded against consumer protection goals. But when the issue goes to the WTO one of the two views will have to prevail even though this may be a matter of profound political disagreement.

As we noted above the WTO is not really in the business of positive integration, with the perhaps unfortunate exception of the TRIPs agreement, but it does come close to creating a mechanism for common standards in the SPS agreement.

The beef hormone case is only one example of the way the Appellate Body had to decide what was really intended. Another example is the *Asbestos* case[51] in which the DSB had to decide whether a ban on all sales of asbestos (including imports) in France was a trade barrier, and if so was it a legitimate one.

Equally problematic is the issue of what is to happen when a case like this is decided. There seems little doubt that member states of the WTO were not entirely agreed whether a negative ruling should lead to automatic compliance or the automatic payment of "compensation" (for rexample, "withdrawal of concessions").[52]

This is not the place to review the full history of the WTO dispute settlement system. Reference to three cases will illustrate the argument.

The *Japanese Alcoholic Beverages* Case set a very major precedent. Serena B. Wille notes[53]:

> The most important question in the dispute was not, however, whether the Japanese Liquor Tax Law discriminated against imported liquors under Article III:2. Rather, the most important question, and the one whose implications were overlooked, was how to design a test for Article III: 2 that does not encroach upon the fiscal sovereignty of the Contracting Parties to the Agreement. As the Panel in Malt

---

[51] See Howse and Tuerk at ch. 12 in this volume.
[52] Jackson, *supra* n. 8.
[53] S.B. Wille, "Recapturing a Lost Opportunity: Article III:2 GATT 1994 Japan—Taxes on Alcoholic Beverages" (1998) 9 *European Journal of International Law* 182.

Beverages stated, "[it is] imperative that . . . determinations [made] in the context of Article III . . . not unnecessarily infringe upon the regulatory authority and domestic policy options of contracting parties." The Panel and the Appellate Body, however, employed a test that restricts the fiscal sovereignty of the Contracting Parties both prior to and during a dispute.

The Appellate Body in this case declared:

The broad and fundamental purpose of Article III is to avoid protectionism in the application of internal tax and regulatory measures. More specifically, the purpose of Article III "is to ensure that internal measures 'not be applied to imported or domestic products so as to afford protection to domestic production' ".[54] Toward this end, Article III obliges Members of the WTO to provide equality of competitive conditions for imported products in relation to domestic products.[55] "[T]he intention of the drafters of the Agreement was clearly to treat the imported products in the same way as the like domestic products once they had been cleared through customs. Otherwise indirect protection could be given".[56] Moreover, it is irrelevant that "the trade effects" of the tax differential between imported and domestic products, as reflected in the volumes of imports, are insignificant or even non-existent; Article III protects expectations not of any particular trade volume but rather of the equal competitive relationship between imported and domestic products. Members of the WTO are free to pursue their own domestic goals through internal taxation or regulation so long as they do not do so in a way that violates Article III or any of the other commitments they have made in the *WTO Agreement.*

Any domestic regulation is subject to this test,[57] and a violation can be shown even with no proof of injury here. With this case in mind a WTO Panel has recently addressed Canada's complaint against French rules outlawing all use of asbestos, wherever produced.[58] The panel had to decide whether this amounted to *de facto* (and hence *de jure*) discrimination by treating Canadian asbestos less favourably than other "like" products. There was no suggestion that this measure had a protectionist intent, but Canada in effect challenged France's right to use this internal health and safety measure. The panel decided that the French measure was a violation of Article III (GATT), *but* that it was justifiable under Article XX on public health grounds. Few would quarrel with the panel's judgment on what scope for national autonomy should be read into Article XX, once that became the issue, but there are serious grounds for wondering whether the WTO should be deciding on what public health measures of this kind are acceptable.[59]

---

[54] *United States—Section 337 of the Tariff Act of 1930,* BISD 36S/345, para. 5.10.

[55] *United States—Taxes on Petroleum and Certain Imported Substances,* BISD 34S/136, para. 5.1.9; *Japan—Customs Duties, Taxes and Labeling Practices on Imported Wines and Alcoholic Beverages,* BISD 34S/83, para. 5.5(b).

[56] *Italian Discrimination against Imported Agricultural Machinery,* BISD 7S/60, para. 11.

[57] It is potentially much more sweeping than under the "non-violation" rules of GATT Art. XXIII.

[58] Howse and Tuerk, *supra* n. 50.

[59] At the time of writing the case had gone to appeal, the Canadians challenging the panel's rejection of their claim that having done a risk assessment on asbestos the French authorities should also have done an equivalent risk assessment on the alternative products that were permitted.

In the case of the SPS agreement it is very difficult for the WTO to avoid having to make such judgments. The SPS Agreement effectively commits countries to accepting into their markets any product produced to *Codex Alimentarius* standards unless they can show that there is scientific evidence that any more restrictive regulations in place are likely to reduce risk. In the *Beef Hormones* case, the panel and the AB ruled that an EU ban on the sale of beef treated with growth hormones (wherever produced) violated the WTO rules because the EU could show no scientific evidence of a (more than merely theoretical) risk if such beef were consumed.

A careful reading of the decisions, not only of the Appellate Body, but also the Panel, reveals that the WTO gave a very broad interpretation of what could constitute scientific evidence, and did not say the EU had to *prove* such beef was unsafe. In fact the AB drew back from what the Panel had appeared to say and stressed the quasi-procedural nature of the obligations, but it could not draw back from the requirements of the SPS agreement which mean that the WTO will have to decide what is and is not appropriate scientific evidence on which a measure can be based. The members of the WTO agreed that scientific evidence should be the basis of SPS measures, even though some argue that public perceptions of risk should be treated as cause for action in their own right.[60]

But the fundamental problem is whether the WTO's dispute settlement system should be the place to resolve such enormously sensitive issues as whether the public authorities have properly evaluated the evidence on food safety. In this case this problem was also a long-standing bilateral one between the EU and the USA, which they had not been able to solve in the Uruguay Round.

Joanne Scott has suggested that in some cases the ECJ has actually been more deferential to the political imperatives affecting the government which introduce health and safety measures.[61]

Clearly part of the problem is that the negotiators of the Uruguay Round did not do their job properly. Ambiguous agreements were signed without anyone appreciating the consequences of them being subject to a legalistic interpretation. The Appellate Body has drawn on the Vienna Convention to insist that it must first and foremost make a literal reading of the wording of the agreements, which may well not have been drafted to take such weight. It would be virtually impossible for the AB to base a decision on the "intentions" of the parties since many or most of the signatories of most of the agreements were not there when they were signed!

The DSB is going to have to solve more and complex new issues. It is being called upon to decide especially under Article XX what other agreements justify overriding trade priorities. Shapiro, comparing the ECJ and the US Supreme Court, notes that even where a tribunal set up to interpret an agreement that has

---

[60] R. Pollak, "Risk Regulation" in P. Newman (ed.), *New Palgrave Dictionary of Economics and the Law* (London, Macmillan, 1998).

[61] J. Scott, "On Kith and Kine (and Crustaceans): Trade and Environment in the EU and the WTO" in J.H.H. Weiler (ed.), *The EU the WTO and the NAFTA* (Oxford, OUP, 2000) 125–68.

one specific aim in mind introduces a "balancing test" to take account of other objectives, as indeed the Appellate Body has done, it will start off with a bias in favour of the objectives of the agreement of which it is guardian.[62]

Shapiro points out that a constitutional court has most legislative power when the texts it interprets are vague and when there is limited scope for the body that agreed it to meet and amend (which may have been a reason for the initial vagueness). There is deep reluctance at the WTO to re-open agreements already concluded.

CONCLUSIONS

We should bear in mind the cautionary comments of North on the evolution of economic institutions: the actors involved learn from experience but do not have perfect information about what they are doing, and do not always get it right first time.[63] It is clear that the experience of the EU influenced the way in which the WTO was set up. In principle the two entities are "comparable" in the sense that the WTO, like the EU, is a form of preferential trading arrangement and the two can be compared with each other. The comparison reveals that, not unlike the EU, the WTO has headed off in the direction of a rule-based dispute settlement system with something resembling a constitutional court. Weiler notes:

> Panels and the Appellate Body fulfil the same function and cover the same issue based on similar norms that national courts and the ECJ fulfil in the European Union.[64]

The big difference is that in the EU the ECJ sits at the head of a complex and subtle political process, and even if many writers argue that the EU does not have a *demos* that can sustain a "federal government", this issue can at least be raised in the EU context; no-one would suggest that the WTO has a *demos* or a polity that can or should make rules for all members. One should hesitate before saying that the Judges of the ECJ are in some way politically accountable, but they are at least aware of the need to secure acceptance of their rulings.

And yet in the absence of any political legislative organ the judicial arm of the WTO is forced to take on some such roles, precisely at a time when the ECJ is being increasingly prudent. Weiler has written:

> As the convergence process progresses, the simplistic dream of "constitutionaliz-ing" the GATT in structural terms and in some ways using the EU as a "model" for the WTO (and for other transnational regimes) through the advocacy of Article 177-type procedures, will become far more nuanced. European constitutionalism is

---

[62] M. Shapiro, "The European Court of Justice" in P. Craig and G. De Búrca (eds.), *The Evolution of European Law* (Oxford, OUP, 1999).

[63] North, *supra* n. 10.

[64] Weiler, *supra* n. 25.

undergoing a certain crisis and reformation conditioned by the tension and gap between its legal imperatives and its social and political reality. The appellate body decision in Hormones, which clawed back some of the more audacious aspects of the Panel, was apparently mindful of the problems of giving binding constitutional force to standards adopted by faceless officials and enforced by adjudicatory bodies whose legitimacy is a matter of some considerable delicacy. This sounds familiar.[65]

We have however already set off down that road. The WTO has set up a binding rule-based system to ensure that the world pursues what appears to be a general consensus to sustain and further pursue trade liberalisation. It is clear that if this process is to be effective, it needs the credibility that a rule-based system can give, but as the protestors in Seattle and Prague insist we have privileged one global objective, namely freer trade, and given its enforcement teeth while leaving other worthy aims to voluntarism. Howse and Nicolaidis point out that the EU was never just about trade liberalisation.[66] But as Rollo and Winters suggest, one must be very wary of addressing the problem by loading extra tasks on to the WTO. It would be folly to imagine that the WTO can solve its problems by being given more powers and greater legislative capacity.[67] This argument is distinct from, but has implications for, the debate about the status of the WTO agreements within EU law, but the implications of this chapter are clearly in support of those who believe this relationship should remain flexible.

---

[65] Weiler, *supra* n. 25.

[66] Howse and Nicolaidis, *supra* n. 2.

[67] J. Rollo and L. A. Winters, "Subsidiarity and Governance Challenges for the WTO: The Examples of Environmental and Labour Standards" (2000) 23 *The World Economy* 561–576.

4

European and International Constitutional Law: Time for Promoting "Cosmopolitan Democracy" in the WTO

ERNST-ULRICH PETERSMANN

EUROPEAN AND INTERNATIONAL CONSTITUTIONALISM: NEED FOR EU LEADERSHIP FOR CONSTITUTIONAL REFORMS OF WORLDWIDE ORGANISATIONS

IMMANUAL KANT WAS the first philosopher who explained, in his essay on *Perpetual Peace* (1795), why human rights, rule of law and democracy inside states cannot remain effective without *international constitutional guarantees* of "democratic peace" among republican states and *cosmopolitan guarantees of human rights* also *vis-à-vis* foreign governments.[1] The EC Treaties have progressively evolved into a new kind of *peace treaties* that reflect, and go far beyond, the Kantian recommendations for protecting perpetual peace on the basis of national and international constitutional guarantees of human rights, rule of law, separation of powers, democracy and cosmopolitan integration law. The contribution of EC law to more than 50 years of democratic peace among the 15 EC Member States—"founded on the principles of liberty, democracy, respect for human rights and fundamental freedoms, and the rule of law, principles which are common to the Member States" (Article 6 EU)—is no less important an achievement of European integration than the progressive extension of functional economic and legal EC integration, from the coal and steel community, customs union, common market and economic and monetary union to the emerging political union with a common foreign and security policy.

Kantian legal theory proceeds from the premise that the rational and moral autonomy and dignity of human beings require them to act in conformity with

---

[1] On Kantian legal theory see e.g. E.-U.Petersmann, "How to Constitutionalize International Law and Foreign Policy for the Benefit of Civil Society?" (1998) 20 *Michigan Journal of International Law*, 1–30.

self-imposed moral and legal rules that respect and protect maximum equal liberty for the personal development of every individual.[2] According to Kant, the legitimacy and "justice" of national and international constitutional law depend on "a constitution allowing the greatest possible human freedom in accordance with laws which ensure that the freedom of each can coexist with the freedom of all the others".[3] By protecting human rights, non-discrimination and free movement of goods, services, persons, capital and payments as fundamental individual liberties inside the EC and the European Economic Area, EC law offers principles for a just constitutional order to which rational citizens can voluntarily agree because the liberties protect their individual freedom, legal equality, personal development and economic welfare across frontiers.[4]

By its network of free trade or customs union agreements with almost all European and Mediterranean countries, and by including "human rights clauses" and "democracy clauses" into most of the international agreements concluded by the EC with countries in Europe, Africa, Asia and Latin-America, the EC has also contributed to the progressive "constitutionalisation" of international relations with third countries and to the emergence of a cosmopolitan integration law and "democratic peace" throughout Europe. The EC's common commercial policy in the WTO, by contrast, continues to remain "power-oriented" in several respects.[5] For instance:

— Notwithstanding more than a dozen GATT and WTO panel, appellate and arbitration findings since 1993 on the illegality of the EC's import restrictions on bananas and, since 1998, additional WTO panel, appellate

---

[2] On the various formulations of Kant's moral "categorical imperative" see H. Reiss (ed.), *Kant—Political Writings*, (Cambridge, CUP, 1991), at 18 (e.g. "act according to that maxim which we can at the same time will should become a universal law"; "act always so that you treat humanity whether in your own person or in that of another always as an end, but never as a means only").

[3] Quoted from Reiss (*supra* n. 2), at 23. For Kant, "the state has three principal functions and obligations: a duty of justice to ensure a condition of maximum law-governed freedom; a duty of benevolence to provide for the needs of its subjects; and a teleological responsibility to create the framework within which all forms of human rationality can flourish" (A.D. Rosen, *Kant's Theory of Justice* (Ithaca, NY: Cornell University Press, 1993), at 218). J. Rawls, *A Theory of Justice* (Oxford: OUP, 1973), proceeds from a similar "first principle of justice": "each person is to have an equal right to the most extensive basic liberty compatible with a similar liberty for others" (at 60). Yet, in his recent book on *The Law of Peoples* (Cambridge, MA: Harvard UP, 1999), Rawls does not apply the principle of maximum equal liberty of every individual to international law which, according to Rawls, should tolerate non-liberal but "decent" conceptions of justice.

[4] On the link between theories of justice and social contract theories of rational choice cf. e.g. Rawls, *A Theory of Justice* (*supra* n. 3), at 11: "Just as each person must decide by rational reflection what constitutes his good, that is the system of ends which it is rational for him to pursue, so a group of persons must decide once and for all what is to count among them as just and unjust. The choice which rational men would make in this hypothetical situation of equal liberty... determines the principles of justice". Also Kant's constitutional theory uses the historical fiction of a *social contract* and requires every citizen to be his own law-giver (*volenti non fit injuria*). For the Hobbesian view that the social contract cannot be extended beyond the state's frontiers see H. Bull, *The Anarchical Society* (London: Macmillan, 1977).

[5] Cf. E.-U. Petersmann, "The Foreign Policy Constitution of the EU: A Kantian Perspective" in U. Immenga, W. Möschel and D. Reuter (eds.), *Festschrift für E.J. Mestmäcker* (Baden Baden: Nomos, 1996), 433–447.

and arbitration rulings on the illegality of the EC's import restrictions on hormone-fed beef, the EC continues to maintain its import restrictions notwithstanding their clear violation of both WTO law and EC law (e.g. Article 300(7)).

—According to the EC Court of Justice, EC law must be construed and applied in conformity with international law binding on the EC.[6] Nowhere does EC law grant discretion to EC institutions to violate international treaties ratified by the EC as well as by national parliaments for the benefit of EC citizens. Yet, both the EC Commission and the EC Council have argued long since *against* rights of EC citizens and rights of EC Member States to invoke precise and unconditional WTO guarantees of freedom and non-discrimination before EC courts against the frequent violations of WTO rules by the EC executives. The ECJ's persistent refusal to apply precise and unconditionally binding GATT and WTO rules, including legally binding WTO dispute settlement rulings on the illegality of EC restrictions of individual freedoms, is clearly inconsistent with the Court's mandate to "ensure that in the interpretation and application of this Treaty the law is observed" (Article 220 EC).[7] Again, the "judicial protectionism" and treatment of EC citizens as mere objects of EC power politics runs counter to the EC law requirements to protect maximum equal liberties and rule of law for the benefit of EC citizens.

—In WTO practice, the EC has declined US proposals to make WTO dispute settlement proceedings between the EC and the USA open to the public, as it is possible pursuant to Article 12 of the WTO's Dispute Settlement Understanding. Why does the EC not lead by example in promoting constitutional reforms of worldwide organisations based on the EC's own constitutional principles of individual rights, rule of law, democracy, and transparency also of court proceedings?

The main thesis of this contribution is that, as a legal community with clearly limited competencies and limited democratic legitimacy deriving from respect for human rights and for the rule of law, EC violations of international law undermine legal and democratic legitimacy also *inside* the EC.[8] The effectiveness of the EU's foreign policies—notably the EU's participation in worldwide organisations like the UN, the IMF and the WTO—will depend on EU leadership in

---

[6] Cf. Case C–162/96 A. *Racke GmbH & Co.* v. *Hauptzollamt Mainz* [1998] ECR I–3655.

[7] For a criticism of the ECJ's WTO case law, notably Case C–149/96, *Portugal v. Council*, 23 November 1999, see S. Griller, "Judicial Enforceability of WTO Law in the European Union", (2000) 3 *Journal of International Economic Law* 441–472. In Case C–149/96, the ECJ ignored the legally binding effect of WTO law and the WTO obligation to terminate illegal measures by misinterpreting Art. 22 of the WTO Dispute Settlement Understanding (which cannot legalise violations of WTO law but relates to the different problem of voluntary compensation as a means of averting countermeasures).

[8] This was, e.g., illustrated by the refusal of German courts to apply the manifestly illegal EC regulations on the discriminatory restrictions of banana imports, cf.: E.-U.Petersmann, "Darf die EG das Völkerrecht ignorieren?" [1997] *Europaische Zeitschrift für Wirtschultsrecht*, 325–31.

promoting constitutional reforms of the law of worldwide organisations based on human rights, rule of law and "cosmopolitan democracy". The full membership and active role of the EC in the WTO should serve as a model for an active EU policy aiming at similar adaptations to the IMF Agreement and UN Charter so as to enable the EU to exercise its common monetary policy and common foreign and security policy by means of EU membership in these state-centred postwar organisations. The WTO itself also requires constitutional reforms so as better to protect human rights across frontiers and promote more active democratic participation of individuals and parliaments in WTO matters.

Developing an EU strategy for "constitutionalising international law" beyond Europe is confronted, *inter alia*, with the problem that "constitutionalism", human rights and democracy mean different things to different people. The second part of this chapter gives a brief overview of nine core principles of constitutionalism and of the different possible levels and strategies of constitutional reforms of international organisations. The third describes the six basic functions of human rights, including the three major constitutional functions of the emerging right to democracy, as a basis for democratic reforms of the law of worldwide organisations. The concluding part provides concrete proposals for promoting *cosmopolitan democracy* in the WTO.

PRINCIPLES, LEVELS AND STRATEGIES OF CONSTITUTIONALISM: A BRIEF OVERVIEW

Human rights law proceeds from the premise that "recognition of the inherent dignity and of the equal and inalienable rights of all members of the human family is the foundation of freedom, justice and peace in the world" (Preamble to the 1948 Universal Declaration of Human Rights). The universal recognition, since the "1989 revolution", of human rights as part of general international law requires a *human rights approach* to international law.[9] In most constitutional democracies, human dignity and human rights are now rightly construed in conformity with Kant's moral *categorical imperative*[10] to the effect that governments should aim at protecting maximum equal liberties of citizens, including both "negative" and "positive freedoms".[11] Some federal constitutions (for example, in Germany and Switzerland) and European constitutional law recognize that guarantees of equal freedoms can be invoked also *vis-à-vis foreign*

---

[9] Cf. E.-U. Petersmann, "Human Rights and International Economic Law in the 21st Century", in (2000) 4 *Journal of International Economic Law*, 3–39.

[10] *Supra* n. 2.

[11] According to C.B. Macpherson, *The Life and Times of Liberal Democracy* (Oxford: OUP, 1977), in "most of the English-speaking world and most of Western Europe . . . there is general acceptance of a principle of maximum individual freedom consistent with equal freedom for others" (at 7).

policy powers and must be protected *across* frontiers (for example, freedom to import and export subject to lawful governmental trade restrictions).[12]

The "paradox of freedom", i.e. the inherent tendency of liberty without legal safeguards to destroy itself through abuses of power, was described already by Plato.[13] In order to solve the constitutional problem of "who guards the guardians?", Plato recommended a *government of laws* rather than of men, based on a "mixed constitution" with monarchic, oligarchic and democratic elements.[14] From the Greek city republics during the fifth century BC up to the post-war institutions (such as the UN, the IMF and the GATT) which, for the first time in history, attempted to limit abuses of foreign policy powers through *worldwide legal and institutional restraints*,[15] the progressive and continuing evolution of *constitutionalism* has focused on the following nine "core principles".[16]

Rule-of-law

Human rationality, morality and "dignity" call for rule-oriented rather than power-oriented behaviour. Rule-of-law has been described already by Plato[17] as a moral and legal prerequisite for democratic self-government and individual self-development. Contrary to Plato's earlier recommendation in favour of a government by philosophers, Plato emphasised in his later writings that person-oriented "political ethics" needs to be supplemented by general legal rules and institutional safeguards so as to protect citizens from arbitrary abuses of power and transform their "natural freedom" (based upon physical power) into "legal freedom" (based upon general legal rules and mutual respect).

Limitation of Government Powers by Checks and Balances

Plato's *Nomoi* and Aristoteles' *Politeia*[18] emphasised the need for different governmental institutions for rule-making, rule-application and peaceful settlement

---

[12] For comparative legal analyses see E.-U. Petersmann, *Constitutional Functions and Constitutional Problems of International Economic Law* (Fribourg: Fribourg University Press, 1991), at 314–354, as well as: M. Hilf and E.-U. Petersmann (eds.), *National Constitutions and International Economic Law* (Deventer, The Netherlands: Kluwer, 1993).

[13] See K.R. Popper, *The Open Society and its Enemies*, Vol. I *Plato* (Amsterdam: North-Holland Pub. Co., 1952), at 123.

[14] See Plato, *The Laws* (trans. by T.L. Pangle, Chicago, IL: University of Chicago Press, 1988), at 136–174.

[15] Cf. E.-U. Petersmann, "Constitutionalism and International Organizations" (1997) 17 *Northwestern Journal of International Law and Business* 398–469.

[16] For a detailed description of these major constitutional principles and their relevance for international law, with detailed references to the vast literature, see E.-U. Petersmann, *supra* n. 1.

[17] In his last book on *Nomoi, supra* n. 14.

[18] See Aristotle, *The Politics* (T.A.Sinclair trans., Harmondsworth: Penguin Books, 1981).

of disputes. Since the sixteenth century, many political philosophers (such as Gianotti and Montesquieu) explained why legislative, executive and judicial powers should be institutionally separated and restrained by mutual "checks and balances" so that "power stops power" (Montesquieu: *le pouvoir arrête le pouvoir*). According to Kant, a state without separation of powers (including a democracy without constitutionally guaranteed civil liberties) risks being "despotic" because the concentration of the entire state authority leaves no effective restraints on arbitrary exercise of power.[19] More recently, the vertical "separation of powers" in federal states has inspired many "unitary" states to reinforce institutional "checks and balances" by decentralising government powers based on principles of *federalism* and *subsidiarity*.

Democratic Self-government

Democracy was an ideal already of the ancient Greek city republics, albeit subject to numerous limitations (such as discrimination against women and slaves). Modern constitutional and contract theories (for example, from Kant to Rawls) explain why democratic legitimacy of rules and government powers depends upon whether rational citizens can agree on them because the rules and institutions are designed to protect the equal liberty, legal security and individual welfare of every citizen. Even though the constitutional concept of a "social contract" remains a historical fiction, numerous human rights treaties and regional integration agreements recognise that human rights and popular sovereignty include citizens' rights to participate in the election of governments and in the exercise of government powers which must be based on "the will of the people" (Article 21 of the Universal Declaration on Human Rights (UDHR)). Without "participatory democracy" and transparent "deliberative democracy" respecting human rights, national and international rule-making lacks "democratic legitimacy" and runs counter to the modern "right to democracy".[20]

Democracies are arenas for interest group politics. A "government of the people, by the people, for the people" (A. Lincoln) can remain sustainable only in "constitutional democracies" which limit democratic procedures (such as popular referenda and parliamentary majority votes) by inalienable human rights of the citizens. Without such constitutional restraints, a "tyranny by the majority" (Tocqueville) risks emerging as in the case of the "paradox of democracy" already described by Plato that a democratic majority may decide to delegate powers to a dictator (as in Germany in 1933). Yet, inside these constitutional restraints, democratic rules and institutions tend to vary from

---

[19] Cf. e.g. Rosen (*supra* n. 3), at 33–34.

[20] On the emergence of a "right to democracy" in modern human rights law and regional integration law see: G.H. Fox and B.R. Roth (eds.), *Democratic Governance and International Law* (Cambridge: CUP, 2000).

one country to the other according to the particular preferences and historical experiences of the people concerned.

National Constitutionalism

The need for long-term constitutional restraints of a higher legal rank, even with regard to democratic government powers, was emphasised already by Aristoteles in his *Politeia*. Today, virtually all 189 UN member states have written or (for example, in the case of England and New Zealand) unwritten national constitutions which recognise the primacy of constitutional guarantees over post-constitutional legislation, executive and judicial measures. Self-imposed constitutional commitments to freedom, non-discrimination and rule-of-law are based on rational psychological techniques ("pre-commitments") to protect the long-term interests of individuals against the temptations of selfish human short-term interests (for example, in abuses of power and interest group politics).

Human Rights

Human rights are not only universal moral entitlements deriving from respect for the moral autonomy, rationality and "dignity" of human beings. They have also become recognised in national constitutions and worldwide and regional international law as inalienable "birth rights" of every individual to legally protected freedom, equality and participation in the exercise of government powers and in the distribution of collective "public goods". The inalienable nature of human rights implies that, even if democratic legislatures may define the legal limits of human rights in a manner differing from country to country, human rights are not conferred by governments; their "inalienable", essential core and functions prohibit "unnecessary" and "discriminatory" limitations, and require procedural guarantees of due process of law and individual access to courts. Many human rights instruments recognise that human rights constitute not only individual rights (for example, of a "defensive", participatory or re-distributive nature) but also objective constitutional principles and corresponding obligations on the part of governments: "[t]he final end of every political institution is the preservation of the natural and imprescriptible rights of man" (Article 2 of the French Declaration of the Rights of Man and the Citizen of 1789).

International Constitutionalism

Wars and international treaties (for example, among the Greek city republics and Persia) have been reported since the beginnings of written history. Yet, neither Plato, Aristoteles, the Roman *ius gentium*, the Hobbesian theory of the sovereign state, nor the Lockean theory of constitutional democracy recognised the need for *international legal restraints* on the foreign policy powers of states as a condition for peaceful co-operation and rule of law in international relations. The interrelationships between national and international rule of law were first explained in the legal philosophy of I. Kant. "Classical" international law doctrines (for example, of Grotius and Vattel) considered the different forms of government as a problem only of national law and did not envisage international institutions for the enforcement of international law and of its underlying moral and "natural law" principles. Kant, by contrast, emphasised the need for a confederation among republican states so as to extend and protect rule-of-law and "democratic peace" across frontiers also in international relations.[21] This Kantian theory of mutually complementary national and "international constitutional law" inspired not only the "treaty constitution" of the EU. Also the worldwide WTO guarantees of freedom and compulsory adjudication of international disputes have constitutional functions for the protection of individual freedom and rule of law across frontiers.[22]

Social Justice

National and international human rights instruments emphasise the "indivisibility" of civil, political, economic, social and cultural human rights, i.e. that the objective of individual self-determination and self-development requires not only "negative" freedoms but also "positive" economic and social rights enabling citizens to acquire the economic resources and social means necessary for actually using their human rights.[23] Most modern national constitutions commit governments to the promotion of "social justice" so as to help needy citizens to live a life in dignity. Modern legal "theories of justice" emphasise, however, that "positive" social rights must be based on generally applicable principles which may differ from country to country depending on their respective resources and political cultures.[24] On the international level among states, the scope of international duties of assistance and of income redistribution among countries remains politically and also morally controversial especially

---

[21] *Supra* nn. 1 and 2.

[22] On the "human rights values" underlying the law of the Bretton Woods institutions and GATT, and on the need for "international constitutional law", see Petersmann (*supra* n. 12), chs. VII–IX.

[23] See, e.g., Art. 22 of the UDHR: "Everyone, as a member of society, has the right to social security and is entitled to realization, through national effort and international co-operation and in accordance with the organization and resources of each State, of the economic, social and cultural rights indispensable for his dignity and the free development of his personality".

[24] See, e.g., the "second principle of justice" defined by J. Rawls (1973) *supra* n. 3, 60: "Social and economic inequalities are to be arranged so that they are both (a) reasonably expected to be to everyone's advantage and (b) attached to positions and offices open to all".

vis-à-vis governments which do not protect human rights.[25] The concept of "positive freedoms" implies that, as stated in Article 29 of the Universal Declaration of Human Rights of 1948:

(1) Everyone has duties to the community in which alone the free and full development of his personality is possible.

(2) In the exercise of his rights and freedoms, everyone shall be subject only to such limitations as are determined by law solely for the purpose of securing due recognition and respect for the rights and freedoms of others and meeting the just requirements of morality, public order and the general welfare in a democratic society.

Cosmopolitan Constitutional Law

The need for protecting rule-of-law and human rights also in transnational relations between individuals and foreign states was emphasised first in Kant's theory of international cosmopolitan law. As shown above, the EC guarantees of human rights and the free international movement of goods, services, persons, capital and payments go far beyond Kant's proposal for a universal cosmopolitan right to visit foreign states.[26]

Variety of Constitutional Architectures and Need for Coherence

National constitutions differ from country to country according to their particular historical experiences, legal traditions and political preferences. Human rights instruments recognise (for example, in Article 28 UDHR) that the human rights objective of treating individuals as legal subjects, rather than as mere objects of paternalistic government policies, requires a citizen-oriented restructuring of national as well as international law and organisations so as to make universal enjoyment of human rights possible and secure.[27] The 1993 Vienna Declaration on Human Rights, for instance, emphasises the "need for States and international organizations, in cooperation with non-governmental organizations, to create favorable conditions at the national, regional and international

[25] See: J. Rawls (1999) *supra* n. 3, e.g. 113–120. The *Human Development Report 2000* (UNDP, 2000) and Nobel Prize economist A. Sen, *Development as Freedom* (Oxford: OUP, 1999), have convincingly argued that human rights and democracy are not only moral and legal values, but also constitutive of the very process of development and instrumental for economic and social welfare.

[26] See, e.g., P. Alston, M. Bustelo and J. Heenan (eds.), *The EU and Human Rights* (Oxford: OUP, 1999); L. Betten and N. Grief, *EU Law and Human Rights* (London: Longman, 1998).

[27] The UN General Assembly "Declaration of the Right to Development" (Resolution 41/128 of 4 December 1986) sets out obligations of states and international organisations for promoting and implementing civil, political, economic, social and cultural human rights. Yet, by mixing individual and collective rights and obligations without a clear indication of who owes what to whom, the Declaration adds little to the effective protection of individual rights.

levels to ensure the full and effective enjoyment of human rights".[28] In the "European house" called for by former Soviet President Gorbatov, the more than 40 member states of the Council of Europe have committed themselves to human rights, rule-of-law and democracy as part of national laws, European integration law, international treaties concluded in the Council of Europe and legal instruments in the context of the Organization on Security and Co-operation in Europe.

The image of a "multi-storied constitutional house" is useful for illustrating the "layered structure" of constitutional systems and the need for ensuring the overall consistency of the "constitutional building blocks", as recognised in national constitutions (for example, Article 23 of the German Basic Law on the conditionality of transfers of government powers to the EU), regional integration agreements (for example Article 6 EU Treaty) and worldwide human rights instruments. The survey of the historical evolution of "constitutionalism" demonstrates that the needed constitutional reforms of international law and international organisations can be pursued through a large variety of different strategies:

(a) *Variety of constitutional principles*: the historical development and legal recognition of the abovementioned "constitutional core principles" tend to vary from country to country and from organisation to organisation due to their particular political circumstances and legal traditions. General treaty references to "respect for human rights and fundamental freedoms" (cf. Article 6 EU) or to the "Fundamental Principles and Rights at Work" adopted by the International Labour Organisation in June 1998, appear more appropriate in worldwide organisations than references to "the general principles common to the laws of the Member States" (Article 288 EC) as a basis for judicial determination of, for example, reparation of injury in case of non-contractual liability.

(b) *Variety of levels and strategies of constitutional protection*: the needed *constitutionalisation* of all local, national and international government powers can be pursued at different national and international levels of political and legal systems by a variety of "constitutional strategies" and combinations of principles. National constitutional systems cannot realise the human rights objective of maximum equal liberties of their citizens without complementary international and cosmopolitan constitutional guarantees. Yet, constitutional reforms of international organisations may be politically easier to achieve by using existing national institutions (for example, stricter control of the law of international organisations by national parliaments, national courts, national central banks and national competition authorities) than by establishing

---

[28] S. 13 of the Vienna Declaration and Programme of Action adopted by more than 170 states at the UN World Conference on Human Rights on 25 June 1993, cf. *The United Nations and Human Rights 1945–1995* (United Nations, 1995), at 449.

supra-national international institutions on a worldwide level (for example, a WTO competition authority).[29]

(c) *Human rights functions of constitutional principles:* even though all the
above-mentioned "constitutional principles" derive democratic legitimacy from their common function to protect human rights at the national
level of states and at the international level of international organisations,
views about the functions and legal interpretation of human rights continue to differ from country to country. From a human rights perspective,
international organisations may be perceived best as a "fourth branch of
government" which, albeit necessary for protecting human rights and
rule of law across frontiers, must be subject to the same constitutional
restraints as national governments so as to protect human rights against
abuses of power.

NEED FOR ADJUSTING STATE-CENTRED INTERNATIONAL ORGANISATIONS
TO THE "HUMAN RIGHTS REVOLUTION" AND TO THE EMERGING
"RIGHT TO DEMOCRACY"

Legal theories of "justice" emphasise that rules derive legitimacy from their
function to protect maximum equal liberty and other human rights.[30] The
democratic legitimacy of rules depends on the consent of the citizens and, in the
absence of unanimous consent, on whether rational citizens can agree to the
rules because they protect the liberty, equal rights and individual welfare of
every citizen. Before discussing the need for democratic reforms of WTO law (in
the concluding part of this chapter), it is useful to recall six major functions of
human rights and the three basic tasks of the emerging "right to democracy".

Six Basic Functions of Human Rights

The constitutive functions of human rights for the "justice" of legal systems, and
the conceptualisation of human rights as moral, constitutional and legal "birth
rights" of every human being, have important consequences for the necessary
restructuring of international law:

(a) As *moral rights*, human rights derive from "human dignity", i.e. the rational and moral autonomy of human beings to think for themselves and to
live and develop their personalities in accordance with self-imposed rules

---

[29] See, e.g., the proposals for stronger involvement of national parliaments and for judicial pro-
tection of individual rights as means of strengthening the foreign policy constitution of the EU in:
E.-U. Petersmann, "Proposals for a New Constitution of the EU" (1995) 32 *Common Market Law
Review* 1123–1175; E. Smith (ed.), *National Parliaments as Cornerstones of European Integration*
(London: Kluwer, 1996).

[30] Cf. *supra* nn. 1 to 3.

which respect equal rights and human self-development for all others. Moral and legal theories of "justice" require governments to promote and protect maximum equal liberties of all citizens across frontiers, including freedom of trade subject to democratic legislation.[31]

(b) As *inalienable constitutional citizens' rights* and corresponding *legal obligations of governments* that are explicitly recognised in many national constitutions and international treaties, human rights constitutionally limit public and private power and commit governments to the promotion of human rights as constitutive elements of "justice". Their inalienable character and recognition as constitutional rights "retained by the people"[32] make clear that human rights precede the constitution and delegation of government powers and are not conferred by governments. Human rights tend to be of a defensive ("negative"), procedural (for example, participatory) or re-distributive ("positive") nature and include rights of access to courts and judicial protection against abuses of power.

(c) Also beyond the historical human rights instruments there are numerous other national and international *"rules with human rights functions"* that protect individual freedom and non-discrimination under the rule-of-law inside and across national frontiers. Such fundamental legal freedoms (for example, for the free movement of goods, services, persons, capital and payments inside the EC) also derive moral legitimacy from the "categorical imperative" of maximising equal liberties of the citizens under the rule of law.

(d) "Bills of Rights" (for example, 1689 in England), Declarations of the "Rights of Man and of the Citizen" (for example, 1789 in France) and other historical human rights instruments emerged from revolutionary struggles for constitutional democracy. They reflect *political claims* that later became recognised in legal texts focusing on the particular political priorities of a given historical moment (for example, freedom of religion in England during the seventeenth century, civil and political liberties in the USA during the eighteenth century, economic and social rights in modern EC law).[33] From a policy perspective, the progressive realisation of the human rights objectives of maximum equal liberties and "justice" in all fields of national and international law remains a never ending challenge which can be realised only progressively to the extent that individuals, governments and courts defend human rights. This dynamic

---

[31] See Kant and Rawls (*supra* nn. 2 and 3) and, for a comparison of Kantian and Rawlsian constitutional theories, e.g. D. Boucher and P. Kelly (eds.), *The Social Contract from Hobbes to Rawls* (London: Routledge, 1994), 132 *et seq.*

[32] Cf. the Ninth Amendment to the US Constitution and, e.g., W.D. Moore, *Constitutional Rights and Powers of the People* (Princeton, NJ: Princeton UP, 1998).

[33] On the many incoherences in the historical development of human rights instruments see, e.g., J. Gordon, "The Concept of Human Rights: The History and Meaning of its Politicization" (1998) 23 *Brooklyn Journal of International Law* 689.

function of human rights justifies "functional" legal and judicial interpretations rather than merely "historical" and "textual" interpretations
of human rights instruments.[34] For example, the guarantees of individual
liberty in German and Swiss constitutional law, as well as in the EC
Treaty, have been construed by German, Swiss and EC courts as protecting also individual "freedom of trade as a fundamental right" across
national frontiers even though such "functional" interpretations were not
explicitly mandated by the wording of the constitutional provisions concerned and were politically opposed by protectionist governments.[35]

(e) Modern economic theory rightly emphasises the *instrumental role of
human rights* for economic and personal development, for example as
incentives for savings and investments, as legal preconditions of professional freedom and transfer of property rights in an exchange economy,
and as defensive rights promoting the "internalization of external effects"
through contractual agreements or court litigation: "Freedoms are not
only the primary ends of development, they are also among its principal
means . . . Freedoms of different kinds can strengthen one another".[36]
Hence, "Rights make human beings better economic actors. You cannot
legislate good health and jobs. You need an economy strong enough to
provide them—and for that you need people economically engaged.
People will work because they enjoy the fruits of their labour: fair pay,
education and health care for their families and so forth. So, economic
and social rights are both the incentive for, and the reward of, a strong
economy".[37] Recognition of human rights, such as freedom of producers
and consumers, gives rise to market competition and calls for legal rules
enabling mutually agreed market transactions (for example, liberty
rights, contract law, property rights), limiting abuses of market power
(for example, by means of consumer protection law), and promoting
monetary stability and undistorted competition (for example, by means
of monetary, securities and competition laws).

(f) All human rights need to be mutually balanced and reconciled through
democratic legislation. The general obligation to promote human rights,
and the existence of certain core human rights (such as prohibition of
slavery and torture), are today recognised as *ius cogens* in international

---

[34] On the importance of functional, teleological interpretations in the jurisprudence of the ECJ
see, e.g., H.G. Schermers and D. Waelbrock, *Judicial Protection in the European Communities* (5th
edn., Deventer, The Netherlands: Kluwer Law and Taxation, 1992), 18–26.

[35] For references to the case-law see Petersmann (n. 12), chapter VIII. Kantian legal theory, like
modern economic theory, emphasizes that conflicts of interests and antagonism among men are
major driving forces for mutually beneficial competition, progress towards rationality, and progressive extension of constitutional guarantees of equal liberties (cf. e.g. Reiss, n. 2, at 38).
Individual rights and their judicial protection, like market competition, are important safeguards of
protecting individual preferences.

[36] A. Sen, *supra* n. 25, at 10–11.

[37] *Human Development Report 2000, supra* n. 25, at iii and 57.

law. Yet, the mutual delimitation and progressive development of human rights by means of democratic legislation and international treaties differ from country to country depending on the political circumstances concerned. All constitutional democracies recognise the principle that human rights may be restricted by governments only on the basis of public legislation and only to the extent necessary for the protection of other human rights. For domestic policy reasons, national governments often find it easier to abolish welfare-reducing restrictions and discrimination against foreigners by means of *reciprocal international guarantees of freedom and non-discrimination* (for example, in EC law, GATT and WTO law) rather than unilaterally through national legislation.[38] The progressive development and extension of human rights law in all fields of national and international law remain a permanent legal and political challenge for satisfying basic human needs, protecting "democratic peace", and for promoting self-government and self-development of all human beings.

The Emerging "Right to Democracy" and its Three Major Constitutional Functions

The 1948 Universal Declaration of Human Rights protects not only "freedom of thought" (Article 18), "freedom of opinion and expression" (Article 19) and "freedom of peaceful assembly and association" (Article 20). According to Article 21:

(1) Everyone has the right to take part in the government of his country, directly or through freely chosen representatives.

(2) Everyone has the right of equal access to public service in his country.

(3) The will of the people shall be the basis of the authority of government; this will shall be expressed in periodic and genuine elections which shall be by universal and equal suffrage and shall be held by secret vote or by equivalent free voting procedures.

The 1966 UN Covenant on Civil and Political Rights confirms these and additional "democratic rights", for instance in Article 25:

Every citizen shall have the right and the opportunity, without any of the distinctions mentioned in Article 2 and without unreasonable restrictions:

(a) To take part in the conduct of public affairs, directly or through freely chosen representatives;

(b) To vote and to be elected at genuine periodic elections which shall be by universal and equal suffrage and shall be held by secret ballot, guaranteeing the free expression of the will of the electors;

(c) To have access, on general terms of equality, to public service in his country.

---

[38] Cf. E.-U. Petersmann, "National Constitutions and International Economic Law" in Hilf and Petersmann (eds.), *supra* n. 12, at 46–47.

The emerging "right to democracy",[39] regardless of particular cultures and history, has been recognised not only in numerous subsequent UN human rights instruments, such as the 1993 Vienna Declaration on Human Rights:

> Democracy, development and respect for human rights and fundamental freedoms are interdependent and mutually reinforcing. Democracy is based on the freely expressed will of the people to determine their own political, economic, social and cultural systems and their full participation in all aspects of their lives.[40]

There are also an increasing number of multilateral and bilateral international treaties (notably by the EC) that include "democracy clauses" and authorise suspension of treaty provisions in case of violation of human rights and "democratic principles".[41] The "right to democracy" is increasingly recognised as a necessary component and requirement of human rights and as an effective means of promoting "democratic peace" not only among democracies but also *vis-à-vis* non-democratic governments (for example, so as to prevent internal armed conflict and external intervention in support of human rights struggles). Just as market economies are the only form of economic regime compatible with respect for human rights, democracy is the only political form of government respecting the human right to individual self-determination and collective self-government.

Since the Athenian paradigm of direct democracy during the time of Pericles, numerous different kinds of direct and/or representative forms of democratic self-government have developed at national and international levels. There are also different concepts of the relationship between human rights and democracy depending on whether democracies focus on "parliamentary sovereignty" (as in England), "popular sovereignty" (as in the USA) or "individual sovereignty" protected by inalienable human rights even against abuses of power by parliaments and "We the People" (as in Germany). Yet, all constitutional democracies appear to recognise at least three basic functions of democracy:[42] first, to legitimise "government of the people" on the basis of popular sovereignty and equal human rights that require a "government for the people"; secondly, to constitute and limit "government by the people" through democratic institutions (for ecxample, political parties, representative parliaments) and procedures (for example, popular referenda, parliamentary elections, majority votes, public legislation); and thirdly, to promote *participatory deliberative democracy* based on public discourse in an informed civil society and active citizen participation in public rule- and policy-making in a way promoting "democratic peace" and tolerance *vis-à-vis* minorities.

[39] See Resolution 1999/57 on "Promotion of the Right to Democracy" adopted by the UN Commission on Human Rights in 1999 (UN Doc. E/CN.4/1999.SR 57). Cf. also T.M. Franck, "The Emerging Right to Democratic Governance" (1992) 86 *American Journal of International Law* 46.

[40] Vienna Declaration (*supra* n. 28), s. 8.

[41] For an overview of this treaty practice see: Fox and Roth (*supra* n. 20).

[42] On the vast literature on democracy see, e.g., *supra* nn. 11, 20, 26, 39 and *infra* nn. 45, 46 and O. Höffe, *Demokratie im Zeitalter der Globalisierung* (Munich: Beck, 1999), at 107–120.

The more government powers are collectively exercised in international organisations, the more civil society claims to democratic participation and more effective protection of human rights in international organisations are likely to increase.[43] If values can be derived only from individuals and from their human rights, and the end of states and of international law is only to serve individuals by protecting their human rights (as legal preconditions for the moral and democratic ideal of "active citizens" and legally protected self-government), then individuals and their human rights—rather than states, "nations" or "people" (*demos*), whose collective rights are merely derivative of the human rights of their citizens—must be recognised as primary normative units in international law and organisations.[44] The increase in the number of democratic states must be accompanied by democratic reforms of international organisations leading to mutually complementary forms of "cosmopolitan democracy" at national and international levels.[45] This need for democratic politics also at the international level calls for democratic reforms of international law and international organisations so as to give citizens, NGOs and the "nascent global civil society"[46] more voice and input, more effective political representation in international affairs, and also more effective human rights and legal remedies to hold national and international decision-makers accountable. Just as judicial protection of individual rights has predated parliamentary democracy in many countries and in the EC, constitutional reforms of international law are easier to achieve through legal and judicial protection of human rights and of spontaneous co-operation among citizens across frontiers ("democratisation and globalisation from below") than through premature initiatives for a world parliament and for other worldwide democratic institutions without adequate "democratic infrastructure".

NEED FOR DEMOCRATIC REFORMS OF
THE GLOBAL INTEGRATION LAW OF THE WTO

The universal recognition of human rights as part of modern general international law requires a *human rights approach* also to WTO law.[47] If the value

---

[43] On the participation of NGOs in the UN system see: UN Non-Governmental Liaison Service, *The NGLS Handbook of UN Agencies, Programmes and Funds Working for Economic and Social Development* (United Nations, 1997).

[44] If human dignity, as the central concept of human rights law, is interpreted in conformity with Kant's categorical imperative (see *supra* n. 2), then respect for the dignity of persons and for the effectiveness of human rights law calls for treating individuals as subjects rather than mere objects also of international law.

[45] Cf., e.g., D. Archibugi and D. Held (eds.), *Cosmopolitan Democracy* (Cambridge: Polity Press, 1995); D. Held, *Democracy and the Global Order* (Oxford: Blackwell, 1995).

[46] Cf. R. Falk, "The World Order between Inter-State Law and the Law of Humanity: the Role of Civil Society Institutions" in Archibugi and Held (*supra* n. 45), 163–179.

[47] This follows also from the general international rules on treaty interpretation which require international treaties to be construed "in good faith in accordance with the ordinary meaning to be

of governments derives from maximising human rights as a legal precondition for enabling individuals fully to develop their personalities and participate in democratic governance, then also *international organisations* derive their value from enhancing human rights. What are the consequences of a human rights approach for the global integration law of the WTO, for example for the interpretation of WTO guarantees of freedom, non-discrimination and property rights, the numerous "public interest" and safeguard clauses in WTO law, the treatment of individuals in WTO law and for the two-thirds majority of less-developed WTO member countries? How can WTO member states be induced to adjust the WTO legal and institutional system in a way recognising legitimate claims for democratic participation and protection of human rights? How can human rights be integrated into relations between democracies and non-democracies?[48]

Freedom of Trade, Non-discrimination, Rule-of-law and Compulsory Adjudication as Constitutional Achievements of WTO Law

The transition from GATT 1947 to the WTO offers the so far most successful example for the "constitutionalisation" of a worldwide organisation based on constitutional principles of freedom and non-discrimination, "rule-of-law", compulsory adjudication, "checks and balances" between legislative, executive and judicial powers, and the legal primacy of the "WTO Constitution" *vis-à-vis* the Agreements listed in the Annexes to the WTO Agreement and "secondary WTO law" (such as GATT Schedules of Concessions, GATS Protocols, DSB dispute settlement rulings). Due to its unique compulsory dispute settlement and appellate review system, and its complementary guarantees of access to domestic courts, WTO law appears to protect "rule of law" more effectively than any other worldwide treaty.

However, the increasing focus of WTO law on *harmonisation* of rules beyond the trade policy area (for example, in the field of technical and (phyto)sanitary regulations, telecommunications, competition and investment rules, intellectual property rights), and the rapid development of WTO jurisprudence through the already more than 40 panel and more than 30 appellate

given to the terms of the treaty in their context and in the light of its object and purpose", including "any relevant rules of international law applicable in the relations between the parties" (cf. Art. 31 of the 1969 Vienna Convention on the Law of Treaties which is widely recognised as reflecting customary rules of treaty interpretation).

[48] J. Rawls, in his recent book *The Law of Peoples* (*supra* n. 3), bases his theory of international law and global "justice" on a global contract between representatives of states (rather than a social contract among individuals) and on a distinction (e.g. at p. 4) between "liberal peoples", "decent peoples" , "outlaw states" and "societies burdened by unfavorable conditions" or by "benevolent absolutisms". Rawls emphasises the need for inter-societal toleration of non-liberal but "decent" conceptions of justice. This Rawlsian theory of international law appears, however, inconsistent with the universality, inalienability and indivisibility of civil, political, economic, social and cultural rights recognised in modern human rights law by virtually all states.

review reports adopted by the Dispute Settlement Body so far, constitute new "constitutional challenges" which call for additional "constitutional reforms" of WTO law. The apparent political difficulties in many WTO members to comply with their WTO obligations (for ecample, under the TRIPS Agreement) and with WTO dispute settlement rulings (for example, on the illegality of the EC's import restrictions on bananas and hormone-fed beef), and the political disagreement on a future "WTO Round" of multilateral negotiations on additional rules, have made WTO member governments increasingly conscious of the need for a *new political consensus* on the future legal evolution of the WTO. Should the WTO, like the old GATT, continue to focus on *discriminatory trade restrictions and trade distortions* whose reciprocal liberalisation is obviously beneficial for consumers? Are WTO rule-making procedures adequate for worldwide *non-discriminatory regulations* (for example on health standards) which go far beyond trade policy concerns and may undermine parliamentary and other democratic procedures for the balancing of competing "human rights interests" (for example in economic liberty and protection of health)?

From "Negative" to "Positive" Integration in the WTO: Need for Promoting Democratic Governance in the WTO

The 1944 Bretton Woods Agreements, the 1945 UN Charter and the 1948 Havana Charter for an International Trade Organisation (ITO) pursued not only economic but also political objectives, such as the prevention of another worldwide economic and political crisis (as in the 1930s) and the creation of "conditions of stability and well-being which are necessary for peaceful and friendly relations among nations" (Article 1 of the Havana Charter). The preamble to the GATT 1947 referred exclusively to *economic* objectives. The numerous safeguard clauses in the General Agreement gave, however, clear priority to national sovereignty to pursue *non-economic* policies, for instance so as to prevent "serious injury to domestic producers" (Article XIX), to protect "public morals" (Article XX,a) and "human, animal or plant life or health" (Article XX,b), "conservation of exhaustible natural resources" (Article XX,g), or national security (Article XXI).

Need for Better Democratic Legitimisation of WTO Rule-making Procedures

The 1994 Uruguay Round Agreements were ratified by national parliaments in most WTO member countries without thorough examination of the more than 25,000 pages of treaty text and without real possibility of modifying the treaty provisions agreed among trade experts from 124 countries and the EC.[49] Also

---

[49] See the comparative country studies in J. Jackson and A. Sykes (eds.), *Implementing the Uruguay Round* (Oxford: Clarendon Press, 1997).

during the eight years of multilateral trade negotiations, most national parliaments (with the exception of the US Congress) exercised little, if any, political influence on the contents of the Uruguay Round negotiations. As long as GATT negotiations focused on reciprocal tariff liberalisation, subsequent parliamentary ratification of mutually beneficial GATT agreements was considered as conferring sufficient democratic legitimacy. The "positive integration law" of the WTO, however, goes far beyond the trade liberalisation rules of GATT 1947.[50] In contrast to GATT 1947, WTO law:

—liberalises and regulates the various kinds of division of labour (for example, trade in goods and services, licensing of know-how, foreign investments) in a much more comprehensive manner;

—requires far-reaching legislative, administrative and judicial measures for the implementation of WTO rules in domestic laws;

—prescribes substantive and procedural individual rights (notably intellectual property rights) and their protection by domestic courts; and

—has introduced far-reaching new limitations on national sovereignty over non-discriminatory internal regulations (as protected under GATT Article III) and national safeguard measures (as protected, for example, by GATT Articles XIX–XX), for instance by new WTO legal requirements of "necessity"; "sufficient scientific evidence"; "harmonisation" of national measures on the basis of "international standards"; "agreements on recognition of the equivalence of specified sanitary or phytosanitary measures"; "assessment of risk and determination of the appropriate level of sanitary or phytosanitary protection"; "consistency in the application of the concept of appropriate level of sanitary or phytosanitary protection"; participation in "appropriate international standardising bodies of international standards"; requirements, for example, for the preparation, adoption and application of technical regulations by central, local and non-governmental bodies, or for government procurement procedures by central and sub-central government entities.[51]

In the context of the old GATT 1947, the USA and other GATT member countries had introduced special "fast-track legislation" facilitating reciprocal tariff liberalisation agreements in GATT and their speedy incorporation into national implementing legislation. The main political motivation for these special legislative procedures had been the traumatic US experience with the Smoot–Hawley–Tariff Act of 1930 by which protectionist interest groups and political "log-rolling" had prompted Congress to introduce the highest tariffs in US history, triggering retaliatory trade and payments restrictions by other countries leading to a worldwide economic crisis and finally World War II.

---

[50] For a detailed analysis see: E.-U. Petersmann, "From 'Negative' to 'Positive Integration' in the WTO: Time for Mainstreaming Human Rights into WTO Law?" (2000) 37 *Common Market Law Review* 1363–1382.

[51] The quotations are illustrations from the WTO Agreements on Sanitary and Phytosanitary Measures, Technical Barriers to Trade, and Government Procurement.

Rather than "circumventing democracy", such special legislative and political procedures for reciprocal tariff liberalisation have proven to be effective "pre-commitments" for protecting the general citizen interest in transnational legal freedom, liberal trade and welfare-increasing legislation.[52]

The Uruguay Round Agreements suggest, by contrast, that the special national and international rule-making procedures for reciprocal tariff-liberalisation are hardly appropriate for legislation in fields such as sanitary and phytosanitary standards, technical regulations, investment rules, environmental rules and intellectual property rights. GATT negotiations used to be politically driven by export industries interested in access to foreign markets. WTO rule-making requires more active involvement by national parliaments and a much broader democratic representation and balancing of all interests involved, for instance because industries may have no self-interest in negotiating effective competition and environmental rules.

Should Freedom of Trade be Protected as a Human Right?

Does the human right to self-development include freedom of trade across frontiers? Or do the human rights guarantees of "liberty" (for example, in Article 3 UDHR) end at national borders? If the moral and legal purpose of human rights is to empower and enable citizens to a maximum equal liberty (including positive rights to satisfy basic human needs) for the development of their human potential, then billions of citizens demonstrate day by day (for example, by using foreign transport, postal, telephone, radio, television and internet services) that access to foreign markets (for example, to food, books, medicines, education, jobs, technology, information systems, tourism, development assistance abroad) is highly valued by citizens, including the more than one billion of poor people whose well-being depend on food aid, financial aid and medical assistance from abroad. There is worldwide consensus today also among economists that division of labour through liberal trade increases real income and consumer welfare, and that trade restrictions are hardly ever an optimal policy instrument for promoting public interests. Political scientists confirm that mutually beneficial trade co-operation across frontiers contributes to "positive peace". If moral, legal, economic and political theory all support the view that individual freedom to import and export should be protected as an individual right unless governmental restrictions are necessary for the protection of more important human rights values: Has it not become anachronistic today that trade politicians and most judges outside the EC interpret constitutional guarantees of liberty as protecting freedom of trade only among *domestic citizens* but not with *foreigners* across frontiers?[53]

---

[52] See R.E. Hudec, "Circumventing Democracy: The Political Morality of Trade Negotiations" in R.E. Hudec, *Essays on the Nature of International Trade* (London: Cameron May, 1999), 215–25.

[53] For a detailed comparative analysis of constitutional protection of freedom of trade see Petersmann (*supra* n. 12).

Need for More Effective Protection of the Human Rights Objective of Maximum Equal Freedom of Citizens Across Frontiers

The secrecy of the Uruguay Round negotiations, and the one-sided political influence of powerful producer lobbies on the negotiators (for example, of the Antidumping, Textiles and TRIPS Agreements), resulted in one-sided protection of *producer interests*: for instance, GATT and WTO law and domestic implementing legislation in many WTO member countries provide for "producer rights to import protection" (for example, in anti-dumping and safeguards legislation) without corresponding "rights to import" by traders and consumers. Also the TRIPS Agreement focuses one-sidedly on the rights of intellectual property holders with few safeguard clauses protecting broader social and consumer interests.

The numerous "protectionist biases" in WTO rules indicate that the self-interests of producers and also of trade bureaucracies in discretionary import protection conflict with the human rights interests of consumers in maximum equal liberty and open markets. For instance, both the EC and US legislation on the domestic implementation of the Uruguay Round Agreements prevent individual citizens invoking WTO rules before domestic courts in order to hold domestic governments accountable for their frequent violations of the WTO guarantees of freedom and non-discrimination.[54] As a result of bureaucratic self-interest in "rights of governments" rather than "rights of citizens", the guarantees of intellectual property rights in the TRIPS Agreement—unlike the corresponding guarantees in WIPO conventions which used to be protected by domestic courts in Europe as "directly applicable individual rights"—may no longer be directly applicable by domestic courts and by the citizens concerned. Treating one's own citizens as mere objects rather than legal subjects of WTO rules is hardly consistent with the human rights ideal of maximum liberty, equal rights and self-determination of citizens.

The large number of more than 200 inter-governmental WTO dispute settlement proceedings since 1995 reflects the determination of many WTO governments to clarify and further develop WTO law through quasi-automatic judicial interpretations and "case law" rather than by recourse to the rigid WTO rules for "authoritative interpretations" and amendments of WTO law (cf. Articles IX and X of the WTO Agreement). Again, there is legitimate and increasing concern that the lack of transparency, one-sided trade-orientation and state-centred design of WTO dispute settlement proceedings may be inconsistent with the requirements of transparent, democratic rule-making and public judicial review in constitutional democracies. Both multilateral rule-making and dispute settlement proceedings in the WTO require more transparency and more effective democratic "checks and balances".

[54] Cf. E.-U. Petersmann, *The GATT/WTO Dispute Settlement System* (London: Kluwer Law International, 1997), at 18–22.

Need for Protecting Freedom of Trade also against Private Restraints of Competition

The GATT guarantees of freedom, non-discrimination and rule-of-law contributed to preventing a recurrence of a worldwide economic crisis as in the 1930s when the US Smoot–Hawley Tariff Act triggered a spiral of protectionist countermeasures by other trading countries resulting in a breakdown of the international trading and payments system. Yet, the "paradox of freedom" is characteristic also for *private* markets and *private* restraints of competition: without competition safeguards, economic markets risk to destroy themselves through abuses of private market power (such as economic cartels and monopolies) and through other "market failures" (for example, "external effects" and non-supply of "public goods" such as "social justice").

"Constitutional economics" and "*ordo*-liberalism"[55] emphasise the need for protecting market economies by means of an "economic constitution" based on a coherent set of "constituent principles" (such as monetary stability, open markets, private ownership, freedom of contract, liability, policy coherence) and "regulative principles" (for example, independence of monetary and competition authorities *vis-à-vis* "rent-seeking" interest group pressures). According to the US Supreme Court, "antitrust laws . . . are the Magna Carta of free enterprise. They are as important to the preservation of economic freedom and our free enterprise system as the Bill of Rights is to the protection of our fundamental freedoms".[56] The historical experience with the comprehensive EC Treaty guarantees of "a system ensuring that competition in the internal market is not distorted" (Articles 3(g), 81 *et seq*.) confirms that the economic objective of maximising consumer welfare and competition through liberal trade cannot be achieved without competition laws and institutions.

It is characteristic for the "producer bias" of GATT and WTO rules that the long-standing proposals for multilateral competition rules—for example, in the 1948 Havana Charter, in GATT and WTO negotiations—continue to be resisted by trade politicians in GATT and the WTO.[57] Trade negotiators have strong self-interests in their power to negotiate market-sharing agreements (for example, for textiles, maritime and air transports) and other trade restrictions by which they can distribute "protection rents" to their trade "clientèles". For decades, they have circumvented liberal GATT rules through protectionist "voluntary export restraints" and "orderly marketing arrangements", thereby distributing billions of dollars to rent-seeking lobbies, often without transparent

---

[55] Cf. E.-U. Petersmann (*supra* n. 12), 61–72; D.J. Gerber, *Law and Competition in Twentieth Century Europe* (Oxford: Clarendon, 1998), ch. VII.

[56] *United States* v. *TOPCO Assoc. Inc.*, 405 US 596, 610 (1972).

[57] Cf. E.-U. Petersmann, "Competition-oriented Reforms of the WTO World Trade System—Proposals and Policy Options" in R. Zäch (ed.), *Towards WTO Competition Rules* (Bern: Kluwer, 1999), 43–71; Petermann, "Legal, Economic and Political Objectives of National and International Competition Policies: Constitutional Functions of WTO 'Linking Principles' for Trade and Competition" (1999) 34 *New England Law Review* 145–162.

democratic discussion, without legislative authorisation and without parliamentary and judicial control.

Even though many sectors of international trade are subject to international cartelisation (for example, by "shipping conferences"), monopolies (for example, for telephone and other telecommunications, railway services) and bilateral market-sharing agreements (e.g. for air and maritime transports), the General Agreement on Trade in Services (GATS) does not include effective competition rules. The TRIPS Agreement acknowledges that "appropriate measures . . . may be needed to prevent the abuse of intellectual property rights by right holders or the resort to practices which unreasonably restrain trade or adversely affect the international transfer of technology" (Article 8). Yet, even though "nothing in the Agreement shall prevent Members from specifying in their legislation licensing practices or conditions that may in particular cases constitute an abuse of intellectual property rights having an adverse effect on competition in the relevant market" (Article 40), the WTO offers no effective help to the numerous WTO member countries without national competition laws to protect themselves against anti-competitive restraints of competition. In July 2000, the worldwide International Law Association adopted detailed proposals for introducing competition rules into WTO law and for liberalising "parallel imports" that are often prevented by private holders of intellectual property rights to the detriment of domestic consumers.[58] Yet, such recommendations from nongovernmental organisations are unlikely to be taken up in the WTO as long as WTO bodies focus so one-sidedly on the interests of producers and trade bureaucracies.

"Paradoxes of Discrimination": Need for a "Self-enforcing Foreign Policy Constitution" Based on Citizens' Rights and Access to Courts

"Human rights revolutions" and "constitutionalism" have usually been "bottom-up movements" in response to citizens' complaints and citizens' struggles in defence of human rights. The progressive evolution of human rights protection can be seen as a continuing struggle against power-oriented *discrimination*, for instance discrimination against slaves, minorities, colonial people, coloured people, workers, women, children, political dissenters and foreigners. Trade policy and WTO are about discrimination against foreign goods, foreign services, foreign investments and foreign economic operators, as they have been practised for centuries by nationalist governments to the detriment of the economic welfare and personal freedom of their citizens. Economic globalisation and the global integration law of the WTO offer the possibility for another "human rights revolution" liberating citizens from arbitrary, welfare-reducing

---

[58] The text of these ILA resolutions adopted on 29 July 2000 can be visited at the ILA web site: www.ila-hq.org.

government restrictions and extending individual freedom and mutually beneficial citizen co-operation across frontiers.

"Foreign Policy Dilemmas" of Constitutional Law

Foreign policy powers are powers to tax and restrict *domestic citizens* (for
example, by taxing domestic consumers and importers through an import
tariff). Like other foreign policy powers, trade policy powers suffer from "constitutional dilemmas" that favour discriminatory policy abuses and render
constitutional reforms difficult:

—First, most national constitutions tend to grant discretionary foreign policy
  powers to governments without effective constitutional restraints (for
  example, without effective judicial protection of human rights in the foreign policy area and, in many countries, without effective parliamentary
  control).[59]
—Secondly, trade policies are exposed to the "Janus face problem"[60] that discrimination among 200 trading countries offers more than 200 possibilities
  of discriminating among *domestic* citizens trading with these countries,
  and of redistributing thereby income among domestic groups without
  effective parliamentary and judicial control;[61] for centuries, governments
  have arbitrarily limited the freedom and welfare of their citizens by restricting imports and exports.
—Thirdly, human rights law permits governmental limitations of individual
  freedom only to the extent "necessary" for the protection of other human
  rights. This "balancing test" requires defining and balancing the constitutional values of freedom of trade and non-discrimination (for example, as
  protected in GATT Articles II, III and XI) *vis-à-vis* the human rights values
  of trade restrictions (for example, as permitted under GATT Article XX
  to the extent "necessary" to protect, for instance, "public morals").
  Unfortunately, in most countries (including the USA), judges decide this
  balancing test without regard to the fact that freedom is not only the primary end of human rights but also the principal means for personal development.[62] In WTO negotiations, developing countries fear that proposals
  by trade unions in developed countries for integrating "social clauses" and

---

[59] On this "Lockean dilemma" see, e.g., Petersmann (*supra* n. 15) at 415.

[60] Janus, the Roman god of doors, was portrayed with two faces looking inside as well as outside
the door.

[61] The EC's longstanding import restrictions for bananas from Latin-American countries in
favour of bananas from producers in the EC, Africa, the Caribbean and the Pacific offer ample evidence of how illegal discriminatory import restrictions can be abused for redistributing billions of
dollars among domestic citizens for the benefit of powerful "rent-seeking" importers in a few EC
member countries.

[62] For a comparative analysis and criticism of this jurisprudence in the USA and Europe see
Petersmann (*supra* n. 12) as well as Hilf and Petersmann (*supra* n. 12).

"human rights clauses" into WTO law may be prompted more by protectionist objectives than by human rights concerns.

The success of rights revolutions in general, and of a rights-based approach to international trade law in particular, depends on incentives and support structures in civil society, such as rights-advocacy organisations, rights litigation and protection of citizens' rights by courts (including the ECJ and the European Court of Human Rights) against unnecessary limitations of rights and other abuses of powers by the rulers. The history of trade liberalisation *inside* federal states and *inside* customs unions (like the EC) shows that freedom of trade for the benefit of the citizens has usually been achieved *not* by reliance on the benevolence of the rulers, but rather by the struggle of courageous citizens and judges defending individual freedom against discriminatory governmental and private restrictions of trade.[63] GATT and WTO dispute settlement bodies have rightly practised judicial deference *vis-à-vis non-discriminatory* national legislation and invocations of the general exceptions and "public interest clauses" of GATT and WTO law (for example, GATT Articles XX and XXI). Yet, there is much less reason for judicial deference *vis-à-vis discriminatory* national restrictions in clear violation of WTO guarantees of freedom and non-discrimination.

Should Precise and Unconditional WTO Guarantees of Freedom and Non-discrimination be Protected by Domestic Courts?

The 1999 Panel Report on *US Sections 301–310 of the Trade Act of 1974* noted the contrast between the *inter-governmental nature* of WTO rights and obligations and their *individualist economic and legal function* to create "market conditions conducive to individual economic activity in national and global markets" and "protect the security and predictability of the multilateral trading system and through it that of the market-place and its different operators".[64] According to the Panel, WTO law is based on a "principle of indirect effect" in the sense that "the GATT/WTO did *not* create a new legal order the subjects of which comprise both contracting parties or Members and their nationals".[65] This obiter dictum of the Panel appears, however, premature and should not be abused by national and EC judges as a justification of their introverted habits of ignoring GATT and WTO law.

The WTO Agreement is not only "a treaty the benefits of which depend in part on the activity of individual operators", and whose treaty obligations (for

---

[63] For a comparative analysis of these experiences in US, Swiss, German and EC law see Petersmann (*supra* n. 12), chs. VIIII and IX. On the importance of the democratisation of access to the judiciary, rights litigation and judicial leadership see also C.R. Epp, *The Rights Revolution* (Chicago: University of Chicago Press, 1998), e.g. at 197 *et seq.*

[64] WTO document WT/DS152/R (adopted, without appeal, on 27 January 2000), at paras. 7.71–7.75.

[65] See *supra* n. 64, at paras. 7.72 and 7.78.

example, GATT Article III:2) are "designed to give certain guarantees to the market place and the operators within it", as recognised by the Panel.[66] If, as the Panel rightly emphasises, the protection of individuals and the market-place "is one of the principal objects and purposes of the WTO"[67]: why should this WTO law objective be achieved exclusively "indirectly" *vis-à-vis* individuals and the market place? Does human rights law not suggest that WTO guarantees of freedom and property rights should be presumed to protect also individual rights of the citizens? The TRIPS Agreement explicitly recognises "that intellectual property rights are private rights" (Preamble). Even though "Members shall be free to determine the appropriate method of implementing the provisions of this Agreement within their own legal system and practice" (Article 1), several WTO members (such as Germany and Switzerland) have recognised in their implementing measures that TRIPS provisions on intellectual property rights and legal remedies may be directly applicable in domestic courts.[68] WTO law hinders member states and courts neither from interpreting domestic law in conformity with WTO obligations nor from recognising precise and unconditional WTO guarantees of freedom, non-discrimination or rule-of-law as being directly applicable in favour of individual citizens.[69]

The continuing illegality of the EC's import restrictions on bananas—notwithstanding more than 12 successive GATT and WTO panel reports, Appellate Body report and arbitration awards since 1993 on the GATT and WTO inconsistencies of these import restrictions[70]—illustrates the need for additional constitutional restraints for the benefit of EC citizens. As stated by J. S. Mill, "The very principle of constitutional government requires it to be assumed that political power will be abused to promote the particular purposes of the holder; not because it always is so, but because such is the natural tendency of things, to guard against which is the especial use of free institutions".[71]

---

[66] See *supra* n. 64, at paras. 7.81, 7.85, 7.95.

[67] *Ibid.*, para. 7.86.

[68] See, e.g., *Botschaft des Schweizerischen Bundesrates zur Genehmigung der GATT/WTO-Uebereinkommen vom 19. September 1994*, p. 329 (noting that "many mandatory provisions of the TRIPS Agreement are directly applicable").

[69] On the application of TRIPS provisions by the ECJ see Case C–53/98, *Hermès* [1998] ECR I–3603. On the misconceived refusal by the ECJ to apply WTO rules in Case C–149/96, *Portugal* vs. *Council*, of 23 November 1999 (not yet reported) see S. Griller, "Judicial Enforceability of WTO Law in the European Union" (2000) 3 *JIEL* 441–472. As Arts. 220 and 300(7) of the EC Treaty also require the ECJ to respect international treaties ratified by all parliaments within the EC and EC Member States, and nothing in the EC Treaty authorises EC institutions manifestly to violate precise and unconditional WTO guarantees of freedom and non-discrimination, the ECJ's arbitrary misinterpretations of GATT and WTO rules (e.g. of Art. 22 of the WTO Dispute Settlement Understanding in Case C–149/96) reflect a regrettable "judicial protectionism" and violation of the rule of law.

[70] Cf. E.-U. Petersmann, "The WTO Panel and Arbitration Reports on the EC Banana Regime", in (1999) 3(3) *Bridges between Trade and Sustainable Development* 3–4.

[71] J. S. Mill, "Considerations on Representative Government" in J.M. Robson (ed.), *Essays on Politics and Society*, Vol. 19 (Toronto: University of Toronto Press, 1977), at 505.

Just as trade protectionism inside federal states and inside the EC could be overcome only by constitutional guarantees of freedom of trade that could be enforced by self-interested citizens and domestic courts, trade protectionism *vis-à-vis* third countries will continue as long as governments and judges treat citizens as immature objects rather than legal subjects. The human rights objective of maximum equal liberty, empowerment and self-development of citizens across frontiers clearly requires the protection of freedom of trade, without prejudice to non-discriminatory constitutional and legal restraints designed to prevent "market failures" and supply agreed "public goods". Just as constitutional law and, for example, competition law are based on individual citizens' rights enabling a decentralised "self-enforcing constitution", citizens have every reason to insist also on the "democratisation" of international trade law and on constitutional limitations of the protectionist and wasteful abuses of trade policy powers by trade politicians.

Need for Advisory Parliamentary and Civil Society Institutions in the WTO so as to Promote Better Representation of Citizen Interests

International law assumes (for example, in Article 7 of the Vienna Convention on the Law of Treaties) that ministers of trade and ambassadors, if they produce appropriate full powers, are representing a state for the purpose of adopting an international treaty. This rule reflects the traditional disregard of international law for the *democratic legitimacy* of governments. Also GATT and WTO have never scrutinised the agency relationship between governments and citizens; they do not ensure that WTO negotiators respect human rights and take into account all national and private interests involved.

Need for Promoting More "Participatory Democracy" in the WTO

Constitutionalism and democracy require the control of power wherever it is exercised, and the possibility for all citizens affected by governmental decisions of voicing their concerns, participating in the exercise of government powers, and seeking judicial protection from violations of their human rights. How can we deal with the "democratic deficit" of international organisations which allocate one vote to each state regardless of its population and do not afford citizens adequate possibilities for "democratic participation" in, and democratic control of, secretive international negotiations on collective international rule-making? How can we overcome the resistance to protecting human rights, including the "right to democracy" more effectively in WTO law and practice?

Democracy aims at national and international self-government based on transparent discussion and public scrutiny; legislation by representative parliamentary bodies maximising the human rights of the citizens; and procedural due process based on respect for principles of "inclusiveness",[72] transparent policy-making and public access to judicial proceedings. "International legislation" through worldwide treaties involves a delegation of rule-making powers to government executives which are rarely effectively supervised by national parliaments and by public opinion due to the confidentiality, length and complexity of worldwide negotiations and the frequent, practical impossibility of reopening negotiations after the final text has been approved at the international level. The Uruguay Agreements illustrate how democratic principles can easily be circumvented through confidential negotiations among more than 120 government representatives. For instance, between the signing of the Agreements in April 1994 and their entry into force on 1 January 1995, there remained so little time for translating the 25,000 pages of treaty text that some national parliaments (for example, in Germany) had to discuss the agreements without a complete translation of the texts into their national language, and this within only a few days which did not enable parliaments to fully understand, evaluate, discuss or criticise such complex and important "international legislation".

Proposals for Advisory WTO Bodies Representing Civil Society Interests

In order to enhance information on and transparency of international rule-making in international organisations, an increasing number of international organisations provide for advisory parliamentary assemblies (for example, in the Council of Europe) and advisory "Economic and Social Committees" (for example, in the EC) consisting of "representatives of the various categories of economic and social activity, in particular, representatives of producers, farmers, carriers, workers, dealers, craftsmen, professional occupations and representatives of the general public" (Article 257 EC Treaty). Proposals for the establishment of similar advisory bodies in the WTO have been made long since in order to strengthen parliamentary and private participation in WTO activities and, by requiring special interests to balance their views among each other, to contain one-sided protectionist pressures.[73] In July 2000, the International Law Association has recommended that:

> WTO members should strengthen the rule of law in international trade by enhancing the legitimacy and acceptance of WTO rules by in particular:
>
> (a) Improving the transparency of the WTO rule making process i.a. by increasing the participation of national representatives of the economic and social activi-

---

[72] On the "principle of democratic inclusion" and accountability to those affected by government activities see e.g., S. Marks, *The Riddle of All Constitutions* (New York: Oxford University Press, 2000), at 88–92, 109 *et seq*: " 'democratic inclusion' is used to refer to the idea that all should have a right to a say in decision-making which affects them, and that systematic barriers to the exercise of that right should be acknowledged and removed" (p.119).

[73] Cf. E.-U. Petersmann, "Trade and the Protection of the Environment after the Uruguay Round" in R. Wolfrum (ed.), *Enforcing Environmental Standards: Economic Mechanisms as Viable Means?* (Heidelberg: Springer, 1996), 165–197, at 189.

ties in the work of the WTO, for instance by creation of an Advisory Economic and Social Committee or an advisory parliamentary body of the WTO to be consulted regularly by the WTO organs.

(b) Opening the WTO dispute settlement system for observers representing legitimate interests in the respective procedures, and promoting full transparency of WTO dispute settlement proceedings.

(c) Allowing individual parties, both natural and corporate, an advisory locus standi in those dispute settlement procedures where their own rights and interests are affected.[74]

Unlike the UN and many other worldwide organisations, the WTO has so far made only inadequate use of its authority to "make appropriate arrangements for consultation and cooperation with non-governmental organizations concerned with matters related to those of the WTO" (Article V:2 WTO Agreement).[75] Whereas the annual meetings of the Bretton Woods institutions and of the International Labour Organisation and World Intellectual Property Organisation benefit from the presence and expertise of NGOs, the WTO's "public relations policy" appears comparatively underdeveloped. Past WTO initiatives for meetings and symposia with environmental and developmental NGOs have enhanced public understanding and transparency of WTO activities. Such sporadic and selective meetings are, however, no substitute for institutionalising civil society representatives as an advisory body with access to WTO documents and with the right to submit recommendations to all WTO bodies subject to procedures which ensure more accountability and representativeness of NGOs and check their democratic legitimacy.[76] There are also no convincing reasons why meetings of WTO bodies should not be open to the public, including meetings of WTO dispute settlement bodies. For, "justice should not only be done, but should manifestly and undoubtedly be seen to be done".[77]

CONCLUSION

The universal recognition of human rights calls for the interpretation of WTO provisions in conformity with human rights law and requires democratic reforms of the WTO, for instance, the establishment of an advisory parliamentary WTO body and an advisory WTO Economic and Social Committee

---

[74] *Supra* n. 58.

[75] On the 1996 WTO Guidelines for Arrangements on Relations with NGOs, the improved transparency of WTO documents, and for other changes in the public relations policy of the WTO: see G. Marceau and P.N. Pedersen, "Is the WTO Open and Transparent?" (1999) 33 *Journal of World Trade* 5–49; W. Benedek, "Developing the Constitutional Order of The WTO—The Role of NGOs" in W. Benedek, H. Isak and R. Kicker (eds.), *Developing and Development of International and European Law* (Frankfurt am Main: P. Lang, 1999), 313–35; D. Esty, "Non-Governmental Organizations and the WTO" (1998) 1 *JIEL*, 123–148.

[76] See *supra* n. 75 and J. Scholte, R. O'Brien and M. Williams, "The WTO and Civil Society" (1999) 33 *Journal of World Trade* 107–123.

[77] Dictum of Lord Hewart CJ in *R. v Sussex Justices, ex parte McCarthy* [1924] 1 KB 256.

institutionalising active, yet more representative and more responsible, participation of NGOs in the WTO. Meetings of the WTO Council and of WTO dispute settlement bodies should, as a matter of principle, be open to the public. In order to promote "participatory democracy" and protect human rights more effectively, precise and unconditional WTO guarantees of freedom and non-discrimination should be protected by domestic laws and judges as individual rights. The numerous "public interest clauses" and safeguard clauses of WTO law grant governments ample opportunities to apply WTO rules with due regard to social and other human rights.

5

Fundamental Right or Political Whim? WTO Law and the European Court of Justice

STEVE PEERS

INTRODUCTION

WHAT STATUS SHOULD World Trade Organisation (WTO) rules have in the European Community (EC) legal order? The answer to this question has been the subject of a number of judgments by the European Court of Justice (ECJ), to say nothing of a voluminous academic literature.[1] The objections to the Court's conservative case law on the legal effect of WTO rules can be

---

[1] K.J. Kuilwijk, *The European Court of Justice and the GATT Dilemma: Public Interest* v. *Individual Rights* (Beuningen, The Netherlands: Nexed, 1996), 79–160; J. Bourgeois, "The European Court of Justice and the WTO: Problems and Challenges", in J.H.H. Weiler (ed.), *The EU, the WTO and the NAFTA: Towards a Common Law of International Trade* (Oxford, OUP, 2000) 72 at 103–123; J. Eeckhout, "The Domestic Legal Status of the WTO agreement: Interconnecting Legal Systems" (1997) 34 *CMLRev.* 11; N. Neuwahl, "Individuals and the GATT: Direct Effect and the General Agreement on Tariffs and Trade in Community law" in N. Emiliou and D. O'Keeffe (eds.), *The European Union and World Trade Law* (Chichester, Wiley, 1996); M. Hilf, "The Role of National Courts in International Trade Relations", (1997) 18 *Mich LRev.* 321; P. Lee and B. Kennedy, "The Potential Direct Effect of GATT 1994 in European Community Law" (1996) 30 *JWT* 67; F. Castillo de la Torre, "The Status of GATT in EC Law, Revisited" (1995) 29 *JWT* 53; M. Montana I. Mora, "Equilibrium: A Rediscovered Basis for the Court of Justice of the European Communities to Refuse Direct Effect to the Uruguay Round Agreements" (1996) 30 *JWT* 43; O. Berkey, "The European Court of Justice and Direct Effect for the GATT: A Question Worth Revisiting" (1998) 9 *EJIL* 626; I. Govaere, "The Reception of the WTO Agreement in the European Union: The Legacy of GATT" in P. Demaret, J.F. Bellis and G. Garciá Jimenez (eds.), *Regionalism and Multilateralism after the Uruguay Round* (Brussels: EIP, 1997) 703; W.E. Kuiper, "The New WTO Dispute Settlement Mechanism—The Impact on the European Community" (1995) 29 *JWT* 49 at 64; T. Cottier, "Dispute Settlement in the World Trade Organisation: Characteristics and Structural Implications for the European Union" (1998) 35 *CMLRev.* 325 at 365–377; J. Scott, "The GATT and Community Law: Rethinking the 'Regulatory Gap', in J. Shaw and G. More (eds.), *New Legal Dynamics of European Union* (Oxford, OUP, 1995) at 147; S. Peers, "Banana Split: WTO Law and Preferential Agreements in the EC Legal Order" (1999) 4 *EFARev.* 195. On the issue of direct effect of the WTO in any legal system, see T. Cottier, "The Relationship Between World Trade Organization Law, National Law and Regional Law" (1998) 1 *JIEL* 83 at 103–123.

classified as either legal or constitutional.[2] "Legal" critiques have focussed largely on the alleged deficiencies in the Court's characterisation of the WTO (formerly GATT) rules in its judgments, along with the alleged inconsistency between the Court's case law on the legal effect of association and free trade agreements which the EC has agreed, and the case law on the GATT/WTO. "Constitutional" critiques have focussed on the Court's failure to pay due regard to the fundamental importance of liberal trading rules within modern economies.

Surprisingly, given the level of academic interest in the status of human rights in the EU legal order, there has been far less discussion of the latter critique than the former. It is therefore long past time for an examination of the constitutional critique, in particular taking into account the Court's recent reaffirmation of the limited effect of GATT/WTO rules in the EC legal order.[3] The legal critiques are in many respects well founded, although they fail to take account of the political arguments in defence of the Court's case law. On the other hand, the constitutional critique has not demonstrated that the Court's case law violates the principles of human rights law forming part of Community law or shown convincing grounds to reconsider those principles.

SUMMARY OF THE COURT'S JURISPRUDENCE

The most controversial aspect of the Court's rulings on the legal effect of GATT 1947 (and now GATT 1994 and the other WTO agreements) is the denial of direct effect of GATT rules within the Community legal order. Beginning with *International Fruit*,[4] the Court argued that GATT 1947 rules could not be directly effective in the EC legal system, because of the nature of such rules, particularly the great flexibility of the GATT system, the possibility of safeguards and waivers and the nature of the dispute settlement process. The Court reaffirmed this principle in a number of later cases, [5] and ultimately ruled that for the same reasons, Member States could not use the provisions of GATT 1947 to attack the validity of Community legislation.[6] However, in parallel to this case law, the Court carved out two exceptions to its rulings. GATT 1947 rules could

---

[2] The important issues of the Community's competence over WTO matters and the ECJ's jurisdiction to interpret WTO rules outside the exclusive competence of the Community are outside the scope of this ch. See respectively *Opinion 1/94* [1994] ECR I–5267 on competence and Case C–53/96, *Hermès International* [1998] ECR I–3603; Advocate General's Opinion in Case C–293/98, *Egeda* [2000] ECR I–629; and the judgment of 14 December 2000 in Cases C–300/98, *Christian Dior* and C–392/98, *Layher* (not yet reported) on jurisdiction.

[3] Case C–149/96, *Portugal* v. *Council* [1999] ECR I–8395 and judgment in *Christian Dior* and *Layher, supra* n. 2.

[4] Joined Cases 21–24/72, [1972] ECR 1219.

[5] Case 9/73, *Schluter* [1973] ECR 1135; Joined Cases 290 and 291/81, *SPI/SAMI* [1983] ECR 801; Case 266/81, *SIOT* [1983] ECR 731; Joined Cases 290 and 291/81, *Singer* [1983] ECR 847; Case C–469/93, *Chiquita Italia* [1995] ECR I–4533.

[6] Case C–280/93, *Germany* v. *Council* [1994] ECR I–4973.

be used to attack Community acts where those acts were either intended to implement a GATT obligation or made reference to specific provisions of the GATT.[7] I call these exceptions "implementation exceptions".[8]

Despite the lack of direct effect, the Court has ruled that there is an "indirect effect" of GATT 1947 rules in Community law, requiring EC measures to be interpreted in light of GATT measures.[9] In fact, this obligation of consistent interpretation applies "as far as possible".[10] In addition, the Court has found that Community secondary legislation is hierarchically subsidiary to the Community's international obligations, including its GATT 1947 obligations.[11] Finally, the Court has ruled that the EC Commission can use the EC Treaty's infringement proceedings system to sue Member States for infringement of Community rules implementing GATT 1947 rules. [12] However, it is clear that Member States cannot take the opportunity of the infringement proceeding to question the validity of Community acts in light of the WTO as a defence to the infringement proceeding.[13]

The advent of the WTO agreements reopened the debate over the effect of GATT rules in the Community legal order. Many commentators argued that with the radical change in the GATT (now WTO) dispute settlement system, coupled with tight new rules on waivers and safeguards, the Court of Justice would be forced to reconsider its prior position rejecting the direct effect of GATT.[14] At the very least, some argued that panel reports adopted by the WTO Dispute Settlement Body should have direct effect in the Community legal system.[15] For several years, the ECJ and CFI avoided (sometimes clumsily) the issue of the direct effect of WTO rules, even when the national courts expressly asked questions about direct effect or when the issue was expressly raised by the Commission or Member States submitting observations in cases before the Court.[16] It also avoided the issue of the legal effect of WTO panel reports,[17] although the CFI later ruled that the 1997 report on the EC's banana regime

---

[7] Case 70/87, *Fediol* [1989] ECR 1781; Case C–69/89, *Nakajima* [1991] ECR I–2069.

[8] Following Eeckhout, *supra* n. 1 at 56.

[9] Case 92/71, *Interfoods* [1972] ECR 231.

[10] Case C–61/94, *Commission* v. *Germany* [1996] ECR I–3989.

[11] See *ibid*.

[12] See *ibid*.

[13] This is because Member States cannot invoke a defence of invalidity in any infringement claim. See Case C–404/97, *Commission* v. *Portugal* [2000] ECR I–4897.

[14] See Govaere, Eeckhout, Cottier, Lee and Kennedy, Kuiper, Berkey and Montana I Mora (all *supra* n. 1).

[15] See Eeckhout, 51–55, Cottier, 369–375 and Peers, 205–212 (all *supra* n. 1).

[16] Case C–183/95, *Affish* [1997] ECR I-4315; *Hermes International* (*supra* n. 2); Joined Cases C–364/95 and C–365/95, *T. Port III* [1998] ECR I–1023; Case C–106/97, *Dutch Antillean Dairy Industry* [1999] ECR I–5983; Case T–120/96, *Lilly Industries* [1998] ECR II–2571. In Case C–352/96, *Italy* v. *Council* ([1998] ECR I–6937), the Court simply applied the case law on the legal effect of GATT 1947 without properly considering whether the case law should be altered. Following the *Portugal* v. *Council* judgment, see Joined Cases T–32/98 and T–41/98, *Netherlands Antilles* v. *Commission* [2000] ECR II–201, para. 87.

[17] Case C–104/97 P, *Atlanta* [1999] ECR I–6983. However, see the Advocate-General's Opinion in that case.

could not be invoked by individuals, without ruling on the broader question of the legal effect of panel reports.[18]

The issue could not be avoided forever, and the Court squarely addressed it in its *Portugal* v. *Council* judgment.[19] The Court found that despite the huge changes introduced by the Uruguay Round, WTO rules *still* could not be used by Member States to attack the legality of Community acts, unless the two "implementation exceptions" applied.[20] Although this judgment addressed only the ability of Member States to invoke WTO rules, it nevertheless implicitly rules out direct effect of the WTO rules also; this was duly confirmed in the subsequent judgment in *Christian Dior* and *Layher.*[21] However, according to this judgment, direct effect is precluded only in areas where the Community has already legislated; in other areas, Member States are free to determine whether or not WTO obligations are directly effective.[22]

While the outcome of *Portugal* v. *Council* essentially extended the *status quo* on the legal effects of GATT/WTO rules, the Court supplied new reasoning for this finding. Although the WTO system did "differ significantly from the provisions on GATT 1947", particularly as regards safeguards and dispute settlement rules, the WTO system "nevertheless accords considerable importance to negotiation between the parties".[23] The Court accepted that "the main purpose of the [Understanding on the WTO dispute settlement system is] . . . to secure the withdrawal of the measures in question if they are found to be inconsistent with the WTO rules", but noted that "that understanding provides that where the immediate withdrawal of measures is impracticable compensation may be granted on an interim basis pending the withdrawal of the inconsistent measure".[24] Indeed, while it admitted that "compensation is a temporary measure" and that the Understanding "shows a preference for full implementation of a recommendation to bring a measure into conformity" with WTO rules,[25] WTO members breaching WTO rules could negotiate with winning parties to compensate them for the breach, instead of amending the infringing domestic measure.[26] It is thus clear that the Court did *not* assert that the WTO Dispute Settlement Understanding "may justify violations of WTO law";[27] if anything

---

[18] Case T–254/97, *Fruchthandelsgesellschaft Chemnitz* [1999] ECR II–2743. On this case and the *Atlanta* Opinion, see G.A. Zonnekeyn, "The Status of Adopted Panel and Appellate Body Reports in the European Court of Justice and the European Court of First Instance" (1999) 34 *JWT* 93.

[19] *Supra* n. 2.

[20] On this point, see para. 49 of the judgment.

[21] *Supra* n. 2.

[22] It is arguable that Member States' freedom on this matter will be reduced as a consequence of the extension of the scope of the EC's common commercial policy that will follow ratification of the Treaty of Nice.

[23] Para. 36 of the judgment.

[24] Para. 37 of the judgment.

[25] Para. 38 of the judgment.

[26] Para. 39 of the judgment.

[27] E.-U. Petersmann, "From Negative to Positive Integration in the WTO: Time for 'Mainstreaming WTO Rights' into WTO Law?" (2000) 37 *CMLRev.* 1363, n. 81 at 1381.

the judgment goes further than the literal wording of the Understanding in stating that compensation could be agreed only where implementation of a ruling was "impractical".[28] Rather, the Court simply noted that a winning party can agree temporarily to accept compensation from a losing party pending full implementation of its obligations: in the words of the Understanding, compensation is a "temporary measure . . . available in the event that [panel] recommendations and rulings are not implemented within a reasonable period of time".[29]

In the Court's logic, this choice, made available by the WTO dispute settlement system, required restraint on judicial power:

> to require the judicial organs to refrain from applying the rules of domestic law which are inconsistent with the WTO agreements would have the consequence of depriving the legislative or executive organs of the contracting parties of the possibility afforded by [the dispute settlement rules] of entering into negotiated arrangements even on a temporary basis.[30]

Moreover, the WTO was still founded on the principle of reciprocity, and was therefore different from the treaties agreed by the EC with third states "which introduce a certain asymmetry of obligations, or create special relations of integration with the Community".[31] Some of the EC's most important contracting parties had already excluded the WTO rules from being invoked before domestic courts to review the legality of domestic law.[32] While the Court had earlier ruled that such lack of reciprocity in legal status of a treaty between the EC and the other signatory should not automatically lead to a lack of direct effect within the Community,[33] there was in this case a risk of "disuniform application of the WTO rules".[34] Again this led to the conclusion that there must be judicial self-restraint:

> To accept that the role of ensuring that those rules comply with Community law [sic] devolves directly on the Community judicature would deprive the legislative or executive organs of the Community of the scope for manoeuvre enjoyed by their counterparts in the Community's trading partners.[35]

The Court concluded by noting that its findings corresponded with that suggested by the Council in the preamble to the Decision approving the WTO agreement and its Annexes on behalf of the Community.[36]

[28] There is no requirement in paras. 22.1 or 22.2 of the Understanding that full implementation be "impractical" before compensation is agreed; a literal reading of those sub-paragraphs does not suggest any grounds limiting recourse to compensation besides the compensation being "temporary", "voluntary", "consistent" with WTO obligations and "mutually acceptable".

[29] Para. 22.1 of the Dispute Settlement Understanding.

[30] Para. 40 of the judgment.

[31] Para. 42 of the judgment.

[32] Para .43 of the judgment.

[33] Para. 44 of the judgment, referring to Case 104/81, *Kupferberg* [1982] ECR 3641.

[34] Para.45 of the judgment.

[35] Para. 46 of the judgment. Surely the Court meant to refer to "the role of ensuring that *Community law complies with those rules*".

[36] Para. 48 of the judgment; see Decision 94/800 [1994] OJ L336/1.

THE CURRENT STATUS OF WTO LAW

Where do we stand after *Portugal* v. *Council?*[37] At first sight, it appears that with this judgment the Court has not only precluded any attack on the validity of Community acts in light of WTO rules (save where the "implementation exceptions" apply), but also precluded any attack on the validity of Community acts in light of a WTO panel report (except perhaps where those same exceptions apply).[38] This seems to follow both from the Court's "reciprocity" argument against the use of WTO rules to attack EC law (although the Court said nothing about the status of adopted panel reports in the legal system of the other contracting parties), and from its detailed examination of the WTO dispute settlement system. The Court explicitly refers to the legal position of the Community *after* the adoption of a panel report, and indeed to the legal position *after the expiry of the "reasonable period"* allowed by WTO rules for the implementation of a panel report.[39] This goes further than the ruling of the CFI in *Fruchthandelsgesellschaft Chemnitz,* which stopped short of ruling out the direct effect of all panel reports and left open a possible *a contrario* argument that *Member States* could use panel reports as a grounds for claiming the invalidity of a Community act. Clearly the Court has ruled out the direct effect of panel reports as a general rule, as suggested by Eeckhout.[40]

However, at no point does the Court mention the possibility of authorised retaliation under the WTO rules against the EC for failure to implement an adopted panel report or agree compensation with affected parties. Therefore, it might still be argued that WTO rules should have direct effect where the Community has made no attempt either to implement a panel report or to agree compensation, or where the Community has not tried to implement the report and negotiations on compensation have failed. In such cases, would the Court rule that it would be inappropriate to allow the judicial authorities to intervene? Did the Court refrain from mentioning the possibility of retaliation only because it was too shy to mention such an aggressive gesture?[41] Or did it wish to leave open the possibility that panel reports could have direct effect in such circumstances?

It seems likely that the Court did not really wish to leave this issue open. For one thing, its separate conclusions on the reciprocity issue logically apply to all circumstances where the Community has not implemented a panel report, unless perhaps a future plaintiff is able to provide evidence that the

---

[37] I address here the effect of the judgment; for comments on the Court's reasoning, see part 4 below.

[38] I am grateful to Miguel Poaires Maduro for his comments on this issue, although the analysis in this ch. is my own.

[39] Para. 39 of the judgment.

[40] *Supra* n. 1 at 51–55.

[41] This prospect was mentioned by Advocate-General Mischo in his Opinion in *Atlanta* (*supra* n. 17), but it did not alter his suggested conclusions.

Community's main trading partners provide for the direct effect of panel reports. Moreover, it would be difficult to distinguish between cases where the Community had tried to negotiate compensation with third states and failed because they would not enter into talks, and cases in which the Community had refused to negotiate or had negotiated in bad faith. Such judgments would involve the Court in second-guessing the *bona fides* of Community and third-state negotiators, something it is ill-equipped to do.

Alternatively, it might be argued that if the Community does not even attempt to negotiate compensation as regards an adopted panel report, but simply fails to implement it by the relevant deadline, that report would be directly effective. Cottier has argued for a variant of this approach, suggesting in effect that where the Community has failed to implement a report without agreeing compensation, the report should have direct effect where the Community has ignored the report or where there are "bad" reasons for such non-implementation.[42] But any legal distinction between different types of non-implementation is, in my view, problematic.[43]

The strongest argument against any of these approaches is that they would place tremendous power in the hands of third states. Why should third states bother to negotiate compensation with the Community, or negotiate in good faith, if they know that the Court of Justice will do their job for them by enforcing the panel report if negotiations fail or never begin? Such a finding would therefore profoundly undercut the principles of judicial restraint and political discretion underlying both main arguments in the Court's judgment.

On the other hand, there is nothing in the judgment to prevent the application of the "implementation exceptions" to adopted panel reports. Put another way, if the Community institutions refer to a specific adopted panel report when adopting a measure or adopt a measure which attempts to implement that report, it should be open to Member States to rely on that adopted panel report as grounds to consider a Community act invalid. Similarly, individuals should be able to rely on direct effect of the reports in such circumstances.[44] The point is not hypothetical: it will likely be tested in the ongoing "banana" litigation, where the Community institutions attempted to implement the 1997 WTO panel report and were condemned by WTO arbitrators for continuing breaches of WTO rules. However, there are certain difficulties facing the application of this principle. Three scenarios are possible, inevitably following a traffic-light analogy. In the first ("red") scenario, the Community has purported to implement a panel report but its implementation attempts have subsequently been condemned for a continuing breach of that report by WTO arbitrators (as in the banana saga). In the second ("green") scenario, the Community has purported to implement a panel report and it has been agreed at WTO level that the implementation is correct. In the third ("amber") scenario, the Community's

---

[42] *Supra* n. 1 at 369–375.
[43] See comments in "Banana Split", *supra* n. 1, at 207.
[44] I have developed this point in "Banana Split", *supra* n. 1, at 209–212.

purported implementation has been attacked at WTO level but the Community is defending itself.

There is a strong argument for giving direct effect to a panel report in the first scenario, but for denying it in the second scenario, even if litigants within the Community legal system disagree with the WTO-compatibility of the agreement reached at WTO level. If the Court were to rule against the WTO-compatibility of EC acts in such circumstances, it would be invading the jurisdiction of the WTO dispute settlement system to determine when breaches of the WTO rules have ceased or the ability of WTO members to settle disputes as provided for in the WTO agreements. As for the "amber" scenario, in practice there may be few cases falling within this category because WTO proceedings in such cases are simplified and will likely be concluded before any challenges within the EC legal system. If the EC proceedings do move more quickly, then it may be preferable for the EC courts to suspend the case until the conclusion of the WTO dispute. If EC court proceedings do go ahead before WTO proceedings are complete, the outcome most compatible with the principles underlying the *Portugal* v. *Council* judgment would be to hold that the panel report was not directly effective as long as the Community's failure to implement it has not yet been definitively established at WTO level.[45]

In any event, there is no reason to preclude interpretation of EC acts in light of panel reports as far as possible, in accordance with the general "indirect effect" rule applying to international law in the Community legal order.[46]

Finally, it is striking that the Court draws a distinction not between the WTO and agreements aimed at *accession* to the Community (or granting asymmetrical treatment), but between the WTO and *special integration agreements* (or agreements granting asymmetrical treatment). This confirms that the key test for direct effect is *not* whether an agreement aims to prepare a state for accession,[47] but whether it creates a "special relationship" going beyond multilateral obligations. This strengthens the argument that the Europe Agreements have direct effect,[48] and that new and planned agreements with Mediterranean states, the African, Caribbean and Pacific (ACP) countries and Mexico will confer direct effect.[49] But since a treaty designed to prepare a third country for acces-

[45] Zonnekeyn (*supra* n. 18 at 106) appears to argue that in "amber" cases the EC should be considered not to have implemented a panel report at all if it is "obvious" that its purported implementation is still in breach of WTO rules. In my view, the practical evidential difficulties of determining in practice whether the EC has or has not "obviously" failed to implement a panel report are too great to consider applying such a rule.

[46] See *Interfoods* (*supra* n. 9); *Commission* v. *Germany* (*supra* n. 10); and Case T–256/97, *BEUC* v. *Commission* [2000] ECR II–101, which confirms the application of this principle to WTO rules.

[47] The Court had hinted in the past that treaties aiming to prepare a third state for accession were particularly likely to confer direct effect (see Case 17/81, *Pabst and Richarz* [1982] ECR 1331; Case C–416/96, *El-Yassini* [1999] ECR I–1209).

[48] In any event, subsequent behaviour by the parties indicates that they treat the Europe Agreements as measures intended to prepare the associates for EU membership.

[49] In the former two cases, the new or planned agreements have replaced or will replace existing "asymmetrical" treaties.

sion is a particularly close form of "special relationship", the Court still has the possibility of adopting a more *communautaire* interpretation of treaties which aim to prepare a state for accession to the Community, in comparison with treaties with more limited objectives.[50]

LEGAL CRITIQUES

The Court's case law on the direct effect of GATT 1947 was subject to stringent and justified critiques on legal grounds. Its greatest weakness was the stark distinction that the Court consistently drew between GATT rules and the rules imposed by other treaties agreed by the Community. If the Court had been consistently monist or consistently dualist, there would have been less criticism. As regards other treaties concerning trade in goods (often also addressing movement of persons), the Court has consistently found that, unlike the GATT, the "nature and purpose" of such treaties did not preclude direct effect. This was the case for simple free trade agreements signed by the Community,[51] for association agreements intended to lead to membership,[52] and for association agreements conferring non-reciprocal advantages on third states.[53]

As many critics observed, the Court's distinction between the two types of agreement was unconvincing. The Community's bilateral agreements usually allow for some form of safeguard measure in the event of economic disturbances, usually differing little from Article XIX GATT. Moreover, most Community agreements provide for an Association Council or Co-operation Council of some form, made up of delegates of the parties, which can settle disputes on the interpretation or application of each agreement. If such a body cannot settle a dispute, each party is usually allowed to take retaliatory action against the others. Under most agreements, arbitrators can be appointed to settle disputes, and the parties must apply such arbitrators' decisions. But no such arbitrators have ever been appointed to date. It is hard to see how this system is less "political" than the system under GATT 1947.[54] It is true that the

---

[50] See particularly *El-Yassini* (*supra* n. 47).

[51] *Kupferberg*, *supra* n. 31; the same held true for all the free trade agreements signed by the Community with member states of the European Free Trade Agreement (EFTA).

[52] Case 12/86, *Demirel* [1987] ECR 3719 and subsequent case law (Turkey); Case C–432/92, *Anastasiou I* [1994] ECR I–3087 (Cyprus); see Opinions of 14 and 26 September 2000 on the Europe Agreements (Cases C–63/99, *Gloszczuck*; C–257/99, *Barkoci and Malik*; C–235/99, *Kondova*, all pending). On the European Economic Area (EEA), contrast Case T–115/94, *Opel Austria* [1997] ECR II–39) with the Opinion in Case C–321/97, *Andersson* [1999] ECR I–3551 and *Opinion 1/91* [1991] ECR I–6079.

[53] Case C–18/90, *Kziber* [1991] ECR I–199 and later case law (Maghreb agreements); Case 87/75, *Bresciani* [1976] ECR 129 (Yaoundé Convention); *Chiquita Italia*, supra n. 5 (Lomé Convention); Case C–162/96, *Racke* [1998] ECR I–3655 (agreement with Yugoslavia).

[54] For a detailed examination of dispute settlement and safeguards under the Community's bilateral agreements, see S. Peers, *Trade Agreements of the European Community* (Oxford, OUP, forthcoming).

Community's bilateral agreements do not provide for "waivers" in the sense of Article XXV GATT, but the Court never placed great stress on this feature of the GATT system. In any event, in one case the EC and its associate state have agreed a Protocol delaying the full implementation of a treaty indefinitely, an act indistinguishable from a waiver.[55]

Moreover, the Court never took note of the relationship between the Community's bilateral agreements and its multilateral obligations. Since the EC's bilateral agreements have been concluded pursuant to GATT Article XXIV (the exception for customs unions and free trade areas) and/or Part IV of the GATT (special treatment for developing countries), they form part of the overall system of international trade regulation. So they pursue the same aims as the GATT, but go further, subject to authorisations contained in the GATT itself. Most of the bilateral agreements contain versions of Articles 28 (ex Article 30) and 90 (ex Article 95) EC, which were themselves based on Articles XI and III GATT.

What about the Court's new arguments for rejecting the direct effect of the WTO?[56] As regards the first argument (the nature of the WTO dispute settlement system), it is true that the Community has the discretion, according to WTO rules, to negotiate compensation with aggrieved parties after an adverse WTO panel report. The Court's argument on this point did not make any comparison with bilateral agreements agreed by the Community, but such a comparison cannot be avoided as long as the latter can confer direct effect but EC rules cannot. Under bilateral agreements, this level of discretion is not available if arbitrators are appointed to settle a dispute under a bilateral Community agreement and issue a ruling. But in practice the Community prefers to retaliate against its partners and associates under bilateral agreements if it believes they have violated the agreement, without recourse to arbitration.[57] Disputes under bilateral agreements could also, as noted above, be settled by Association or Co-operation Councils—an essentially *political* process. Whatever the position on paper, the WTO system is far more "judicial" and less political in practice than the Community's special relationships. In granting direct effect, the Court is thus still fettering the discretion of the EC's political institutions.

What about the Court's second argument, concerning the difference between the WTO rules and "special relationships"? There are really two heads to this argument: the assertion that the WTO rules are distinct in nature from the Community's bilateral treaties and the conclusion that the Community should not grant direct effect to WTO rules as long as its trading partners do not.

---

[55] Protocol with Malta [1991] OJ L116/66.

[56] For other comments on the judgment, see G.A. Zonnekeyn, "The Status of WTO Law in the EC Legal Order: The Final Curtain" (2000) 34 *JWT* 111; *ibid.*, "The Status of WTO Law in the EC Legal Order: Some Comments in Light of the *Portuguese Textiles* Case" (2000) 25 *ELRev.* 293; and S. Griller, "Judicial Enforceability of WTO Law in the European Union: Annotation to Case C–149/96, *Portugal* v. *Council*" (2000) 3 *JIEL* 441.

[57] See Peers, *supra* n. 54.

The first head is not a credible argument. As noted above, the Community's bilateral treaties were always closely connected to the GATT rules allowing for further economic integration. This connection has been strengthened by the Uruguay Round, with the adoption of rules on economic integration and services (Article V GATS), coupled with the controls imposed by GATS on exceptions from its Most Favoured Nations principle. In fact, since many EC bilateral agreements contain no provisions (or very limited provisions) on services, the GATS *goes beyond* the integration commitments in many bilateral agreements. In any case, a number of Community bilateral agreements contain references to GATS rules. As for GATT, the Understanding on Article XXIV of GATT strengthens the effect of that important clause, and it is widely understood that the Community's retreat from treaties granting third states non-reciprocal preferential treatment has been hastened by the new disciplines. Moreover, the additional liberalisation commitments which the Community and third states have agreed during the Uruguay Round have lessened the gap between the EC's bilateral agreements and multilateral rules. Finally, the Court's use of the preamble to the WTO agreement is bizarre. Surely the Community's bilateral treaties providing for mutual trade liberalisation are also "reciprocal and mutually advantageous arrangements", even if the preambles to those treaties do not use the same words? True, the EC's non-reciprocal preferential agreements cannot be described as "reciprocal and mutually advantageous". However, since 1995 the Community has signed only a few such agreements,[58] and these could arguably be described as "interim agreements" designed to lead to agreements on full free trade later. In any event, developing members of the GATT/WTO have traditionally had far less onerous commitments in comparison with developed members, and developed states have been authorised to offer them discriminatory concessions by means of a GATT waiver and now the GATT Enabling Clause. So for *the majority of WTO Members*, the WTO *does* contain a "certain asymmetry of obligations", just like the Community's bilateral non-reciprocal treaties.

The second, more political, head is the Court's strongest argument for refusing direct effect of WTO rules. Even so, its conclusion is problematic for two reasons. First, the argument is not applied consistently. Does the Court know whether the Court's main trading partners also apply an "implementation exception"? If not, there will still be a risk of non-uniform application of sorts, because the trading partners' implementation will not be subject to potential invalidity under domestic law. Trading partners would then be free to purport to implement WTO rules in their domestic law, while in fact implementing

---

[58] See the agreement with the Former Yugoslav Republic of Macedonia [1997] OJ L348/2, which will be replaced by a Stablisation and Association Agreement incorporating full free trade signed in April 2001 (COM(2001)90, 26 February 2001); the update of the Lomé IV Convention [1998] OJ L156/3, which only extended the pre-1995 non-reciprocal treaty [1991] OJ L229/1; and the recently agreed Lomé replacement (COM(2000)324, 23 May 2000), which is expressly intended to be replaced by free-trade agreements.

those rules very badly, without any possibility of judicial review. Meanwhile, the Community legislative measures adopted in the same circumstances might be struck down. A parallel objection applies to the "indirect effect" of WTO rules upon domestic law.

Secondly, several of the Community's largest trading partners already have bilateral agreements with the Community, most notably Switzerland (its second largest partner) and Norway.[59] These bilateral agreements confer direct effect.[60] Why does the lack of guaranteed reciprocity of enforcement of the Community's bilateral agreements with these countries not bother the Court? Since the bilateral treaties in question go further than WTO rules (at least as regards trade in goods), the EC has *more to lose* from the inability to ensure enforcement of a bilateral treaty within its partner's legal system than it has to lose from that partner's non-enforcement of WTO rules. True, the Community can begin dispute settlement proceedings under the bilateral agreements, but it could also bring proceedings to enforce its WTO rights. Why tie one hand behind its back in the former case, but not the latter?

Since both arguments of the Court are unconvincing, its underlying concern must therefore be that the Community's other large trading partners, lacking any general preferential agreement with the Community and accounting for much of its external trade, would take advantage of the "scope for manœuvre" which the lack of domestic direct effect affords them if the WTO rules were directly effective in the Community. Put very bluntly, the Americans and the Japanese (and likely soon the Chinese and Taiwanese) could reap huge commercial advantages from one-sided direct effect of WTO rules. Job losses and consumer safety fears which allegedly followed as a consequence would be blamed on the Court, which would be characterised by critics as the unelected enforcer of illegitimate agreements.[61] Of course, the apparent disadvantage of the Community might be remedied by a broader agreement between all (or the most important) WTO parties to make WTO rules directly effective in each of their legal systems, perhaps inspired by the Court's (hypothetical) brilliant radical judgment. But this seems unlikely for the foreseeable future. First, it would be hard to sell to domestic audiences, given the present unpopularity of the WTO. Secondly, the Community's negotiating position in such talks would obviously be weak. Put bluntly, why would the Community's main trading partners buy the cow, if they could have the milk for free?

So despite the many weaknesses of the Court's legal reasoning, there is considerable force to its most political argument in *Portugal* v. *Council*. Judges

---

[59] Before membership, Sweden, Austria and Finland (enjoying directly effective treaties with the Community) were also among the EC's largest trading partners.

[60] On the EC–Swiss free trade agreement see the reference in *Anastasiou* (*supra* n. 52) to Case 218/83, *Les Rapides Savoyards* [1984] ECR 3105; on the EEA, see *supra* n. 52.

[61] The *Portugal* v. *Council* judgment was delivered during widespread heavy criticism of the WTO, only two weeks before the "Battle of Seattle" forcefully questioned the legitimacy of the WTO before a worldwide audience.

should not disarm politicians and civil servants, leaving them "naked in the conference chamber" before the Community's aggressive, heavily armed trading partners, who will pounce on any sign of weakness. Pacifism is a laudable policy, but it works only if everyone practises it: if they will not, we cannot send Gandhi forth to do battle with Rambo. So far, so *realpolitik*. But such deference to politicians and civil servants cannot be justified if we are dealing not simply with the economic interests of Community industry, but with a fundamental human right. This brings us to the second type of critique of the Court's GATT/WTO case law: its alleged failure to give effect to the constitutional status which the GATT/WTO should be accorded.

CONSTITUTIONAL CRITIQUES

Is there, or should there be, a fundamental constitutional right to trade with third countries, or is such trade instead governed largely by the discretion of the legislature and executive? In a number of articles, Petersmann has contended that within the Community legal order, there is either a pre-existing fundamental right to trade with third states that the Court of Justice has refused to recognise, or at least that such a right should be recognised.[62] If such a right does exist or were recognised, it would not only address the argument that the application of WTO rules in the Community should be left to politicians. Recognition of such a right would also dramatically increase the status of WTO rules in the Community legal order, for human rights are part of the general principles of Community law. General principles have the same rank in the Community legal order as the EC Treaty; indeed it could now be argued that protection of human rights is an enforceable Treaty obligation.[63] This would not confer direct effect as such on the WTO rules, but it would mean that conflicting rules of secondary Community law could be set aside on application by Member States or individuals.[64] Indeed, the Treaty and general principles have a status even above international agreements agreed by the Community, so inclusion of WTO rules within the former categories of acts would mean that international agreements conflicting with WTO rules would have to be set aside. This might include the preferential treaties such as the Lomé Convention, as well as environmental

[62] See, e.g., "Constitutional Principles Governing the EEC's Commercial Policy", in M. Maresceau (ed.), *The European Community's Commercial Policy After 1992: The Legal Dimension* (Dordrecht: Martinus Nijhoff, 1993), 21; *ibid.*, "The EEC as a GATT Member: Legal Conflicts Between GATT Law and European Community Law", in M. Hilf, F.G. Jacobs and E.-U. Petersmann (eds.), *The European Community and GATT* (Deventer, Kluwer, 1986), 23; *ibid.*, "National Constitutions and International Economic Law" in M. Hilf and E.-U. Petersmann (eds.), *National Constitutions and International Economic Law* (Deventer, Kluwer, 1993), 3.

[63] See Arts. 6(2) and 47 EU, as cited by the Court in its Order in Case C–17/98, *Emesa Sugar* [2000] ECR I–665 and the judgment in Case C–7/98, *Krombach* [2000] ECR I–1935.

[64] See *Opinion 2/94*, [1996] ECR I–1759, confirming that Community acts breaching human rights principles might be held invalid by the Court.

treaties. Moreover, if the "right to trade" is a free-standing right in Community law, the content of the right may differ from the rules set out in WTO agreements, conferring even greater rights to trade freely than allowed in WTO rules. Petersmann accepts that WTO rules (and presumably also any free-standing "right to trade") should be subject to derogations on certain grounds,[65] which should include protection of (other) human rights, but it is clear that, in his view, the WTO breaches and infringements of the "right to trade" resulting from the EC's external trade policies could not be justified *holus bolus* by any such derogation.

Petersmann's case is that the right to trade should be recognised as a fundamental right in EC law for a number of reasons. His philosophical justification is that the right to trade with third states has domestic constitutional functions. It protects individual rights to property and equality from the vagaries of politicians who would otherwise be captured by rent-seeking protectionist lobbies which would induce executives and legislatures to agree trade rules redistributing wealth within a state from consumers and more efficient companies to less efficient companies, infringing individual rights in the process.

There are several issues here. The first issue is whether the concept of a "right to trade" with third countries can be found by examining the sources of the human rights recognised as general principles of law by the EC legal order. Secondly, in the event that the right cannot be found by such examination, the next issue is whether the sources of law are defective. Thirdly, the case for a general "right to trade" should be subject to normative analysis.

First, then, is there a "right to trade" in the sources of human rights law recognised by the Court of Justice as general principles of human rights law? According to Article 6(2) of the Treaty on European Union (TEU), the Community must respect the rights found in national constitutions of the Member States and the 1951 European Convention of Human Rights as general principles of Community law. The Court of Justice has described Article 6(2) TEU as confirming its prior case law,[66] which is not correct: the prior case law additionally provided that other international human rights treaties in which the Member States had participated formed part of EC human rights law. One can now question whether the EU Charter of Fundamental Rights will form part of or influence the general principles of Community law[67]; but the point is moot in this discussion, because the agreed Charter makes no reference to any "right to trade".[68]

---

[65] See particularly "From Negative to Positive Integration", *supra* n. 27.

[66] See *Emesa Sugar* and *Krombach*, *supra* n. 63.

[67] [2000] OJ C364/1.

[68] The closest reference is a preambular assertion that "[t]he Union . . . ensures free movement of persons, goods, services and capital, and the freedom of establishment". There is no reference to the EC Treaty as regards these concepts, but it is clear that the Charter does not require the Union to ensure at least movement of persons as regards entry from third countries into the Union (see Arts. 15 and 45); and surely in the absence of express wording we cannot assume that the preamble is referring to entry from third countries as regards *some* of such forms of movement but not others.

So is there a "right to trade" in international human rights treaties? Such a right cannot be found as such in the ECHR or any of its Protocols, or any other international human rights instrument. Nor can that right be found in the jurisprudence of the bodies interpreting those treaties. Alternatively, it might be arguable that the GATT, now the WTO, is itself an international human rights treaty. However, there is no formal link between the WTO and other international human rights instruments. The text of the GATT/WTO agreements does not suggest that the parties see such agreements as human rights treaties. Nor does Petersmann refer to any indication from the behaviour of the parties to such agreements to indicate that state practice, *opinio juris* or WTO panel reports (with their scrupulous references to the rules of international treaty law) support this interpretation. Indeed, he has recently recognised that "[s]ince the inception of GATT 1947, WTO diplomats have conspicuously avoided any references to human rights law".[69]

This brings us to national law. Petersmann argues that a right to trade can be found in the national constitutions of France, Germany and Luxembourg.[70] However, he does not provide further examples, and since other research indicates that the German courts do not treat the GATT as directly effective,[71] any "right to trade" is therefore weakened in parallel with the limited legal effect of GATT in EC law. Other analyses of the French constitution make no mention of any "right to trade".[72] In any event, the Court now appears to reject the prospect that rights recognised by only some Member States can form part of the general principles of Community law.[73]

It is true that notwithstanding the paucity of references to the "right to trade" in international or national human rights instruments, the Court of Justice has recognised such a right in the *ADBHU* judgment.[74] This is an odd reference, which the Court has been reticent to repeat.[75] The Court did not defend the existence of such a right by reference to the usual sources of Community human rights law, obviously because it could not. In any event, there is nothing to indicate that the Court recognised that such a right extended to a right for *third-country* goods to enter or leave the Community. Petersmann has objected that failure to extend the right to third-country goods would be a breach of the principle of equality,[76] but this argument is unconvincing. The EC Treaty draws a clear distinction between the *obligation* to establish free trade within the

---

[69] "From Negative to Positive Integration", *supra* n. 27 at 1374.

[70] For instance, see "Constitutional Principles" (*supra* n. 62) at 41.

[71] M. Hilf, "The Application of GATT Within the Member States of the European Community, with Special Reference to the Federal Republic of Germany" in Hilf, Petersmann and Jacobs (*supra* n. 62) 153 at 157–158. Petersmann, in "National Constitutions" (*supra* n. 62) at 22, refers to several economic liberties in the German constitution but makes no reference to a right to trade as such.

[72] Zoller, in Hilf and Petersmann (*supra* n. 62) at 265.

[73] Joined Cases 46/87 and 227/88, *Hoechst* [1989] ECR 2859.

[74] Case 240/83, [1985] ECR 513.

[75] See the description of free movement of goods as a fundamental *principle* of Community law, for example in Case C–265/95, *Commission* v. *France* (revolting farmers) [1997] ECR I–6959.

[76] For instance, see "Constitutional Principles" (*supra* n. 61) at 41.

Community and the *objective* of gradually liberalising trade with third states.[77] As such, the Court was simply interpreting and giving effect to a distinction embedded within the Community's "constitutional charter".

Most of Petersmann's arguments have focussed on other specific rights that might be described as bolstering or amounting to an *indirect* right to trade. These are, in particular, equality rights, the right to property and the right to carry on a business. First of all, it is difficult to derive a "right to trade" from the individual rights set out in the ECHR. The right to carry on a business is not mentioned in the ECHR, but because of its existence in national law, the Court of Justice has recognised it as forming part of the general principles of EC human rights law.[78] As for the other rights, property is certainly protected under the First Protocol to the ECHR, which has been ratified by all Member States, but not in a form which supports its extension to a general "right to trade". The ECHR right does not protect the right to *acquire* possessions, and does not protect expectations.[79] Moreover, it allows for very broad exceptions, which leave great discretion to states to regulate the use and even the ownership of property. As for equality, under the ECHR system, there is no free-standing right to equality, only a derivative right connected to each of the substantive rights set out in the Convention and its Protocols pursuant to Article 14 ECHR, or (for states ratifying the Twelfth Protocol to the Convention) connected to any right guaranteed by law. This new Protocol could be considered a more promising route to guaranteeing a form of "right to trade" by connection with rights to carry on a business as guaranteed by national law. However, it has not been signed by all the Member States, and so in accordance with the *Hoechst* judgment should not be a source of inspiration for the general principles of Community law. As for the new EU Charter, it recognises "the freedom to conduct a business *in accordance with Community law and national laws and practices*"; it guarantees the right to property in wording similar to the ECHR Protocol; and the equality rights are not generalised to all situations.[80]

This leaves us with the prospect that the separate rights protected in national constitutions can constitute an indirect right to trade. The principle of equality, long accepted by the Court of Justice as a general principle of Community law and applying well beyond the scope of Article 14 ECHR or the Twelfth Protocol,[81] does not generally apply to trade with third countries, in accordance with the political discretion which the EC Treaty grants to the Community insti-

---

[77] Compare Arts. 28 and 29 (ex Arts. 30 and 34) with Art. 131 (ex Art. 110) EC.

[78] For example, see *Germany* v. *Council (supra* n. 6).

[79] For analysis, see D.J. Harris, M. O'Boyle and C. Warbrick, *The European Convention on Human Rights* (London, Butterworths, 1995), ch. 18.

[80] See respectively Arts 16, 17(1) and 20–21 (*supra* n. 67).

[81] It does not appear to be linked to other rights, although conversely the Court has not usually referred to the equality principle in all cases as a "human right". For discussion, see T. Tridimas, "The Application of the Principle of Equality to Community Measures" in S. O'Leary and A. Dashwood (eds.), *The Prinicple of Equal Treatment in EC Law* (London, Sweet and Maxwell, 1996) 214.

tutions as regards such trade.[82] While German constitutional case law has traditionally left the executive much discretion over external trade, and refused consistently (even before German membership of the Community) to give direct effect to the GATT, the "banana saga" has led to a more robust approach to the alleged vested rights of German banana importers.[83] But even the most committed critics of the EC banana legislation do not claim that this form of right to trade is a right also protected by other Member States' constitutions. As such it should not form part of the general principles of Community law, for the reasons set out in *Hoechst*.[84]

One additional source of human rights principles could be the EC Treaty itself, which of course satisfies the *Hoechst* test of receiving the imprimatur of every Member State.[85] However, as observed above, the EC Treaty does *not* guarantee a right to trade freely with third countries.

We appear to be trapped by the definition of the sources of human rights in EC law. This brings us inevitably to the second, more fundamental question: is the Court's traditional definition of those sources correct? In a detailed analysis, Besselink has argued that the "common minimum standard" approach to the role of human rights in Community law (as represented by *Hoechst*) is deficient, for a Community concept of human rights applying as the sole source of standards within the scope of Community law runs the risk that national constitutions and national obligations under human rights treaties will be infringed to the extent that Community standards are lower than such national standards.[86] Member States cannot escape their international obligations by transferring powers to an international body,[87] any more than they can escape their national constitutions by doing so. The solution is either to adopt a "universalised maximum standard" approach and protect simultaneously all national human rights obligations and the supremacy of Community law by accepting all national human rights concepts as part of the Community system of general principles, *or* to accept that "local maximum standards" apply, at the expense of the supremacy of Community law when it results in infringement of such national rules.

There is much to be said for these suggestions, but there are difficulties with both of them. The "local maximum standard" approach is vulnerable on grounds of democratic legitimacy, for it would result in all Member States

[82] See discussion by Tridimas (*ibid.*).

[83] See U. Everling, "Will Europe Slip on Bananas? The Bananas Judgment of the Corut of Justice and National Courts" (1996) 33 *CMLRev.* 401; N. Reich, "Judge-made Europe à la Carte: Some Remarks on Recent Conflicts Between European and German Constitutional Law Provoked by the Banana Litigation" (1996) 7 *EJIL* 103.

[84] *Supra* n. 72.

[85] And see now Arts. 52(2) and 53 of the EU Charter of Rights (*supra* n. 67).

[86] "Entrapped by the Maximum Standard: On Fundamental Rights, Pluralism and Subsidiarity in the European Union" (1998) 35 *CMLRev.* 629.

[87] This position is now to some extent at least confirmed by the *Matthews* v. *UK* judgment of the European Court of Human Rights (No. 24833/94, ECHR 1999–I), and see also Art. 53 of the EU Charter (*supra* n. 67).

having to accept, at least as far as Community law is concerned, other Member States' constitutional concepts and other Member States' international obligations that the newly obligated Member State deliberately refrained from enshrining as a constitutional rule or accepting as an international obligation. But it is also problematic for two further reasons, at least as applied to the present issue, because it is contradictory in two different ways.

First of all, a broad concept of the "right to trade" as effectively developed by the German courts that protects the market share of market participants would have the effect of precluding the Community not only from protectionism but also from further market *liberalisation*, whether at multilateral, bilateral or Community level. Secondly, in the particular case of bananas, the principles defended by the German courts would inevitably mean that the market shares of EC companies in *other Member States* would be dramatically reduced once the EC established a common policy. Given the massive differences in the banana regimes established in the different Member States, there was no way to create a common policy as required by the EC Treaty without reducing the market shares of market participants.

A "local maximum standards" approach would have the same effect. Here it might be argued that there is no conceptual contradiction: while a Community concept of the right to trade *à la* Kirchberg would have to protect the market shares of all Community nationals, a purely national version of that concept need only protect the market shares of its nationals. The ensuing demise of the common agricultural market in bananas would simply have to be accepted by the other Member States, leaving it to the EC institutions to choose between replacing that system with a regime that meets the standards of the German courts or re-introducing internal border controls to re-establish separate markets for external banana trade. Either way, the German courts' decision would have extra-territorial effects on the Community legal system and on other Member States, so the concept of "*local* maximum standards" is a misnomer. I leave aside here the question of the application of Besselink's principles in cases where Community law has set only minimum standards for Member States (for example, in immigration and asylum law), but most human rights disputes within the EC courts involve such matters as the common agricultural and common commercial policies which function across the Community only if uniformly applied in each Member State.

As a result, the so-called "local maximum standards" approach would suffer from similar problems of democratic legitimacy as the "universal maximum standards" approach. Even if we dismiss the Community legislative institutions as inherently undemocratic, so that one national court's *de facto* override of their measures is unobjectionable or even welcome, the "local maximum standard" effect will mean that purely national concepts of human rights protection will have a substantial effect upon other Member States' territories. Moreover, a compelled re-imposition of border checks and the partial dismantling of the common commercial policy would respectively frustrate the Single European

Act and the original EC Treaty, both of which were ratified by national parliaments of each Member State and public referenda in several.

It might be argued that the democratic legitimacy of finding a right to trade is not significant, given that an inherent purpose of any human rights guarantee is to protect certain fundamental rights against interference, to some extent, by democratic institutions. But even human rights protection in primary law usually has its origin in some form of democratic process,[88] and so the idea of a "right to trade with third countries" should need a similar imprimatur. Another means of circumventing democratic affirmation of rights is the development of *jus cogens*; but Petersmann makes no argument that the "right to trade" has become *jus cogens*.

The third aspect of this issue is a normative analysis of the prospect of a right to trade with third countries. Even if we accept that the right to trade is not found, directly or indirectly, among the rights protected by EC law at present, and that there is no case at present for overturning the method of recognising these rights in order to secure a "right to trade", that is not the end of the discussion of the issue. Any commentator is of course free to suggest that the international community, and the EU in particular, should consider recognising the protection of *new* rights. Here the key issues are the method of recognising such a right and the extent to which it applies as a free-standing rule.

First, it would be highly undesirable to accept any form of "right to trade" with third states without a proper democratic process. Traditionally, the development of international human rights law has depended upon the treaty-making process, beginning with civil society in many countries pressing for recognition of human rights principles, the negotiation of relevant treaties by states' representatives and ratification of the results (or not) by national procedures. It is hard to see why recognition of any "right to trade" should not also be subject to such a process, particularly given the numbers of protestors with grave misgivings about further world trade integration on economic, environmental and development grounds. If the advocates of recognition of a new "right to trade" cannot win the argument in the normal forums available for the development of international or national human rights law, no "right to trade" deserves to be recognised.

Even if that argument could be won, we have a second question: should a *free-standing* "right to trade" be developed? What would its relationship be with WTO rules? How should conflicts between the right to trade and other rights be reconciled? What "derogations" would be allowed, and how should they be interpreted?[89] What legal form would recognition of the right to trade take? Of

---

[88] A rather glaring example to the contrary is, of course, the pre-1993 development of the protection of human rights within the EC legal system.

[89] Since many of the "derogations" from the right to trade would exist for the purpose of protecting other human rights (including the right to development) or important economic or environmental interests, it would usually be inappropriate to interpret them narrowly, in the way that one would normally interpret derogations from human rights.

course, in theory it would be possible to find answers to such questions; but is there a purpose in seeking those answers given that we have an existing trading agreement with nearly universal membership?

The way forward to any international recognition of a "right to trade" is to place it firmly in the framework of the World Trade Organisation, on condition that the grave concerns about the legitimacy of that organisation and the issues of derogations and relationship with other rights can be fully addressed. But if the WTO agreements contained an enforceable "right to trade" independent of their specific provisions, the result would be a substantial transfer of power to an international "judiciary", with considerable legal uncertainty and even further doubts about the legitimacy of the Dispute Settlement Body's decisions. It would be preferable rather to recognise "the right to trade" freely as a non-justiciable principle underlying the framework of the WTO decisions, with due recognition to the "derogations" from that right set out in the WTO agreements and parallel consideration of the development of an international right for individuals to *move* freely.

CONCLUSION

The Court's previous legal rationales for lack of direct effect of the GATT were deeply unconvincing, and became more so over time. Much of its revised argument for lack of direct effect of the WTO is equally unconvincing. But its core argument that the Community should be awarded some political discretion as long as many of its largest trading partners fail to provide for direct effect is persuasive. Such political discretion could be trumped by a constitutional "right to trade", but this would preclude democratic determination of the appropriateness of such a right, for the recognition of a "right to trade" is not supported by precedents in most national or international human rights law. Nor, at least where the Community has exclusive competence, is a rethink of the application of human rights rules justified, for the result would be contradictory and raise serious problems of democratic legitimacy by any standard of assessment. In short, if the Court of Justice were at present to recognise a fundamental right to trade with third countries, it would not be "taking rights seriously". Rather it would be "making rights up".

6

Collision, Co-existence or Co-operation? Prospects for the Relationship between WTO Law and European Union Law

ARMIN VON BOGDANDY and TILMAN MAKATSCH

INTRODUCTION

THE EUROPEAN UNION—usually using the EC's legal personality[1]—maintains a number of treaties which allow its partners' products preferential access to the European single market. There is significant tension between these treaties and their implementing regimes, on the one hand, and fundamental WTO obligations on the other, since equal treatment in international trade is the fundamental principle of WTO law. This tension between specific trade agreements which promote deeper economic integration and global trade law has been hotly debated for years, and especially so with respect to European integration and European foreign trade policy.[2] On the one hand, the WTO is weakened when a large portion of world trade is conducted under special preferential rules. On the other hand, regional economic co-operation areas[3] and specific treaties allow for a greater liberalisation due to the smaller number of

---

[1] For the theoretical background to this terminology see A. von Bogdandy, "The Legal Case for Unity" (1999) 36 *CMLRev.* 887 at 905–907, in more detail see *ibid.*, "Organizational Proliferation and Centralization under the Treaty on European Union" in N.M. Blokker and H.G. Schermers (eds.), *Proliferation of International Organizations* (The Hague, Kluwer Law, 2001), 177.

[2] T. Askey, C.A.P. Braga, H.A. Brigera Naón, A. Porges and C. Roh, "Regional Trade Organisations: Strengthening or Weakening Global Trade?" (1994) *ASIL Proceedings* 309; K.W. Dam, "Regional Economic Arrangements and the Gatt: The Legacy of a Misconception" (1963) 30 *University of Chicago Law Review* 615; M. Hart, "The WTO and the Political Economy of Globalization" (1997) 5 *Journal of World Trade* 75; M. Hilf and E.-U. Petersmann (eds.), *GATT und die Europäische Gemeinschaft* (Baden-Baden, Nomos Verlagsgesellschaft, 1986); F. Jaeger, *GATT, EWG und EFTA* (Bern, Stämpfli, 1970); T. Mulat, "Multilateralism and Africa's Regional Economic Communities" (1998) 4 *Journal of World Trade* 115; T. Oppermann, "Die Europäische Gemeinschaft und Union in der Welthandelsorganisation (WTO)" (1995) *RIW* 919; H. Steinberger, *GATT und regionale Wirtschaftszusammenschlüsse* (Cologne, Heymanns, 1963).

[3] The term "regional economic co-operation area" refers to a broad spectrum of arrangements, from highly integrated customs unions (e.g., the EU) to free trade areas (e.g., NAFTA, EFTA).

members. Furthermore, they permit a harmonization of legal orders and are able to take specific circumstances into account.[4] Moreover, regional economic co-operation areas often make it possible for their members to pursue political goals of a non-economic nature, for example, environmental protection, human rights, democratisation and development.[5]

In this briefly described area of tension, WTO law and the law of the European Union must find solutions which make regional integration and specific bilateral trade relations possible, while yet at the same time protecting against unwelcome international effects (market protection, diversion of trade or trade conflicts). This contribution will critically analyse how the relevant judicial or quasi-judicial bodies (the WTO panels, the WTO Appellate Body and the ECJ) are developing their case law in this complex field. The guiding thesis is that the WTO bodies aim at a critically dense form of juridification (*Verrechtlichung*) to which the ECJ responds through a strategy which is generally convincing except in one point, and which lacks, moreover, a solid dogmatic basis. Trouble ahead.

TIGHTENING THE ROPE: REGIONAL INTEGRATION AS AN EXCECPTION TO THE GATT

The most important provisions of WTO law with respect to regional integration are contained in Article XXIV of GATT 1994 (hereafter "GATT"), Article V and Article V*bis* of GATS, as well as in the Understanding on Article XXIV GATT 1994. Under specific circumstances they allow for exceptions to the fundamental principle of equal treatment. The WTO's Dispute Settlement Organs have recently added greatly to our understanding of Article XXIV GATT. However, two preliminary issues must first be addressed: the justiciability of exceptions to substantive obligations under WTO law, and the related question of burden of proof.

On the Justiciability of Exceptions and the Provision of Sufficient Evidence

The Treaty Provisions and Dispute Settlement Procedures

According to the conventional viewpoint, the legal quality of WTO law is dependent upon the extent to which resort to claiming an exception, which would otherwise constitute a breach of WTO duties, is subject to legal review.[6]

---

[4] J.H. Jackson, "Foreword, Perspectives on Regionalism in Trade Relations" (1996) 27 *Law & Policy in International Business* 873 at 874.

[5] P. Hilpold, *Die EU im GATT/WTO-System* (Frankfurt am Main, Lang, 1999) 25.

[6] Most important are Cases 21–24/72, *International Fruit Company NV v. Produktschap voor groenten en fruit* [1972] ECR 1219, para. 21 *et seq.*; Case C–280/93 *Germany v. Council* [1994] ECR I–4973, para. 103 *et seq.*

This question has been clarified by *India—Quantitative Restrictions on Imports of Agricultural, Textile and Industrial Products*.[7] India had introduced quantitative restrictions on agricultural, textile and industrial products with the defence that they were justified by the balance-of-payments provisions in Article XVIII:B GATT. India's proposal to phase out these restrictions after seven years appeared to some WTO Members, above all the USA, to be unsatisfactory. After fruitless consultations, a panel was established to determine whether India's balance of payments restrictions were consistent with its obligations arising out of Article XI and Article XVIII:B GATT, Article 4(2) of the Agreement on Agriculture and Article 3 of the Agreement on Import Licensing Procedures.

Pursuant to Article XII and XVIII:B GATT, as well as the Balance of Payments Understanding, a WTO member which is a developing country may impose import restrictions owing to balance-of-payments difficulties.[8] However, such restrictions must, according to Article XVIII:9 GATT, be necessary to prevent the threat of a serious decline of monetary reserves or to increase inadequate monetary reserves. The qualifications contained in Article XVIII:9 as well as in paragraphs 10 to 12, are therefore limits to the extent to which an exception may be used: they are limits on exceptions. Article XVIII:B GATT provides for a special procedure for the introduction of such restrictive measures, in which the General Council, the Committee on Balance-of-Payments Restrictions (BOP Committee) and the IMF (Article XV:2 GATT) participate. In these proceedings the nature of the balance-of-payments difficulties, possible alternative measures and the effect of the proposed restrictions on the other Members are to be examined.[9] This case is of general significance since similar procedures are foreseen for a number of other exceptions, for example, Article XXIV:7 GATT.

The Scope of Legal Review

In its report, the Panel found that the contested measures taken by India were inconsistent with Articles XI and XVIII:11 GATT and were not justified by Article XVIII:B GATT. The India appeal is remarkable for its reasoning concerning the question of justiciability. India argued that the Panel lacked the competence to review India's justification of its balance-of-payments restrictions under Article XVIII:B GATT. According to Article XIII:12 GATT and the BOP Understanding, the General Council and the BOP Committee have, as political organs, exclusive jurisdiction over such matters. There is, India's argument continues, a fundamental principle of institutional balance which requires that the

[7] Panel Report WT/DS90/R dated 23 August 1999 and Appellate Body Report WT/DS90/AB/R dated 22 September 1999; on the internet at www.wto.org/wto/dispute/dispute.htm.

[8] In detail see M. Trebilcock and R. Howse, *The Regulation of International Trade* (2nd edn., London and New York, Routledge, 1999), 101 *et seq.*

[9] Art. XVIII(12)(a) GATT.

Panel exercise its powers with due regard to the powers of other WTO organs when assessing and determining its own competence. This principle is only then respected if assessment of the justification of balance-of-payments restrictions is attributed exclusively to the General Council and the BOP Committee as political bodies.

According to the Report of the Appellate Body, the scope of the legal review is to be determined in the light of Article XXIII GATT, which is concretised in the Understanding on Rules and Procedures Governing the Settlement of Disputes (DSU), and footnote 2 of the BOP Understanding. This provision, together with the review mandate (Article 7 DSU), describes the scope of judicial review competence. According to sentence 1 of Article I:1 DSU, its rules and procedures are applicable to all disputes brought pursuant to the consultations and dispute settlement provisions of the agreements listed in Appendix 1. In Appendix 1 the Multilateral Agreements on Trade in Goods is listed, to which GATT also belongs. As neither special nor additional dispute settlement rules or procedures are applicable (cf. Sentence 1 of Article I:2 DSU), the DSU is fully applicable to disputes arising out of Article XIII:B GATT.[10]

According to the Appellate Body, the scope of application of Article I DSU is not limited by a principle of institutional balance as India had argued. Such a principle is not to be found either in the general principles of international law or in WTO law. Thus, the WTO dispute settlement bodies are not forbidden from reviewing the justification of balance-of-payments restrictions according to Article XVIII:B GATT for reasons of institutional balance.[11] On the contrary: if the Panel were to refrain from reviewing the justification of the balance-of-payments restrictions, the procedural and substantive rights of the Members would, under Articles XXIII and XVIII:11 GATT, be significantly diminished. The Appellate Body also sees no conflict between the Panel's competence and the powers of the General Council and BOP Committee.[12] It justifies this by reference to the different functions of the Committee and the Council as political organs on the one hand and the dispute settlement organs on the other.[13] The WTO members have a choice of whether they utilise the procedures under Article XVIII:12 GATT to have the justification for balance-of-payments restrictions reviewed, or whether they have recourse to the procedures established by Article XXIII GATT. Exercising the latter option does not prejudice the competence of either the BOP Committee or the General Council to consider the same matter in accordance with Article XVIII:12 GATT.[14]

The Appellate Body left undecided which decision takes precedence in the case of a conflict: the political or the legal settlement. It is, however, certain, that a political dispute settlement does not prejudice a legal review of the same

---

[10] Appellate Body Report (*supra* n. 7) paras. 4.6 and 4.7.
[11] *Ibid.*, para. 4.26.
[12] *Ibid.*, para. 4.24.
[13] *Ibid.*, para. 4.25.
[14] *Ibid.*, para. 4.18.

matter, which indicates that the latter takes precedence. Political settlements, so the Appellate Body implies, do not provide sufficient protection for Members. In particular, disputes involving controversial political subjects, such as national development programmes, can be translated into legal terms in dispute settlement proceedings and, with the aid of, for example, the IMF, handled on an "expertocratic" basis. This strengthens the principle contained in Article 3:2 DSU, according to which the dispute settlement system is a central element for the provision of security and predictability in the multilateral trade system.

Equally important is the finding of the Appellate Body concerning India's argument that the Panel's decision required India to use certain macro-economic instruments to meet its balance-of-payments difficulties, and thus required it to change its development programme, this being inconsistent with WTO law. This implicitly raises the critical question whether the scope of judicial review must be limited if important national policies are at stake. The IMF, in response to questions put to it by the Panel, was of the opinion that quantitative restrictions were not necessary for improving India's balance-of-payments situation. India's situation could be improved by macro-economic policy instruments alone. The Panel accordingly found that the continuation of quantitative restrictions was inconsistent with WTO law. The Appellate Body agreed.[15] Thus, when reviewing the necessity (or proportionality) of such restrictions, macro-economic instruments must, as a general rule, also be taken into account as possible alternatives. The scope of judicial review is thereby significantly increased in dispute settlement proceedings.

Creating a Prima Facie Case and the Burden of Proof

Of even greater importance are the statements concerning the provision of sufficient evidence and burden of proof.[16] India had understood that the burden of proof had been placed upon it, which, in view of Article XVIII:11 GATT, is a legal error. The Appellate Body emphasised, by way of introduction, the general principle that "the burden of proof rests upon the party, whether complaining or defending, who asserts the affirmative of a particular claim or defense".[17] Thus, it was the USA which, as complainant, was originally obliged to provide sufficient evidence that India's policies were inconsistent with those conditions of Article XVIII:1 GATT which limit the admissibility of trade restriction measures.[18] If, however, the complainant succeeds in establishing a *prima facie* case the burden of proof passes to the respondent. Concretely, the developing country must prove that the removal of contested instruments would be inconsistent

---

[15] *Ibid.*, para. 6.10.
[16] The Appellate Body does not clearly distinguish between burden of proof and providing sufficient evidence, cf. *ibid.*, para. 7.7.
[17] *Ibid.*, para. 7.5.
[18] *Ibid.*, para. 7.8.

with Article XVIII:11 GATT, i.e., that removal would require it to change its development policy.[19]

In its appeal, India argued that the Panel committed a legal error by not analysing whether the USA had brought sufficient evidence to create a *prima facie* case prior to considering the IMF's response, and prior to shifting the burden of proof to India. Furthermore, the USA was, according to India, unable to adduce sufficient evidence that India's balance-of-payment restrictions were not justified under the Ad Note to Article XVIII:11 GATT. The Appellate Body conceded that the Panel had not expressly established whether the USA had brought forward sufficient evidence to create a *prima facie* case prior to considering the IMF's and India's responses. This procedure is, however, not objectionable, according to the Appellate Body. The Appellate Body thereby modified its previous statements, whereby the complaining party must provide evidence sufficient to create a *prima facie* case *before* the burden of proof shifts to the respondent.[20] According to the opinion of the Appellate Body, the Panel was justified in considering the answers of the IMF to its questions prior to the determination of whether the complainant had established a *prima facie* case. Moreover, India's responses to the USA's arguments could be considered in deciding whether a *prima facie* case had been made.[21]

The understanding of the law reached by the Appellate Body deserves further enquiry. The Panel had not expressly found that the complainant had provided sufficient evidence for a *prima facie* case. India, on the other hand, was required to demonstrate that the removal of the quantitative restrictions would have required it to change its development programme. India was thus placed in a disadvantageous position. If the Panel considers the responses of the respondent and other experts in its analysis of whether a *prima facie* case has been established, the risk arises that vague allegations may be brought for investigatory purposes. The question of the burden of proof—an extremely important question which had heretofore been settled—is thus potentially destabilised by this decision.

The Scope of Article XXIV GATT

The Treaty's Provisions and the Dispute Settlement Procedures

The decisions relating to Article XXIV GATT must be evaluated against the background developed above, concerning the broad justiciability of exceptions. Article XXIV GATT provides justification for inconsistencies with the primary GATT obligations caused by the creation of a customs union or a free trade

---

[19] Appellate Body Report (*supra* n. 7) para. 7.6.
[20] See the Appellate Body in *EC Measures Concerning Meat and Meat Products (Hormones)*, WT/DS48/AB/R dated 13 Febuary 1998 para. 109.
[21] Appellate Body Report (*supra* n. 7) paras. 7. 12 *et seq*.

area. The core idea behind Article XXIV GATT is that the trade-creating effects of a regional economic co-operation organisation must be greater than its trade diverting effects.[22] Article XXIV GATT thus allows the formation of such organisations, but requires an extensive opening of the internal markets between the participants in the regional agreement and disallows the creation of new trade barriers vis-à-vis other WTO members. The aim of these requirements is to ensure that such agreements promote a positive trading environment, and an expansion of world trade.

Although the basic logic is clear, the interpretation of Article XXIV GATT gives rise to a number of difficult questions. Until recently, the WTO or GATT legal bodies had not offered a *legal* opinion on the compatibility of the E(E)C, or the EC's association policies, with Article XXIV GATT.[23] Instead, GATT members had sought to find pragmatic solutions to disputes arising out of customs unions and free trade areas through political processes. Article XXIV GATT was analysed for the first time by the WTO dispute settlement organs in the *Turkey—Restrictions on Imports of Textiles and Clothing Products*.[24] The decision will have far-reaching implications for the EU's eastward expansion as well as for its entire network of Association Agreements which the EU has wrapped around the single market and intends to expand to the ACP States and the Mediterranean area.

In 1961 the EEC and Turkey concluded an Association Agreement to create a customs union.[25] On 6 March 1995 the EC–Turkey Association Council adopted Decision 1/95, which regulates the implementation of the final phase of the customs union between Turkey and the EC. Article 12(2) of this Decision states that Turkey, as from the entry into force of the Decision and in conformity with Article XXIV GATT, will apply substantially the same commercial policy in the textile sector as does the EC.[26] To implement this Decision, on 1 January 1996 Turkey introduced various quantitative restrictions on textile and clothing products imports from India.[27]

The WTO Panel, established at India's request, found in its Report that the quantitative restrictions introduced by Turkey were inconsistent with the provisions of Articles XI and XIII GATT as well as with Article 2(4) of the Agreement on Textiles and Clothing (ATC).[28] Turkey did not question this

---

[22] Jackson (*supra* n. 2) 875.

[23] An overview of the GATT practice can be found in *Analytical Index, Guide to GATT Law and Practice* (Geneva: GATT Secretariat, 1994) 735 *et seq.*, 790 *et seq.* A brief description in Panel Report, *EEC—Member States' Import Regimes for Bananas*, DS32/R of 3 June 1993 para. 358 (non-binding).

[24] Panel Report WT/DS34/R of 31 May 1999 and Appellate Report WT/DS34/AB/R of 22 October 1999; for the agreement see C. Hartler and S. Laird, "The EU Model and Turkey. A case for Thanksgiving?" (1999) 3 *Journal of World Trade* 147; Jaeger (*supra* n. 2) 322 *et seq.*

[25] Signed on 9 July 1961 [1964] OJ L217 3687.

[26] Art. 12(2) of Decision 1/95 [1996] OJ L35 1.

[27] For further detail see Panel Report (*supra* n. 24), paras. 2.2–2.46 and 4.1–4.3.

[28] *Ibid.*, para. 9.86.

finding on appeal. The central question was whether Article XXIV GATT could justify the restrictions at issue.

WTO Jurisdiction over Regional Integration?

Both the Panel and the Appellate Body discuss the fundamental question whether a regional economic association as such can be adjudicated in a dispute settlement proceeding only *in passim*. The Panel's statements are ambivalent and leave the question open.[29] The Appellate Body is, however, clear: recalling its jurisdiction as developed in *India—Quantitative Restrictions on Imports of Agricultural, Textile and Industrial Products*, it indicates that, in the future, it will—if required—assess the overall compatibility of regional associations with WTO law.[30]

It is doubtful whether the overall compatibility of regional associations with WTO law is an appropriate object of decision for the dispute settlement organs. When the vital interests of an entire region are predicated on the formation or development of a regional association, a satisfactory conciliation of interests can be difficult to achieve by means of a dispute settlement which usually has a winner and a loser. If such a fundamental undertaking as a regional association were to be found inconsistent with WTO law and therefore forbidden according to international law, the consensual basis for participating in dispute settlement proceedings and even the WTO system as a whole could be eroded. Such critical issues should be assigned to the appropriate political body or bodies, for example, to the Committee on Regional Trade Agreements. The political process offers the attractive solution of agreeing to disagree.[31] Such a result will better achieve the overall goals of the WTO.

It is therefore recommended that the WTO Members refer only implementing decisions to the dispute settlement bodies for ruling, as India did in the case at hand. As the dispute settlement organs are strictly bound by Article 7:1 DSU to the referral, this recommendation offers a solution. Whether the dispute settlement organs are capable of developing their own internal mechanisms against more far-reaching findings is, in view of *India—Quantitative Restrictions*, questionable.

Article XXIV GATT as an Exception

The Panel Report builds on the understanding that the creation of a customs union authorises the violation of primary GATT rules only within strict limits. According to this view, Article XXIV GATT does not authorise, in particular, the introduction of the disputed quantitative restrictions.[32] The Panel inter-

---

[29] For further detail see Panel Report (*supra* n. 24) para. 9.153.
[30] Appellate Body Report (*supra* n. 24) para. 60.
[31] This has been the result in numerous cases, cf. the evidence in n. 24.
[32] Panel Report (*supra* n. 24) paras. 9.109 ff., especially paras. 9.134, 9.154 and 9.188 *et seq.*

preted Article XXIV:5(a) and 8(a) according to semantic, systematic and teleo-logic analyses. It found in this analysis, which is well worth reading, that Article XXIV GATT only provides customs unions with a basis for measures otherwise incompatible with the Most Favoured Nation (MFN) principle in Part I of GATT. The background to this interpretation is the fact that the Panel under-stands regional economic associations to be closely bound up with the WTO system.[33] With the closely circumscribed exception regarding the MFN princi-ple, WTO obligations always take precedence over interests in creating and deepening regional economic integration.

The Appellate Report differs in two respects from that of the Panel: (1). it expands the applicability of grounds for justification and (2) it tightens, how-ever, the requirements which an association must meet in order to qualify as a customs union. To put it differently, it loosens one rope, but tightens the other.

The Appellate Body expands the applicability of Article XXIV GATT beyond Part I of GATT. Its argument rests on the "chapeau" of Article XXIV:5 GATT, which, according to the Appellate Body, the Panel had failed to take adequate account of in its legal reasoning. The Appellate Body found that the "chapeau" of Article XXIV:5 GATT leads to the conclusion that Article XXIV GATT may be invoked as a defence, the scope of which goes beyond Part I of GATT.[34] However, it also states—in an ambivalent way—that this does not necessarily apply to measures which are incompatible with Articles XI and XIII GATT.[35]

The Concept and Admissibility of a Customs Union

The Appellate Body applies stricter criteria for meeting the definition of a com-mon external trade regime in the sense of Article XXIV GATT. Article XXIV:8 GATT establishes the standards for the internal and external trade regimes which must be met to satisfy the definition of a customs union. To qualify as a customs union, Article XXIV:8(a)(i) requires that duties and other restrictive regulations of commerce be eliminated with respect to "substantially all the trade" as between the constituent members. The Appellate Body states that the key term "substantially" is not identical to "all the trade", yet more than merely "some of the trade".[36] The members of the customs union may retain certain restrictive regulations of commerce in their internal trading provided that these are permitted under Articles XI–XV GATT and Article XX GATT, which thus allows for a certain flexibility in the liberalisation of internal trade.[37] This leaves open the problematic question whether agricultural products can also be excluded, a situation which likely to arise frequently.

[33] In detail see Panel Report (*supra* n. 24) paras. 9.157 *et seq.*
[34] Appellate Body Report (*supra* n. 24) para.45.
[35] *Ibid.*, para. 65.
[36] *Ibid.*, para. 48.
[37] *Ibid.*, para. 48.

With respect to external commerce, according to Article XXIV:8(a)(ii) GATT, in order to qualify as a customs union the constituents must apply "substantially the same duties and other regulations of commerce" with third countries. The term "substantially" contains a quantitative and a qualitative aspect.[38] It requires that common external trade regimes practised by the members be substantially the same. According to the Appellate Body, it does not, however, require that the members always apply the *same* duties and other regulations. There is, according to the Appellate Body, a certain flexibility in the creation of a common commercial policy. However, the Appellate Body leaves less room for play than the Panel. The latter required only "comparable trade having similar effects".[39] The Appellate Body, in contrast, states: "it must not be forgotten that the word 'substantially' qualifies the words 'the same'. Therefore, in our view, something closely approximating 'sameness' is required".[40] This requires a higher degree of sameness in external commercial policy. The Appellate Body was no more specific than this.

According to Article XXIV:5(a) GATT a further criterion is an economic test.[41] The application of duties and other regulations of commerce attendant upon the creation of a customs union should not, overall, be more restrictive with respect to trade with non-member countries than prior to the creation of the union. With regard to duties, paragraph 2 of the *Understanding on Article XXIV GATT* states that the general incidence of the duties applied before and after the creation of the customs union shall be evaluated according to an "overall assessment of weighted average tariffs and of customs duties collected". The assessment is based on trade-weighted averages for a representative period of time, provided by the customs union, calculated from individual tariff lines in value and quantity and broken down by the WTO country of origin.[42]

Prevention of the Formation of the Customs Union as a Defence

The Party which invokes Article XXIV GATT as a defence must demonstrate that the formation of the customs union would be prevented if the introduction of the contested measures were disallowed.[43] Turkey was of the opinion that, had it not introduced the quantitative restrictions against India, the EU would have excluded these products from the EU–Turkey customs union in order to prevent trade diversion.[44] According to Turkey's own calculations, these products account for 40 per cent of its exports to the EU. Turkey expressed its doubts that it could meet the requirements of Article XXIV:8(a)(i) GATT were it not

[38] Panel Report (*supra* n. 24) para. 9.148, Appellate Body Report (*supra* n. 24) para. 49.
[39] Panel Report (*supra* n. 24) para. 9.151.
[40] Appellate Body Report (*supra* n. 24) para. 50.
[41] Panel Report (*supra* n. 24) para. 9.120; Appellate Body Report (*supra* n. 24) para. 55.
[42] No. 2 Sentence 2 of the Agreement on the Interpretation of Article XXIV GATT (Geneva: GATT Secretariat, 1994).
[43] Appellate Body Report (*supra* n. 24) para. 58.
[44] *Ibid.*, para. 61.

allowed to introduce quantitative restrictions on textiles and clothing from India. Turkey would thus be prevented from creating a customs union with the EU. This is, according to Turkey, in conflict with Article XXIV:5 GATT, which states, Turkey argued, that GATT rules may not impede the formation of a customs union.

The Panel addresses this defence in a rather general manner. It observes that there are other methods open to Turkey which would have satisfied the EU's requirement of preventing a diversion of trade in Indian textiles via Turkey.[45] In other words: the specific shape of a customs union, namely its specific policies, regulations and measures applied both with respect to internal and external trade, must be evaluated in light of fundamental WTO duties. The implicit effect of this doctrine is that a complete customs union is, in the end, only realisable if it realises the WTO ideal with respect to external commerce, namely, the transformation of all barriers to trade into duties.

The Appellate Body is also of the opinion that the elimination of quantitative restrictions does not prevent the formation of a customs union between Turkey and the EU. It refers to Article XXIV:8(a)(i) GATT which allows the members of a customs union a certain flexibility in the formation of internal trade policy, and requires that an alternative measure which is less disadvantageous to trade with third countries than quantitative restrictions be chosen.[46] Turkey could have adopted a certificate of origin system which would have allowed the EU to distinguish between those textile and clothing articles originating in Turkey— and which therefore would have enjoyed free access to the EU upon completion of the final phase of the customs union—and those textiles which originated in third countries, such as India. Turkey was thus unable to demonstrate that the customs union with the EU would be prevented if the quantitative restrictions were to be declared to be inconsistent with GATT obligations.[47] However, the Appellate Body did not assess whether such measures would conform with the requirement of Article XXIV:8(a)(ii) GATT. In any case, there remains only a small "corridor" within which measures can be adopted in order to form a customs union, in a manner which is in keeping with Article XXIV GATT.

Concluding Assessment

By way of concluding assessment, it may be remarked that there are significant differences between the Panel and the Appellate Body. In the Panel's eyes, a regional economic association must conform to a very large extent with the WTO objectives. Exceptions are admissible only with respect to the MFN principle. Article XXIV GATT cannot justify inconsistencies with other WTO obligations. Thus, there is a clear hierarchy of trading systems. The multilateral WTO system enjoys primacy over regional economic systems. One could even

[45] Panel Report (*supra* n. 24) para. 9.150.
[46] Appellate Body Report (*supra* n. 24) para. 62.
[47] *Ibid.*, para. 63.

understand the Panel in a way in that it conceives a regional association as some kind of a sub-regime to the WTO. Article XXIV GATT serves only as a criterion for closer examination of the compatibility of a regional economic association with the primary GATT obligations. At the same time it is, according to the Panel report, quite easy to qualify as a customs union. The underlying logic could be that the Panel wants to facilitate WTO members in forming regional associations (as sub-systems of the WTO) which serve to further the aim of transforming all trade restrictions into tariffs.

The decision of the Appellate Body also aims at furthering the objectives of the WTO, however in a different and probably more pragmatic way. In one crucial respect it is more open. The formation of customs unions and free trade areas may serve as a basis for justifying inconsistencies with primary WTO obligations. Members may invoke Article XXIV GATT as a defence not only for violations of Part I GATT (the MFN principle) but also for other GATT norms.[48] Article XXIV GATT is thereby a general exception.[49] There is less of a categorical insistence upon the primacy of multilateral primary duties, and also less insistence as regards the primacy of the WTO system. The Appellate Body recognised that regional economic co-operation associations with preferential regulations can create positive effects for world trade in general. A regional integration association will be evaluated principally on the basis of whether it contributes positively to the highest WTO objectives (a raising of the standard of living, and an increase in the volume of world commerce), and only secondarily according to whether or not it gives rise to new preferential treatment and is therefore discriminatory. The Appellate Body has thus developed an interpretation of Article XXIV GATT which lessens the tension between regionalism and universalism. At the same time, it rendered stricter the requirements which an association must meet in order to rely upon the justification provided by Article XXIV GATT. One can understand this as an attempt to push a regional association further down the path of integration, as the Panel did. Summing up, it loosens one rope, but tightens the other on the basis of a more pragmatic view of how to increase international trade. What effect these reports may have on future EU practice and policies is difficult to assess, not least because the Appellate Body leaves crucial issues deliberately vague, thereby creating a critical burden on any further negotiations on regional integration. The European Union must, nevertheless, orient its external trade regime accordingly, as the WTO Dispute Settlement organs will evaluate the formation and practice of customs unions or free trade areas by means of the criteria discussed above. In one respect, however, the European Union can see confirmed its basic position that there is no fundamental or unqualified primacy of the WTO mul-

---

[48] As Jackson previously argued: see J.H. Jackson, *World Trade and the Law of GATT* (Indianapolis,Ind., Bobbs-Merrill, 1969) 576.

[49] In more detail see A. von Bogdandy, "Eine Ordnung für das GATT" (1991) *RIW* 55 at 59. This construction follows the general principles of international responsibility: International Law Commission, "Draft Articles on State Responsibility" (1998) 37 ILM 440 *et seq.*

tilateral trade system over more developed regional economic co-operation areas.[50]

THE ECJ'S STRATEGY OF AVOIDING CONFLICT

The Problem of Direct Applicability

The decisions discussed above, like so many other decisions of the WTO Dispute Settlement Body, add further momentum to the process of bringing world trade under legal control, thereby restricting the legal room for manoeuvre in the formation and practice of external trade policies. The probability of collisions between the external trade regime of a WTO member and WTO law is proportionally increased. This gives rise to the question of how to cope with possible collisions.

In the 1960s, when the EEC has faced with the analogous problem of how to cope with collisions between the EEC Treaty and national laws, in two revolutionary decisions, the ECJ developed the concepts of the direct applicability and supremacy of Community law.[51] Thus far the WTO dispute settlement bodies have not developed similar legal institutions for WTO law; probably Article 3(2) DSU even excludes such a development. The legal orders of the WTO members could, however, do this themselves. The question whether WTO law should enjoy direct applicability within the legal order of the European Union is the subject of significant controversy.[52] The ECJ had rejected the direct applicability of the GATT 1947.[53] In view of the wholesale transformation of GATT 1947 into the WTO and particularly the far more highly developed system of dispute settlement, direct applicability of WTO law could have been reached on the basis of the ECJ's former arguments.[54]

---

[50] The Union did not participate in the case, but rather responded to some questions pursuant to Art. 13 DSU; Panel Report (*supra* n. 24), para. 4.2; there is no duty to participate: *ibid.*, para. 9.5.

[51] Case 26/62, *Van Gend & Loos* [1963] ECR 1; Case 6/64, *Flaminio Costa* v. *ENEL* [1964] ECR 1251.

[52] For this discussion see G.M. Berrisch and H.-G. Kamann, "WTO-Recht im Gemeinschaftsrecht—(k)eine Kehrtwende des EuGH" (2000) *EWS* 89 *et seq.*; T. Cottier, "Dispute Settlement in the World Trade Organisation: Characteristics and Structural Implications for the European Union" (1998) 35 *CMLRev.* 325; P. Eeckhout, "The Domestic Legal Status of the WTO Agreement: Interconnecting Legal Systems" (1997) 34 *CMLRev.* 11; W. Meng, "Gedanken zur Frage unmittelbarer Anwendung von WTO-Recht in der EG" in U. Beyerlin *et al.* (eds.), *Recht zwischen Umbruch und Bewahrung, Festschrift für Bernhardt* (Berlin, Springer, 1995); J. Sack, "Von der Geschlossenheit und den Spannungsfeldern in einer Weltordnung des Rechts" (1997) *EuZW* 650.

[53] Case 21–24/72, *International Fruit Company NV* v. *Produktshap voor groenten en fruit* [1972] ECR 1219, para. 21 *et seq*; Case C–280/93, *Germany* v. *Council* [1994] ECR I–4973, para. 103 *et seq.*

[55] In detail see Advocate General Saggio's Opinion of 25 February 1999 in Case C–149/96, *Portugal* v. *Council*, paras. 14 *et seq.*, 24.

Perhaps it was precisely for this reason that the Council sought to decide this matter negatively. Pursuant to the last recital of Council Decision 94/800, neither the Agreement for the Establishment of the WTO nor its Annexes are of such a nature to be directly applied by the European Courts or the courts of the Member States.[55] Yet this by no means settled the legal argument.[56] So all depends on the ECJ. Only a few points of the ECJ's strategy of avoiding collision have been clearly developed; important elements are only vaguely presented. A tendency has, however, emerged from the *Fediol* and *Commission v. Germany, Nakajima* and recently in *Portugal* v. *Council* decisions.[57] In so far as WTO law conflicts with the law of an EU *Member State*, the ECJ attempts to resolve the conflict pursuant to WTO law and applies WTO law against the Member State; this entails some form of direct application. In so doing it avoids liability on the part of the Union under international law (possibly under the legal personality of the EC), since the Union is generally responsible also for ensuring respect for WTO law by Member State institutions.[58]

As regards the solution of conflicts between WTO law and measures adopted by the EU organs, by contrast, the ECJ will leave resolution to the WTO dispute settlement process or to the political process, unless the EU organs decide in a specific case to concede greater relevance to WTO law in the EU legal order. The following considerations demonstrate that this strategy is tenable, with one exception: if a Member State institutes legal proceedings pursuant to Article 230(2) (ex Article 173(2)) EC it would be far more convincing if an EU act were to be assessed according to WTO law.

Conflict Avoidance through Inapplicability of WTO Law

The core of the controversy was always centred on how the ECJ can control the *Union's* organs on the basis of WTO law. Going against the Opinion of Advocate General Saggio, the ECJ decided in its leading case of 23 November 1999, *Portugal* v. *Council*, that it will not oversee decisions of the EU institutions on the basis of WTO law. The central statement in paragraph 47, with which the ECJ obviously intends to settle the matter for future disputes, reads:

It follows from all those considerations that, having regard to their nature and structure, the WTO agreements are not in principle among the rules in the light of

---

[55] Council Decision 94/800/EC, [1994] OJ L336/1.

[56] Cf. the "de-bunking" by Advocate General Tesauro [1996] ECR I–3989, paras. 23 *et seq.*, *Hermès*; Advocate General Saggio, Opinion of 25 February 1999 in C–149/96, *Portugal* v. *Council*, paras. 19 *et seq.*

[57] Respectively, Cases 70/87, 69/89, 61/94 and 53/96, [1989] ECR 1781; [1991] ECR I–2069; [1996] ECR I–3989; [1998] ECR I–3603; the Judgment of 23 November 1999 in Case C–149/96, *Portugal* v. *Council* is not yet reported.

[58] Panel, 5 Febuary 1998, *USA* v. *EC, UK and Ireland, Customs Classification of Certain Computer Equipment*, paras. 8.15 *et seq.*

which the Court is to review the legality of measures adopted by the Community institutions.

The ECJ thereby continues its case law developed with respect to the GATT 1947, while putting its conclusion on a different basis.

One reason given by the ECJ for disallowing WTO law as a ground for legal complaint is that the direct applicability of WTO law would, should the Union lose in a WTO dispute settlement, render it impossible for the Union to make use of the room for manoeuvre provided by Article 22(1) DSU.[59] More important—and more convincing—is the reference to the lack of reciprocity, if one were to assume the applicability of the WTO law. The most important trading partners have disallowed direct applicability.[60] The WTO has no power to change US law. In the event of a conflict between US law and any of the Uruguay Round agreements, section 102(a) of the implementing Bill makes it clear that US law will take precedence: no provision of any of the Uruguay Round agreements, nor the application of any such provision to any person or circumstances, that is inconsistent with any law of the United States shall have effect. Moreover, as explained in greater detail in this Statement in connection with the Dispute Settlement Understanding, WTO dispute settlement panels will not have any power to change US law or to order such a change. Only Congress and the administration can decide whether to implement a WTO panel report and, if so, how to implement it.[61]

The European Court's solution is not persuasive (nor that of the American government) if one sees as inherent in WTO obligations subjective rights of the market citizen.[62] That WTO law enjoys this attribute is, however, by no means expressly stated, but rather must be discovered by the usual methods of interpretation. The ordinary meaning, system and State practice, denying direct applicability, speak against the law of the WTO being invested with this quality. A further element must be added to this: were the direct applicability of WTO law to be affirmed, the Union would be more strictly bound than most of the other WTO members. According to majority opinion, Article 300(7) EC (previously Article 228(7) EC) implies that international agreements enjoy primacy over secondary law.[63] It would thus be impossible for any Union organ to free the Union internally from its WTO obligations by unilateral means,

---

[59] Paras. 36–41; for a critical view see S. Griller, "Judicial Enforceability of WTO Law in the European Union" (2000) 3 *JIEL* 441 *et seq.*

[60] Paras. 42–46; see pathbreaking C.-D. Ehlermann, "Die innergemeinschaftliche Andwendung der Regeln des GATT in der Praxis der EG" in Hilf and Petersmann (*supra* n. 2), 203 *et seq.*, 216; Advocate General Tesauro (*supra* n. 57), para. 35.

[61] The Uruguay Round Agreements Act, 103D Congress, 2nd Session, House Document 103–316, Vol. 1, 1994, 659.

[62] E.-U. Petersmann, "The Transformation of the World Trading System throught the 1994 Agreement Establishing the World Trade Organization" (1995) 6 *EJIL* 161 *et seq.*

[63] Cases 21–24/72, *International Fruit* [1972] ECR 1219, para. 5 *et seq.*; this "self-binding" is not mandatory: see Ch. Tomuschat, "Art. 228 EGV", para. 74 in H. von der Groeben, J. Thiesing and C.-D. Ehlermann, *Kommentar zum EU-, EG-Vertrag* (5th edn., Baden-Baden, Nomos, 1997).

whereas most WTO members can do so because, in these legal systems, a later national parliamentary act enjoys internal primacy over prior international agreements.

This lack of direct applicability makes it impossible for the market citizen to mount a legal challenge to a Union measure on the basis of WTO law. When a claim brought by an EU Member State based on WTO law comes before the ECJ—as in the case of *Portugal* v. *Council*—it is unconvincing when the Court dismisses the claim on the basis of an absence of direct applicability. First of all, this solution is not convincing from a dogmatic point of view, because direct applicability is a legal institution which, according to the dominant theory, concerns the position of the market citizen, not, however, that of the Member States. Direct applicability is not a general condition for ECJ jurisdiction in direct actions for judicial review, in particular for those brought by the Member States.[64] The Court's judgment in *Germany* v. *Council* has already been convincingly criticised for this reason.[65]

Moreover, the ECJ's decision fails to take into account the special nature of the European Union's foreign relations. In contrast to all other federations, in the European Union the Members remain full subjects of international law.[66] Not only is the European Union (under the legal personality of the EC) a WTO Member, but the EU Member States are full WTO members too. Moreover, there is no WTO provision which states that in the case of an infringement of a WTO rule by the Union, WTO responsibility is limited to the Union as such and that an internally objecting Member State is free of any responsibility. Each Member State carries full international liability for any WTO-inconsistent measure adopted by the Union's organs. The ECJ's decision in *Portugal* v. *Council* prevents this problem from being addressed internally and denies Member States one last opportunity to ensure conformity with international law, thus avoiding their liability under international law. The Court did not consider Portugal as a subject of international law, but rather as a banana importer only. In any case, mechanisms within the EU should be considered such as to release objecting EU Member States (and also perhaps their citizens) from the consequences of international liability, such as punitive duties by the United States. It is notable in this respect that the United States carefully targeted its threatened sanctions against those Member States which had supported the ACP-friendly bananas regime.

---

[64] This results from the case law on Arts. 2 und 3 EC Treaty: A. von Bogdandy, "Art. 2 EG" in E. Grabitz and M. Hilf, *Das Recht der Europäischen Union* (Munich, Beck, 2000), paras. 4 *et seq.*

[65] U. Everling, "Will Europe Slip on Bananas?" (1996) 33 *CMLRev.* 401 at 421–422.

[66] Advocate General Tesauro (*supra* n. 53), para. 21; see in greater detail M. Cappelletti, M. Secombe and J.H.H. Weiler, "Integration through Law: Europe and the American Federal Experience" in *ibid.* (eds.), *Integration Through Law I* (Berlin, de Gruyter, 1986) 3, 51 *et seq.*

Conflict Avoidance through Direct Applicability of WTO Law

It would, however, be a grave error to conclude from this that WTO law is irrelevant to the commercial law practitioner in the European Union. First, there is the principle of indirect applicability by construing Union law in the light of international and therefore WTO law (*völkerrechtskonforme Auslegung*). In so far as a Union act or a national act provides an interpretative margin or discretionary authority, the interpretation which conforms to the Union's international obligations is to be preferred.[67]

Moreover, there are two constellations in which *Union acts* must yield before WTO law in case of a collision. The ECJ confirmed the principles developed in the *Fediol* and *Nakajima* cases[68] in its decision of 23 November 1999 in paragraph 49:

> where the Community intended to implement a particular obligation assumed in the context of the WTO, or where the Community refers expressly to the precise provisions of the WTO agreements, that it is for the Court to review the legality of the Community measure in the light of the WTO rules.

This formulation leaves many questions open beyond the decided cases (antidumping and the Trade Barriers regulation) and offers only rough indications of the circumstances in which WTO law shall provide legal control for the Union's organs through the ECJ.[69] It should, however, be noted that the direct applicability of WTO law depends on a special (and revocable) act of the Union's organs.

It appears that in the ECJ's conception, WTO law is of far greater significance for the control of *Member State* measures. This possible distinction between acts of the Union's organs and those of the Member States has not yet been sufficiently noted. It is remarkable how much emphasis the ECJ places—in the decisive paragraph 46 of *Portugal* v. *Council*—on the fact that the lack of direct applicability of WTO law concerns the WTO compatibility of "Community law" and of acts of the "Community's legislative and executive organs". What is missing? The Member States! Member State measures are, in contrast to the recital of Council Decision 94/800, noted above, not mentioned by the ECJ. This leads to the question whether control of Member State measures is to be regulated on the basis of other principles.

Thus far there has been no clear answer to this question. On the one hand, it is hardly defensible according to current theory concerning international

---

[67] Case C–83/94, *Leifer* ECR I–3231, para. 24; Case C–53/96, *Hermès* [1998] ECR I–3603, para. 28; P. Manin, "A propos de l'accord instituant l'Organisation mondiale du commerce et de l'accord sur les marchés publics: la question de l'invocabilité des accords internationaux conclus par la Communauté européenne" (1997) 33 *RTDE* 401 at 412 *et seq.*

[68] Case 70/87, *Fediol* [1989] ECR 1781; Case C–69/89, *Nakajima* [1991] ECR I-2069.

[69] Instructive are Berrisch and Kamann (*supra* n. 52).

agreements that an international treaty in the sense of Article 300(7) EC (formerly Article 228(7) EC Treaty) has different legal consequences, depending on whether it is being applied to Union or Member State measures.[70] On the other hand, however, there are clear signs that the ECJ has precisely this solution in mind. In the *Hermès* case (significantly itself an Article 234 EC case) the question at issue was whether Article 50 TRIPS rather than a Dutch civil procedural norm was to be applied by the Dutch court.[71] The ECJ interpreted Article 50 TRIPS, which implies that it was of direct relevance for the decision of the Dutch court. As a construction of the Dutch Civil Procedure Code in conformity with international law was not possible, the reasoning of the ECJ makes sense only if the direct applicability of the WTO norm in question is assumed.

An application of WTO law for the ECJ's control of Member States is also the basis of the decision of 10 September 1996, in which the Commission, in a process pursuant to Article 169 EC (now Article 226 EC), charged Germany with a breach of the International Dairy Agreement, a part of the GATT Tokyo Round.[72] Without any discussion of the problem of applicability, the ECJ evaluated the German measures on the basis of the Agreement, which, as part of the Tokyo package, belongs to the GATT. This implies that, in terms of intra-Union control, WTO law has the character of being a yardstick for the legality of Member States' measures.[73] This is—by pure accident?—exactly the sole situation in which US law gives effect to WTO law in its internal legal order: the US administration can enforce it against a disobedient state.[74]

One can conclude from these two judgments and the carefully limited reasoning in case *Portugal* v. *Council* that the ECJ is quite prepared to control acts of EU Member States on the basis of WTO law or to have the national courts apply WTO law against national measures. However, the ECJ, by means of the preliminary ruling procedure, remains at the helm. This quest for control is understandable if one considers the Union's responsibilities under public international law and the internal mechanisms for ensuring conformity within it.

The European Union is a WTO member and is liable for all violations of WTO law within its jurisdiction. Violations can occur, however, not only through acts of the Union's organs but also as a result of those of the Member States. The Union's direct instruments (i.e. the Commission) for supervising the Member States are weak. The most important instrument for ensuring respect for Community law has always been its decentralised application via its direct

---

[70] Case 81/73, *R & V Haegeman* [1974] ECR 449, para. 2(6); Case 104/81, *C.A. Kupferberg & Cie KG* [1982] ECR 3641, paras. 13 *et seq.*

[71] [1998] ECR I–3603; cf. also A. von Bogdandy, "Case C–53/96, *Hermès International* v. *FHT Marketing Choice BV*, Judgment of the Court (Full Court) of 16 June 1998; [1998] ECR I–3603" (1999) 36 *CMLRev.* 663–672.

[72] Case C–61/94, *Commission* v. *Germany* [1996] ECR I–3989.

[73] See, for a position from within the EU Commission, J. Sack, "Noch einmal: GATT/WTO und europäisches Rechtsschutzsystem" (1997) *EuZW* 688.

[74] Sec. 102 (b) Uruguay Round Agreements Act, Public Law 103–465 (1994).

applicability, and complementary legal institutions (for example state liability in damages); this is also valid for the Community's international obligations.[75] Against this background, the reason why the ECJ tends toward control of Member States' acts in the light of WTO law is apparent. This compensates for the Commission's weak supervisory powers and helps to avoid national acts which violate international law, and which could be attributed to the Union.

Furthermore, it is of fundamental importance to the formation of a Union's political identity that the Union and its members be represented to third parties as a unity.[76] Divergent lines of applicability of WTO law would gravely damage this unity and with it the already difficult formation of an external political identity.

Seen from this angle, the ECJ's diverse judgments and its differentiated approach to WTO law make sense. Nevertheless, there remains a tension between the judgments *Hermès* and *Commission* v. *Germany* judgments on the one side, and *Portugal* v. *Council* on the other; moreover the overall legal situation remains fraught with doubts. One reason is that dominant understandings of Article 300(7) EC and of the concept of direct applicability leave no room for such differentiation. Legal scholarship may investigate whether the ECJ's strategy is capable of being formulated in a legally consistent way.

CONCLUSION

The reports of the dispute settlement organs discussed above demonstrate a considerable keenness for, and remarkable level of, legal control. They weigh micro-economic against macro-economic instruments when analysing the "necessary" clause and interpret Article XXIV GATT as imposing strict criteria on the formation of a customs union and its foreign trade policies. The ECJ follows a differentiated strategy with regard to this rapidly expanding body of law, which still requires clarification in a variety of points. One can state with certainty, however, that neither the ECJ nor national courts can control the WTO compatibility of acts of the Union's *organs*, except in narrowly circumscribed situations. By contrast, it is apparent that such control in the case of acts of the Member States should, in principle, be possible. This differentiated strategy reflects the Union's internal constitution and its unique international status. However, it has thus far lacked any theoretical foundation. Yet, as the basic thrust is convincing, it is likely that such theoretical underpinnings will be developed in the future. By contrast, the ECJ's strategy appears deficient in so far as the Member States are deprived of the possibility of instituting legal proceeding pursuant to Article 230(2) EC against violations of WTO law by acts of the Union's organs.[77] As a whole, these new developments reveal elements not only

---

[75] For liability created by treaties see P. Gasparon, "The Transposition of the principle of Member State Libility into the context of External Relations" (1999) 10 *EJIL* 605.

[76] Editorial comments (1999) 36 *CMLRev.* 881.

[77] Everling (*supra* n. 66), 421 *et seq.*; Ehlermann (*supra* n. 61) 220 *et seq.*

of collision, but also of peaceful coexistence and even co-operation between the legal order of the European Union and the international trade regime. Further developments may be awaited with anticipation.

7

Neutrality or Discrimination? The WTO, the EU and External Trade

MARISE CREMONA

INTRODUCTION

Historically, the EU (or Community, as it was) has never made liberal trade its highest priority. It is no accident that the hallmark of the EU's external trade policy is not neutrality but discrimination—of an exceptionally developed kind—among its various trading partners.[1]

THIS COMMENT BY an anonymous *Economist* writer was made in 1994, in the context of the conclusion of the Uruguay Round and an assessment of the European Community's role in the negotiations and the outcome. The link made here between trade liberalisation and neutrality or non-discrimination is a link found within the logic of both the GATT—and now WTO—and the EC. The Preamble to the Agreement establishing the WTO, in almost the same words as in the original Preamble to GATT 1947, asserts the desire of the Contracting Parties to enter into "reciprocal and mutually advantageous arrangements" with the aim of substantially reducing tariffs and other trade barriers and "the elimination of discriminatory treatment in international trade relations". The GATT 1994, its related Annex 1A Agreements, the GATS and TRIPS Agreements are all built upon the foundational principles of MFN (Most Favoured Nation) and national treatment. Within the European Community the principle of equal treatment, the prohibition of discrimination on grounds of nationality,[2] is one of the fundamental principles in Part I of the EC Treaty alongside the liberal trade agendas of Articles 2 and 3, and has played a crucial role in the creation of an integrated market, as an instrument for securing market access in each of the "four freedoms". It is placed among the principles of the EU (economic) constitution.[3] It is easy in this way to see the EC, or at least its earlier incarnation, the European Economic Community, as a child of the

---

[1] *The Economist*, 16 April 1994.
[2] Now found in Art. 12 EC.
[3] See G. More, "The Principle of Equal Treatment: From Market Unifier to Fundamental Right?" in P. Craig and G. de Búrca (eds.), *The Evolution of EU Law* (Oxford, OUP, 1999).

GATT, a regional integration agreement based on non-discrimination and market access among a number of regionally linked participants.

And yet . . . when we turn to the EC Treaty provisions dealing with external trade policy, the pattern shifts. The link between trade liberalisation and non-discrimination appears to be broken. Against a background of commitment to the principles of trade liberalisation, the emphasis is on the development of a *common* commercial policy, *uniform* principles, and presenting a united front to trading partners in international negotiations. The Member States declare in Article 131 that their "aim" is to contribute to the "harmonious development of world trade, the progressive abolition of restrictions on international trade and the lowering of customs barriers". This aspirational but non-prescriptive adherence to the objectives of the GATT/WTO is understandable given the reciprocal and negotiated nature of trade liberalisation within GATT: the WTO is not about unilateral dismantling of tariff barriers. However, within the WTO negotiated liberalisation takes place in the framework of a commitment to MFN which is unconditional and not dependent on reciprocity of advantage. Article 133 of the EC Treaty strikingly says almost nothing about the content of the common commercial policy, except that it should be based on uniformity as between the Member States (in this way complementing the common external tariff).[4] There is certainly no incorporation of the unconditional MFN obligation, or Treaty-based commitment to national treatment for third country goods (or services).

This is not necessarily to say either that these principles are not followed by the EC in its trade practice or that they are absent from its formulation of autonomous and contractual external trade policy measures. However their absence from the Treaty has implications when considering the question of hierarchies of norms, both internal and external, and in particular in the context of assessing the legality of institutional acts in the external trade sphere. The location of a non-discrimination *obligation* has to be sought outside, thus raising issues of enforceability of these external obligations within the Community legal order. It is also more difficult to identify a coherent approach to non-discrimination in external trade, as the roles played by the principle of non-discrimination in the development of the Community legal order have been defined largely in terms of its application internally.

The question of the effect of WTO obligations on EC external trade policy is a very large one. This chapter will explore one facet of the question: the EC's approach to non-discrimination in its external trade policy, and the link between non-discrimination and trade liberalisation in the light of WTO rules. It will not attempt to assess the compatibility of the whole range of the Community's commercial policy with WTO obligations. But because non-discrimination is such a central, "constitutional" obligation within both the EU

---

[4] The list in Art. 133(1) is essentially a list of instruments, including tariff and trade agreements and trade protection measures.

and the WTO, it is a useful window through which to consider the relationship between these inter-connected legal orders; what has been called "the tension between internal Community legitimacy and external legitimacy derived from the global commercial system and its institutions".[5] However, before we turn to EC policy we should first look briefly at non-discrimination within the WTO.

THE WTO AND NON-DISCRIMINATION

Non-discrimination is, alongside reciprocity, market access and fair competition, an essential ingredient of the WTO system.[6] To an EC lawyer, the most striking aspect of non-discrimination within the WTO system is the differentiation between MFN treatment and national treatment (NT). MFN requires equality of treatment on the part of each contracting party with respect to all other parties; all trading partners who are also WTO members must be treated alike. Under this principle all import controls (tariff and non-tariff) will be origin-neutral:

> any advantage, favour, privilege or immunity granted by any contracting party to any product originating in or destined for any other country shall be accorded immediately and unconditionally to the like product originating in or destined for the territories of all other contracting parties.[7]

The basic MFN rule found in Article I GATT 1994 applies to customs duties and charges, including methods of levying duties, all import and export formalities, internal taxation and regulatory requirements within Article III:4 of GATT 1994. It operates together with Article XIII which requires that no prohibitions or restrictions on imports or exports (such as quantitative restrictions) may be applied to products of other contracting parties unless the same restrictions are applied to "like products" from all third countries. MFN is also explicitly included within a number of the Annex 1A Agreements, especially those dealing with quantitative restrictions and other import licensing regimes; for example, the Safeguards Agreement requires that safeguard measures shall be applied to an imported product "irrespective of its source".[8] The Import Licensing Agreement extends the MFN principle applied to quantitative restrictions in Article XIII to the application and administration of *procedures* for import licensing; it requires that these procedures "shall be neutral in application and administered in a fair and equitable manner".[9]

---

[5] M. Smith and S. Woolcock, "European Commercial Policy: A Leadership Role in the New Millennium?" (1999) 4 *EFA Rev.* 439 at 461.

[6] M. Farrell, *EU and WTO Regulatory Frameworks: Complementarity or Competition?* (London: Kogan Page, 1999), 1.

[7] GATT 1994 Art. I:1.

[8] Agreement on Safeguards, Art. 2:2.

[9] Agreement on Import Licensing Procedures, Art. 1:3. The Agreement covers not only import licensing procedures in relation to quantitative restrictive but also procedures for the administration

The MFN rule in GATT applies a non-discrimination test in favour of products of contracting parties as against products of *any other* country (WTO member or not). In contrast, national treatment is by its nature restricted to products and services of the contracting parties themselves. Article III of GATT 1994 requires "no less favourable treatment" to imported goods as compared with domestic goods, and applies essentially to "behind the frontier" measures, such as internal taxation, standards and other regulatory requirements. The TBT[10] and SPS[11] Agreements apply national treatment rules to technical regulations and standards and sanitary and phytosanitary measures and the TRIMS Agreement expressly applies Article III of GATT 1994 with an illustrative list of measures that are inconsistent with Article III:4 in an Annex.[12] Article III:1 prohibits internal taxes, laws, and regulations affecting internal sale which are applied "so as to afford protection to domestic products", and this is referred to explicitly in the second sentence of paragraph 2 which deals with certain internal taxes. However a specific consideration of protectionist application is not necessarily required for Article III:4, which is drafted in terms of "no less favourable treatment".[13]

The GATS deals with MFN and national treatment somewhat differently from the GATT. Unconditional MFN forms the basis of the GATS, under Article II:

> With respect to any measure covered by this Agreement, each Member shall accord immediately and unconditionally to services and service suppliers of any other Member treatment no less favourable than that it accords to like services and service suppliers of any other country.[14]

The national treatment obligation, on the other hand, is subject to country and sector-specific schedules of commitments, under Article XVII:

> In the sectors described in its Schedule, and subject to any conditions and qualifications set out therein, each Member shall accord to services and service suppliers of any

---

of tariff quotas: *European Communities—Regime for the Importation, Sale and Distribution of Bananas*, Appellate Body Report WT/DS27/AB/R, 9 September 1997, at para 194. See also Art. X:3(a) GATT 1994.

[10] Agreement on Technical Barriers to Trade, Art. 2:1.

[11] Agreement on the Application of Sanitary and Phytosanitary Measures, Arts. 2:3 and 5:5.

[12] Agreement on Trade-related Investment Measures, Art. 2. The Annex includes measures which require the purchase or use by an enterprise of domestic products, or which link the quantity of imported products purchased or used to the volume or value of domestic products exported.

[13] *Bananas* AB Report, n. 9 *supra*, at paras. 215–216, explaining *Japan—Alcoholic Beverages*, Appellate Body Report, WT/DS8/AB/R, WT/DS10/AB/R, WT/DS11/AB/R, adopted 1 November 1996.

[14] GATS Art. II:1. "Measures" covered by the Agreement are defined broadly in Art. I. Limited exemptions are provided for under Art. II:2 and the Annex on Article II Exemptions. In the *Bananas* case, the AB held that Art. II must cover *de facto* as well as *de jure* (indirect and direct) discrimination, although interestingly it refused to argue this by analogy from the express provision in relation to national treatment in Art. XVII:2, as the Panel had done, and instead argued from earlier Panel reports on MFN within the GATT: *Bananas*, AB Report at paras. 229–234, citing *EEC—Beef from Canada* adopted 10 March 1981, BISD 28S/92.

other Member, in respect of all measures respecting the supply of services, treatment no less favourable than that it accords to its own like services and service suppliers.

It is not possible in a chapter this length to analyse fully these provisions; I want to highlight only a couple of points that are particularly relevant to my theme. The first relates to discrimination in the context of the determination of prohibited conduct under GATT/GATS rules. The second relates to discrimination in the context of the express exception found in Article XX of GATT 1994.

The first issue focuses on the fundamental issue of the relevance (or otherwise) of the aims of the legislature when enacting a measure which is then challenged as discriminatory. The Appellate Body (AB) in the *Bananas* case discusses this issue in the context of the GATS.[15] The EC had argued that its licensing system for bananas was not discriminatory under Articles II and XVII of the GATS, because the various rules "pursue entirely legitimate policies" and "are not inherently discriminatory in design or effect".[16] The AB rejected this argument, holding that the "aims or effects" of the measure are not relevant in establishing discrimination, and instead relying on evidence of indirect discrimination which "modifies the conditions of competition" between service suppliers.[17] Although the AB was here discussing the GATS non-discrimination rules, it explicitly relies on an earlier AB report which rejected the "aims and effects" approach in the context of Article III:2 GATT 1994.[18] The approach to non-discrimination under the GATT is carried over and applied in the context of the GATS. And the "legitimate objectives" of establishing a common organisation of the market in bananas are rejected as irrelevant when considering the discriminatory effect of the import licensing system and in particular the operator category and activity function rules.[19] What is significant is the Panel's factual finding that most of the suppliers of the complainants' origin were classified in one category, and that most of the suppliers of EC (or ACP) origin were classified in another: "We see no reason to go behind these factual conclusions of the Panel".[20] This contrasts strikingly with the European Court of Justice's

---

[15] *Bananas* AB Report, *supra* n. 9. Although the EC had argued that the GATS should not apply to its import licensing regime, the AB supported the Panel in finding that the operators covered by the EC's Regulation were engaged in wholesale trade services and that GATS would therefore apply: *Bananas*, AB Report at paras. 217–228.

[16] *Bananas*, *supra* n. 9, AB Report at para. 240, citing EC's appellant's submission, para. 301.

[17] Modification of the conditions of competition by either formally identical or formally different treatment (indirect or direct discrimination) amounts to less favourable treatment under GATS Art. XVII:3.

[18] *Bananas*, AB Report, *supra* n. 9, at para. 241, citing *Japan—Alcoholic Beverages,* Appellate Body Report, WT/DS8/AB/R, WT/DS10/AB/R, WT/DS11/AB/R, adopted 1 November 1996.

[19] The EC argued that the operator category system had the objective of "integrating the various national markets" and "distributing quota rents among the various operators in the market" in order to "develop market structures without disrupting existing commercial links": *Bananas*, AB Report, *supra* n. 9, at para. 242.

[20] *Bananas*, AB Report, *supra* n. 9, at para. 243, citing Panel Reports, WT/DS27/R/ECU, WT/DS27/R/MEX, WT/DS27/R/USA, para. 7.334.

approach to the relationship between non-discrimination and Community, or Member State, market objectives. As we shall see, in ECJ jurisprudence, legitimate objectives (legitimate in the view of the Court) even where they do not appear among the Treaty-based exceptions to free movement, may be accepted as an "objective justification" for differential treatment and thus counter an allegation of indirect discrimination.[21]

The second issue that I wish to highlight here is the concept of discrimination as it appears in the express exemption found in Article XX of GATT 1994 and as it is discussed by the Appellate Body in the *Shrimp–Turtles* case.[22] This provision permits the parties, for certain legitimate objectives (public health, the conservation of exhaustible natural resources etc.), to adopt measures which would otherwise be inconsistent with provisions of the Agreement, as long as the measures:

> are not applied in a manner which would constitute a means of arbitrary or unjustifiable discrimination between countries where the same conditions prevail, or a disguised restriction on international trade.

This "chapeau", which was placed at the head of Article XX (as compared with its equivalent in "second sentence" place in Article 30 EC) was said by the Appellate Body in *Shrimp-Turtles* to embody a different concept of discrimination from that found in Article I, III or XI—a concept that is "but one expression of the principle of good faith".[23] Nevertheless, where the European Court has used concepts of proportionality to determine whether national measures are "justified" and has arguably effectively combined the proportionality test in the first sentence of Article 30 with the proviso of the second sentence,[24] the Appellate Body insists that these are separate questions—so that justifiability under paragraphs (a) to (j) does not necessarily imply compliance with the "chapeau"—and has then interpreted the "chapeau" in terms of discrimination.[25] According to the AB, the "chapeau" recognises the need to maintain a balance between the right of members to invoke the allowed exceptions in order to protect legitimate policies and interests, and the substantive rights of other members. However, where the European Court of Justice would speak of the balance between legitimate national policies and interests on the one hand and the aims of market integration on the other, the Appellate Body sees the balance in terms of the competing interests of the WTO members:

---

[21] See, e.g., Case 21/79, *Commission* v. *Italy (regenerated petroleum products)* [1980] ECR 1, in the context of Member State policy on taxation; Case C–280/93, *Germany* v. *Commission (Bananas I)* [1994] ECR I–5039, in the context of Community policy establishing the common organisation of the market. See further discussion in the text at n. 68 *et seq.*

[22] *United States—Import Prohibition of Certain Shrimp and Shrimp Products*, Appellate Body Report, WT/DS58/AB/R, 12 October 1998.

[23] *Ibid.*, at para. 158.

[24] See, e.g., Case 40/82, *Commission* v. *United Kingdom* [1982] ECR 2793.

[25] *Shrimp-Turtles*, AB Report, *supra* n. 22, at para. 149.

The task of interpreting and applying the chapeau is, hence, essentially the delicate one of locating and marking out a line of equilibrium between the right of a Member to invoke an exception under Article XX and the rights of the other Members under varying substantive provisions (e.g., Article XI) of the GATT 1994, so that neither of the competing rights will cancel out the other. . . . The location of the line of equilibrium, as expressed in the chapeau, is not fixed and unchanging; the line moves as the kind and the shape of the measures at stake vary and as the facts making up specific cases differ.[26]

Marking out a line of equilibrium, rather than merely calling for an examination of differential treatment, requires an assessment of both the underlying objectives and the actual effects of the measure (as well as the legitimacy of its policy goals). So, in *Shrimp–Turtles*, the factors which lead the Appellate Body to determine that the United States had failed to meet the requirements of the "chapeau" to Article XX are instructive. First, the AB stresses that in its view the US objective was not only conservation *per se* but, in addition, the export of its own particular standard as *the* way of achieving its objective. This was problematic both because it did not allow its partners to demonstrate the potential compatibility of alternative methods, and because no account was taken of the appropriateness of the US approach for other countries:

discrimination results not only when countries in which the same conditions prevail are differently treated, but also when the application of the measure at issue does not allow for any inquiry into the appropriateness of the regulatory program for the conditions prevailing in those exporting countries.[27]

The AB is implying that good faith and non-discrimination impose an obligation to recognise the equivalence of comparable standards; the "rigid and unbending standard" applied by US officials in certifying countries for the purposes of exporting shrimp to the US failed to take into account other, possibly comparable, methods. The reasoning is reminiscent of the ECJ in *Commission v. Ireland*[28] in the context of a finding of indirect discrimination, and in the application of justification tests under Article 28 or 30 EC.[29]

Secondly, the AB condemns the "singularly informal and casual" procedures for certification of exporting countries; problems included the lack of procedural transparency, the absence of an opportunity to make representations, the

---

[26] *Shrimp-Turtles*, AB Report, *supra* n. 22, at para. 159.

[27] *Ibid.*, at para. 165.

[28] Case 45/87, *Commission* v. *Ireland (Dundalk Water Supply)* [1988] ECR 4929 at para. 22. The SPS Agreement in Art. 4 also contains an obligation to recognise as equivalent standards which reach the importing member's "appropriate level" of protection. The TBT Agreement in Art. 2:7 merely requires members to give "positive consideration" to accepting alternative standards as equivalent.

[29] In order to rely on a "mandatory requirement" to justify a barrier to trade under Art. 28 EC, the importing state will need to show that the regulations in force in the exporting state do not provide an equivalent level of protection: Case 120/78, *Cassis de Dijon* [1979] ECR 649 at para. 14; see also on justifications under Art. 30: Case 188/84, *Commission* v. *France* [1986] ECR 419 at para. 16.

absence of a reasoned decision, and of any review or appeal procedures.[30] Article X:3(a) requires laws and regulations to be administered in a "uniform, impartial and reasonable manner" and this requirement must also apply to laws adopted under the aegis of Article XX. Even where legislating within the scope of an exemption provision, member countries are bound by fundamental procedural obligations, and a denial of "basic fairness and due process" thus results in "arbitrary discrimination". Again, the reasoning recalls the ECJ, in *Heylens*, applying due process standards to Treaty-based exceptions.[31]

Thirdly, unjustifiable discrimination results from the failure of the USA to make a real effort to negotiate bilateral or multilateral agreements with exporting countries which would incorporate agreed standards. The reasoning here is multi-faceted and in part relies on the emphasis on negotiation of multilateral agreements within environmental initiatives and fora, such as the WTO Decision on Trade and Environment and the Rio Declaration on Environment and Development. From the perspective of discrimination, the crucial argument was that by concluding one agreement, the Inter-American Convention for the Protection and Conservation of Sea Turtles of 1996, with five exporting countries (Brazil, Costa Rica, Mexico, Nicaragua and Venezuela) the USA discriminated against those other states with which it had not attempted to negotiate:

> The United States negotiated seriously with some, but not with other Members (including the appellees), that export shrimp to the United States. The effect is plainly discriminatory and, in our view, unjustifiable.[32]

The effect was not merely that some countries had an agreed solution, and some did not; there were consequent differences between exporters about the periods allowed for phasing in the new systems and in relation to assistance with technology transfer. Most important, the AB contrasts the possibility of a negotiated agreement with the alternative, for the USA, recourse to the unilateral measures complained of. "The unilateral character of the application of section 609 heightens the disruptive and discriminatory influence of the import prohibition and underscores its unjustifiability".[33] In the EC context, of course, measures justified under Article 30 EC will by their nature be unilateral; once concerted action has been taken in the form of a Community instrument recourse to Article 30 will no longer be justified.[34] In the context of the multilateral dimension of the WTO, the link made here between unilateralism and unjustifiable discrimination is significant.

---

[30] *Shrimp-Turtles*, AB Report, *supra* n. 22, at paras. 180–181.

[31] Case 222/86, *UNECTEF* v. *Heylens* [1987] ECR 4079.

[32] *Shrimp-Turtles*, AB Report, *supra* n. 22, at para. 172. C.f. the AB finding in the *Bananas* case that the conclusion by the EU of the Framework Agreement on Bananas with some but not all of the non-ACP exporters was contrary to the MFN non-discrimination principle of Art. XIII:1.

[33] *Shrimp-Turtles*, AB Report, *supra* n. 22, at para. 172.

[34] Case C–5/94, *R.* v. *MAFF, ex parte Hedley Lomas* [1996] ECR I–2553.

In assessing the role played by the principle of non-discrimination within the EC's external trade policy, I have found the categorisation used by More helpful.[35] She identifies three roles for the principle of equal treatment (which she holds as synonymous with non-discrimination—I have used the term non-discrimination rather than equal treatment, because it more naturally encompasses both the most-favoured-nation and national treatment principles):

—The market-unifying role, which contributes to the creation of an integrated market by ensuring equality of market access, addressing primarily the actions of the Member States (negative integration) and which is reflected in the Treaty provisions on the four freedoms (and consequent secondary legislation) as well as in the general statement of the principle in Article 12 EC.
—The regulatory role, which operates as a principle guiding Community legislative intervention in the market (positive integration) and thus acts to protect equality of competition in the market.
—The constitutional role, within which equal treatment is developing into a general and autonomous (not market-based) right, emerging from legislative and judicial initiatives in the context of sex discrimination, citizenship and Article 13 EC.

Mapping these roles onto the WTO, we can see that non-discrimination plays essentially a market-unifying or market-creating role. It is designed to ensure equal access to the market both as compared with other exporters (MFN) and as compared with national producers (national treatment). Whether in GATT 1994, the Annex 1A Agreements, GATS or TRIPS, it is directed at the actions of the WTO Member States. In the absence of autonomous law-making institutions, non-discrimination does not yet possess a regulatory role within the WTO system, in the sense of a role which would constrain the executive discretion of those institutions. Neither has non-discrimination broken free of its market context to become a "fundamental right" outside the market access rights granted by the WTO Agreements.[36]

How then does non-discrimination operate in the context of EC external trade? It is in fact in looking at the position of third country goods and people that we can see the limitations of EC non-discrimination as a principle of even the economic constitution. In its market-unifying role, non-discrimination serves to ensure market access for all *Community-origin* goods and *Union*

---

[35] More, *supra* n. 3.
[36] For discussion of this issue, see E.-U. Petersmann, "The WTO Constitution and Human Rights" (2000) 3 *JIEL* 19; E.-U. Petersmann, "Human Rights, Cosmopolitan Democracy and the Law of the World Trade Organization" in M. Cremona, I.F. Fletcher and L. Mistelis (eds.), *Foundations and Perspectives of International Trade Law* (London, Sweet and Maxwell, 2001).

citizens, but not for those of third country origin until they are in free circulation within the Community (which is why the EC customs union needs the exemption from the MFN rule granted by Article XXIV GATT 1994). The Community, as a unified market, is interested in free movement for third country goods and people only in so far as this is necessary to ensure the removal of all internal barriers to free movement. Hence the principle of freedom of movement for goods in free circulation found in Articles 23 and 24 EC and the *Donckerwolcke* case.[37] Hence the rationale for the provisions on third country nationals found in Article 61 EC with its express link to Article 14 (the area without internal frontiers).[38] When it comes to the crossing of the *external* borders of the Community, the important principle is not non-discrimination but uniformity: a common external tariff, common commercial policy and common immigration and visa controls, as it is this uniformity which enables *internal* free movement to take place. It is this uniformity which is stressed in Article 133(1) and which provides the justification for the exclusive nature of the Community's external commercial competence.[39]

The example of internal indirect taxation of goods will serve to illustrate this point. Discriminatory internal taxation is prohibited by Article III of GATT 1994. The EC Treaty, however, does not contain any provision requiring non-discrimination in relation to third country goods on entry onto the Community market. Article 90 EC, which prohibits discriminatory internal taxation, refers to "products of other Member States". This has been interpreted by the Court of Justice to include goods from third countries which are in free circulation within the Member States, although the Treaty provisions on the customs union and free circulation (Articles 23 and 24) make no reference to internal taxation.[40] The rationale is based on the need to ensure freedom of movement of goods within the internal market itself with Article 90 acting "to fill in any breaches which a fiscal measure might open in the prohibitions [of customs duties and charges] laid down". This rationale does not however apply to goods on their *initial import* into the Community. In *Simba SpA*—which concerned the Italian consumption tax on fresh bananas—Article 90 was held not to prohibit discrimination against third country bananas which were not in free

---

[37] Case 41/76, *Donckerwolcke* [1976] ECR 1921.

[38] Under Art. 61 the Council is to adopt "measures aimed at ensuring the free movement of persons in accordance with Article 14, in conjunction with directly related flanking measures with respect to external border controls, asylum and immigration". Under Art. 62 these measures are to be enacted "with a view to ensuring, in compliance with Article 14, the absence of any controls on persons, be they citizens of the Union or nationals of third countries, when crossing internal borders".

[39] *Opinion 1/75* (OECD Agreement) [1975] ECR 1355. See also M. Cremona, "External Relations and External Competence: The Emergence of an Integrated Policy" in P. Craig and G. de Búrca (eds.), *The Evolution of EU Law* (Oxofrd, OUP, 1999) at 152–155; M. Cremona "EC External Commercial Policy after Amsterdam: Authority and Interpretation within Interconnected Legal Orders" in J.H.H. Weiler (ed.), *Towards a Common Law of International Trade?: The EU, the WTO and the NAFTA* (Oxford, OUP, 2000).

[40] Case 193/85, *Cooperativa Co-Frutta (bananas)* [1987] ECR 2085 at paras. 24–29.

circulation.[41] The Court also held that Article 133 did not of itself prohibit such discrimination:

> The Treaty provisions concerning the common commercial policy, and in particular Article 113 [now 133], do not of themselves prohibit a Member State from levying on products imported directly from a non-member country a duty such as the national tax on consumption. . . . [F]or trade with non-member countries, and as far as internal taxation is concerned, the Treaty itself does not include any rule similar to that laid down in Article 95 [now 90].[42]

The Court does however point out that account should be taken of any non-discrimination rules in international agreements entered into by the Community relating to the goods in question. We will consider the effect of such clauses, and their absence, below.[43]

· So, we do not find, expressly in the EC Treaty, in relation either to the Community institutions or to Member State legislative activity, either MFN or national treatment for third country goods or service providers at their point of initial entry into the Community market. The level of compliance of the Community, as a member of the WTO, with its principles and rules is to be found not in the Treaty itself but in the secondary legislation by which the Community conducts its external trade policy.

Autonomous Measures

The Regulation on common rules for imports[44] was adopted following the conclusion of the WTO Agreements by the Community and was intended to bring Community rules into line with WTO requirements, especially in the area of safeguard measures. The Regulation, in its Preamble, acknowledges (as well as the requirement of uniform principles found in Article 133 EC) the objectives of trade liberalisation:

> Whereas the starting point for the common rules for imports is liberalization of imports, namely the absence of any quantitative restrictions;

Accordingly, under Article 1 all products covered by the Regulation are to enter the Community freely and without being subject to any quantitative restrictions, subject to safeguard measures adopted under the relevant provisions in the Regulation. Products excluded from the scope of the Regulation are limited to (a) textile products in so far as they have not yet been integrated in GATT 1994, these being subject to a specific Regulation; and (b) products "originating

---

[41] Case C–228/90, *Simba SpA (bananas)* [1992] ECR I–3713 at paras. 14–15.

[42] *Ibid.*, at paras. 17–18. See also Case C–130/92 [1994] ECR I-3281.

[43] See text *infra* at n. 97.

[44] Council Regulation 3285/94/EC of 22 December 1994 on the common rules for imports and repealing Regulation 518/94 [1994] OJ L349/53, as amended by Regulation 139/96 [1996] OJ L21/7 and by Regulation 2315/96 [1996] OJ L314/1.

in certain third countries listed in Council Regulation (EC) No 519/94", these being countries not members of the WTO.[45] The Community is thus complying with its MFN obligation under GATT 1994 in so far as imports from all WTO members are covered by the same Regulation. MFN also underlies the provisions on safeguard measures in the same Regulation, as where these are adopted they will apply to all imports of a particular product, whatever its origin.[46]

As far as autonomous measures are concerned, the major exception to MFN in the application of the common external tariff is of course the GSP system (Generalised System of Preferences). This has been in operation since 1971, and operates within the framework of the GATT "Enabling Clause".[47] The EC's GSP scheme[48] discriminates in favour of developing countries in modifying the normal common customs tariff rates for exports from those countries. This is envisaged by the GATT enabling clause. However, the Regulation also discriminates *between* developing countries, by granting extra reductions as "incentives" to certain countries. These include "special arrangements supporting measures to combat drugs" available to certain Latin American countries.[49] These arrangements, which have been in place since 1990, are unusual in that they are available only for a limited group of countries and the Regulation does not itself set out the basis on which the extra concessions are granted. Brazil, not one of the countries covered, has initiated WTO dispute settlement proceedings against the EC on the basis of this aspect of the GSP system, arguing that the resultant duty-free entry onto the EC market of soluble coffee from the Andean

[45] Council Regulation 519/94/EC of 7 March 1994 on common rules for imports from certain third countries and repealing Regulations 1765/82, 1766/82 and 3420/83 [1994] OJ L67/89, see text *infra* at n. 60.

[46] We are here focusing not on WTO compatibility generally, but only on the issue of discrimination. There are other ways in which the provisions on safeguards in the Regulation seek to comply with the WTO Agreement on Safeguards, e.g. Art. 16(1) and (2) requiring a cumulation of conditions before the imposition of safeguard measures against products originating in a WTO member country.

[47] Differential and More Favourable Treatment, Reciprocity and Fuller Participation of Developing Countries, Decision of the Contracting Parties of 28 November 1979, L/4903, Art. 1: "Notwithstanding the provisions of Article I of the General Agreement, contracting parties may accord differential and more favourable treatment to developing countries, without according such treatment to other contracting parties". This exception, known as the "Enabling Clause", expressly included the GSP under which non-reciprocal preferential tariff treatment is accorded on an autonomous basis by developed contracting parties to products originating in developing countries. The Decision also covered differential and more favourable treatment with respect to non-tariff measures, and special treatment for the least developed countries in the context of any general or specific measures in favour of developing countries.

[48] Council Regulation 2820/98/EC of 21 December 1998 applying a multiannual scheme of generalised tariff preferences for the period 1 July 1999 to 31 December 2001 [1998] OJ L357/1.

[49] Regulation 2820/98/EC Art. 7 and Annex V. The countries covered are the Andean Group (Colombia, Venezuela, Ecuador, Peru, Bolivia) and the Countries of the Central American Common Market (Guatemala, Honduras, El Salvador, Nicaragua, Costa Rica, Panama). EU involvement in action against illegal drugs within the region takes place within the context of the "Coordination and Cooperation Mechanism on Drugs between the EU, Latin American and Caribbean States", and the Action Plan on Drugs agreed in Panama in April 1999; see COM(1999)239 final, Communication from the Commission to the Council and the European Parliament on a European Union Action Plan to Combat Drugs (2000–2004), 26 May 1999.

and Central American states is inconsistent with Article I of GATT 1994 and the Enabling Clause.[50] Other incentive arrangements in the GSP Regulation, linked to compliance with certain international labour and environmental standards, are more transparent.[51] Here the Regulation contains detailed provisions governing the standards in question, investigation by the Commission, and monitoring and enforcement provisions.[52] These incentives are more defensible in MFN terms, being based on arguably objective standards, open to all GSP beneficiaries, and subject to procedural requirements.

Following the TBT Agreement, originally concluded as part of the Tokyo Round negotiations within GATT, the Council enacted a Decision designed to ensure national treatment for third country imports in relation to technical standards.[53] The Decision also deals with the possibility of mutual recognition of both standards and conformity assessment procedures, mutual recognition being closely connected with national treatment in both the Community and the WTO regimes.[54] As far as standards harmonised at Community level are concerned:

> The technical regulations, standards and certification and verification procedures laid down in the Directives for the removal of technical barriers to intra-Community trade shall apply . . . to all products on the Community market irrespective of their origin . . .[55]

Where there are no Community harmonised standards, Member States are to apply their national technical regulations, standards and certification and verification procedures on a non-discriminatory basis.[56]

As the Preamble to the Decision states, however, the TBT Agreement is based on the principle of reciprocity and so (in contrast to the position between Member States of the Community) where there is evidence of a lack of reciprocity, or discriminatory treatment applied by a trading partner, then appropriate measures may be taken which may derogate from the national treatment principle of Article 1, although they must nonetheless be taken "in accordance with" the provisions of the TBT Agreement.[57] This will include, for the

---

[50] *European Communities—Measures Affecting Differential and Favourable Treatment of Coffee*, complaint by Brazil (WT/DS154/1), 7 December 1998. See also WT/DS209/1, dated 12 October 2000.

[51] Regulation 2820/98/EC, *supra* n. 48, Arts. 8–21.

[52] The labour standards refer to implementation of ILO Conventions No 87 and No 98 concerning application of the principles of the right to organise and to bargain collectively and Convention No 138 concerning the minimum age of admission to employment. The environmental provisions refer to implementation of ITTO standards of forestry protection and apply to products originating in tropical forests (Art. 9 and Annex VIII).

[53] Council Decision 80/45/EEC of 15 January 1980 laying down provisions on the introduction and implementation of technical regulations and standards [1980] OJ L14/36.

[54] As discussed above, effective non-discrimination may require a willingness to recognise equivalence of different standards: see text at n. 29ff.

[55] Council Decision 80/45/EEC, *supra* n. 53, Art. 1(1).

[56] *Ibid.*, Art. 1(2).

[57] *Ibid.*, Art. 5.

Commission, taking account of the recommendations of the Committee on Technical Barriers to Trade provided for in Article 13 of the TBT Agreement. In comparison with the 1994 Trade Barriers Regulation, however, there is no explicit reference to the prior use of international trade dispute settlement procedures.[58]

Measures may also be taken by national customs authorities on grounds of product safety, and the Preamble to the general Council Regulation on safety of products imported from third countries indicates that the Community institutions were aware of their non-discrimination obligations and in particular of Article 2.2 of the TBT Agreement and Article XX of GATT 1994:

> such controls should comply with obligations incumbent upon the Community under GATT to conduct trade on a non-discriminatory basis and under the GATT Code on Technical Barriers to Trade, according to which standards should not be applied as a means of creating obstacles to international trade.[59]

So far, then, the general autonomous trade provisions we have considered in this Section appear to operate within the WTO framework of non-discrimination. What about countries which do not have the protection of WTO membership? Here a distinction is made between MFN and national treatment. While the Community adheres to the principle of national treatment in applying technical standards to products coming from *all* third states (see Decision 80/45 mentioned above), the same is not true of MFN treatment as regards quantitative restrictions. The general Regulation on common rules for imports does not apply to a group of non-WTO members, countries which are regarded as non-market economy states by the EU and which may be the subject of quantitative restrictions. These states are covered by a separate Regulation which was intended to establish uniformity between Member States in their treatment of imports from these countries and to remove derogations in favour of national commercial policies that had existed in former regulations.[60] A number of these

---

[58] Compare Council Regulation 3286/94/EC of 22 December 1994 laying down Community procedures in the field of the common commercial policy in order to ensure the exercise of the Community's rights under international trade rules, in particular those established under the auspices of the World Trade Organisation [1994] OJ L349/71, as amended by Regulation 356/95/EC [1995] OJ L41/3, Art. 12(2). This difference reflects the fact that Decision 80/45 was adopted prior to the establishment of the WTO dispute settlement procedures, whereas the Trade Barriers Regulation was adopted immediately following the conclusion of the WTO Agreements.

[59] Council Regulation 339/93/EEC of 8 February 1993 on checks for conformity with the rules on product safety in the case of products imported from third countries [1993] OJ L40/1. It should be noted, however, that Art. 24(2)(a)(i) of the common import Regulation 3285/94/EC, which allows Member States to restrict imports from third countries on grounds which mirror Art. 30 EC does not contain any equivalent to the second sentence of Art. 30 prohibiting "arbitrary discrimination or a disguised restriction on trade".

[60] Council Regulation 519/94/EC of 7 March 1994 on common rules for imports from certain third countries and repealing Regulations 1765/82, 1766/82 and 3420/83 [1994] OJ L67/89. Countries covered include Russia and other states of the former Soviet Union, North Korea, Vietnam and China. The only quotas currently actually imposed under the regulation relate to imports of certain products from China.

countries however, are entitled to MFN treatment (for their imports of industrial products at least) under bilateral agreements.

Non-discrimination in Agricultural Market Organisations

The picture becomes less clear when we move away from quantitative restrictions as such and on to tariff quotas which may be imposed in the context of an agricultural market organisation. We have already seen that such tariff quotas, involving import licensing systems, will be subject to WTO non-discrimination rules found, *inter alia*, in Articles I, III and XIII of GATT 1994. As far as the Community dimension of non-discrimination is concerned, the principle is here playing a regulatory role, to use More's terminology. Market organisations involve legislative and executive interventions in the market, interventions which distinguish between different sectors and economic activities in order to achieve specific objectives. Non-discrimination thus operates as a constraint on the discretion of the legislative institutions, imposing, at least in principle, the requirement of objective justification for differential treatment. The EC Treaty is explicit about one form of non-discrimination: under Article 34(2) common organisations of agricultural markets "shall exclude any discrimination between producers and consumers within the Community". The Court of Justice has built on this to create a generalised principle of equality. In *Ruckdeschel* the Court held:

> The prohibition of discrimination laid down in [Article 34(2)] is merely a specific enunciation of the general principle of equality which is one of the fundamental principles of Community law. This principle requires that similar situations shall not be treated differently unless differentiation is objectively justified.[61]

The requirement of objective justification allows the Court (and the legislator) to take into account the particular needs of the market in question and the efficient operation of the system:

> [the difference in treatment] is justified by the need to limit the number of years which may be taken as reference years, in the interests of both legal certainty and the effectiveness of the additional levy system. The resulting difference in treatment is therefore objectively justified and consequently may not be regarded as discriminatory within the definition of that concept as established by the Court.[62]

It can indeed be argued that the Court is so willing to take these considerations into account, and to recognise a wide executive discretion in formulating policy

---

[61] Joined Cases 117/76 & 16/77, *Albert Ruckdeschel & Co. et Hansa-Lagerhaus Ströh & Co.* v. *Hauptzollamt Hamburg-St. Annen; Diamalt AG* v. *Hauptzollamt Itzehoe* [1977] ECR 75, at para. 7.
[62] Case 84/87, *Marcel Erpelding* v. *Secrétaire d'Etat à l'Agriculture et à la Viticulture* [1988] ECR 2647 at para. 30.

objectives, that the principle of non-discrimination has become, in this area at least, little more than a "symbolic reminder" of the rule of law.[63]

It is this ability of the Community legislator to put forward internal policy objectives as "objective justifications" for differential treatment (and thereby rebut the allegation of discrimination) which the Community tried without success to rely on in the *Bananas* case before the WTO Appellate Body.[64] Before the European Court, the Council's arguments notoriously met with more success and the Court's reasoning sheds light on the principle of non-discrimination as it applies to the Community's external trade policy.

We should start with the case of *Faust*, an action for damages brought by a German importer in relation to protective measures adopted by the Commission with respect to imports of preserved mushrooms from third countries, in this case from Taiwan.[65] Protective measures were applied to those countries that had not entered into voluntary export restraints to the Commission's satisfaction. The Commission, the Court held, had not acted outside the scope of its discretion, since "the Council Regulations pursuant to which those measures were adopted expressly permitted a selective application in favour or to the detriment of certain non-member countries, thus leaving to the Commission a wide measure of discretion".[66] Nor had the Commission misused its powers under the Regulation by acting, not solely in order to avoid internal market disturbance, but also for external commercial objectives. The external objective in question, Faust alleged, derived from the recently concluded trade agreement with China. The Court pointed out that the relevant regulations (from which the Commission derived its powers to take protective measures) contained, in their Preambles, references to both Article 131 (ex Article 110) EC and the need to respect the Community's obligations under international agreements. The Court recognised "two equally legitimate objectives" of the measure, "namely stabilization of the market and implementation of a community policy relating to external trade". In a crucial passage, the Court then rejects the complaint on the basis of discrimination on the ground that there is no general principle of non-discrimination with respect to non-Member States:

> Although Taiwan certainly appears to have been treated by the Commission less favourably than certain non-member countries, it should be remembered that there exists in the Treaty no general principle obliging the Community, in its external relations, to accord to non-member countries equal treatment in all respects. It is thus not necessary to examine on what basis Faust might seek to rely upon the prohibition of discrimination between producers or consumers within the community contained in

---

[63] More, *supra* n. 3, 517 at 549, citing *inter alia* R. Barents, "Recent Developments in Community Case Law in the Field of Agriculture" (1997) 34 *CMLRev.* 811.

[64] It will be recalled that the Appellate Body took the view that the objectives of a measure were not relevant in determining the existence of discrimination under the GATS rules: see text *supra* at n. 17.

[65] Case 52/81, *Offene Handelsgesellschaft in Firma Werner Faust* v. *Commission* [1982] ECR 3745.

[66] *Ibid.*, at para. 9.

Article 40 [now Article 34] of the Treaty. It need merely be observed that, if different treatment of non-member countries is compatible with Community law, different treatment accorded to traders within the Community must also be regarded as compatible with Community law, where that different treatment is merely an automatic consequence of the different treatment accorded to non-member countries with which such traders have entered into commercial relations.[67]

In the absence of an overriding obligation to accord equal treatment to non-member countries, the conclusion of the trade agreement with China should have alerted traders to the likelihood of changes in import policy and patterns of trade; the Court was thus also able to reject an argument based on protection of legitimate expectations. According to this case, therefore, there is no general principle of non-discrimination with respect to non-member countries deriving from Community law *per se*. Non-discrimination in relation to specific third countries will thus have to be derived from contractual obligations, if any, either under bilateral agreements with the Community, or through membership of the WTO.

In *Germany* v. *Council (bananas I)*[68] the challenge by Germany was to the regulation adopted in 1993 which established a common organisation of the market for bananas. The regulation[69] was an attempt to harmonise the very different pre-existent policies in the Member States with respect to banana imports while complying with Community obligations under the Lomé Convention.[70] A complex series of arguments was put forward by Germany supporting its view that certain aspects of the regulation were invalid, in particular those which removed the German right to import a quota of non-ACP bananas tariff-free under the so-called "Banana Protocol" annexed to the (then) EEC Treaty in 1957. These included allegations of breaches of essential procedural requirements, of substantive rules and of fundamental principles of Community law, the Lomé Convention, the GATT and the Banana Protocol. We are here concerned with the principle of non-discrimination, applied as a fundamental principle of Community law.

Non-discrimination was at issue here, as in *Faust*, in the context of the operation of a common organisation of the market for an agricultural product. Germany had argued that the 1993 Regulation discriminated against traders in third country (non-ACP) bananas by subdividing the tariff quota in favour of importers of Community and/or traditional ACP bananas. The Court starts with the "general principle of equality which is one of the fundamental principles of Community law" and which requires that "comparable situations are

---

[67] *Ibid.*, at para. 25.

[68] Case C–280/93, *Germany* v. *Council* [1994] ECR I–4973.

[69] Council Regulation 404/93/EEC of 13 February 1993 on the common organisation of the market in bananas [1993] OJ L47/1.

[70] The Fourth Lomé Convention was signed at Lomé, Togo, on 15 December 1989 [1991] OJ L229/3; a revised text of Lomé IV following mid-term review was signed in Mauritius 4 November 1995, Council and Commission Decision of 27 April 1998 [1998] OJ L156/1.

not treated in a different manner unless the difference in treatment is objectively justified". Given the very different situations of the different categories of traders before the introduction of the common organisation, it is to be expected that some will be more adversely affected than others:

> It is true that since the Regulation came into force those categories of economic operators have been affected differently by the measures adopted. Operators traditionally essentially supplied by third-country bananas now find their import possibilities restricted, whereas those formerly obliged to market essentially Community and ACP bananas may now import specified quantities of third-country bananas.
>
> However, such a difference in treatment appears to be inherent in the objective of integrating previously compartmentalized markets, bearing in mind the different situations of the various categories of economic operators before the establishment of the common organization of the market. The Regulation is intended to ensure the disposal of Community production and traditional ACP production, which entails the striking of a balance between the two categories of economic operators in question.[71]

The Court appears to be arguing both that the categories of trader were not "comparable" because of earlier differences between national markets (thus arguably perpetuating the differences), and that differential treatment is objectively justified ("striking a balance" between the traders) in terms of the Regulation's objectives. We have already seen that differential treatment may be justified in terms of the objectives of the common organisation in question[72] and thus the framing of the objectives of the Regulation is crucial here. The reference in the passage just quoted is to "the disposal of Community production and traditional ACP production" (no commitments in relation to non-ACP third country production). Earlier in the judgment the Court had expanded on this point in discussing whether the legal basis of Article 37 (formerly Article 43) was adequate where the common organisation had a development policy dimension. The Court accepts that in some cases "the internal and external aspects of the common policy cannot be separated" and that therefore "the creation of a common organisation of the market requires, alongside the regulation of Community production, the establishment of an import regime to stabilize the markets and ensure sales of Community production", while at the same time recognising the obligation not to disregard the Community's international obligations under the Lomé Convention.[73] The Court here strikingly frames the objectives of the external dimension of the common organisation in terms of the needs of the internal market—stabilisation of markets and ensuring sales of Community production. This is, essentially, a recognition of the principle of Community preference, subject to the overriding demands of a specific contractual obligation towards certain non-member countries. Where there are no such overriding obligations, then the internal needs of the Community market may—

---

[71] Case C–280/93, *Germany* v. *Council, supra* n. 68 at paras. 73–74.
[72] See Case 84/87, *Marcel Erpelding* v. *Secrétaire d'Etat à l'Agriculture et à la Viticulture* [1988] ECR 2647.
[73] Case C–280/93, *Germany* v. *Council, supra* n. 68 at paras. 55–56.

legally as far as Community law is concerned—result in discrimination against third country products and those importing them.

The next two cases also arose out of the bananas dispute. In *Germany v. Council (Bananas II)*[74] and *T. Port III*[75] the Court applies *Faust*, but this time in its application of the principle of non-discrimination it makes a distinction between different aspects of Community policy which is significant for this discussion. Germany brought an action for the annulment of the Council Decision concluding the Framework Agreement on Bananas (FAB) between the EC and Costa Rica, Colombia, Nicaragua and Venezuela, designed to settle the dispute concerning the EC's banana import regime which had led to the (unadopted) Panel Report January 1994.[76] Germany had already—unsuccessfully— requested an Opinion on the compatibility of the FAB with the Treaty under Article 300(6) EC.[77] In *T. Port III* the referring court questioned the legality of the Regulation implementing the FAB.[78] In both cases the claim was based on allegations of breaches of Community law principles in the system set up by the FAB and its implementing regulations: discrimination against certain categories of trader (Category A and C operators) as compared with Category B operators, their fundamental rights, namely their freedom to pursue a trade or business and their right to property, and contravention of the principles of the protection of legitimate expectations and of proportionality. In considering the possibility of discrimination the Court follows identical reasoning in the two cases, making a critical distinction between the country-based quotas established by the FAB, and the export licence system which applied to all FAB countries and to some but not all Community operators.

The allocation of quotas on a country-of-export basis does not contravene the Community concept of non-discrimination because it is merely the inevitable internal reflection of the discrimination between third countries which, as the Court had held in *Faust*, is not prohibited under the general principle of non-discrimination. The Court had held, in the *Bananas I* case, that it was legitimate in Community law terms to differentiate between third-country and non-traditional ACP bananas on the one hand and traditional imports from the ACP countries on the other by introducing a global tariff quota for the former group of imports. The allocation of this quota among importers was the natural consequence of that distinction:

> there is no general principle of Community law obliging the Community, in its external relations, to accord third countries equal treatment in all respects. Therefore . . . if different treatment of third countries is compatible with Community law, then

[74] Case C–122/95, *Germany v. Council* [1998] ECR I–973.
[75] Joined Cases C–364/95 and C–365/95, *T. Port GmbH & Co. v. Hauptzollamt Hamburg-Jonas* [1998] ECR I–1023.
[76] DS 38/R.
[77] *Opinion 3/94* [1995] ECR I–4577. The Court rejected the request as Art. 300(6) EC only applies to "envisaged" agreements and by this stage the FAB had already been concluded. The action for annulment under Art. 230 EC is the proper recourse in these circumstances.
[78] Commission Regulation 478/95/EC of 1 March 1995 [1995] OJ L49/13.

different treatment accorded to traders within the Community must also be regarded as compatible with Community law where that different treatment is merely an automatic consequence of the different treatment accorded to third countries with which such traders have entered into commercial relations.[79]

The export-licence system, on the other hand, creates a difference in treatment which "is not . . . the automatic consequence of any difference of treatment of some third countries as compared with others". The Court is at pains to distinguish between differential treatment which results from Community policy towards different groups of third countries, and differentiation between groups of Community traders as regards imports from the same (non-ACP) country— some (Categories A and C) will require export licences but some (Category B) will be exempt. The former is not inherently discriminatory in Community law terms; the latter must be objectively justified.

The Council based its justification on the need to maintain, in the context of the quota increase for the FAB parties, the "balance" between categories of trader established by the 1993 Regulation. This "balance" had been accepted by the Court in *Bananas I* ("balance" here being used to describe an inequality of treatment which was justified in terms of the needs of the internal market organisation). The Court was not convinced: Category B operators also benefited from the increased quota and did not need this additional benefit of exemption from paying for export licences that their competitors would have to buy. In so far as the export licence system was intended to benefit the FAB exporting states, it was not permissible to achieve this in a way which burdened some Community operators and not others. Note that the Court does not hold that *any* differential treatment between categories of trader is discriminatory: rather, it confirms the need for the differential accepted in *Bananas I* and holds that the Council had not shown why the objective situation had changed to the extent that a further "re-balancing" was required.

Four fundamental points emerge at this stage from this case law. First, there is in Community law no general Treaty-based principle of non-discrimination, or equal treatment, applicable to third countries. Secondly, as a result, differential treatment between Community operators that is merely an automatic consequence of difference of treatment between third countries will not be regarded as discriminatory. Thirdly, in other cases differential treatment between Community operators will require objective justification. Fourthly, such objective justification, although it may well affect the position of third country exporters, may (in the absence of a general principle of non-discrimination) legitimately be defined entirely in terms of internal Community policy needs, including market integration, the protection of Community producers, and the protection of producers from other favoured third countries. The needs of internal market integration may take precedence over external trade liberalisation.

[79] Case C–122/95, *Germany* v. *Council, supra* n. 74, at para. 56.

How do these conclusions relate to the WTO principle of non-discrimination? The (internal) Community concept of non-discrimination does not distinguish between MFN and national treatment. However the lack of such a distinction arguably accounts for some of the difficulties in the Court's reasoning in these cases involving tariff quotas. National treatment applies, as we have seen, to measures affecting the internal sale of products, such as technical standards and regulatory requirements. It is understandable that Community law should not contain a general national treatment rule with respect to the *quantitative* aspects of the treatment of third country imports, any more than for tariffs.[80] To exclude MFN is another matter. Quantitative restrictions are *prima facie* abolished under the WTO rules, but where they still operate (safeguard measures, tariff quotas) they should be applied on an MFN basis (Article XIII of GATT 1994). Community secondary legislation applies MFN to safeguard measures, as we have seen, but in the case of tariff quotas the legislator (backed up by the Court) has been prepared to subordinate MFN to the objectives of common market organisations. This goes beyond Community preference in the sense of denial of national treatment; discrimination *between* trading partners may be acceptable under Community law where this serves internal market objectives or, as in *Faust*, external trade policy.

In *Faust*, the two non-member countries concerned were China and Taiwan, neither of them GATT parties, neither of them with agreements with the Community that required non-discriminatory treatment as far as quantitative restrictions were concerned.[81] In the following section we will examine the non-discrimination principle as it operates within a number of Community agreements. In the final section we will consider the interaction between the EC and WTO legal orders. At this point, we can briefly consider whether the approach of the Court outlined above takes account of the fact that WTO member countries are in question.

In none of the banana cases does the Court of Justice consider that the operation of the Community concept of non-discrimination as it applies to third country imports (and traders in those goods) is affected by WTO rules of MFN

---

[80] Under the WTO regime, national treatment within Art. III:4 GATT 1994 does not apply to an import licence regime *per se*: "the fact that imported products may be subject to . . . the imposition of a licensing requirement taken as such, whereas the marketing of domestic products is obviously not, cannot per se violate Article III:4 of GATT": *European Communities—Regime for the Importation, Sale and Distribution of Bananas*, Panel Report *supra* n. 0 at para. 7.173. Art. III:4 may however apply to the distribution of import licences to operators within the Community, where they "go beyond the mere import licence requirements needed to administer the tariff quota" and are intended as an instrument of cross-subsidisation by favouring domestic operators who imported EC bananas: *Bananas*, AB Report, *supra* n. 9, 9 September 1997 at para. 211.

[81] The 1978 Trade Agreement between the European Economic Community and China [1978] OJ L123/2, contained a reciprocal MFN clause applicable to tariffs and charges (Art. 1); under Art. 4(2) the EC will "strive for an increasing liberalization of imports from the People's Republic of China" and "will endeavour progressively to introduce measures extending the list of products for which imports from China have been liberalized and to increase the amounts of quotas". This agreement was replaced by a Trade and Economic Cooperation Agreement in 1985 OJ 1985 L250/2, with similar trade provisions. There is no agreement with Taiwan.

or national treatment. This issue was raised in *Germany* v. *Council (Bananas I)*[82] but the fact that the third country bananas came from countries that were parties to the GATT is not even discussed. International obligations under the GATT are not taken into account because "it is only if the Community intended to implement a particular obligation entered into within the framework of GATT, or if the Community act expressly refers to specific provisions of GATT, that the Court can review the lawfulness of the Community act in question from the point of view of the GATT rules".[83] Neither of these conditions applied, the Court held. After the coming into force of the WTO Agreements, in *Germany* v. *Council (Bananas II)*[84] and *T. Port III*,[85] the Court again ignores the possible implications of WTO membership. In the former case, compatibility with the GATT was not argued by Germany and the Court merely refers to its earlier judgement. In *T. Port III* the national referring court raised the question in the context of Article 307 EC which preserves the rights of third countries under international agreements concluded by the Member States before the entry into force of the EC Treaty (or before the date of their accession to the Community). The Court was able to discount the question because the third country whose exports were in question—Ecuador—had acceded to the WTO (and therefore the GATT) only in 1996, after the date of the relevant banana exports to the Community.[86] Since these cases, the Court has held in a different context that "the WTO Agreements are not in principle among the rules in the light of which the Court is to review the legality of measures adopted by the Community institutions".[87]

Non-discrimination in Community Agreements

In contrast to the Court's approach to the GATT and WTO, in *Bananas I* it was accepted that the Council, in determining the common organisation for the market in bananas, was bound to ensure compliance with the Community's obligations under the Lomé Convention.[88] The Lomé obligations at issue in this case centred on the preferential trade provisions: a general ACP preference clause in Article 168(2)(a), and the specific provisions relating to bananas under Protocol 5 to the Convention. Preferential agreements such as the Lomé Convention, or

---

[82] Case C–280/93, *Germany* v. *Council* [1994] ECR I–4973.

[83] *Ibid.*, at para. 111, citing Case 70/87, *Fediol* v. *Commission* [1989] ECR 1781 and Case C–69/89, *Nakajima* v. *Council* [1991] ECR I–2069.

[84] Case C–122/95, *Germany* v. *Council* [1998] ECR I–973.

[85] Joined Cases C–364/95 and c–365/95 *T. Port GmbH & Co.* v. *Hauptzollamt Hamburg-Jonas* [1998] ECR I–1023.

[86] *Ibid.*, at paras. 58–64; Elmer AG had argued that the earlier case law denying any direct effect to the GATT should be confirmed as regard GATT 1994: paras. 28–29.

[87] Case C–149/96 [1999] ECR I-8395, *Portuguese Republic* v. *Council*, judgment of 23 November 1999, at para. 47. See further the contribution by S. Peers in this volume.

[88] Case C–280/93, *Germany* v. *Council* [1994] ECR I–4973.

the Europe Agreements, clearly go beyond MFN treatment in at least some areas of trade with the EU. Hence the need for exemption from the normal WTO MFN obligation, either through the general Article XXIV GATT 1994 (or Article V GATS) exception, or via a specific waiver. The EC needed a specific waiver for the Lomé Convention, since this non-reciprocal preferential agreement with a group of developing countries does not qualify for an Article XXIV GATT 1994 exemption; and by favouring only certain developing countries it does not fall within the GSP Enabling Clause or other provisions accommodating non-MFN preferential treatment for developing countries. This waiver, agreed under Article XXV(5) of GATT, allowed an exception to the MFN obligation in Article I of GATT 1994:

> Subject to the terms and conditions set out hereunder, the provisions of paragraph 1 of Article I of the General Agreement shall be waived, until 29 February 2000, to the extent necessary to permit the European Communities to provide preferential treatment for products originating in ACP States as required by the relevant provisions of the Fourth Lomé Convention, without being required to extend the same preferential treatment to like products of any other contracting party.[89]

It is the scope of this waiver, and the tension between the fundamental WTO non-discrimination rules and the special preferences given to some, but not all, developing country exporters, that have given rise to the disputes over the Community's banana regime.[90] The new Partnership Agreement between the EC and the 71 ACP states, designed to replace the fourth Lomé Convention, envisages the continuation of non-reciprocal preferences during a "preparatory period" of eight years, during which the parties will conclude an agreement on WTO-compatible trading arrangements. The EC and the ACP have made an application under Article IX:3 of the WTO Agreement for a waiver for the new Agreement to cover this preparatory period.[91]

Apart from such preferential trading arrangements, however, the Lomé Convention, the new EU–ACP Partnership Agreement and other preferential agreements also contain non-discrimination provisions. In this section we will examine the role of such non-discrimination clauses in Community agreements by looking at two examples, from the Lomé Convention, and from the

[89] The Fourth ACP–EEC Convention of Lomé, Decision of the Contracting Parties of 9 December 1994, L/7604.

[90] As an exception to a fundamental principle, this waiver was interpreted strictly by the Appellate Body in the *Bananas* case, both in holding that it applied only to Article I and not to Article XIII (*Bananas*, AB Report, *supra* n. 9, at para. 183) and in its interpretation of the phrase "as required by" the Lomé Convention in the context of the EC's import licensing regime for traditional and non-traditional ACP and third country bananas (*Bananas*, AB Report, *supra* n. 9, at paras. 167–178). See S. Peers, "Banana Split: WTO Law and Preferential Agreements in the EC Legal Order" (1999) 4 *EFA Rev.* 195; F. Smith, "Renegotiating Lomé: the Impact of the World Trade Organisation on the European Community's Development Policy after the Bananas Conflict" (2000) 25 *EL Rev.* 247.

[91] The new Agreement was signed in June 2000, in Cotonou, Benin; the trade provisions of the new Agreement were applied provisionally from 1 March 2000 following a Decision of the ACP–EC Committee of Ambassadors on 29 February 2000.

Association Agreement with Cyprus, against the background of the conclusions we have drawn in the context of autonomous measures.

Non-discrimination, Taxation and the Lomé Convention

The first example brings together two of the topics we have already discussed: internal taxation and bananas. Most Community trade agreements do contain a prohibition on discriminatory internal taxation and some of these reflect the wording of Article 90 EC. They have been held to be directly effective.[92] However, this does not necessarily imply that they will be interpreted in the same way as Article 90: "the interpretations given to Article 95 [now 90] of the Treaty cannot be applied by way of simple analogy to the Agreement on free trade".[93] Provisions of this Article 90-type are found in, for example, the EEA Agreement, the Association Agreement with Turkey, the Europe Agreements, and the Free Trade Agreement with Switzerland. Other agreements, particularly those with non-WTO members, reflect the wording of Article III of GATT, thereby (as with the MFN provisions in these agreements) bringing these states into a level of trading relationship equivalent to GATT rules (for example the Partnership and Cooperation Agreement with Russia).

Although the Fourth Lomé Convention does not contain a general non-discrimination clause apart from the statement in Article 2 that "equality between partners" is a fundamental principle of the Convention, there are a number of provisions dealing with non-discrimination in specific sectors. In the field of trade the ACP states are to accord the Community treatment "no less favourable than" MFN treatment; this MFN obligation in practice relates to developed states: it does not apply to trade between ACP states or between one or more ACP states and other developing countries.[94] The ACP states also undertake not to discriminate among the EU Member States.[95] The Community, which undertakes the removal of all customs duties and quantitative restrictions on ACP products (with special provision for agricultural products), "shall not discriminate between the ACP States".[96]

---

[92] Case 104/81, *Hauptzollampt Mainz* v. *Kupferberg* [1982] ECR 3641 at para. 27.

[93] *Ibid.*, at para. 30.

[94] Fourth Lomé Convention as amended at Mauritius November 1995 [1998] OJ L156/1, Art. 174(2)(a) and (c). There is also a more specific MFN clause relating to the tax and customs treatment of contracts financed by the Community: Art. 308.

[95] *Ibid.*, Arts. 25 and 174(2)(a).

[96] *Ibid.*, Art. 174(2)(b). There are, however, provisions which make special provision for the least developed, the landlocked and the island states: see Art. 8 and Part III, Title IV. The trade provisions in Annex V to the new EU–ACP Partnership Agreement (the successor to the Lomé Convention), replace this Community obligation with a Joint Declaration on non-discrimination which reflects the existing Article 174(2)(b), but with an increased emphasis on the need for differentiation in favour of the least-developed countries:

"The Parties agree that notwithstanding specific provisions of Annex V to this Agreement, the Community shall not discriminate between ACP States in the trade regime provided for in the framework of that Annex, taking account however of the provisions of this Agreement and of

A notable absence from the current Lomé Convention is any provision on non-discrimination in relation to internal taxation, equivalent to either Article III:2 of GATT 1994 or Article 90 EC. We have already seen that Article 90 does not apply to third country goods directly imported into an EU Member State, and that Article 133 does not itself contain any presumption or rule of non-discrimination.[97] However, in the *Simba* case, the Court went on to point out that provisions in international agreements to which the Community is a party may be relevant. It even invited the national court (and by implication the parties) to look at the Lomé Convention, referring to the obligation not to use protectionist measures found in (what is now) Article 177(2) of Lomé and reminding the national court that it had already declared the banana tax to be of a protectionist nature in the context of Article 90(2) EC.[98]

However when the challenge was taken up in *Chiquita Italia*, a case brought the following year, the Court accepted that the Lomé Convention was relevant, but would not interpret any of its general trade provisions so as to prohibit the protectionist tax.[99] In the first place, the Convention contained no direct prohibition of discriminatory taxation, and the Court refused to imply such a provision into the Convention. Whereas Article 90 EC has been interpreted broadly by the Court in order to ensure that it serves to fill up any gaps in the Treaty prohibition on barriers to free movement,[100] interpretation is more constrained within the context of a Community agreement:

> if the Community and the ACP States had wished to deal with the question of internal taxation in the framework of the general trade arrangements put in place by the Convention, they would have done so precisely by adopting a provision modelled on Article 95 [now 90] of the EC Treaty.[101]

For similar reasons the Court would not apply the anti-protectionist provision in Article 177(2) or the prohibition of quantitative restrictions in Article 169(1) of the Lomé Convention to the tax. Although within the EC Treaty these provisions (and especially Article 28 EC) could be seen as a connected whole with an overall objective of achieving free movement of goods, this was not the case here:

specific autonomous initiatives in the multilateral context, such as that in favour of the least developed countries pursued by the Community."

[97] See discussion of Case C–228/90, *Simba SpA (bananas)* [1992] ECR I–3713 in text *supra* at n. 41.

[98] Case C–228/90, *Simba SpA* [1992] ECR I–3713 at paras. 20–21.

[99] Case C–469/93, *Amministrazione delle Finanze dello Stato v. Chiquita Italia SpA* [1995] ECR I–4533.

[100] See, e.g., Case 142/77, *Statens Kontrol med ædle Metaller v. Preben Larsen* [1978] ECR 1543 at paras. 20–25; Case 193/85, *Cooperativa Co-Frutta Srl v. Amministrazione delle finanze dello Stato* [1987] ECR 2085 at paras. 24–29.

[101] Case C–469/93, *Amministrazione delle Finanze dello Stato v. Chiquita Italia SpA* [1995] ECR I–4533 at para. 43. The Court was also influenced by the fact that the Second Yaoundé Convention (precursor to Lomé) does contain an equivalent to Art. 90 EC; the omission thus appears deliberate.

That argument of Chiquita Italia presupposes that both the EC Treaty and the Fourth ACP-EEC Convention seek to ensure a free movement of goods which is exempt from any obstacle whatsoever, including those resulting from discriminatory internal taxation.

That line of argument cannot be adopted. It follows from the settled case-law of the Court that the extension of the interpretation of a provision in the Treaty to a comparably, similarly or even identically worded provision of an agreement concluded by the Community with a non-member country depends inter alia on the aim pursued by each provision in its particular context and that a comparison between the objectives and context of the agreement and those of the Treaty is of considerable importance in that regard . . .[102]

Nevertheless, the banana importers were not finally disappointed. They could, the Court held, rely on Article 1 of Protocol 5, which provides that "In respect of its banana exports to the Community markets, no ACP State shall be placed, as regards access to its traditional markets and its advantages on those markets, in a less favourable situation than in the past or at present". In so far as the tax was introduced after the coming into force of the first Lomé Convention in 1976, it was a breach of that obligation. The absence of any reference to internal taxation in the general trade provisions was not an obstacle here, since the provisions on bananas (and rum) were explicitly declared to be "special undertakings" and could therefore operate as a *lex specialis* in relation to the general trade provisions.

The absence of any general non-discrimination clause in a Community agreement may give rise to difficulties where there is no clause covering a particular sector, as we have just seen in relation to internal taxation in context of the Lomé Convention. It also means that there is little scope for non-discrimination to move from operating in the economic sphere as an instrument of market access to becoming a fundamental right as part of a constitutional framework, or even emerging as a regulatory principle; non-discrimination is tied to specific economic activities, such as trade in goods.

Non-discrimination in the Association Agreement with Cyprus

Even where there is a general non-discrimination clause in a Community agreement, this does not necessarily mean that it will possess the status of a fundamental and overriding principle. The clause will take on a role and colour in the context of a trade agreement which may be rather different from the autonomous nature of the non-discrimination rule in Article 12 EC, for example. The *Anastasiou* case illustrates this point well.[103] The case arose out of the UK customs authorities' practice of accepting origin and phytosanitary certifi-

---

[102] Case C–469/93, *Amministrazione delle Finanze dello Stato* v. *Chiquita Italia SpA* [1995] ECR I–4533 at paras. 51–52.

[103] Case C–432/92, *R.* v. *Minister of Agriculture, Fisheries and Food, ex parte S.P.Anastasiou (Pissouri) Ltd and Others* [1994] ECR I–3087.

cates issued by the authorities in the northern (Turkish-occupied) zone of Cyprus (TRNC) in the name of the "Republic of Cyprus" or the "Cyprus Customs Authorities". A number of producers and exporters of citrus fruit and potatoes from the southern zone sought to ensure that the UK Minister of Agriculture, Fisheries and Food (MAFF) would only accept certificates actually issued by the Republic of Cyprus (and not those issued from the northern zone without the authority of the Republic of Cyprus). The UK, supported by the Commission, centred its argument on the non-discrimination provision in Article 5 of the EC–Cyprus Association Agreement, under which the fruit and vegetables were entitled to preferential access to the Community market (access that was dependent on the origin certificates):

> The rules governing trade between the Contracting Parties may not give rise to any discrimination between . . . nationals or companies of Cyprus.

According to this argument, the Agreement applied to trade between the EC and the whole of Cyprus, and so any commercial benefits of the Agreement should benefit the entire population of Cyprus; the policy of the Community and its Member States not to recognise the TRNC should not deprive the people (nationals or companies) in the northern zone of the benefits of the Agreement. The Court did not agree. It gave priority to the rules of origin contained in a Protocol to the Agreement, and to the need for a reliable certification system to determine origin. These rules could not be altered unilaterally by one party to the Agreement and had certainly not been altered by agreement with the Republic of Cyprus. Consequently they must be applied strictly, and the principle of non-discrimination, although important, must be balanced against the other general aims of the Agreement, in particular the need for certainty in the operation of preferential trade measures. This was a matter of "the proper operation of the trade arrangements" and not "mere administrative arrangements". Reliability and confidence in the system are not the only factors however: the Court also stressed the need for unity between the Member States in the application of the Agreement and the uniformity of the common commercial policy:

> the practice followed . . . reflects the absence of a uniform approach on the part of the Member States. Although some Member States have accepted certificates issued by authorities other than those of the Republic of Cyprus, others have not. The existence of different practices among the Member States thus creates uncertainty of a kind likely to undermine the existence of a common commercial policy and the performance by the Community of its obligations under the Association Agreement.[104]

Non-discrimination, as a principle in a Community Agreement, therefore, is to be seen as "only one of its objectives" and will not necessarily override others, including the "proper operation" of the agreement and the need for uniformity in Community policy and practice.

---

[104] *Ibid.*, at paras. 52–53.

INTERCONNECTED LEGAL ORDERS

We have seen that although the fundamental principle of non-discrimination in the EC Treaty as it applies as between the Community Member States reflects (although is not identical to) the non-discrimination obligations under the WTO Agreements, the same is not the case for non-discrimination in the context of the EC's external trade relations.

The absence of any generalised statement of principle in the commercial policy provisions of the Treaty itself leads to the unwillingness of the Court to imply such a principle either to acts of the Member States (the *Simba* case) or the Community institutions (the bananas cases) where there is no explicit commitment in the secondary legislation. Even though Community policy and legislation is circumscribed by obligations entered into within bilateral agreements, non-discrimination clauses in these agreements are linked to specific economic activities as only one among the many objectives, rather than expressed as a general constitutional principle (*Chiquita Italia, Anastasiou*).

Community preferential agreements relate to WTO concepts of non-discrimination in another way. By definition they offer more than MFN treatment to the Community's trading partner. They may be defensible in WTO terms by virtue of Article XXIV of GATT 1994 or Article V of GATS, or as a result of an agreed specific waiver (such as is being sought for the new EU–ACP Partnership Agreement). Nevertheless, they—and particularly their proliferation—undermine the concept of multilateral unconditional non-discrimination (MFN) by replacing it with a myriad of bilateral highly conditional preferences, reciprocal or not. In one sense, the stronger the non-discrimination clauses in such agreements are, the greater the derogation from the basic WTO MFN-based system.

This is in part a question of the uncertainty surrounding the proper scope and operation of Article XXIV but it is not just about a failure of the rules. It is a challenge to the idea of classic MFN as a basis for trade liberalisation. Nor is it only a problem at the global level: as Sapir has pointed out, the proliferation of preferential (mainly free trade) agreements within Europe itself creates an inherently discriminatory system.[105] Not only does each state within Europe not have an agreement with every other state, not only is each agreement different in terms of coverage and preferences (what the *Economist* called "highly developed" discrimination); there is also an imbalance in the EC's favour: the EC has by far the highest number of such agreements,[106] creating a hub and spoke effect which favours the centre at the expense of the rim. Sapir suggests the possibility

---

[105] A. Sapir, "Trade Regionalism in Europe: Towards an Integrated Approach" (2000) 38 *JCMS* 151 at 158. Looking only at agreements between Council of Europe members, Sapir estimates 90 RTAs of which 86 are bilateral agreements.

[106] The EC has bilateral RTAs with 20 out of the 25 European states which are Council of Europe members (and one with one other European state which is not yet a Council of Europe member: Belarus): Sapir, *ibid.*, n. 105 at 152.

of creating a regional MFN clause for Europe, which would generalise the existing preferences and effectively create a pan-European free trade area.[107] Such a possibility of course highlights the difficulty such regional agreements create for WTO-based MFN. John Jackson also suggests the need for a new approach to MFN:

> there are so many variations and so many possible preferential arrangements, that nations entering them may find it necessary to develop a new type of MFN clause: a clause that will ensure to the preference parties preferences at least as favourable as those granted to other potential preferential parties when a nation belonging to one enters into additional similar arrangements.[108]

This relationship between the bilateral and regional trade agreements and the multilateral MFN-based system suggests that we need finally to turn to a brief examination of the interaction between the bilateral and multilateral legal orders from the particular perspective of the European Union.

Where a new member accedes to the EU, it joins the EU customs union aligning its external tariffs to the EU's common external tariff and becoming a part of the EU's extensive preferential trade regime. This affects the EU's other trading partners, and negotiations with other WTO members will be necessary with a view to achieving "mutually satisfactory compensatory adjustment" under Article XXIV:6 of GATT 1994 and paragraph 5 of the Understanding on the Interpretation of Article XXIV of the General Agreement on Tariffs and Trade 1994. According to the European Court of Justice in *Italy* v. *Council*, the concept of a "mutually satisfactory compensatory adjustment" does not constitute an "objective criterion" against which the legality of a specific agreement can be measured.[109] For compliance with Article XXIV, it is necessary to show only that an agreement has been reached.

However, it is not only when new members join the Union that Article XXIV comes into play. In entering into new customs union or free trade agreements, the Community itself is bound by Article XXIV, as are its contractual partners if also members of the WTO. In *Italy* v. *Council* the Court of Justice was ready to interpret Article XXIV in order to determine whether WTO law had been complied with. The WTO dispute settlement panels and the Appellate Body are in their turn prepared to interpret the requirements of Community agreements

---

[107] *Ibid.*, n. 105 at 160.

[108] J.H. Jackson, *The World Trade Organization: Constitution and Jurisprudence* (London, RIIA, Pinter, 1998) at 57.

[109] In Case C–352/96, *Italy* v. *Council* [1998] ECR I–6937, Italy challenged the legality of a Council Regulation implementing agreements entered into by the EC with Thailand and Australia consequent upon the accession of Austria, Finland and Sweden. The Court was prepared to examine the legality of the Regulation for compatibility with the WTO commitments, under the so-called Nakajima principle (the agreements and implementing Regulation were explicitly designed to ensure compliance with Art. XXIV of GATT 1994) but held that "if the parties themselves have reached agreement on the question of mutually satisfactory compensatory adjustment, the requirement referred to in Article XXIV:6 of GATT must be regarded as fulfilled and cannot therefore serve as a basis for examining the legality of the Regulation" (at para. 23).

in order to determine what precisely they require in the context of an exception to MFN. In the *Bananas* case, the Appellate Body took a view on what was, and what was not, required by the Lomé Convention in its application of the Lomé waiver.[110] In *Turkey: textile imports from India* the Appellate Body interpreted Turkey's customs union agreement with the EC in order to apply Article XXIV.[111] Under the customs union agreement, Turkey is required to align its commercial policy to that of the EC, thus implying not only alignment to the common external tariff but also the adoption of trading rules reflecting the Community's import policy. Article 12 provides that "in conformity with the requirements of Article XXIV of the GATT Turkey will apply as from the entry into force of this Decision, substantially the same commercial policy as the Community in the textile sector". In implementation of this provision Turkey introduced new quotas on its imports of textiles from India. The WTO Panel concluded that these quantitative restrictions were contrary to Articles XI and XIII of GATT 1994 (and Article 2.4 of the Agreement on Textiles and Clothing) and were not covered by the customs union exemption in Article XXIV of GATT 1994, and the Appellate Body confirmed these findings (although with some disagreement over the interpretation of Article XXIV).

The Panel and Appellate Body Reports raise a number of interesting questions around such issues as the scope of Article XXIV, the proper forum for determining compatibility and the impact of these for EC external policy.

The first question is jurisdictional. To what extent does the WTO's dispute settlement procedure apply to issues of Article XXIV compliance? It had been argued that the application of Article XXIV was essentially a political issue, to be determined by the Committee on RTAs. In so far as this Committee is a subordinate body of the Ministerial Conference and General Council, Article IX:2 of the WTO Agreement could be said to support this proposition, as could the approach to Article XXIV:6 adopted by the European Court of Justice in *Italy v. Council*. In *Turkey: textile imports* the Panel nevertheless held that it could decide on the compatibility with the WTO of a specific measure adopted on the formation of a customs union:

> Although the right of WTO members to form regional trade arrangements is "an integral part" of the set of multilateral disciplines of GATT and now WTO, the DSU procedures can be used to obtain a ruling by a panel on the WTO compatibility of any matters arising from such regional trade arrangements. For us, the term "any matters" [in paragraph 12 of the Understanding on Article XXIV of GATT 1994] clearly includes specific measures adopted on the occasion of the formation of a customs union or in the ambit of a customs union.[112]

---

[110] *European Communities—Regime for the Importation, Sale and Distribution of Bananas*, Appellate Body Report WT/DS27/AB/R, 9 September 1997, para 167; see *supra* n. 90.

[111] *Turkey—Restrictions on Imports of Textile and Clothing Products*, Appellate Body Report WT/DS34/AB/R, 22 October 1999. See also the contribution by A. von Bogdandy to this volume.

[112] *Ibid.*, at para. 9.50.

The Panel was however of the view that the overall compatibility of an agreement with Article XXIV was a matter for the Committee on RTAs and not a "measure" to be determined by an individual Panel established under the DSU. This issue of overall compatibility is, the Panel said, a "very complex undertaking" involving economic, legal and political perspectives and "a broad multilateral assessment" which concerns the WTO membership as a whole.[113] The Appellate Body agreed with the Panel on the first point: specific measures adopted by a WTO member in the context of a customs union agreement could be considered by a DSU Panel; it did not feel the need to express an opinion on the second point as it was not necessary to the reasoning of the Panel. The Appellate Body thus confirmed its willingness to exercise jurisdiction over the compatibility with Article XXIV of measures designed to implement a customs union agreement, albeit with some remaining uncertainty about the scope of this jurisdiction.[114] Given the importance of Article XXIV for the EU's external trade regime, this is a significant development.

The second, substantive, question raised by this case concerns the scope of the exception created by Article XXIV. Article XXIV:5 provides:

> the provisions of this Agreement shall not prevent, as between the territories of contracting parties, the formation of a customs union or of a free trade area . . .;

The Appellate Body gives this a restrictive interpretation: it is not a general exception to all WTO rules; it will act as an exemption only where it can be shown that the application of the rule (*in casu* Articles XI and XIII on quantitative restrictions) would *prevent* the formation of the customs union. The "measure" will therefore benefit from the provision only if it is essential, or necessary, for the formation of a customs union; it is not enough that it is part of the customs union agreement. The Appellate Body then goes further: in order to decide what is *necessary* to a customs union, it looks to other elements of Article XXIV for a definition of customs union. What is "necessary" is thus determined by reference to the GATT concept of customs union, not the content of the specific customs union agreed by the parties (in this case, Turkey and the EC).

The Appellate Body, relying particularly on Article XXIV:4, sees this provision as striking a balance: "a customs union should facilitate trade within the customs union, but it should *not* do so in a way that raises barriers to trade with

---

[113] *Ibid.*, at paras. 9.52–9.53.

[114] The AB does, however, refer (at para. 60) to its own earlier report in *India—Quantitative Restrictions on Imports of Agricultural, Textile and Industrial Products*, WT/DS90/AB/R, adopted 22 September 1999, at paras. 80–109, in which India had unsuccessfully relied on arguments based *inter alia* on principles of institutional balance. Moreover, in saying (at para. 58) that the party claiming the benefit of Article XXIV must demonstrate that the measure at issue was introduced upon the formation of a customs union that fully meets the requirements of Article XXIV:8(a) and 5(a), the AB implies that this issue is within the jurisdiction of a dispute settlement panel. Jackson points out that the reference in the Understanding on the Interpretation of Article XXIV to the application of dispute settlement procedures was a deliberate attempt to strengthen this provision: J.H. Jackson, *The World Trade Organization: Constitution and Jurisprudence* (London, RIIA, Pinter 1998) at 55.

third countries".[115] Hence the provisos in Article XXIV:5 and the definition of a customs union and free trade area in Article XXIV:8. And in striking the balance, the AB uses the flexibility provided by terms such as "substantially" in Article XXIV:8.[116] Something interesting is happening here: it is the vagueness of a word such as "substantially" which has led to criticisms of the inadequacy of a provision which has never been effectively enforced. Here it is being used by the AB to justify a flexibility of interpretation in defining what is really "necessary" for a customs union: and thus to set clear boundaries to the exception. This is very different from the hands-off approach to political discretion evidenced by the Court of Justice in *Italy* v. *Council*.

According to the AB, the precise alignment of Turkey to the EU's quota system for textile imports was not "necessary" for a workable customs union within the meaning of Article XXIV:8. Here, the AB interprets the customs union Decision as well as the GATT: the word "substantially" also occurs in Article 12 of the customs union Decision, reflecting the wording of Article XXIV:8(a)(ii). "Substantially the same"—the AB holds—means more than merely comparable but does not require identical duties or other trade regulations. Although Turkey had argued that the adoption of the quantitative restrictions was necessary for the full operation of the customs union in order to avoid trade diversion, the Panel and the AB both disagreed: they held that there were other less restrictive means of avoiding deflection of trade, such as certificates of origin, which would allow the Community customs authorities to distinguish between Turkish-origin textile imports and those from other third countries, such as India.[117]

In this way the Appellate Body is defining, not only the scope of Article XXIV (the measure must be necessary), but the nature of a customs union. It points to a type of customs union that actually reflects the nature of the Community customs union itself *before* the completion of the common commercial policy: where differences between the commercial policies of the constituent parties may necessitate origin checks (and barriers) at internal borders. With the completion of the internal market and the removal of internal borders at least for trade in goods, the European Union has moved towards a more "complete" form of customs union which requires a fully common commercial policy based on uniform trade rules. This degree of uniformity, necessary if internal border controls are to disappear, and the only characteristic of the EC's commercial policy defined in the Treaty, is not—the Appellate Body says—"necessary" for an Article XXIV-type customs union. In the case of the EC–Turkey customs union, this conclusion does not do violence to the parties' objectives (there are

---

[115] *Turkey: textile imports*, AB Report, *supra* n. 111, at para. 57.

[116] Under Article XXIV(8) restrictions must be eliminated in "substantially all the trade" between the constituent parties to the customs union or free trade area.

[117] The Appellate Body alludes to the fact that this would be a temporary measure, in that the Community will have to remove its quantitative restrictions in time under the WTO Agreement on Textiles and Clothing.

other ways in which the customs union is not a mirror of the internal market, for example in the retention of anti-dumping measures). The AB is careful to say that "we make no finding on the issue of whether quantitative restrictions found to be inconsistent with Article XI and Article XIII of the GATT 1994 will *ever* be justified by Article XXIV".[118] But an important step has been taken even in asking the question: the case implies a constraint on the type of economic integration agreement entered into by the Community—a constraint which is not just a matter of having to demonstrate that "substantially all" trade is covered, or that a common external tariff is "not on the whole higher or more restrictive" than pre-customs union duties. Where courts (or dispute settlement organs) speak of striking a balance between competing goals they are generally making a claim to—at least—set out the framework for the balancing exercise.

The balance referred to by the WTO Appellate Body reflects the tension between regional trade liberalisation and multilateral MFN. Regional trade agreements are inherently discriminatory. The traditional link that this chapter started with, between trade liberalisation and non-discrimination, is challenged by the increasingly complex network of regional trade agreements generally and those of the European Union in particular. This is not the only challenge: the *Banana* cases demonstrate the need to re-examine the role of MFN-based trade liberalisation in the context of trade-based development policies.

In what forum will the necessary re-working of these relationships take place? The WTO Appellate Body has, in *Turkey: textile imports* and the *Bananas* cases, put down a marker. The willingness of the Appellate Body to engage in this way with the Community's legal order (and, in *Turkey: textile imports*, the extension of its legal order to a non-EU State) is in striking contrast to the caution of the European Court of Justice when faced with the interaction of the WTO and Community legal orders.[119] The European Union response is limited in two ways: by the reluctance of the Court of Justice to get involved in judicial assessment of the relationship, expressed in terms of the need to give room to executive and legislative discretion[120] and by the lack of any general constitutional principles governing its external trade policy and in particular the lack of any worked-out principle of non-discrimination in the external context. The two are almost certainly linked; the second is the more fundamental. As we have seen, in the external trade context, the place of non-discrimination as a guiding principle (or right) will depend on its inclusion in specific legislative provisions and agreements, and even then it will be balanced against other objectives. The Court of Justice, in addressing allegedly discriminatory acts, will give weight to "objective justifications" for differential treatment that are based on the

---

[118] *Turkey: textile imports*, AB Report, *supra* n. 111, at para. 65.

[119] See, most recently, Case C–149/96 [1999] ECR I-8395, *Portugal* v. *Council*, 23 November 1999.

[120] Case C–149/96 [1999] ECR I-8395, *Portugal* v. *Council*, 23 November 1999 at para. 40. Both the Panel Report and the AB in the *Turkey: textile imports* case show awareness of this issue in discussing the relationship between dispute settlement panels and other WTO institutions in the operation of Art. XXIV: see text *supra* at n. 112ff.

Community interest as defined by the exercise of political and executive discretion. This is hardly surprising given the absence of enforceable principles (comparable to the fundamental freedoms) in the Community's external commercial policy.

Advocate General Saggio, in *Portugal* v. *Council*, argues that the provisions of an international agreement such as the WTO should be capable of constituting a basis for a challenge to the legality of a Community act, but that priority should be given, within the Community legal order, to primary Treaty law and constitutional norms over obligations contained in international agreements.[121] The implication is that while compliance with international obligations is one foundational element within the Community's legal order,[122] it cannot be elevated into a norm which replaces the need for the Community to establish its own constitutional and regulatory principles. If this argument, based on the autonomy of the Community legal order, is accepted, it becomes all the more important for that legal order to develop its own constitutional principles which are designed to underpin the external dimension of Community policy. The commitment to trade liberalisation coupled with uniformity found in Articles 131–133 EC is not adequate to resolve the tension between non-discrimination and preferential free trade. It does not, for example, reflect the Community's own experience—that trade liberalisation may go beyond the abolition of discriminatory barriers; or that regional trade agreements may serve integration and other social and political objectives which go beyond trade liberalisation. This is not to say that it would be sufficient or even helpful merely to incorporate WTO-derived principles of non-discrimination into the Community's external trade policy; the point is rather that at present the Community lacks the normative tools to make a reasoned case at the global level for (for example) principled exceptions to MFN. Only on the basis of such constitutional principles will it be possible for the Community to develop its own response to the crucial questions of the balance between regional and multilateral trade liberalisation and between trade liberalisation and non-discrimination.

---

[121] Case C–149/96, *Portugal* v. *Council*, Opinion of AG Saggio, para. 22; the AG accepts that this may entail a breach by the EC of international obligations but argues that an international agreement should not be applied in such a way as to require the institutions to compromise the proper functioning and objectives of the Community.

[122] Cf. Art. 300(7) EC.

8

The WTO and EU Distributive Policy: the Case of Regional Promotion and Assistance

THOMAS COTTIER and CHRISTOPHE GERMANN

INTRODUCTION

T RADE LIBERALISATION HAS been a common and historic trait of federal structures. For example, the creation of a common market was one of the driving forces in the founding of the United States of America in the eighteenth Century, the Swiss Confederation and Germany in the nineteenth Century, and the European Communities and Union in the twentieth Century. While constitutional programmes dismantling interstate trade barriers can frequently be found at the beginning and early stages of developing federal structures, it is interesting to observe that such narrow functionalism eventually gives way to broader, and more extensive, policies.[1] As time passes federations turn increasingly to flanking policies accompanying the dismantling of trade barriers, and creation of appropriate conditions of competition. It seems that such flanking policies generally become necessary to counterbalance national, regional or sectoral disadvantages brought about for the weaker parts of a federation. In the European Community, such mechanisms were most visible from the very beginning in the guise of common policies for agriculture and mining. Eventually, a more targeted and nuanced approach was developed in the context of policies for cohesion and regional policies.

This chapter seeks to explore EU and WTO rules with respect to regional policies, and the scope these systems currently offer, and should offer in the future, for flanking policies which differ among different regions of a Member of the WTO. The EU cohesion policy programmes, specifically designed to promote economic development in the poorer Member States and regions, shall thereby serve as an example. Evidently, it is a matter of balancing interests, advantages and disadvantages. The capacity of regional policy to comply with WTO law must be

---

[1] See J.H.H. Weiler, "The transformation of Europe", in *The Constitution of Europe, "Do the New Clothes have an Emperor?" and Other Essays on European Integration* (Cambridge, CUP, 1999), 10–102.

considered in the light of its discriminatory effects towards those entities which are not recipients of the benefits conferred by such policies. On the other hand, history suggests that regional policies are an inherent condition further to promote open markets. We analyse in particular to what extent EU regional policies of promotion and assistance are compatible with WTO law, and whether or not WTO law is sufficiently flexible to accommodate such policies in the future. It goes without saying that the issue is of importance in the light of current enlargement processes which will eventually bring about an expanded EU membership characterised by great diversity in levels of social and economic development.[2]

Regional policies take the form of interventions by public entities on different levels such as nations (federal or quasi-federal level), communities of nations (supranational organisations), infranational entities (states such as the German or Austrian *Bundesländer*, the Swiss cantons, etc., or even larger municipalities), or in between these levels. As a matter of fact, regions may also extend across constitutionally defined territories, since a *dynamic* component is inherent in the concept of region which may be variable in time and space. Therefore, this chapter first seeks to define the legal concept of region. In this context, by means of the example of the European cohesion policy programmes, the chapter focuses on the interaction between Member States, their regions and the Commission. In a second part, the WTO rules on national treatment and subsidies are outlined as the constraining legal framework for regional policy intervention in the context of international trade. Eventually, in a third concluding part, the chapter examines whether the core principles of non-discrimination, in particular national treatment, and rules on subsidies specifically applicable to regional policies are sufficiently nuanced, and whether the current disposition of WTO law, anchored to the construct of the nation state, is sufficiently elaborate to enforce necessary disciplines with a view to successfully balancing interests relating to level playing fields on the one hand, and goals of distributive justice pursued by regional policies on the other hand.

THE DEFINITION OF REGIONS

Regions on the Supranational and Transnational Level

The GATT and the WTO have a long tradition of dealing with regions on a supranational and transnational level.[3] For the purposes of trade relations, they

---

[2] With respect to the enlargement process, see European Commission, *EC Structural Funds, European Union Assistance for Regional Development: A Brief Guide for Future Member States* (Brussels, European Commission, 2000). See also Erik Evtimov, Rechtsprobleme der Assoziierung der Mittel-und Osteuropäischen Länder und der Voraussetzung für ihren Beitritt zur Europäischen Union (Bern, Peter Lang Verlag, 1999).

[3] For an overview, see P. Demaret, J.F. Bellis and G. Garcia Jimenez, *Regionalism and Multilateralism after the Uruguay Round, Convergence, Divergence and Interaction* (Brussels, Europeam Interuniversity Press, 1997), and J.A. Frankel, *Regional Trading Blocks in the World Economic System* (Washington, Institute for International Economics, 1997).

are defined in and contained by WTO rules. One of the most significant excep-
tions to the Most-Favoured Nation (MFN) clause of Article I GATT 1994
Agreement refers to preferential trade arrangement (PTAs) as addressed in its
Article XXIV. A corresponding regime is provided for in Articles II and V of the
GATS.

Article XXIV GATT grants legal status to Free Trade Areas (FTAs), and also
to Customs Union (CUs) by allowing contracting parties to form such arrangements, provided they eliminate, rather than just lower, tariff and non-tariff
trade barriers on substantially all of the trade among members, and do not render protection against non-members more restrictive, specifically (FTAs) or on
the whole (CUs).[4] In the area of trade in services, Article V GATS includes provisions that essentially parallel those in Article XXVI GATT. Both rule out
partial preferential trade agreements (PTAs). Because PTAs are inherently discriminatory, their proliferation has led to legitimate fears that they may undermine the multilateral process of trade liberalisation. By liberalising trade among
members preferentially, PTAs create new trade between members and divert
trade from low-cost, non-member suppliers to high-cost, member suppliers.
Since this change is trade diversion, it is commonly viewed as imposing a welfare cost on the PTAs and on the world as a whole. In FTAs as opposed to CUs,
goods destined for a high-tariff member may enter through a low-tariff member.
To avoid trade deflection, when a low-tariff country imports a product in
almost finished form, adds a small amount of value to it, and then exports it to
the high-tariff country duty free, FTAs usually include rules of origin according
to which products receive duty-free status only if a pre-specified proportion of
value added in the product originates in member countries.[5] For a long time, it
was unclear whether regional arrangements must cover substantially all trade in
terms of quantitative or qualitative requirements in the field of goods. The matter is of particular importance for agriculture which has, traditionally, been
excluded from FTAs concluded by the European Community. Unlike the
GATT, the WTO no longer excludes this issue from dispute settlement. Recent
rulings of the Appellate Body, taking into account also the dual corresponding
provision of Article V GATS, suggest that discipline is being tightened and a bla-
tant exclusion of agricultural trade would no longer be tolerated. In *Turkey—
Restrictions on Imports of Textile and Clothing Products*, the Appellate Body
of the WTO held that the notion of "substantial" comprises both quantitative

---

[4] T. Cottier, "The Challenge of Regionalization and Preferential Relations in World Trade Law
and Policy" [1996] *European Foreign Affairs Review*, 149–167.

[5] See T. Cottier, "Das Ende der bilateralen Ära: Rechtliche Auswirkungen der WTO auf die
Integrationspolitik der Schweiz", in T. Cottier and A.R. Kopse (eds.), *Der Beitritt der Schweiz zur
Europäischen Union* (Zurich, Schulthess, 1998), 87; Palmeter, "Rules of Origin in Regional Trade
Agreements" in P. Demaret, J.F. Bellis, G. García Jiminéz (eds.), *supra* n. 3, 341; Panargariya and
Srinivasan, "The New Regionalism: a Benign or Malign Growth?" in J. Bhagwati and M. Hirsch
(eds.), *The Uruguay Round and Beyond: Essays in Honour of Arthur Dunkel* (Berlin and
Heidelberg, Springer Verlag, 1999), 223.

and qualitative aspects.[6] The ruling will not remain without practical implications for many preferential agreements, in particular those concluded by the European Community. For example, the 1999 secotorial agreements concluded with Switzerland are not fully compatible with WTO law and may trigger claims for MFN treatment by non-EU WTO member states.[7] In this chapter, we shall not further address regionalism and its legal problems on the supranational level, since our aim is to focus on regions on the subnational level.

Regions on the Subnational Level in Europe

Unlike supra- and transnational regions, subnational regions are not defined by WTO law. Thus, we turn for guidance to other sources of international and regional law.

The concept and notion of the "region" vary in terms of size and functions. With respect to functional criteria, one can distinguish between geographical, economic and political regions. In EU law, there is a tendency to focus upon two criteria: an economically orientated definition gives the basis for regional policy, whereas a narrower institutionally orientated definition refers to the entity which is to be found on the level immediately below the central (federal) level.[8]

The Definition of the Council of Europe

The European Charter of Local Self-Government of 15 October 1985[9] adopted by the Council of Europe gives an example of a definition of regions on the infranational level. According to Articles 13 and 16 of this Charter, the states are exclusively competent to define the regional authorities and territories within their national territory to which this Charter shall apply. Thus, the parties to this Charter, which are exclusively Member States, autonomously define the regions. To the extent that these national states constitutionally control the subnational level, they are also responsible in accordance with Article XXIV:12 GATT. The responsibility for policy-making in the regions falling under the scope of application of the Charter will be analysed in further details under point 4.3 below. These states are also likely to be held accountable for the part

---

[6] WT/DS34/ASB/R, of 22 October 1999, para. 49; see also T. Cottier and E. Evtimov, "Präferenzielle Abkommen der EG: Möglichkeiten und Grenzen im Rahmen der WTO" [2000] *Zeitschrift für Europarechtliche Studien* ZEuS 477–505; and T. Cottier, "Das Ende der bilateralen Ära: Rechtliche Auswirkungen der WTO auf die Integrationspolitik der Schweiz", in T. Cottier and A. Kopse, *Der Beitritt der Schweiz zur Europäischen Union* (Zurich, Schulthess, 1998), 87.

[7] See T. Cottier and M. Panizzon, "Die bilateralen Verträge und das Recht der WTO: Grundlagen und Spannungsfelder" in D. Felder and C. Kaddous (eds.), *Accords bilatéraux Suisse—UE (Commentaires), Dossier de droit Européen* (Basel and Brussels, Helbing and Lichtenhahn, Bruylant, 2001) (forthcoming), viii.

[8] Bolz, "Die Regionen in der Europäischen Union" (1994) 11 *Aktuelle Juristische Praxis* 1394, with further refernces to case law and doctrine.

[9] Council of Europe, European Treaty Series 122.

of the regional territories that are located on their own national territories in the case of a transborder region.

In addition, regions can also come into existence spontaneously, without the approval of the national state in whose territories they are located. In particular, regional entities may come into existence as transnational entities, growing across national borders. Special problems of state responsibility may arise in such constellations. Any policy-making not compatible with international rules would possibly extend the responsibilities of states beyond their own territory, to jurisdictions over which they do not have full domestic control. In addition, discriminatory effects resulting from such constellations may also affect the interests of their own nationals not directly benefiting from these transnational regional advantages.

The EC Treaty Definition

The EC Treaty, in light of subsidiarity, recognises the concept of subnational regions—however without actually defining it—and establishes the Committee of the Regions (Articles 263 *et seq.*, EC) in order to give subnational authorities a formal position in the framework of EU institutions. It is interesting to observe that both the Community and the formal recognition of regions by it have contributed to, and facilitated, the emergence of new regional structure in particular in states traditionally characterised by centralised governance, such as the United Kingdom and Ireland.

Created as a consultative body by the Treaty on European Union, the Committee[10] appears as a guardian of the principle of subsidiarity.[11] The Treaty requires the Committee to be consulted on matters relating to trans-European networks, public health, education, youth, culture and economic and social cohesion (Article 265 EC). But the Committee can also take the initiative and give its opinion on other policy matters that affect cities and regions, such as agriculture and environmental protection.

The Committee's work is based on a structure of seven standing Commissions[12] and a Special Commission on Institutional Affairs, which is

[10] As regional presidents, mayors of cities or chairmen of city and county councils, the 222 members of the Committee are elected officials from the levels of government closest to the citizen. With such resources, the Committee is able to bring its expertise and influence to bear on the Union's other institutions.

[11] We recall that subsidiarity is enshrined in the Treaty and means that decisions should be taken by those public authorities which stand as close to the citizen as possible. It is a principle which resists unnecessarily remote, centralised decision-making.

[12] These Commissions are as follows:
(A) Regional policy, structural funds, economic and social cohesion, cross-border and interregional cooperation;
(B) agriculture, rural development, fisheries;
(C) trans-European networks, transport, information society;
(D) spatial planning, urban issues, energy, the environment; *over/*

responsible for contributing to the debate on the reform of the EU institutions.[13] The Bureau, elected for a two-year term, organises the work of the Committee.

The EU's Structural and Cohesion Policies Programmes

Redistributive policies, flanking the process of trade liberalisation and economic and legal integration within the European Union, are pursued on all levels of governance. Subsidies in the European Community are granted both at Community level, i.e. out of the Community budget, and by the Member States, at the level of national, regional or local government. And indeed, in view of the principle of additionality, these two levels often work in consort.

While the Committee on the Regions provides an important forum for discussion and policy formation, the bulk of regional policies pursued by the EU are realised by the EU's structural and cohesion policy programmes. Pursuant to Article 158 EC, the Community shall aim at reducing disparities between the levels of development of the various regions and the backwardness of the least favoured regions or islands, including rural areas. These regional policies shall serve to strengthen the Community's economic and social cohesion.

The main financial instruments of the EU's economic, social and political cohesion policies set forth in Articles 158 to 162 EC are the four Structural Funds, i.e. the European Regional Development Fund (ERDF), the European Social Fund (ESF), the European Agricultural Guidance and Guarantee Fund (EAGGF) and the Financial Instrument for Fisheries Guidance (FIFG). In addition, the Maastrich Treaty established the European Cohesion Fund as an instrument for support and solidarity, intended to contribute to the strengthening of the economic and social cohesion of the EU and to help the least prosperous Member States take part in the Economic and Monetary Union (EMU). As a matter of fact, the Cohesion Fund was set up to provide assistance to projects in Greece, Ireland, Portugal and Spain for the purpose of contributing to the improvement of the environment or to the development of transport infrastructure and networks.[14] The goals of the European structural and cohesion policies are as follows:

(E)   social policy, public health, consumer protection, research, tourism;
(F)   employment, economic policy, single market, industry, small and medium sized enterprises; and
(G)   education, vocational training, culture, youth, sport, citizens' rights.

[13] Since 1993, the Committee has already dealt with a wide range of issues including guidelines for a trans-European airport network, the development of rural tourism, the right of European citizens to vote in local elections in those Member States of which they are not nationals, and suggestions on Europe's approach to the Information Society.

[14] The Cohesion Fund budget was in excess of 15 billion Euros over 7 years increasing from 1.5 in 1993 to more than 2.6 billion Euros in 1999 (expressed in 1992 prices). The indicative allocation of assistance to each of the eligible Member States has been fixed by the Council as follows: 16–20% for Greece, 7–10% for Ireland, 16–20% for Portugal and 52–58% for Spain.

—Promoting the development and structural adjustment of regions whose development is lagging behind; (Objective 1);

—Supporting the economic and social conversion of regions facing structural difficulties (Objective 2);

—Supporting the adaptation and modernisation of policies and systems of education, training and employment (Objective 3).[15]

Pursuant to Article 160 EC, the ERDF, which was set up in 1975, aims at contributing to the development and structural adjustment of backward regions and to the restructuring of declining industrial regions to balance regional disparities within the Community. The ERDF can support many different measures, in particular productive investments and economy-related infrastructure improvements. In relation to regional assistance granted by the Member States, the ERDF is an additional tool, which shall supplement, i.e. not replace, national efforts.

In particular, the ERDF provides structural aid through regional development programmes targeted at the most disadvantaged regions with a view to helping reduce socio-economic imbalances between regions of the Union. Financial assistance from the ERDF is mainly targeted at supporting small and medium-sized enterprises, promoting productive investment, improving infrastructure and furthering local development.[16]

The ESF promotes employment, in particular through training and recruitment aid, and the EAGGF supports national aid schemes for agriculture and rural development, whereas the FIFG contributes to the modernisation of fisheries equipment.

The financial resources available for the cohesion policies during the programming period of 1994–1999 amounted to almost 170 billion Euros, i.e. one third of the Community budget. The forthcoming enlargement will pose an unprecedented challenge. With a *per capita* GDP of only about 30 per cent of the existing Union's average, the 10 countries of central and eastern Europe lag far behind, in GDP terms, the least developed of the existing Member States. A Union of 26 countries would have an average GDP *per capita* about 15 per cent lower than the present figure.[17]

The EU's structural and cohesion policies are intended to support national and regional aid programmes in the weakest regions and on national and

---

[15] See Art. 1(1) of Council Regulation 1260/99 [1999] OJ L161/1. On the background to these reforms and the reduction of the number of objectives from six to three see J. Scott, "Regional Policy: Evolutionary Perspectives" in P. Craig and G. de Búrca (eds.), *The Evolution of EU Law* (Oxford, OUP, 1998). See also L. Jung and H. Hassold, "Die Neuordnung der deutschen und europäischen Regional-/Strukturförderung vor dem Hintergrund der Beihilfenkontrolle und der Agenda 2000" (2000) 5 *Die öffentliche Verwaltung* 194.

[16] In terms of financial resources, the ERDF is by far the largest of the EU's four Structural Funds, representing almost half of the total budget thereof.

[17] On 16 July 1997 the European Commission adopted the document "Agenda 2000", in which it made proposals to continue its support for the most disadvantaged of its existing regions, and laid the ground for a structural policy for a 26-nation Union.

regional labour markets. Thus, the main aim of these programmes consists in contributing to a reduction of economic and social disparities.[18] The Commission stresses in its Guidelines for programmes in the period 2000–2006 that substantial gaps between the regions in regional incomes, infrastructure and human capital endowments, as well as in terms of the competitiveness of enterprises, still remain. In particular, regional disparities in terms of overall unemployment levels remain at a level which is unacceptable.[19]

Competition and Redistribution

The cohesion and distributive programmes discussed above are controversial by their very nature, in that they have the effect of distorting conditions of competition. On a normative level, according to Article 12 of the General Regulation for the Structural Funds for the period 2000–2006, all structural fund operations must be consistent with EU competition rules, thus including state aid rules. Nonetheless there persist profoundly divergent attitudes to regional policy. Hooghe[20] suggests that there two models of European capitalism exist in connection with EU cohesion policy: neoliberalism and regulated capitalism. The former model is based on the postulate that markets should be insulated from political interference by combining European-wide market integration with sovereign political regulation vested in national governments. This approach should generate competition among national governments in providing a national regulatory climate which is attractive to mobile factors of production. In contrast, proponents of regulated capitalism seek to create a European liberal democracy capable of regulating markets, redistributing resources, and shaping partnerships among public and private actors. Proponents of this latter model contend that the single market works more efficiently if political actors provide collective goods and services such as European-wide transport and communication infrastructure, information networks, workforce skills, and research and development. There is a role for positive as well as negative regulation at the European level. Historically, during the dismantling of the main trade barriers before 1988, there was only a minimal European policy on cohesion: few resources, few common priorities, and no uniform institutional design. The

---

[18] However, the impact of cohesion policies is not limited to these disparities, but also influences the cultural development of the European society, which in turn contributes to cohesion; see J.M. Delgado Moreira, "Cohesion and Citizenship in EU Cultural Policy" (2000) 38 *Journal of Common Market Studies* 449–470.

[19] Communication of the Commission, The structural funds and their coordination with the cohesion fund, Guidelines for programmes in the period 2000–6, 1. The Commission has adopted these Guidelines in accordance with Art. 10(3) of Council Regulation 1260/99, *supra* n. 15; these Guidelines seek to help national and regional authorities to prepare their programming strategies for the objectives categories of the Structural Funds and their links with the Cohesion Fund.

[20] L. Hooghe, "EU Cohesion Policy and Competing Models of European Capitalism" (1998) 36 *Journal of Common Market Studies* 457.

1988 reform overhauled this basic framework. Subsidies were doubled and further significantly increased in 1993, and the criteria and rules of operation changed. In order to obtain funding, a national government was required to design and implement multi-annual EU-funded programmes in partnership with the European Commission and regional and local authorities and social partners.[21] It seems fair to say that practical policies float among and between the two basic schools of thought, but that the school of regulated capitalism, given increased levels of intervention and redistribution, has tended to prevail of late. Such increases are likely to continue in view of the process of enlargement of the Union. While these programmes expand, it is important to monitor them from the point of view of competition under both Community law and the Community's international obligations under WTO law.

The Dynamics of the EU's Cohesion Programmes

It is fair to say that regional policies have a decentralising effect and an inbuilt tendency to enhance a special and differential treatment within the EU not equally extended to products and services originating in other members of the WTO.[22] The question arises what extent such effects may be limited by rules and principles of the WTO for products originating outside the EU. We hasten to add that WTO rules do not apply between Member States of the EU despite the fact that they all are members of the WTO in their own right.[23]

Ansell, Parson and Darden[24] observe that the creation of EU subnational links in recent years has created a structure of "dual networks". Historically, the state (federal level) had a "gateway" role as only national governments enjoyed relationships with other territorial actors at supranational (EU) and subnational (regions) levels, whereas today, each of the three actors in EU regional policy has two direct relationships. These scholars point out that the overall pattern is no longer that of three levels of actors engaged in policy-network co-operation, but of constantly shifting alliances within the triad: "Regions can now potentially mobilise Commission support against their own national governments, and vice versa. But crucially, regions can and do also mobilise their national governments against the Commission, and vice versa". It is interesting to note that the interaction between national, sub- and supranational levels of

---

[21] Besides spatial economic disparities among regions, the EU cohesion policies also address disparities between social groups and individuals within states, regions or locals areas such as deprived urban areas, see Guideslines on State aid for undertakings in deprived urban areas [1997] OJ C146/6.

[22] For environmental subsidies under EC law for example, see J. de Sépibus, *Die Umweltschutzsubvention im Gemeinschaftsrecht, Eine Kritik der europäischen Beihilfekontrolle aus umweltrechtlicher Sicht*, dissertation Bern, to be published in 2001.

[23] E.-U. Petersmann, "The EEC as a GATT Member—Legal Conflicts between GATT Law and European Community Law" in M. Hilf, F. Jacobs and E.-U. Petersmann, *The European Community and GATT* (Deventer, Kluwer, 1986), 23.

[24] K. Ansell, C. Parsons and K. Darden, "Dual Networks in European Regional Development Policy" (1997) 35 *Journal of Common Market Studies* 347.

policy-making illustrates the dynamic features of the principle of subsidiarity as applied on the regional level. In particular, the shift of decision-making from the central, as well as intermediary, powers to regional powers, and back,[25] shows the complexity and volatility of the concept of regional policies which are no longer exclusively determined by the traditional actors of public international law, the nation states.

EU Rules on Subsidies for Regional Policy Purposes

According to Article 87 EC, Member States shall not grant aid in any form whatsoever[26] which distorts or threatens to distort competition by favouring certain undertakings or the production of certain goods, in so far as it affects trade between Member States. Aid addressed by this provision is defined as a specific or selective[27] (as opposed to a general) transfer of state resources[28] which grants an economic advantage[29] having an effect on competition and trade between Member States.[30] Based on Article 87(3)(a) and (c) EC, the Commission may consider intervention to be compatible with the Common Market on a case-by-

[25] Ansell, Parsons and Darden, *supra* n. 24, 359, analyse this shift of decision-making as follows: "For the Commission, regional connections bring new sources of information and political support for its programmes. Information flowing form regions, particularly on the workings of Structural Funds programmes, makes the Commission less directly dependent on national government sources. Politically, Commission officials do little to disguise their attempts to cultivate potential allies in subnational governments, who may ultimately pressure the Commission's main interlocutors at the national level. Regional actors, in turn, may be willing to lend this political support for several reasons. From the Commission they too obtain useful information, not just on Structural Funds policy-making, but on other EU policies from which they are generally excluded. Politically, while the Commission is usually careful not to intrude into general national-subnational conflicts, regions may profit from the support the Commission lends to regional priorities which diverge from national priorities in regional development".

[26] For a definition of aid, see ECJ, Cases C–72/91 and 73/91, *Sloman Neptun Schiffahrts AG v. Seebetriebsrat Bodo Ziesemer of Sloman Neptun Schiffahrts AG* [1993] ECR I–887, paras. 18–22; Case C–387/92, *Banco de credito industrial SA v. Ayuntamiento de Valencia* [1994] ECR I–877; Case C–142/87 *Belgium v. Commission* [1990] ECR I–959; for case law on exceptions to the prohibition of aid see Case 730/79, *Philip Morris BV v. Commission* [1980] ECR 2671, para. 17ff; Case C–122/94 *Commission v. Council* [1996] ECR I–881, para. 9ff.

[27] The criterion of "selectivity" means that state aid must affect the balance between the beneficiary firms and their competitors. It is the element that differentiates state aid from so-called "general measures", i.e. measures which apply in an automatic manner to all firms in all economic sectors in a Member State such as most nationwide fiscal measures.

[28] The aid does not necessarily need to be granted by the state itself, since it can also come from private or public intermediate bodies appointed by the state. Financial transfers that constitute aid can take the form not only of grants or interest rate rebates, but also of loan guarantees, accelerated depreciation allowances, capital injections, etc.

[29] The aid must constitute an economic advantage that the undertaking would not have received in the normal course of business.

[30] This criterion is fulfilled if it can be shown that the beneficiary is involved in an economic activity and that he operates in a market in which there is trade between Member States, which is not the case for *de minimis* aid as defined by the Commission in its notice at [1996] OJ C68/9; such aid, therefore, does not need to be notified in advance to the Commission. Export aid, however, is excluded from the benefit of the *de minimis* rule.

case basis, provided that the measures aim at promoting the economic development of areas where the standard of living is abnormally low or where there is serious underemployment. In addition, measures are lawful for the development of certain economic activities, or of certain economic areas, where such aid does not adversely affect trading conditions to an extent contrary to the common interest. Article 88 EC requires the Member States to give advance notification to the Commission of any plan to grant state aid, and sets forth specific procedural rules under which the Commission monitors new aids, while at the same time keeping existing aid under constant review.[31] The Commission has discretionary powers to decide whether the proposed aid measure qualifies for exemption, or whether the Member State concerned must abolish or alter such aid within a given period of time.[32]

The Commission is aware of policy tensions inherent in the exercise of its discretionary power in the context of Article 87(3) EC. For this reason, it has identified three principal criteria to be applied in the course of assessing the compliance of subsidies with Community law. First, the subsidies in question must serve the purpose of contributing to a goal supported by the treaty provisions (target materialisation). Assessment in this respect must encompass all economic and social values pertaining to the Union as a whole. Considerations which are specific to national undertakings therefore remain relevant only where they also bear some significance in the social and economic context of the Union as a whole. Secondly, the aid must be necessary in order to achieve the targeted development. Thus, the application of Article 87(3) EC implies that the Commission ascertains that free market dynamics alone would not enable the undertakings to achieve such goals on their own. Thirdly, the modalities of the aid, i.e. its concrete form, volume, reimbursement conditions, etc., must comply with the principle of proportionality in respect of the target that the aid is to achieve.[33] Such subsidies shall not contribute to a transfer of existing problems and issues from one Member State to another.[34]

Regional aid is designed to develop the less-favoured regions by supporting investment and job creation in a sustainable manner and context.[35] It is to promote the expansion, modernisation and diversification of the activities of

---

[31] In case of failure to notify, see Case C–301/87, *France* v. *Commission* [1990] ECR I–307; Case C–354/90, *Fédération nationale du commerce extérieur des produits alimentaires and Syndicat national des négociants et transformateurs de saumon* v. *France* [1991], ECR I–5505.

[32] The Commission has developed specific approaches depending on the size of the firms, their locations, the region concerned, the purpose of the aid, etc. To grant transparency and predictability with respect to the exercise of its discretionary powers, the Commission publicises to a broad extent its decisions and criteria. These publications have taken the form of regulations, "communications", "notices", "frameworks", "guidelines", and letters to Member States; see in particular European Commission, Directorate-General for Competition, *Competition Law in the European Communities, Volume IIA, Rules Applicable to State Aid* (Brussels and Luxembourg, 1999), 51 ff.

[33] W. Mederer, "Wettbewerbsregeln, Commentary ad article 92", in H. Groeben, J. Thiesing and C.-D. Ehlermann (eds.), *Kommentar zum EU-/EG-Vertrag, Art. 88–102* (Baden-Baden, Nomos, 1999), 2/1887ff.

[34] Case 730/79, *Philip Morris* [1980] ECR 2671, n. 26.

[35] See Guidelines on national regional aid [1998]OJ C74/9.

establishments located in those regions and encourage new firms to settle there. Such aid, however, is made available to the most disadvantaged regions only. It works as an incentive and should not interfere with the normal interactions of market forces in a way which would result in a reduction of the efficiency of the Community economy as a whole.[36] Balancing interests and equities, the Court of Justice considers that individual *ad hoc* payments made to a single firm or aid limited to one area of activity which could have a major impact on competition in the relevant market, while its effects on regional development are not sufficiently substantial, do not meet the criterion of regional specificity pursuant to Article 87(3)(a) EC:

> That aid is not primarily intended to facilitate the development of certain economic regions, but is granted in the form of aid for the operation of undertaking in difficulty. In those circumstances, it is for the Member State concerned to establish that such aid actually fulfils the regional specificity criterion. None the less, the Commission should first specify the criteria according to which it considers ad hoc aid, exceptionally, to be regional in character.[37]

The Court of Justice further requires that regional aid must contribute to the region's long-term development. This means in the case of aid granted to re-establish the profitability of a single company that such aid should not cause, at the very least, any unacceptable adverse effects on conditions of competition within the Community, in order to be eligible under the exemption of Article 87(3)(a) EC.[38] This case law appears to be in line with the relevant WTO rules on specific "red" or "amber" subsidies described below.

It is interesting to note that the European Court of Justice has upheld a very restrictive interpretation of Article 87 EC. For example, it ruled in a judgment of 19 September 2000 regarding aid granted to undertakings in the new German *Länder,* in the form of tax regulation favouring investment, that state aid is basically incompatible with the Common Market. Since it constitutes a derogation from the general principle laid down in Article 87(1) EC, Article 87(2)(c) must be construed narrowly.[39] This restrictive approach towards subsidies granted by EU Member States contrasts with the generous subsidising activities performed by the Community itself in the name of cohesion policies on the EU level. While the EC is determined to defend these policies against restrictive WTO law requirements, the Court of Justice favours a restrictive handling of EC competition rules on subsidies at the same time. This is a contradiction at first sight, yet it may be explained on two grounds. First, it may be justified in the context of an overall policy which seeks to reduce national programmes to the benefit of EU-wide programmes. Secondly, the global level of the WTO is

---

[36] See Guidelines on national regional aid [1998]OJ C74/9 these Guidelines apply to regional aid granted in all sectors of the economy apart from the production, processing and marketing of the agricultural products listed in Annex II to the Treaty, fisheries and the coal industry.

[37] Joined Cases C–278, C–279 and C–280/92, *Spain* v. *Commission* [1994] ECR I–4105.

[38] Court of Justice, *supra* n. 37, ECR 1–4195f.

[39] Case C–156/98, *Federal Republic of Germany* v. *Commission* [2000] ECR para. 49.

limited to regulating conditions of competition and does not yet offer policies of redistribution and cohesion in its own right which would call for restrictive policies on the regional (and outside the EU on a national) level.

Different layers of governance play an important role in providing vertical checks and balances. While EC law monitors the distributive policies of Member States, this role is essentially assumed by WTO law with respect to the economic and social cohesion policies of the EU. The legitimate scope of EU action is therefore essentially defined by this body of law to which we now turn.

Principle of National Treatment

The first fundamental equalising principle to be discussed is that of national treatment (NT). It is more important in this context than the Most Favoured Nation (MFN) principle as regional policies may lead to differential treatment between domestic products originating in a region and foreign products within the same market. This effect constitutes a *prima facie* violation of Article III GATT. The situation is different in the field of services. As market access rights and national treatment are accorded on the basis of concessions which may be tailor-made, it is possible to build in remaining privileges to regions by way of conditions for and limitations on the full use and application of national treatment in respective schedules (cf. Articles XVI and XVII GATS).

In the area of goods, the principle of national treatment does not allow for differential treatment unless a lawful exception can be invoked. We note that Article XX GATT does not contain exceptions which would fit the needs of regional programmes. Moreover, the disciplines imposed by the Agreement on Trade-related Investment Measures (TRIMs) abolishing local content requirements further indicate a strict application of national treatment which does not leave any scope for preferential regional regimes. Things are, however, partly different in the field of subsidies.

Article III:8:b GATT excludes the application of national treatment to subsidies. Obviously, this is necessary, as application of national treatment would offset all supportive effects. However, the words "payment of subsidies" pursuant to this Article refer only to direct subsidies involving a payment, not to other subsidies such as tax credits or tax reduction. Article III:8(b) limits, therefore, permissible producer subsidies to "payments" after taxes have been collected or payments otherwise consistent with Article III.[40]

---

[40] See the 1992 Panel Report on *United States—Measures Affecting Alcoholic and Malt Beverages* 19 June 1992, BISD 395/206.

The question arises whether some EU programmes are in fact in violation of Article III GATT, and possibly of concessions already made under GATS. This matter requires further examination in specific policy areas.

Rules on Subsidies

Applicable Rules

Within the body of WTO rules, there are several sources of law addressing subsidies: Article VI GATT, the Agreement on Subsidies and Countervailing Measures (SCM Agreement), the Agreement on Agriculture, and the Agreement on Trade in Civil Aircraft. The interrelationship between these rules is sometimes unclear about delimitation between their respective scopes of application.[41] At first sight, the relation between GATT and the SCM Agreement seems clear by virtue of the general interpretative note to Annex 1A to the Agreement Establishing the WTO. This note sets out that in the case of a conflict between a provision of the GATT 1994 and a provision of another agreement in this Annex 1A, the provision of the other agreement shall prevail to the extent of the conflict. However, this relationship requires further elucidation in the absence of such conflict, where the rules of the GATT and the special agreement could be applied independently.

The Appellate Body uses a case-by-case approach to the question whether a provision of GATT must be considered as independent, or whether it must be construed in relation to another applicable sectorial agreement such as the SCM Agreement.[42] Based upon the current practices of Panels and of the Appellate Body, the GATT and specialised agreements as well as GATS are generally applied to deploy utmost effect (*"effet utile"*). They are applied in addition, and in a complementary manner, and not in a mutually exclusive way. As a practical matter, it is fair to say that disputes are primarily resolved on the basis of the specialised agreement and dealt with under GATT only to the extent that the General Agreement offers additional criteria.[43]

Agreement on Subsidies and Countervailing Measures

The GATT rules on subsidies based upon Article XVI were further elaborated during the Uruguay Round by the Agreement on Subsidies and Countervailing

---

[41] See M. Bénitah, *Fondements juridiques du traitement des subventions GATT & OMC* (Geneva and Paris, Librairie Droz, 1998), 175 *et seq.*

[42] For an overview on this question in the light of WTO case law between 1995 and 1999, see D. Falke, "Vertragskonkurrenz und Vertragskonflikt im Recht der WTO, Erste Erfahrungen der Rechtsprechung 1995–1999" [2000] *ZEuS, Zeitschrift für Europarechtliche Studien ZEuS* 307.

[43] The principle of effective interpretation or *"effet utile"* reflects the general rule of interpretation which requires that a treaty be interpreted to give meaning and effect to all the terms of the treaty: see Panel Report, *Korea—Definitive Safeguards Measures on Imports of Certain Dairy Products*, WT/DS98/R, 21 June 1999, nn. 7.32 *et seq.*, and references therein.

Measures (SCM) and the Agreement on Agriculture. The provisions of the SCM Agreement apply, with a few exceptions, to industrial products; those of the Agreement on Agriculture relate to agricultural products. The SCM Agreement recognises that governments utilise subsidies to attain various policy objectives. The aim of the SCM Agreement is not to restrain unduly the right of governments to grant subsidies, but to prohibit or discourage them from using subsidies that have adverse effects on the trade of other countries. The Agreement divides subsidies into prohibited ("red light subsidies") and permissible subsidies. Prohibited subsidies are export subsidies, i.e. subsidies that are contingent on export performance, and subsidies that are contingent on the use of domestic over imported goods, whereas all other subsidies are permissible.[44] Permissible subsidies are divided into two categories: subsidies that are actionable ("amber subsidies") and those that are not actionable ("green subsidies"). The Agreement as it originally entered into force contains the category of green subsidies—non-actionable subsidies. This category (along with a provision establishing a presumption of serious prejudice in respect of certain specified types of actionable subsidies) applied provisionally for five years ending 31 Dec. 1999, and Art. 31 of the Agreement, could be extended by consensus of the SCM Committee. As of today, no such consensus had been reached. Different countervailing measures are allocated to the three categories.

Permissible subsidies are actionable if they are specific, i.e. if they are limited to an enterprise or group of enterprises, to an industrial sector or to a group of industries, or to a designated geographic region within the jurisdiction of the granting authority. However, they are only actionable provided that they cause "adverse effects to the interests of other Members" (Articles 2 and 5 SCM). Adverse effects means serious prejudice or material injury to the domestic industry of the importing country, or nullification and impairment of the benefits of bound tariff rates. In such cases, a member may unilaterally determine injury and levels of countervailing duties. It would then be up to the subsidising member to demonstrate in WTO dispute settlement that the duties imposed are unlawful.

Subsidies are generally not actionable if they are not specific (Articles 2 and 8 SCM). However, certain subsidies that are specific remain non-actionable, provided that the specific conditions governing them comply with the rules of the

---

[44] See Panel Report, *Australia—Subsidies provided to producers and exporters of automotive leather*, WT/DS126/R, adopted 16 June 1999, paras. 9.43–9.76; as regards export subsidies granted by developing countries in the light of Art. 27 SCM, see Panel Report, *Brazil—Export Financing Programme for Aircraft*, WT/DS46/R, paras. 7.1–7.93, as clarified by Panel Report, *Brazil—Export Financing Programme for Aircraft—Recourse by Canada to Article 21.5 of the DSU*, WT/DS46/RW, 9 May 2000, paras. 6.9–6.17 and 6.21–6.67, and as partially modified by the Appellate Body Report, *Brazil—Export Financing Programme for Aircraft*, WT/DS46/AB/R, adopted 20 August 2000; see further Panel Report, *Canada—Measures Affecting the Export of Civilian Aircraft*, WT/DS70/R, 14 April 1999, paras. 9.96–9.123, confirmed by Appellate Body Report, *Canada—Measures Affecting the Export of Civilian Aircraft*, WT/DS70/AB/R, adopted 20 August 2000; see also Appellate Body Report, *Canada—Certain Measures Affecting the Automotive Industry*, WT/DS139/AB/R, WT/DS142/AB/R, 31 May 2000, paras. 87–146.

SCM Agreement. These comprise subsidies:

—for research purposes,
—to adapt existing production facilities to new environmental requirements, provided that the subsidy is a one-off non-recurring measure, and is limited to 20 per cent of the cost of adaptation, or
—to assist in the development of industries in disadvantaged regions, provided that such assistance is not directed to specific enterprises or industries within the region.

Regarding regional subsidies, Article 2(2:2) SCM provides, on one hand, that a subsidy which is limited to certain enterprises located within a designated geographical region within the jurisdiction of the granting authority shall be specific.[45] The provision therefore excludes non-specific, general contributions to regions from the application of the Agreement, while leaving to the regions the possibility of levying their own tax rates.

On the other hand, non-actionable "green" subsidies include, according to Article 8.1(b) and 8.2(b) SCM, specific subsidies in the form of assistance to disadvantaged regions within the territory of a member given pursuant to a general framework[46] of regional development and non-specific within eligible regions provided that:

—such regions are territorially determined as a contiguous geographical area with a definable economic and administrative identity;
—such regions are considered as disadvantaged on the basis of neutral and objective criteria[47] indicating that the region's difficulties arise out of more than temporary circumstances;
—such criteria shall include a measurement of economic development based on at least one of the following factors:

—one of either income *per capita* or household income *per capita*, or GDP *per capita*, which must not be above 85 per cent of the average for the territory concerned;
—unemployment rate, which must be at least 110 per cent of the average for the territory concerned.

---

[45] This provision also sets out that the setting or change of generally applicable tax rates by all levels of government entitled to do so shall not be deemed to be a specific subsidy for the purpose of the SCM Agreement.

[46] According to the interpretative note to this provision, a "general framework of regional development" means that regional subsidy programmes are part of an internally consistent and generally applicable (i.e. non-specific) regional development policy and that regional development subsidies are not granted in isolated geographical points having no, or virtually no, influence on the development of a region.

[47] A further interpretative note to this section specifies that "neutral and objective criteria" mean criteria which do not favour certain regions beyond what is appropriate for the elimination or reduction of regional disparities within the framework of the regional development policy. In this respect, regional subsidy programmes shall include ceilings on the amount of assistance which can be granted to each of the subsidised projects. Such ceilings must be differentiated according to the different levels of development of assisted regions and must be expressed in terms of investment costs or cost of job creation.

The SCM Agreement covers only subsidies for goods, and excludes trade in services from its scope of application. These disciplines are yet to be defined. As a matter of fact, pursuant to Article XV GATS, members shall enter into negotiations with a view to developing the necessary multilateral disciplines in order to avoid distortive effects on trade in services. This programme has not led to any results so far. Nevertheless, trade in services has to comply with other applicable WTO rules such as the principle of national treatment which we have described briefly above.

The margin of manœuvre for regional policies has therefore to be found within the framework of amber and green subsidies. It is defined by the law and the remedies provided for the implementation of the rules. Different options need to be distinguished. The SCM Agreement provides two types of remedies where the subsidies granted by governments cause "adverse effects" to the trade interests of other countries.

Where adverse effects take the form of material injury to a domestic industry in the importing country, the Agreement authorises that country to levy countervailing duties in order to offset the subsidy. Such duties can be levied only if, after duly conducted investigations, the investigating authorities are satisfied that there is a causal link between subsidised or dumped imports and the material injury to the industry concerned. Furthermore, such investigations can normally be initiated only on the basis of a petition from the affected industry alleging that such imports are causing damage to it. Finally, findings have to be made subject to domestic judicial review (Part V, Articles 10–23 SCM). It is unclear to what extent domestic proceedings are equally open to challenge non-actionable subsidies. Part V (which essentially reflects the results of the Tokyo Round) is not well co-ordinated with provisons in Parts I–V (elaborated during the Uruguay Round). The wording does not exclude such measures in the case of non-actionable subsidies as the new categories are not reflected in the text. The very notion of non-actionable subsidies, however, implies that domestic countermeasures should not take place with regard to this category. It was the very object and purpose to create legal security, and to exclude countervailing measures in this field. Earlier and conceptual drafts excluded the possibility of taking such measures. Negotiations, however, settled for the possibility of diplomatic efforts aiming at removing the measures or offering compensation (but short of unilateral trade sanctions) in case these subsidies nevertheless produce serious adverse effects abroad. At any rate, unlawful unilateral action taken by countries may eventually be challenged by the subsidising member before the WTO dispute settlement panels and Appellate Body.

Alternatively, in the case of both serious prejudice to a domestic industry and other adverse effects by actionable (as well as prohibited) subsidies the importing country can bring the matter before the Dispute Settlement Body (DSB) in order to secure withdrawal or modification by the subsidising country of the subsidies that are causing these adverse effects. Members are, as such, not obliged to pass through domestic determination but may challenge a policy directly on the international level. With respect to non-actionable subsidies, one would expect no countermeasures at all to be allowed, and that dispute settlement would be made available to challenge unlawful countermeasures only. However, to the extent that green subsidies cause serious adverse affects, the trading partner concerned may request consultations with a view to finding a solution. The logic of non-actionable subsidies did not fully materialise and negotiations resulted in a compromise. The matter is not subject to dispute settlement before a Panel and the Appellate Body. However, upon consultations, the Party concerned may eventually be authorised by the (political) SCM Committee to take appropriate action (Article 9 SCM). It is unclear to what extent these procedural differences are of importance. The absence of legal dispute settlement and thus of proper enforcement of adopted reports amounts overall to weaker remedies in the field of non-actionable subsidies.

Agreement on Agriculture

Agricultural subsidies are of particular importance for the regional policies of the European Union. It is important to note that they are subject to a special legal regime. Unlike the SCM Agreement, the approach adopted in the Agreement on Agriculture requires from the Members reductions in the use of export and production subsidies. From this perspective, this Agreement divides subsidies into two categories: green and amber.[48] Green subsidies are those which are permitted to be used, and to which reduction commitments do not apply. Amber subsidies include subsidies to which reduction commitments apply.[49]

All subsidies that have "no, or at most minimal, trade-distorting effects or effects on production" and do not have the "effect of providing price support to producers" are considered as green subsidies pursuant to Annex 2, Section 1, of the Agreement on Agriculture. Pursuant to this Annex, green subsidies include payments under regional assistance and environmental programmes, government expenditures on agricultural research and structural adjustment assistance provided through producer retirement programmes, resource retirement programmes or investment aids designed to assist the financial or physical restructuring of producers' production.[50]

---

[48] See R. Horber, "Die Liberalisierung des Agrarhandels: Beweggründe, Auswirkungen und Massnahmen", in T. Cottier (ed.), *GATT-Uruguay Round* (Bern, Verlag Stämpfli, 1995), 51–66.

[49] Under the Agreement on Agriculture, the members are committed to abolish non-tariff measures, such as quantitative restrictions, discretionary licensing and variable levies, by computing their tariff equivalents and adding these to the fixed tariffs. Tariff rates resulting from such tarification as well as tariffs applicable to other products have been bound against further increases. Furthermore, the Agreement on Agriculture lays down rules for subsidies on agricultural products which differ from those applicable to industrial products.

[50] In particular, agricultural programme payments with environmental objectives are granted green box status under two conditions: first, eligibility for the payments "shall be determined as part of a clearly defined government environmental or conservation programme and be dependent on the fulfilment of specific conditions under the government programme, including conditions related to

According to Section 1 of Annex 2 to the Agreement on Agriculture, domestic support measures for which exemption from the reduction commitments is claimed shall have no, or at most minimal, trade-distorting effects or effects on production, and shall meet the basic criteria as follows:

—the support in question shall be provided through a publicly-funded government programme not involving transfers from consumers; and
—such support shall not have the effect of providing price support to producers.

Section 13 of this Annex further lists the additional requirements for payments to be made specifically under regional assistance programmes, which can be summarised as follows:

—eligibility for such payments shall be limited to producers in disadvantaged regions, which are defined in the same way as in the SCM Agreement;
—the amount of such payments shall not be related to, or based on, the type or volume of production, or the prices, domestic or international, applying to any production undertaken in any year after the base period;
—payments shall be available only to producers in eligible regions, but generally available to all producers within such regions;
—where related to production factors, payments shall be made at a digressive rate above a threshold level of the factor concerned;
—the payments shall be limited to the extra costs or loss of income involved in undertaking agricultural production in the prescribed area.

As under the SCM Agreement, the distinction between amber and green subsidies is equally reflected in the remedies available to enforce obligations. Domestic support measures in conformity with Annex A are deemed to be non-actionable subsidies as defined under the SCM Agreement and are exempt from actions based upon Article XVI GATT and the categories of actionable subsidies as well as from non-violation complaints. Equally, direct payments are generally exempted from countervailing duties otherwise allowed with respect to actionable subsidies, and from non-violation complaints. Finally, agricultural export subsidies complying with the provisions of the Agreement are subject to countervailing duties only to the extent that injury is determined (Article 13). In conclusion, regional policies pursued by means of agricultural policies enjoy considerable scope and leeway under current rules of the WTO.

Further WTO Agreements

The Agreement on Technical Barriers (TBT), which provides for non-discrimination in respect of mandatory and voluntary product standards, can,

production methods or inputs"; secondly, the payment amount "shall be limited to the extra costs or loss of income involved in complying with the government programme".

on occasion, be relevant in the context of regional policies. The TBT requires in principle that where technical regulations are necessary, and where relevant international standards exist or their completion is imminent, members shall use them as a basis for their technical regulations. However, Article 2.4 TBT sets out an "exception" addressing the situation where such international standards would be an ineffective or inappropriate means of fulfilling the legitimate objectives pursued, for instance, because of fundamental climatic or geographical factors or fundamental technological problems. States are therefore authorised under the TBT to adopt technical regulations in the context of regional policies that would be based, for example, on geographical or climatic factors being specific to the regions which are concerned by such policies. Pursuant to this exception, technical regulations implemented on a regional basis caused by geographical factors would not need to be in compliance with international standards otherwise relevant by virtue of Article 2.1 TBT. We cannot see much scope for pursuing regional policies by means of standard-setting under this Agreement. But the possibility exists. If a country adopts mandatory technical regulations that are not based on international standards, it must follow the notification procedure described in Article 2.9 TBT to enable the other countries to comment on them. Members shall ensure that products imported from the territory of any member shall, in respect of technical regulations be accorded treatment no less favourable than that accorded to like products of national origin and to like products originating in any other country, and that these regulations do not cause unnecessary obstacles to trade (Articles 2.1 and 2.2 TBT).

The Agreement on the Application of Sanitary and Phytosanitary Measures (SPS) allows the members to adopt measures in the field of foodstuffs that are necessary to protect human, animal or plant life or health (see Annex 1 to the Agreement for a definition of SPS measures). However, such measures shall not be applied in a manner which would constitute a means of arbitrary or unjustifiable discrimination between Members where the same conditions prevail, or a disguised restriction on international trade. According to Article 6, Members shall ensure that their sanitary or phytosanitary measures are adapted to the sanitary or phytosanitary characteristics of the area—whether all of a country, part of a country, or all or parts of several countries—from which the product originated and to which the product is destined. This provision therefore may require a differentiated treatment of such measures according to the relevant specificities of the region concerned. In particular, members shall recognise the concepts of pest- or disease-free areas and areas of low pest or disease prevalence (Article 6(2) SPS) which grant to the concerned regions corresponding facilitations in trade.

The Agreement on Trade-related Aspects of Intellectual Property Rights (TRIPs) contains provisions relating to the protection of geographical indications. These are of some importance for regional policy as the quality of a product, in this case of IPR rights, is essentially linked to and attributed to its geographical origin (Article 21). The protection of such denominations and the obligation to establish specific instruments for the protection of denominations of wines and spirits (Article 23) entails important components and offers significant potential to support the economic performance of regions which produce specialties.

Finally, there is an important angle for regional policies in the plurilateral Agreement on Government Procurement (GPA).[51] According to Article XVI(1), of the agreement, entities shall not, in the qualification and selection of suppliers, products or services, or in the evaluation of tenders and award of contracts, impose, seek or consider offsets. In a footnote related thereto, "offsets in government procurement" are defined as measures used to encourage local development or improve the balance-of-payment accounts by means of domestic content, licensing or technology, investment requirements, counter-trade or similar requirements. Under Article XVI(2) GPA, a developing country may at the time of accession negotiate conditions for the use of offsets, such as requirements for the incorporation of domestic content. This exception is based on general policy considerations, including those relating to development. The scope for regional policies by means of government procurement are limited under WTO law. As a practical matter, local tenders in remote regions may often not be the cheapest, but the economically most efficient ones if services provided in maintaining the product are considered.

Enforcement on the Subnational Level: the Federal Clause

As regions constitute sub-federal or sometimes even transnational entities, it is important to look into the possibility of enforcing WTO disciplines *vis-à-vis* these entities. Normally, full state responsibility under international law rests with the central state encompassing all actions taken by sub-federal levels and entities. The WTO, interestingly, provides for limited responsibility only. Pursuant to Article XXIV:12 GATT, each contracting party shall take such reasonable measures as may be constitutionally available to it in order to ensure observance of the provisions of this Agreement by the regional and local governments and authorities within its territories. The 1985 Panel unadopted report on *Canada—Measures Affecting the Sale of Gold Coins*[52] examined the drafting history of Article XXIV:12 GATT. It noted that this provision "applies only to those measures taken at regional or local level which the federal government cannot control because they fall outside its jurisdiction under the constitutional distribution of competence".[53]

---

[51] The European Community is a signatory to this non-mandatory WTO Agreement.
[52] L/5863, 17 September 1985
[53] See E.-U. Petersmann, "Strengthening the Domestic Legal Framework of the GATT Multilateral Trade System: Possibilities and Problems of Making GATT Rules Effective in Domestic Legal Systems" in E.-U. Petersmann and J. Hilf (eds.), *The New GATT Round of Multilateral Trade Negociations: Legal and Economic Problems* (Deventer, Kluwer, 1991) 93 ff.

This panel report further specified that "if Article XXIV:12 is to fulfil its function of allowing federal States to accede to the General Agreement without having to change the federal distribution of competence, then it must be possible for them to invoke this provision not only when the regional or local governments' competence can be clearly established but also in those cases in which the exact distribution of competence still remains to be determined by the competent judicial or political bodies".

Referring to this report, the 1992 Panel Report on *United States—Measures Affecting Alcoholic and Malt Beverages*[54] stated that:

> As indicated in an earlier panel report, not yet adopted by the contracting parties, the qualification in Article XXIV:12 of the obligation to implement the provisions of the General Agreement grants a special right to federal states without giving an offsetting privilege to unitary states, and has to be construed narrowly so as to avoid undue imbalances in rights and obligations between contracting parties with unitary and federal constitutions. The above-mentioned interpretation—according to which Article XXIV:12 applies only to measures by regional or local authorities which the central government cannot control under the constitutional distribution of powers—meets the constitutional difficulties which central governments may have in ensuring the observance of the provisions of the General Agreement by regional and local authorities, but minimises the risk that such difficulties lead to imbalances in the rights and obligations of contracting parties.

Regarding the meaning of "reasonable measures" in this context, the unadopted 1985 Panel report on *Canada—Measures Affecting the Sale of Gold Coins* specified that the only indication in the General Agreement of what was meant by "reasonable" was contained in the interpretative note to Article III:1 GATT, which defined the term "reasonable measures" for the case of national legislation authorising local governments to impose taxes. The basic principle embodied in this note is, in the view of the Panel, that in determining which measures to secure the observance of the provisions of the General Agreement are "reasonable" within the meaning of Article XXIV:12, the consequences of their non-observance by the local government for trade relations with other contracting parties are to be weighed against the domestic difficulties of securing observance".[55] The Understanding on the Interpretation of Article XXIV GATT, inserted by the Uruguay Round, was essentially informed by these reports and experiences. It does not further specify the concept of reasonableness except for clarifying that action taken by sub-federal entities are subject to dispute resolution (paragraph 13.15 of the Understanding). Some agreements, however, contain somewhat more specific obligations. It is interesting to note that Article 7 of the plurilateral Agreement on Trade in Civil Aircraft expressly

---

[54] DS23/R, adopted on 19 June 1992.

[55] According to J. Jackson, *The Jurisprudence of GATT & the WTO* (New York, CUP, 2000), 255, GATT is directly applicable to state and local governments in the United States, and supersedes state or local law even when that law is not automatically pre-empted by federal law, and even when such law existed prior to GATT.

provides that its "Signatories agree not to require or encourage, directly or indirectly, regional and local governments and authorities, non-governmental bodies, and other bodies to take action inconsistent with provisions of this Agreement". Likewise, Article 7 TBT provides that members shall take such reasonable measures as may be available to them to ensure compliance by the local government bodies within their territories with respect to the set of rules in Articles 5 and 6 addressing the procedures of assessment where a positive assurance of conformity with technical regulations or standards is required, and the recognition of such conformity assessment.[56]

Regarding the determination of references with respect to which differential treatment among regions must be analysed under the principle of national treatment, the 1992 Panel Report on *Canada—Import, Distribution and Sale of Certain Alcoholic Drinks by Provincial Marketing Agencies*[57] is of importance. It addresses measures of Canadian provincial liquor boards which applied both to beer originating outside of Canada and beer from other provinces of Canada. A note to the Panel findings provides that "the reference to domestic beer is a reference to the domestic beer which receives the most favourable treatment by Canada in the province in question, that is in most instances the beer brewed in that province". Furthermore, the 1992 Panel Report on *United States— Measures Affecting Alcoholic and Malt Beverages*[58] considered with respect to differential excise taxes levied by US states as not being relevant to the fact that many of the state provisions at issue in this dispute provide the same treatment to products of other states of the Union as that provided to foreign products. It specified that "national treatment provisions require contracting parties to accord to imported products treatment no less favourable than that accorded to any like domestic product, whatever the domestic origin. Article III GATT consequently requires treatment of imported products no less favourable than that accorded to the most-favoured domestic products". Thus, discrimination against subnational entities (*"discrimination à rebours"*) on the internal level does not legitimate discrimination against other WTO Members.

CONCLUSIONS

The multilateral trading system of the GATT and now the WTO is concerned principally to secure freer trade among its members. It has not been concerned with distributive justice other than in terms of incremental effects on it resulting

---

[56] This rule applies when local regulatory authorities require that imports are allowed to be sold only upon deliverance by the exporter of a certificate of positive assurance from a recognised control body in the importing country according to which the product is in conformity with the standard. Art. 6 TBT requires that Members shall accept, whenever possible, the results of the inspection and tests carried out by competent certifying entities in the exporting countries, even when those procedures differ from their own, provided that they can be considered as equivalent.

[57] DS17/R, adopted 18 February 1992.

[58] DS23/R, adopted 19 June 1992.

from growth and efficient allocation of resources. Moreover, it primarily deals with national levels, leaving disciplines enforceable on the subnational level merely to the extent that constitutional law allows for it (Article XXIV:12 GATT and the Understanding). Regions other than sub-federal entities are mentioned in WTO law by reference to "other authorities within its territory", but not addressed in a more detailed manner. Indeed, it seems that the matter of preferential flanking policies within federal structures has not been an explicit and widely discussed concern so far.

All of this is not astonishing. We should recall that international law essentially deals with international relations. Generally speaking, sovereign states are held responsible in international law for all governmental acts occurring on their territory, irrespective of the level of government involved. The problem of regulating sub-state levels in international law does not normally occur. The WTO is a special case as the GATT, designed from its very beginning as a provisional agreement and applied in the United States, for instance, as an executive agreement only, has limited the scope of application and enforcement essential to the powers of central government.

The WTO core principle of national treatment applies to regional policies as to any other policy of the WTO members. The Agreements do not contain specific exceptions relating to regional policies other than in the field of specific subsidies. The WTO assumes that regional policies are mainly pursued through financial assistance, and does not contemplate other trade-related means to social and economic development. In particular, local content rules and policies are excluded. The same holds true for government procurement which no longer allows to privilege local and regional tenders.

The general rules on subsidies contained in Article VI GATT and the SCM Agreement and those covering the agricultural area allow certain assistance, which may vary in terms of the sector concerned (industry, agriculture, culture) and in the light of their purposes (environment, research and development, etc.). In addition, the rules addressing subsidies, which include tax breaks and other forms of privileges, grant further possibilities specifically with respect to regional policies not yet explored by WTO case law. In this context, the "federal clause" of Article XXIV:12 GATT could well obtain new significance, and become subject to more elaborate interpretation in future cases. The dynamics—which we have illustrated by reference to the concept of "partnership" between the Commission, the EU Members and their regional entities to implement the EU Structural Funds—and which are inherent in the very idea of the region, in particular in the decision-making processes of regional and local authorities, represent in our view a substantial enrichment for the elaboration and enforcement of cohesion policy programmes, since they materialise the principle of subsidiarity. On the other hand, such dynamics are likely to reduce the central (federal) governments' control, to be exercised through "reasonable measures" as defined in the quoted Panel case law over those public interventions on the regional or local level that would not be in compliance with

WTO rules. We therefore expect that the new architectures of regional cohesion policy-making and implementation will increasingly define the scope of application of the WTO rules in this area—and vice versa. It is premature to say whether the current rules of the WTO adequately reflect the need for regional policies or in what ways they may need to be amended. In the long run, we may observe a parallel evolution to the one witnessed in many federal structures and the European Union alike. The process of liberalisation, and the bringing about of equal conditions of competition may eventually require the development of flanking policies and thus regional policies on the part of the WTO itself, in combination with other international organisations. This would be based upon the need to bring about not only an efficient, but also an equitable allocation of resources among the different regions of the globe.

9

Constitutional Concepts for Free Trade in Services

PIET EECKHOUT

INTRODUCTION

THIS CHAPTER IS an attempt to tell the stories of liberalisation of trade in services in the EU and the WTO. It concentrates on the concepts which the EC Treaty and the General Agreement on Trade in Services (GATS) employ to achieve such liberalisation, and seeks to compare those concepts as interpreted by the respective judiciaries—the European Court of Justice and WTO Panels and Appellate Body. The chapter does not examine the actual impact of GATS on the regulation of external trade in services in the EU. Such an examination would require an in-depth study of the EC's commitments under GATS (and those of its Member States), which I am unable to carry out at present, and would perhaps yield fewer results in terms of the constitutional dimension to the relationship between the EU and the WTO. The aim is rather to set up an inquiry into the GATS notions of market access and non-discrimination, whilst contrasting those notions with the EC law experience with basic, constitutionalised legal principles governing free trade. It is argued that the EC law experience may be relevant, particularly in light of the Appellate Body's recent admission that "[g]iven the complexity of the subject-matter of trade in services, as well as the newness of the obligations under the GATS, we believe that claims made under the GATS deserve close attention and serious analysis".[1] It is not however argued that EC law on services is necessarily a model for GATS,[2] or that GATS provisions need to be interpreted along the lines of the interpretation given to the EC Treaty provisions. There are obvious differences, in wording, objectives, context, and scheme of liberalisation mechanisms in the respective systems. But that does not mean that comparison could not be enriching, and this chapter is looking for similarities rather than differences.

---

[1] *Canada—Automotive Industry*, WT/DS139/AB/R and WT/DS142/AB/R, Appellate Body Report, adopted 19 June 2000, para. 184.

[2] See, before the adoption of GATS, C.D. Ehlermann and G. Campogrande, "Rules on Services in the EEC: A Model for Negotiating World-Wide Rules?" in E.U. Petersmann and M. Hilf (eds.), *The New GATT Round of Multilateral Trade Negotiations* (Deventer, Kluwer, 1989) 127–140.

The chapter contains two broad sections. The first explores the development and evolution of liberalisation law, both in the EC and in GATT/WTO, where we can see that the approach to free trade in services follows in the footsteps of the experience with the liberalisation of trade in goods. The second section examines the market access and national treatment (or non-discrimination) concepts which are central to finding a balance between worshipped liberalisation and accepted regulation. There are other issues, such as direct effect, which lend themselves to a comparison, but (to borrow from the Appellate Body again) I leave those to another paper and another day.[3] Also, the chapter has no concluding section, because the subjects which it addresses are open-ended, and because the two main sections each have a concluding sub-section.

FROM GOODS TO SERVICES—AND PERSONS?

From the outset the EEC Treaty provided for the free movement of goods as well as the freedom to provide services. In that respect EC law is markedly different from GATT/WTO law, where it took from 1947 to 1994 before services were expressly and substantially included. But that chronological difference may mask some essential similarities between the EC and the WTO approach. In particular, in both cases the approach to trade in services has followed in the footsteps of the approach to trade in goods.

The EC Treaty defines the freedom to provide services as subsidiary to the other basic freedoms of the internal market (see Article 50 EC). One reason for that may be that when the Treaty was drafted "trade in services" had not been conceptualised. Indeed, the very concept of trade in services did not yet exist, and services occupied a position in industrialised economies not nearly as prominent as at present. No doubt, services were looked at as rather ancillary and insignificant, but they were none the less sufficiently visible for inclusion in the Treaty approach to the establishment of a common market. We still see the traces of this definition of services as a residual freedom: it sits uneasily between free movement of goods, freedom of establishment and free movement of capital. In the relationship with goods, there is the issue of delineation and definition of what constitutes a good and what constitutes a service.[4] With establishment, there is the, in a sense, more artificial delineation of whether an activity is temporary or permanent, and therefore subject to the services or the establishment provisions.[5] It is artificial because in practice there may be a range of forms of foreign presence of a service provider, the intensity and duration of

---

[3] *Canada—Automotive Industry, supra* n. 1, para. 184.

[4] See, e.g., Case 155/73, *Sacchi* [1974] ECR 409, paras. 6–7; Case C–17/92, *Distribuidores Cinematográficos* v. *Spanish State* [1993] ECR I–2239, paras. 10–11; Joined Cases 60 and 61/84, *Cinéthèque* v. *Fédération nationale des cinémas français* [1985] ECR 2605, paras. 9–10.

[5] See, e.g., Case 205/84, *Commission* v. *Germany* [1986] ECR 3755, para. 21; Case C–55/94, *Gebhard* v. *Consiglio dell'Ordine degli Avocati e Procuratori di Milano* [1995] ECR I–4165, paras. 19–28.

which may fluctuate in time. And with capital, the issue of delineation is likely to pop up in many cases involving financial services, where both a service and a capital transaction are performed.[6] In all such cases of delineation a strict reading of the Treaty suggests that the services provisions are to yield to the application of the other freedoms. However, the ECJ's case law does not always reflect the subsidiary character of services, and appears to treat services in their own right. The best example is perhaps *Svensson and Gustavsson*, where a measure discriminating against foreign bank loans was considered to be a restriction of both the free movement of capital and the freedom to provide services.[7] As such, the case law does justice to the economic development and emancipation of services.

The ECJ appears to have taken services seriously from the outset. Its case law on the scope of (now) Articles 49 and 50 EC is quite developed and sophisticated, even if there are not as many judgments as in the case of goods. None the less, in terms of concepts and analytical tools it is fairly clear that the services case law is very much inspired by the goods case law. Goods has been the leading freedom, even if services has tailed it quite closely at times.

The Classic Tale of Tailing Case Law

In the *Dassonville* case of July 1974 the Court gave its first, and still basic, definition of import restrictions concerning goods[8]—all trading rules capable of hindering, directly or indirectly, actually or potentially, intra-Community trade—and in the *Van Binsbergen* case of December 1974 the Court held that the restrictions to be abolished pursuant to Articles 59 and 60 EC (now Articles 49 and 50) include all requirements imposed on the person providing the service by reason in particular of his nationality or of the fact that he does not habitually reside in the state where the service is provided, which do not apply to persons established within the national territory or which may prevent or otherwise obstruct the activities of the person providing the service.[9]

In the *Cassis de Dijon* case of 1979[10] the Court extended the scope of the free movement of goods to "indistinctly applicable measures", i.e. rules or regulations which apply to all products, be they domestic or imported. Such measures may also constitute restrictions on the movement of goods, in particular where they prevent the importation of goods lawfully produced and marketed in another Member State. As such, *Cassis de Dijon* inaugurated the principle of mutual recognition. However, the case is not just significant for the extension

---

[6] See Case C–484/93, *Svensson and Gustavsson* v. *Ministre du Logement et de l'Urbanisme* [1995] ECR I–3955.

[7] *Ibid.*

[8] Case 8/74, *Procureur du Roi* v. *Dassonville* [1974] ECR 837, para. 5.

[9] Case 33/74, *Van Binsbergen* v. *Bedrijfsvereniging Metaalnijverheid* [1974] ECR 1299, para. 10.

[10] Case 120/78, *Rewe* v. *Bundesmonopolverwaltung für Branntwein* [1979] ECR 649.

of the scope of the free movement principle: that extension carries its own limitations with it, because the Court introduced the concept of "mandatory requirements" which, provided the principle of proportionality is observed, may justify restrictions resulting from indistinctly applicable measures. It is arguable that *Cassis de Dijon* was soon followed by comparable rulings as regards services, but it none the less took until 1991 before the Court expressly confirmed that the Treaty's provisions on services also extend to indistinctly applicable measures. In *Säger*, a clear-cut case of legislation which was indistinctly applicable to domestic and foreign service providers,[11] the Court held that Article 59 (now Article 49) EC requires not only the elimination of all discrimination against a person providing services on the ground of his nationality but also the abolition of any restriction, even if it applies without distinction to national providers of services and to those of other Member States, when it is liable to prohibit or otherwise impede the activities of a provider of services established in another Member State where he lawfully provides similar services.[12] But, as in *Cassis de Dijon*, the Court accepted that restrictions can be justified by "imperative reasons relating to the public interest", provided there is no discrimination and provided the principle of proportionality is complied with.[13]

In *Keck and Mithouard* the Court attempted to limit the scope of the free movement of goods, by ruling that the effects on intra-Community trade of what it called "certain selling arrangements" are not such as to justify the application of Article 30 (now Article 28) EC, which prohibits import restrictions, provided such selling arrangements are non-discriminatory. Selling arrangements were contrasted with product regulations, which continue to be subject to the *Cassis de Dijon* approach.[14] The notion of selling arrangements is notoriously difficult in that the Court did not define it in *Keck*. It is beyond this analysis to try to clarify it;[15] suffice it to point out that subsequent case law does shed light on the types of measures covered by the *Keck* limitation.[16] As regards services, the Court seems unwilling so far to apply a *Keck*-type limitation. The leading case is *Alpine Investments*, which concerned a decision by the Netherlands Ministry of Finance to prohibit certain investment firms from contacting individuals by telephone without their prior consent in writing in order to offer them various financial services ("cold calling"). Alpine Investments was of the opinion that such a prohibition, in so far as it extended to contacting potential clients in other Member States, constituted a restriction on the

[11] Case C–76/90, *Säger* v. *Dennemmeyer* [1991] ECR I–4221; see the Opinion of Jacobs AG, para. 18, where the non-discriminatory character of the legislation is emphasised.

[12] At para. 12.

[13] At para. 15.

[14] Joined Cases C–267/91 and C–268/91 [1993] ECR I–6097.

[15] See S. Weatherill, "After *Keck*: Some Thoughts on How to Clarify the Clarification" (1996) 33 *CMLRev.* 885.

[16] For a short analysis of some of the post-*Keck* cases see P. Eeckhout, "Recent Case-law on Free Movement of Goods: Refining *Keck and Mithouard*" (1998) 9 *EBLR* 267.

freedom to provide services. The Netherlands and United Kingdom governments argued before the Court that the prohibition fell outside the scope of
Article 59 (now Article 49) EC because it was a generally applicable measure, it
was not discriminatory and neither its object nor effect was to put the national
market at an advantage over providers of services from other Member States.
Since it affected only the way in which the services were offered, it was analogous to the non-discriminatory measures governing selling arrangements identified by the Court in *Keck*.[17] The Court, however, disagreed. It stated that,
although the prohibition was general and non-discriminatory and neither its
object nor effect was to put the national market at an advantage over providers
of services from other Member States, it could constitute a restriction on the
freedom to provide cross-border services. The prohibition was not analogous to
the legislation concerning selling arrangements held in *Keck* to fall outside the
scope of Article 30 (now Article 28) EC. The reason for *Keck* was that the application of non-discriminatory selling arrangements was not such as to prevent
access by products from other Member States to the market of the Member State
of importation or to impede such access more than it impedes access by domestic products. By contrast, the prohibition in issue in *Alpine Investments*, which
affected not only offers for investment made to addressees established in the
Netherlands but also offers made to potential recipients in other Member States,
directly affected access to the market in services in the other Member States and
was thus capable of hindering intra-Community trade in services.[18]

At first sight, therefore, it may seem that as regards selling arrangements the
services case law does not follow in the footsteps of the goods case law. And
there are indeed good reasons for not extending the *Keck* limitation to services.
In contrast with goods, most services are consumed at the same time as they are
produced; services are invisible, they are not physical objects which may change
hands and be the subject of a series of transactions. The *Keck*-type situation of
a selling arrangement (for example a prohibition of Sunday trading for gardening materials[19]) which may have an effect on the quantity of imports (if we are
not allowed to sell gardening materials on Sunday, we sell fewer gardening
materials, and therefore import fewer gardening materials) does not readily
arise in the case of services. For example, if the cold-calling restriction in *Alpine
Investments* had been limited to contacting potential clients in the Netherlands,
it would have been impossible for Alpine Investments, as a firm established in
the Netherlands, to use the Sunday trading argument of saying: if we are unable
to use cold calling, we sell fewer services, and therefore we import fewer services. The situation would have been purely internal, not involving trade in

---

[17] Case C–384/93, [1995] ECR I–1141, para. 33.
[18] Paras. 35–38.
[19] The example is inspired by the Sunday trading cases which led to *Keck and Mithouard*, i.e.
Case C–145/88, *Torfaen Borough Council* v. *B & Q plc* [1989] ECR 3851; Case C–332/89,
Marchandise and Others [1991] ECR I–1027; Case C–169/91, *Council of the City of Stoke-on-Trent*
v. *B & Q plc* [1992] ECR I–6635.

services between the Member States. If, on the other hand, the cold-calling restriction affected an investment firm established in another Member State, which could not use cold calling to attract new clients in the Netherlands (the reverse of the actual *Alpine Investments*), then again there would obviously be a restriction on the freedom to provide services of the *Säger* type (an "import" restriction, but as regards services it makes little sense to distinguish between imports and exports). A restriction which, obviously, comes within the scope of Articles 49 and 50 EC, and is prohibited if not justified on the basis of imperative requirements in the general interest.

But there is, as regards selling arrangements, less difference between goods and services than may be thought. In *Alpine Investments* the Court emphasised, as we have seen, that the measure direcly affected market access. In the post-*Keck* case law, not only in the field of goods, but also in the field of services and even as regards free movement of workers, the notion of market access has become an important tool for examining whether or not there is a restriction coming within the scope of the Treaty provisions.[20] Increasingly, the central question appears to be whether a measure prevents or significantly impedes market access. That very notion of market access is of course well known to WTO lawyers, especially as regards services, where market access and national treatment are the basic tools for liberalisation—but this analogy will be developed below. At this point it may be sufficient to note that, under the ECJ's case law, the notion of discrimination is not (or no longer) central to determining whether there is a restriction on free movement. Indistinctly applicable measures may constitute restrictions, if market access is in issue, and such restrictions are prohibited where they cannot be justified on grounds of "mandatory" or "imperative" requirements—an open-ended set of non-economic policy concerns which trump the internal market ideal, provided the restrictions are non-discriminatory and proportionate.

From GATT to GATS

The evolution in GATT/WTO law is similar to that in EC law, in the sense that the approach to services has followed in the footsteps of the approach to goods: as is well known the GATS aims to liberalise trade in services through the use of principles and mechanisms similar to those employed by GATT (as even the respective names of the agreements suggest), such as most-favoured-nation treatment (MFN), national treatment, market access, detailed negotiation of

[20] See Eeckhout, *supra* n. 16. Concerning goods, see Case C–368/95, *Familiapress* v. *Bauer Verlag* [1997] ECR I–3689, paras. 11–12; Joined Cases C–34–36/95, *KO* v. *De Agostini and TV-Shop* [1997] ECR I–3843, paras. 39–44; Case C–337/95, *Christian Dior* v. *Evora* [1997] ECR I–6013, para. 5. Concerning services, see *Alpine Investments*, *supra* n. 17 and Joined Cases C–51/96 and C–191/97, *Deliège*, judgment of 11 April 2000, para. 61. Concerning workers, see Case C–415/93, *Union Royale Belge des Sociétés de Football Association and Others* v. *Bosman and Others* [1995] ECR I–4921, para. 103.

commitments, etc. And the footstepping exercise is not confined to the formulation of the provisions in those agreements, but naturally extends to the case law under them. For example, in *Bananas III* the Appellate Body held that:

(a) In construing the "treatment no less favourable" clause in Article II GATS, on MFN, the Panel was mistakenly guided by the same clause in Article XVII GATS, on national treatment; instead, the correct point of reference was Article I GATT, on MFN in the field of goods;[21]
(b) Like the national treatment obligation of Article III GATT, the national treatment principle of Article XVII GATS was foreign to an "aims-and-effects" analysis which would include looking at the regulatory purpose of a measure.[22]

Of course, as was mentioned, there was a huge time-gap between the creation of GATT and of GATS. This time-gap allowed for prior reflection on the conceptualisation of trade in services and its liberalisation. It is notable that the formulation of GATS was preceded by advanced economic research on the service economy, on the position and indeed very definition of "trade" in services, and on the transposability to international trade in services of economic theories demonstrating the advantages of free trade.[23] One could say that GATS is the child of both GATT and the economic research on services.

At this juncture a brief overview of the main GATS principles and mechanisms may be in order. According to Article I, GATS applies to measures affecting trade in services. The latter is defined as the supply of a service by one or more of four "modes":

(1) cross-frontier, i.e. from the territory of one member into the territory of any other member;
(2) consumption abroad, i.e. in the territory of one member to the service consumer of any other member;
(3) commercial presence, i.e. by a service supplier of one member, through commercial presence in the territory of any other member;
(4) presence of natural persons, i.e. by a service supplier of one member, through presence of natural persons of a member in the territory of any other member.

Part II of GATS contains "General Obligations and Disciplines". For our purposes, its most significant provision is Article II on MFN, which provides that with respect to any measure covered by GATS each WTO member shall accord immediately and unconditionally to services and service suppliers of any other member treatment no less favourable than that it accords to like services and

---

[21] *EC—Bananas (III)*, Appellate Body Report, WT/DS27/AB/R, adopted 25 September 1997, paras. 229–234.
[22] Paras. 240–248. On aims-and-effects see below.
[23] See for an overview P. Eeckhout, *The European Internal Market and International Trade* (Oxford, OUP, 1994) at 7–12.

service suppliers of any other member. Granting MFN treatment is an unconditional and unqualified obligation, in contrast with the market access and national treatment commitments referred to below. There is scope for exemptions from the application of Article II, but those must be temporary and are subject to the provisions of the Annex on Article II Exemptions.

Part II also contains provisions on economic integration; on recognition of foreign education etc.; on general exceptions and on security exceptions.

Parts III and IV of GATS deal with specific commitments entered into by members under a process of progressive liberalisation. It is here that GATS ceases to be just a basic text on the liberalisation of trade in services. The specific commitments of market access (Article XVI) and national treatment (Article XVII) apply only to the extent that a member has inscribed a service sector in its Schedule, and under the terms, limitations and conditions agreed and specified there. The basic idea is that liberalisation of trade in services can be achieved only through a gradual process of negotiation, and the Schedules' approach is inspired by the GATT system of negotiating tariff reductions. There are of course no tariffs for services, but there are limitations to the supply of services by foreign service suppliers, and GATS categorises those limitations as either market access restrictions or lack of national treatment. The Schedules in a sense codify and freeze those limitations, and the negotiating process aims at their gradual removal, the end goal being full market access and national treatment in all services sectors.[24]

The provisions of Articles XVI and XVII are therefore relevant only to the extent that actual commitments were made by members. Article XVI mentions six types of measures which a member may not adopt or maintain in those sectors where market-access commitments were undertaken. They include limitations on the number of service suppliers, limitations on the total value of service transactions or the total number of service operations, limitations on the total number of natural persons that may be employed in a particular service sector, measures which restrict or require specific types of legal entity or joint venture, and limitations on the participation of foreign capital.

Article XVII defines national treatment, and that definition has already been crucial in a couple of disputes and therefore warrants closer scrutiny. Article XVII:1 contains the principle: each member shall accord to services and service suppliers of any other member, in respect of all measures affecting the supply of services, treatment no less favourable than that it accords to its own like services and service suppliers (subject of course to the conditions and qualifications set out in the Schedules). A footnote specifies that this does not require any member to compensate for any inherent competitive disadvantages which result from the foreign character of the relevant services or service suppliers. The principle of paragraph 1 is clarified in paragraphs 2 and 3. Article XVII:2 provides that a

---

[24] For a more detailed description see M.J. Trebilcock and R. Howse, *The Regulation of International Trade* (2nd edn., London, Routledge, 1999) at 286–289.

member may meet the requirement of paragraph 1 by according to services and service suppliers of any other member either formally identical or formally different treatment from that it accords to its own like services and service suppliers. Article XVII:3 specifies that formally identical or formally different treatment shall be considered to be less favourable if it modifies the conditions of competition in favour of services or service suppliers of the member compared to like services or service suppliers of any other member. It may be noted here that, again, GATT was the source of inspiration, as the wording of Article XVII:2 and XVII:3 was taken from GATT Panel Reports on the interpretation of Article III GATT, which contains the national treatment principle for goods.[25] In fact, both GATT and GATS distinguish between market access (Article XI GATT on import and export restrictions) and national treatment.

Bringing them Together: EC and GATT/WTO Law—and Goods, Services and Persons

In both cases services follow in the footsteps of goods, even though in EC law the basic provisions were drafted at the same time. One may be tempted to conclude that the EC experience with services is much more developed and covers a much longer time frame than the experience with GATS. But that is only half true. The ECJ's case law concerning Articles 49 and 50 EC is indeed extensive, but in a sense the framework for the real liberalisation of trade in services in the EC was set up at about the same time as GATS was starting to be negotiated. For it is safe to say that it was not the case law which opened up the provision of services in Europe's internal market, but rather the EC's 1992 internal market programme, with its extensive harmonisation of legislation. As is well-known, the cornerstone of that legislation is the principle of mutual recognition, coming from *Cassis de Dijon* and turned into a principle of allocation of supervisory competence by the legislature (the home and host Member State matrix, for example in financial services).[26]

Here there is a difference. To simplify, Europe seems to have put its faith in the generalisation of a principle stemming from case law, whereas GATT/WTO built its approach to trade in services on foundations of economic theory. History will (perhaps) tell which is to be the more successful. Or the difference may turn out to be insubstantial.

---

[25] Panel Report on *Italian Discrimination of Imported Agricultural Machinery*, adopted on 23 October 1958, BISD 7S/60, 63, para. 12 ("adversely modify the conditions of competition") and Panel Report on *US—Section 337 of the Tariff Act of 1930*, adopted on 7 November 1989, BISD 36S/345, 386, para. 5.11 ("effective equality of opportunities" and "there may be cases where application of formally identical legal provisions would in practice accord less favourable treatment to imported products").

[26] On the differences between mutual recognition (or functional parallellism, as some prefer) in the case law and in the legislation, see P. Eeckhout, "The European Court of Justice and the Legislature" (1998) 18 *YEL* at 18–20.

However, there is more to be said on "from goods to services". For services are not goods (indeed, what are they exactly?), and we cannot simply speak of both as products whose circulation is to be liberalised, full stop.

The approach to trade in goods is clearly primarily economic and product-based. It makes absolute sense here to concentrate on removing obstacles to the circulation of products. In order to reap the benefits of free trade goods are to have free market access, they must reach the consumer after having cleared as few hurdles as possible. This has many layers, as goods are traded at various levels and may change ownership several times before reaching the consumer. At each of those levels there may be regulation constituting an "obstacle", "barrier", "impediment", or "restriction". Hence the broad scope of the rule of free movement, for even Sunday trading rules or the prohibition of selling formula milk other than in pharmacies[27] may affect trade between countries. Hence the importance of non-discrimination (or national treatment) at every stage of transportation, distribution, offering for sale, etc., once goods have been imported. It is further important to note here that goods, as traded in current societies, are as a rule fully standardised and homogenised: of each type of goods there is an identical range and goods are highly substitutable. Formula milk for babies will feed (nearly) any baby. There are different brands, with slightly different characteristics,[28] but of any particular brand/type of formula milk there are bound to be huge, perfectly substitutable quantities.

Two footnotes. The first is that the above is of course not intended to suggest that there must be absolutely free market access. There are obviously policy concerns that justify limitations to free trade, and which must be balanced against the free trade rule. The second is that, in the end, any regulation remains regulation of a (natural or legal) person involved in the trading or use of a product. No obligations can be imposed on the goods themselves. None the less, in conceptual terms much regulation does come close to being regulation of the goods themselves.

Services, by contrast, are much more complex. Some types of services are most analogous to goods, in that the service can be separated from the person providing the service, much like goods are separated from their producer. But other types of services are by definition individual, and the emphasis is on the relationship between the supplier of the service and its consumer. This may imply that the service supplier or consumer move to the country where the service is consumed. The *locus classicus* in this respect is the Opinion of AG Jacobs in *Säger*:[29]

> The truth is that the provision of services covers a vast spectrum of different types of activity. At one extreme, it may be necessary for the provider of the service to spend a

---

[27] See Case C–391/92, *Commission* v. *Greece* [1995] ECR I–1621.

[28] The example is admittedly somewhat a-typical, as for parents especially the difference between brands may be tremendous in terms of effect on the baby's digestion and knock-on effect on the parents' peace of mind and night rest.

[29] *Supra* n. 11, at paras. 25–26.

substantial period of the time in the Member State where the service is provided: for example, an architect supervising the execution of a large building project. In that type of case, the border-line between services and establishment may be a narrow one . . . At the other extreme, the person providing the service might transmit it in the form of a product: for example, he might provide an educational service by posting a series of books and video-cassettes: here there is an obvious analogy with the free movement of goods . . .

Because of the generally more personalised character of services most of the "obstacles" to trade in services result from the regulation of the service-producing persons or companies. This arguably raises issues which are different from those raised by liberalising trade in goods.[30] Perhaps the most notable difference lies in the fact that free trade in services involves movement of persons across borders.[31] The above quotation from the Opinion in *Säger* leads one to note a fundamental difference between the EC law approach to the freedom to provide services and the approach under GATS which has not been discussed here yet. The EC Treaty provisions on services do not cover permanent presence in the Member State where the service is provided. Where a service provider is permanently present in that state the Treaty provisions on freedom of establishment apply. By contrast, GATS covers both the temporary supply of a service in the territory of another WTO member and permanent commercial presence there (see the modes of supplying services referred to above). In EC law terms, GATS covers freedom to provide services and freedom of establishment—but the latter only by service suppliers, not of course by goods manufacturers.

This has wider ramifications than are usually noticed. The difference in coverage does *not* mean that in the EC the liberalisation of the provision of services is narrower in scope than the liberalisation of international trade in services through the GATS: services provided in another EC Member State through a permanent presence are simply covered by the Treaty provisions on establishment, which also prohibit discrimination, and which also extend to indistinctly applicable measures which restrict the economic activity concerned.[32] No, the ramifications are in GATT/WTO law. In the EC there is full free movement, not only of goods but also of persons. Indeed such free movement is gradually developing into a general right of European citizens (see Article 18 EC) less and less predicated on economic activity in the internal market. EC law therefore has no difficulty with allowing service providers to establish themselves in another Member State. But in this respect the WTO is of course different. The WTO is about free trade, and does not nurture the ambition of realising free movement of persons on a world-wide scale. Indeed, none

---

[30] See Trebilcock and Howse, *supra* n. 24, at 273–274.

[31] It may be recalled that that was the fundamental reason for the ECJ to consider that GATS does not wholly come within the EC's common commercial policy, see *Opinion 1/94* [1994] ECR I–5267, paras. 42–47.

[32] See, e.g., *Gebhardt, supra* n. 5.

of the WTO agreements seem to have any effect on movement of persons—except for the GATS.

This calls for three further comments. The first is that at present WTO law seems rather imbalanced, in that foreign investment by service suppliers is covered, by GATS, and is liberalised where members have entered into specific commitments, and is subject to MFN, whereas foreign investment by goods manufacturers is not covered, except for the very narrow agreement on trade-related investment measures (TRIMs). Indeed, the investment liberalisation through the application of GATS is not to be underestimated. It is often said that the world lacks a multilateral agreement on investment (which is not deplored by certain sections in society—witness the sinking of OECD negotiations on the subject), but it is not so clear whether that statement is correct in the light of the scope of GATS, especially if one considers the broad view of the scope of GATS which panels and the Appellate Body have so far taken, and which suggests that nearly any goods manufacturer or trader may be able to present itself as also being a service supplier.[33]

The second comment is more in the nature of a question. Is the GATS, or can it become, a vehicle for international migration? If services are to be truly liberalised, does that not extend to individuals seeking to engage in a self-employed economic activity abroad? In principle, at least, GATS does have the vocation to have such broad coverage. The commercial presence mode of Article I:2(b) concerns "any type of business or professional establishment" (see Article XXVIII(d)) by a service supplier, the latter defined as "any person that supplies a service", and the term person "means either a natural person or a juridical person" (Article XXVIII(g) and (j)). Similarly, the presence of natural persons mode of Article I:2(d) covers the supply of a service by a service supplier of a member—so any natural or juridical person supplying a service—through presence of natural persons of a member in the territory of any other member. Presence of natural persons thus covers, for example, an individual service supplier going to a WTO member country to supply a service.

One needs to add immediately that the actual scope for making use of GATS in the above way depends on the commitments entered into. It is fairly clear that, at present, the WTO membership does not seek to have GATS become a real vehicle for international migration. That is confirmed by the Annex on Movement of Natural Persons Supplying Services under the Agreement, which provides that GATS "shall not apply to measures affecting natural persons seeking access to the employment market of a Member, nor shall it apply to measures regarding citizenship, residence or employment on a permanent basis" (paragraph 2). The Annex further indicates that GATS "shall not prevent a Member from applying measures to regulate the entry of natural persons into, or their temporary stay in, its territory, including those measures necessary to

---

[33] See *EC—Bananas III*, *supra* n. 21, and *Canada—Automotive Industry*, Panel Report, WT/DS139/R and WT/DS142/R; but see the Appellate Body Report in the latter case, *supra* n. 1.

protect the integrity of, and to ensure the orderly movement of natural persons across, its borders, provided that such measures are not applied in such a manner as to nullify or impair the benefits accruing to any Member under the terms of a specific commitment" (paragraph 4).

It is thus highly likely that WTO members will attempt to limit the effects of GATS on international migration. But that certainly creates the risk of GATS becoming a migration vehicle for the economically strong—service-supplying companies as well as individuals such as lawyers, accountants, architects, doctors, etc.—and not for the economically weak—those who seek standard employment abroad or engage in service activities which do not carry a high profile. Indeed, the economic, trade-based logic of GATS pushes in the direction of liberalisation in established, easily quantifiable and economically "important" services sectors. If that risk materialises, there is bound to be further critical public debate on the merits of this "purely economic" international organisation. That debate may become much more vociferous than the debate we have within the EU on free movement of persons.[34]

The third comment concerns direct effect. To the extent that GATS has a personal dimension, that it is concerned with movement of persons across borders, there seems to be an enormous tension between its object and its effects. If the object of GATS is partly personal movement, which means that GATS law is at least to some extent about creating benefits for "individuals" (persons, or indeed companies), one would then of course tend to start speaking about "rights" being created. But, in the absence of direct effect, those rights seem largely unenforceable at the mere instance of those who are affected.

MARKET ACCESS AND NATIONAL TREATMENT—LIBERALISATION AND REGULATION

This section essentially aims to compare the legal mechanics of EC law and GATS law in their pursuit of liberalisation of trade in services. The basic rules and concepts are set out above, but more analysis is required to be able to appraise and compare the respective systems. The main focus for such appraisal and comparison is the balance between liberalisation and regulation, which is clearly the overarching policy issue here. Unavoidably, it is submitted, trade liberalisation cuts into the regulatory tissue of legal systems and therefore affects the policies strived at through regulation.[35] The assumption is thus that one cannot speak of trade liberalisation in neutral terms, that concepts such as market access and non-discrimination do affect regulatory policies, even though at first glance they may appear neutral. The relationship is of course not in linear terms;

---

[34] For the EU debate see, e.g., I. Moebius and E. Szyszczak, "Of Raising Pigs and Children" (1998) 18 *YEL* 125.

[35] The term regulation is used here in its most general meaning, as encompassing all forms of rule-making public intervention; I am unable to find a more satisfactory term.

the interplay between liberalisation and regulation is dynamic and multi-faceted, and therefore difficult to analyse. It is none the less hoped that the idea of finding some form of balance between them may serve to elucidate some of the processes at work.

But liberalisation and regulation are not the only focus. Surrounding them are further issues, which can be considered to be constitutional in character. They include the role of the judiciary (including here of course WTO dispute settlement bodies), democratic legitimacy and governance. This section does not aim to come to grips with all of this. Much more modestly, its aim is to carry out some of the groundwork for further analysis and construction.

The section starts off with a recapitulation of the EC law approach to the freedom to provide services. It then describes the GATS case law so far—surprisingly enough in a case involving imports of bananas. The concluding part again tries to bring EC law and GATS law together.

An Introduction on EC Law

We can be brief in this sub-section, as some of the main judgments on the freedom to provide services under the EC Treaty are set out above. As was mentioned, the Treaty does not itself distinguish between, indeed it does not even mention, the notions of market access and national treatment which are the cornerstones of the GATS approach to liberalisation. Article 49 EC simply prohibits "restrictions" on the freedom to provide services. But comparable notions are present in the Court's case law. Already in *Van Binsbergen* the Court distinguished between discrimination (requirements imposed on the person providing the service by reason in particular of his nationality or foreign residence) and restrictions which may prevent or otherwise obstruct the activities of the person providing the service.[36] With the *Säger* case the Court left us in no doubt about the scope of Articles 49 and 50: the restrictions to be abolished pursuant to those provisions require not only the elimination of all discrimination but also the abolition of any restriction, even if indistinctly applicable.[37] The approach is therefore one of "beyond discrimination", where the critical question is very much the notion of what constitutes a restriction. Obviously, there must be boundaries to that notion, as nearly any form of regulation may be seen to have an effect on intra-Community transactions.[38] In fact, there appear to be at least two boundaries.[39] The first is the concept of "imperative requirements", which may justify restrictions on free movement. Those imperative require-

---

[36] *Supra* n. 9.
[37] *Supra* n. 11.
[38] For a recent case acknowledging those boundaries in the context of the legislative action of the Community, see Case C–376/98 *Germany* v. *Parliament and Council*, judgment of 5 October 2000.
[39] There may be others: see A. Biondi, "In and Out the Internal Market: Recent Developments on the Principle of Free Movement" (1999–2000) 19 *YEL* 469–491.

ments are most often looked at as constituting exceptions to free movement, but it is submitted that the analytically orthodox approach is to see them as boundaries to the otherwise unlimited notion of restrictions.[40] This will become clearer when we compare it with GATS law. The second boundary is the notion of market access, developed in the Court's case law sprung off from *Keck and Mithouard*, where it was held that, in relation to goods, non-discriminatory selling arrangements are not such as to prevent access to the market (or to impede access of foreign products any more than access of domestic products).[41] As was mentioned, *Keck* has not been extended to services, but the notion of market access does play an important role in the recent case law on services, where, as with some of the other freedoms, it is a basic tool for analysing the restrictive effect of regulatory measures.[42] Unfortunately, however, the Court has not as yet clearly defined the market access notion, and in EC law it still resembles the distant relative whom everyone likes but nobody really knows well and whose appearances are rather infrequent and unpredictable.[43]

It is true that, at academic level, there is still no universal recognition of the "beyond discrimination" characterisation of the Court's case law.[44] It is still occasionally argued that, *in fact*, the Court's case law revolves around the notion of non-discrimination. The idea here is that one should not take the Court's own language at face value, and that what we *really* see at work is an advanced standard of non-discrimination.[45] Much of such analysis is centred on the notion of mutual recognition. It is argued that where the Court speaks of indistinctly applicable measures, there is none the less a form of discrimination present, because the foreign service (or good, for that matter) is subject to a double regulatory burden, of both the home and host Member State. Where the host Member State does not take that into account, it is in fact discriminating against the foreign service provider (or good). The "importing" Member State needs to look at the regulation in the home Member State, and where it is equivalent to its own, it needs to recognise that and no longer impose its own standard.

Those elements of mutual recognition and double burden are of course present in the Court's case law, but it is submitted that they are not central to the

---

[40] That is the fundamental reason why the imperative or mandatory requirements cannot justify distinctly applicable measures. For an argument challenging that doctrine, at least as regards environmental protection, see Opinion of Jacobs AG of 26 October in Case C–379/98, *PreussenElektra v. Schleswag*, paras. 222–234.

[41] *Supra* n. 14, para. 17.

[42] See *supra* n. 20.

[43] Case C–190/98, *Graf*, judgment of 27 January 2000, was an occasion, but the Court did not seize upon it.

[44] See N. Bernard, "Discrimination and Free Movement in EC Law" (1996) *ICLQ* 82; L. Daniele, "Non-discriminatory Restrictions to the Free Movement of Persons" (1997) 22 *ELRev.* 191; C. Hilson, "Discrimination in Community Free Movement Law" (1999) 24 *ELRev.* 445. To some extent see even J. Weiler, "The Constitution of the Common Market Place", in P. Craig and G. de Búrca (eds.), *The evolution of EU Law* (Oxford, OUP, 1999) 349.

[45] The idea of not accepting the Court's own explicit language is itself quite interesting. Does it imply that the Court does not understand its own reasoning? Or does it imply that the Court is trying to deceive us, by using language which does not correspond to its actual thinking?

mechanics of the Court's test of what constitutes a restriction.[46] Within the scope of this chapter it is not possible to present full argument on this thesis. Instead, let me just try to (re)state shortly how I understand the Court's thinking. As regards services (as well as the other Treaty provisions on free movement of persons) the starting-point was of course the notion of non-discrimination on grounds of nationality or place of residence. But as the Court was pushing for advanced integration, it increasingly employed an advanced notion of non-discrimination.[47] There is a problem with that, because non-discrimination is inherently an elusive concept, and the more advanced and marked its application, the more elusive it seems to become.[48] Moreover, with respect to goods, the Treaty did not seem centred on non-discrimination at all—at least not as concerns regulatory barriers[49]—and the case law on imports of goods had as its starting-point the question whether a measure hinders intra-Community trade (*Dassonville*). That case law, as it developed with *Cassis de Dijon*'s recognition of the fact that indistinctly applicable measures may also hinder trade, became leading, and at some stage the Court decided to transpose it to the other freedoms. The transposition means that the Court is no longer constrained to find discrimination, and it may focus its attention on whether there is a restriction and, if so, whether it is justified.

Bananas and Services

There is so far only one case in which both a WTO Panel and the Appellate Body (AB) made significant statements on the scope and effect of GATS, and in particular on the meaning of the national treatment provision of Article XVII GATS. Surprisingly, perhaps, the case is on the EC's import regime for bananas—*Bananas III* in WTO parlance.[50] The facts are complex, and the reasoning of the Panel and the AB is elaborate, so we need to set those out at some length before being in a position to assess the first steps in the interpretation of some of the key concepts of GATS.

The EC banana import regime, as challenged before the WTO, essentially involved tariff preferences for "traditional" imports of bananas from ACP countries, traditional here meaning the level of exports protected by the Lomé IV

---

[46] See Eeckhout, *supra* n. 26.

[47] Literature spoke of both indirect discrimination and material discrimination. We return to those concepts below.

[48] See, e.g., the case law on sex equality; for a comparison with the case law on free movement see B.J. Drijber and S. Prechal, "Gelijke behandeling van mannen en vrouwen in horizontaal perspectief" [1997] *Sociaal-Economische Wetgeving* 122.

[49] See Art. 90 for tax barriers.

[50] *Supra* n. 21. The reasoning of Panel and AB in *Bananas III* was copied by the Panel in *Canada—Automotive Industry, supra* n. 33, but the AB felt on appeal that the Panel had insufficiently examined the impact of the Canadian import measures on service suppliers as service suppliers, and had limited its analysis to extending its findings concerning goods to services: see Appellate Body Report, *supra* n. 1, paras. 147–184.

Convention. Those preferences were intended to make it easier for those ACP bananas to compete on the European market with imports of so-called third-country bananas, mainly coming from Latin America. The latter type of bananas (together with "non-traditional" ACP bananas, which hereafter we will leave out of account, for ease of reference) were subject to a yearly tariff quota, with imports above the quota being subject to a prohibitively high quota. In effect, therefore, the tariff quota amounted to a quantitative restriction.

Access to imports under the tariff quota thus became a scarce commodity, and a vital issue for banana importers in the EC. Such access was subject to a licensing system. Import licences were essentially granted on the basis of past import performance. To that effect, the EC regime distinguished between three types of "operators" (companies importing and marketing bananas in the EC): Category A operators, consisting of those operators who in the past traded in third-country bananas; Category B operators, consisting of operators who in the past traded in EC and ACP bananas; and Category C, for newcomers. Licences were proportionally divided between those categories of operators, under the following terms: 66.5 per cent for Category A, 30 per cent for Category B, and 3.5 per cent for Category C. This may sound more innocuous than it in fact was, for the 30 per cent given to Category B was in effect a sort of EC subsidy for these operators: they obtained significant access to licences for importing third-country bananas, whereas in the past they (by definition) did not import such bananas at all. Conversely, traditional importers of third-country bananas, in Category A, saw their access to import opportunities drastically reduced. In practice, what happened was that Category B sold much of their licences to Category A, but this of course affected the competition between them, and it effectively raised the price for third-country bananas. There were several other aspects of the licensing regime which were challenged, but for the purpose of our analysis the above may be sufficient.

The banana regime was challenged in the WTO by Ecuador, Guatemala, Honduras, Mexico and the United States. Most claims were centred on the provisions of GATT, but some of the complainants also claimed that the EC regime was inconsistent with the EC's obligations under Articles II (MFN) and XVII (National Treatment) of GATS. The argument was that there was discrimination against distributors of Latin American and non-traditional ACP bananas in favour of distributors of EC and traditional ACP bananas, and that such distributors were suppliers of "wholesale trade services", a service sector in which the EC has undertaken a full commitment on national treatment in its Schedule. The Panel and the AB agreed with that claim. The following are some of the steps in their reasoning.[51]

The EC argued that the banana licensing regime was not a measure "affecting trade in services" in the sense of Article I GATS, and that GATT and GATS

---

[51] For a fuller analysis see W. Zdouc, "WTO Dispute Settlement Practice Relating to the GATS" (1999) 2 *JIEL* 295.

were mutually exclusive. The Panel, however, adopted a broad view of the scope of GATS and of the term "affecting". It came to the conclusion that no measures are excluded *a priori* from the scope of GATS as defined by its provisions, and that the scope of GATS encompasses any measure to the extent it affects the supply of a service regardless of whether such measure directly governs the supply of a service or whether it regulates other matters but nevertheless affects trade in services. The AB essentially confirmed this approach. As regards the respective scope of GATT 1994 and GATS the AB held that they may or may not overlap, depending on the nature of the measures at issue. Certain measures could be found to fall exclusively within the scope of GATT 1994; certain measures could be found to fall exclusively within the scope of GATS; and a third category of measures could be found to fall within the scope of both GATT 1994 and GATS. The latter are measures that involve a service relating to a particular good or a service supplied in conjunction with a particular good. Such measures could be scrutinised under both agreements, but the specific aspects of that measure examined under each agreement could be different. Under GATT 1994, the focus is on how the measure affects the goods involved. Under GATS, the focus is on how the measure affects the supply of the service or the service suppliers involved.

That hurdle having been cleared, the next question was whether the "operators" involved in the banana trade were suppliers of "wholesale trade services", a sector where the EC had entered into a full national treatment commitment. The Panel found that the EC had based its commitments on the Services Sectoral Classification List developed during the Uruguay Round. That List is itself based on the United Nations Central Product Classification system (CPC), and in the relevant part of its Schedule the EC had referred to the relevant CPC item number (622). The Panel therefore analysed the wording of that CPC item, which describes "wholesale trade services" as a sub-set of the broader sector of "distributive trade services". Under this section the CPC contains a sub-sector entitled "wholesale trade services of food, beverages and tobacco", with a further breakdown including a separate item relating to "wholesale trade service of fruit and vegetables", referring to a number of goods in a separate CPC classification, including an item "fruits and nuts", with a sub-classification referring to "dates, figs, *bananas*, coconuts, . . ." etc. (emphasis added).

The Panel then identified the relevant mode of supplying services (see Article I GATS). Here this was the commercial presence mode: it had to be examined whether service suppliers of the complainants' origin, having a commercial presence in the EC, received national treatment, i.e. treatment no less favourable than that accorded to like service suppliers of EC origin.

As regards the "likeness" of the services, the Panel considered that the nature and characteristics of wholesale transactions as such, as well as each of the different subordinated services, were "like" when supplied in connection with wholesale services, irrespective of whether these services were supplied with respect to bananas of EC and traditional ACP origin, on the one hand, or with respect to bananas of third-country or non-traditional ACP origin, on the other. To the extent that entities provided these like services, they were like service suppliers.

The Panel then went on to examine the alleged discrimination. It first established that service suppiers of the complainants' origin were receiving treatment formally identical to the treatment of EC service suppliers. Indeed, the operator category rules did not distinguish between service suppliers on the basis of their origin. However, under Article XVII formally identical treatment may constitute lack of national treatment, where it "modifies the conditions of competition" (Article XVII:3). The Panel found that most of the service suppliers of the complainants' origin were Category A operators, because in the past they had imported nearly exclusively third-country bananas, whereas most of the service suppliers of EC origin were Category B operators—because those operators imported or traded nearly exclusively ACP and EC bananas. The Panel then established that Category A operators were indeed subject to less favourable conditions of competition than Category B operators. The latter obtained a share of the licences for importing third-country bananas, whereas the former did not obtain licences for importing traditional ACP and EC bananas. Given that licences were transferable, the allocation of fixed percentages did not automatically determine the new distribution of market shares. But licences were in fact traded from Category B to Category A, thus giving rise to quota rents for Category B, which Category A could not reap. The EC's argument that the EC market shares of the three major international banana traders (of complainants' origin, i.e. Chiquita, Del Monte and Dole) fell only slightly in the period 1991–1994 (from 43.5 per cent to 41.5 per cent) did not convince the Panel, which pointed out that there were other means for maintaining market share, and that a lack of significant change in market share did not demonstrate that there had not been a significant change in the conditions of competition. The analysis was corroborated by references to EC documents pointing out that the aim of the regime was to "cross-subsidise" EC/ACP operators, and to strengthen their competitive position. Thus there was a breach of Article XVII GATS.

On appeal the EC argued that the banana regime pursued "entirely legitimate policies" and was "not inherently discriminatory in design or effect". The AB rejected that argument by making a significant statement on the "aims and effects" theory.[52] This theory stems from (among others) an unadopted GATT 1947 panel report, *United States—Taxes on Automobiles*.[53] The question in the case was whether US taxes on automobiles were contrary to Article III:2 GATT (national treatment as regards internal taxation), and in particuler whether different tax treatment of autos on the basis of their value or gasoline consumption amounted to discrimination. In deciding this question the Panel looked not only at the competitive effects of this difference in treatment, but also at its

[52] See generally R. Hudec, "GATT/WTO Constraints on National Regulation: Requiem for an 'Aim and Effects' Test" (1998) 32 *The International Lawyer* 619.
[53] DS31/R, 11 October 1994.

regulatory purpose. It held that that purpose was *bona fide*, and found the competitive effects neither clear enough nor inherent enough, and thus concluded that the product distinctions were permissible. However, the theory has so far been unsuccessful in the WTO. In the bananas case the AB stated:[54]

> We see no specific authority either in Article II or in Article XVII of the GATS for the proposition that the "aims and effects" of a measure are in any way relevant in determining whether that measure is inconsistent with those provisions. In the GATT context, the "aims and effects" theory had its origins in the principle of Article III:1 that internal taxes or charges or other regulations "should not be applied to imported or domestic products so as to afford protection to domestic production". There is no comparable provision in the GATS. Furthermore, in our Report in *Japan—Alcoholic Beverages*,[55] the Appellate Body rejected the "aims and effects" theory with respect to Article III:2 of the GATT 1994.

Bringing EC Law and GATS Law Together—Is GATS going Bananas?

This subsection investigates the differences and points of comparison between the ECJ's approach to freedom to provide services and the application of the GATS concepts of national treatment and market access. As regards the latter, admittedly, it is still very early days, as the AB has spoken in only one case, *Bananas III*. Yet there is some reason for concern about the potentially broad scope and the possibly unintended effects of GATS, as interpreted so far. "Is GATS going bananas?" is of course provocative, but precisely because there is still room for manœuvre under GATS it may be good to try to put matters as sharply as possible.

As we noted, the ECJ's case law moved beyond discrimination into a restriction-based approach, where the emphasis is on market access. That approach is far-reaching, with the potential of cutting deep into the regulatory tissue of the Member States, but that potential is checked by the notion of imperative or mandatory requirements.

It seems that in GATS, by contrast, there is no movement from discrimination to restrictions on market access. National treatment and market access appear to be complementary and self-standing notions. Again this is inherited from GATT, where one has the same issue: Article III on national treatment and Article XI on import and export restrictions are separate, but probably complementary notions. The effect of that on GATT case law seems to have been that, for some reason, restrictions whose effects are difficult to gauge are challenged under Article III rather than under Article XI. Indeed, the Article XI case law is fairly limited, and not nearly as sophisticated as the Article III case law.[56] There

---

[54] *Supra* n. 21, para. 241.

[55] [Original n.:] Appellate Body Report, WT/DS8/AB/R, WT/DS10/AB/R, WT/DS11/AB/R, adopted 1 November 1996.

[56] See Weiler, *supra* n. 44, at 374.

appears to be a preference for considering certain types of measures to be discriminatory towards imported goods, rather than looking at them as being a restriction on market access. The best example is, again, *Bananas III*, where with respect to GATT the licensing regime described above was analysed as a violation of the national treatment standard for imported bananas, and was not tested against Article XI—rather difficult to understand when one realises that the licensing regime was part and parcel of the tariff quota system for imports of third-country bananas, a system which obviously did not apply to EC-produced bananas, as those are never imported and thus not subject to the Common Customs Tariff!

If in this respect GATS continues to follow in the footsteps of GATT, this will mean that national treatment will be the most significant test for the GATS-compatibility of national regulation (together with MFN, which is also a non-discrimination standard). The above also means that national treatment is "out there" on its own, and that it cannot move into a restriction-based approach but has to remain within the confines of a non-discrimination standard. At first sight this may seem reassuring in terms of having some measure of deference towards valid regulatory policies, but, as we noted, non-discrimination is a most elusive notion, and great care will have to be taken that the standard is clear and remains within certain boundaries.

Is that the case at present? On the (narrow) basis of *Bananas III* the jury is still out on this question. Let us try to look into the various components of the national treatment test as applied by the Panel and the AB.

The first component is the broad scope of GATS, which extends to measures concerning imports of goods, in so far as they affect suppliers of wholesale trade services. In contrast with EC law, there appears to be no clear delineation of goods and services, and as the scope of GATS was broadly defined so as to reflect economic realities and to capture all forms of service supply, its reach is extensive. After all, services are a form of virtual reality, and perhaps it is possible to characterise nearly any economic activity as including the supply of certain services. Or, to put it differently, it may be difficult to conceive of regulatory measures which do not affect the supply of any service, as covered by GATS. It is beyond the scope of this chapter further to analyse the relationship between GATT and GATS, but the broad scope of GATS does of course increase the significance of the national treatment provision.

The second component concerns the definition of the relevant market, to use a competition law term (which is not far-fetched, as Article XVII:3 expressly refers to conditions of competition). In *Bananas III* that market was very narrowly defined. The Panel looked at the EC's Schedule of Commitments, noted that it covered "wholesale trade services", and then narrowed that down to wholesale trade services in bananas. Without entering into a discussion as to whether that is the correct approach or not, it is obviously far easier to find discrimination against foreign service suppliers where the relevant market is so narrowly defined. If, for example, the Panel had considered that discrimination had to be found throughout the entire sector of wholesale trade services, it might have concluded that the banana regime did not give rise to a significant lack of national treatment. Again, it is not suggested that the latter would be the correct approach; the example merely serves to illustrate that the definition of the relevant services market affects the impact of the national treatment standard.

One also wonders whether this was not the point where the Panel should have examined the likeness of the services being supplied, rather than merely breaking up the sector of wholesale trade services in its myriad components (for that is the effect of the analysis, as there seems to be a wholesale trade services market for hundreds, if not thousands, of types of product). Is not the basic question, in any discrimination analysis, whether persons or facts are sufficiently alike to trigger the equal treatment standard? Yet likeness is not thoroughly analysed by the Panel.[57]

The third component is the actual national treatment standard. Panel and AB agree that Article XVII incorporates a standard of *de facto* national treatment, but they do not seem to clarify what those terms actually imply. It is to be noted that the text of Article XVII does not mention the term *de facto*. Paragraph 2 provides that the national treatment requirement may be met by according either formally identical or formally different treatment and paragraph 3 specifies that formally identical or formally different treatment shall be considered to be less favourable if it modifies the conditions of competition. But what is the meaning of this language? What does *de facto* national treatment imply?

It is submitted that EC law experience with the non-discrimination principle may help to clarify the issues involved. In conceptual terms the basic question, it seems to me, is whether *de facto* national treatment prohibits (a) purely factual or material discrimination or (b) only (direct and) indirect discrimination. What is the difference between those two?

Factual or material discrimination is a concept which was used by EC lawyers to point towards the far-reaching scope of the free movement principle, as developed by the ECJ in cases such as *Cassis de Dijon*.[58] The concept is intimately linked to the treatment of indistinctly applicable measures, i.e. those forms of regulation which apply to all products (or service providers, or workers, etc.). It is clear that an indistinctly applicable measure may, for a number of different reasons, have a negative effect on imported products or "imported" services. (This is to be distinguished from cases where the regulatory measure does not discriminate, but where discrimination occurs in the administration or application of the measure.) At its extreme, the concept implies that one looks only at the effect of a regulatory measure. As such, however, there are two fundamental problems with purely factual discrimination.

The first problem is that, unless there is a mechanism for taking into account the regulatory purpose of the measure, the concept of factual discrimination

---

[57] See also Zdouc, *supra* n. 51, at 331–334.

[58] See, e.g., K. Lenaerts, "L'égalité de traitement en droit communautaire" (1991) 27 *CDE* at 8–17.

seems to put factual trade liberalisation above all else. In EC law, the regulatory purpose is of course taken on board through the idea of mandatory or imperative requirements: if there were a consumer protection justification for reserving the activity of patent renewal to patent agents (*Säger*), then the indistinctly applicable German measure which negatively impacts on the UK service provider would be allowed to stand. Without such a counterbalance, however, the mere fact that a particular measure, which is as to its formulation indistinctly applicable (perhaps the AB would speak of the design and application of the measure which is indistinctly applicable), may be more burdensome for a foreign service provider, is sufficient to conclude to a breach of national treatment. Thus understood, factual discrimination is, as it were, blindfolded with respect to the regulatory policies pursued by a WTO member. To use an example: suppose a WTO member introduces, for perfectly valid policy reasons, a new regulatory condition in the field of insurance, a condition which happens to affect a particular, specialised insurance market more than other insurance markets, and suppose that it so happens that this particular market is dominated by foreign service suppliers. Factual discrimination, as here understood, would have to be found purely on the basis of the effects of the measure. If the particular market involved, on the other hand, were dominated by domestic service suppliers, there would be no factual discrimination.[59] Is such an approach useful?

The second fundamental problem is: if the question is purely one of effect, are we then still speaking of a meaningful form of non-discrimination (or equal treatment)? I have argued above that EC law has moved beyond discrimination into a restriction-based approach where the central question is one of market access. The fundamental reason for this evolution is that, the further one moves, the less helpful the discrimination concept becomes. To find out whether there is discrimination, one has to compare. But if the matter is purely one of effect, whom or what does one compare with whom or what? As regards GATS, does one compare the whole group of foreign service suppliers in a particular sector with the whole group of domestic service suppliers? Is that possible in a purely effects-based analysis? Surely, the effects of a regulatory measure will be varied, unevenly distributed and diverse. Does one weigh up all the effects, or is it sufficient that there is a more negative impact on just one foreign service supplier? Compared to the whole group of domestic service suppliers, or compared to just one domestic service supplier?

Let us now contrast this notion of factual discrimination with the notion of indirect discrimination which, it is submitted, may be more helpful for determining the proper scope of Article XVII GATS. In the case of indirect discrimination, there is a clear difference in treatment, a distinction operated by the regulatory measure in issue. However, the distinction is not formally based on the prohibited factor, but on some other factor which may appear neutral from

---

[59] Note that in GATS the foreign or domestic character of the service provider may simply depend on the location of the parent company.

the perspective of the relevant non-discrimination rule. None the less, there is discrimination because effectively the regulatory distinction means that the two groups which are to be treated equally under the relevant non-discrimination rule are not treated equally. Examples abound in the ECJ's case law on non-discrimination on grounds of sex and non-discrimination on grounds of nationality. In the latter area, the ECJ typically looks at regulatory measures which treat residents and non-residents differently.[60] This is suspect from the perspective of non-discrimination on grounds of nationality because, obviously, most residents are nationals and most non-residents are not nationals. In the field of sex equality, typical cases of indirect discrimination concern wage differences between full-time and part-time workers, where a considerably smaller proportion of women work full-time.[61]

In the ECJ's case law the indirect discrimination standard has the following basic components. First, there is a difference in treatment, but it is not formally based on the prohibited criterion. Secondly, there is a presumption of discrimination if the regulatory distinction which is made has an effect similar to the effect of using the prohibited criterion. Thirdly, the presumption is rebuttable, in that the defending party may be able to show that the regulatory distinction is objectively justified on policy grounds which are unrelated to the prohibited discrimination.

Such an indirect discrimination concept differs significantly from a concept of purely factual or effects-based discrimination. The relevant measures are not indistinctly applicable, applying to all products on the market; there is, instead, a regulatory distinction. Moreover, that distinction produces effects which are similar to the effects of measures of clear-cut discrimination. Exactly how similar is something to be decided by the judicial organ deciding on cases—there is obviously a margin of discretion here, indirect discrimination is stretchable. However, its stretch is limited in that it does require a significant regulatory distinction and cannot be purely based on the effects of the measure. In GATS, for example, if one were to apply an indirect discrimination standard, it would not be possible to argue that a measure discriminates because it happens to have a negative effect on a single foreign service supplier. One would have to show that there is a regulatory distinction (and in the *Bananas* case there was one, between the different categories of service suppliers) which has the effect of treating the group of foreign service suppliers, or at least a significant proportion of them, less favourably than the group of domestic service suppliers.[62] Indirect discrimination is therefore much more restrained than factual discrimination.

---

[60] E.g., Case 152/73, *Sotgiu v. Deutsche Bundespost* [1974] ECR 153.

[61] E.g., Case 96/80, *Jenkins v. Kinsgate* [1981] ECR 911.

[62] There are indications that the Schedules of Commitments are actually based on such a notion of indirect discrimination: see WTO, Committee on Specific Commitments, *Revision of Scheduling Guidelines—Note by the Secretariat*, S/CSC/W/19, 5 March 1999, para. 24, where examples of national treatment limitations are given. The examples are all clearly concerned with regulatory distinctions likely to affect the group of foreign service suppliers more than the group of domestic service suppliers; most of them are residence-based.

It may be noted last that the concept of indirect discrimination, as employed by the ECJ, allows for rebuttal of the discrimination presumption on grounds of "objective justification". This again brings us to "aims and effects". I would subscribe to the comment that it may not have been the AB's wisest move in *Bananas III* to rule out categorically the relevance of "aims and effects".[63] Whichever type of discrimination analysis one adheres to, be it factual or indirect or some other type of discrimination, there seems to be an unavoidable need for some type of counterweight which represents the regulatory policies which are being pursued. "Aims and effects" may therefore have to come in again through some backdoor.

In this context, I cannot refrain from making the comment that the EC may itself be partly responsible for the killing of "aims and effects", because it argued strongly against this theory in the GATT case *Japan—Alcoholic Beverages*,[64] where the AB ruled out the relevance of "aims and effects" in the context of Article III:2 GATT.[65] Given that there was some support for "aims and effects" in the language of Article III GATT, and that there appears to be no support for it in the language of GATS, it is not surprising that the AB rejected the EC's reference in *Bananas III* to "aims and effects". But that leaves us with no real instrument under GATS for acknowledging the regulatory policies pursued by WTO members, in particular since the express exceptions in Article XIV are clearly narrow—probably narrower than those in Article XX GATT.

[63] Zdouc, *supra* n. 51, at 341–342 and Hudec, *supra* n. 52, at 640.
[64] *Supra* n. 56.
[65] See Hudec, *supra* n. 52, for a fuller discussion.

10

Trade in Culture: International Legal Regimes and EU Constitutional Values

BRUNO DE WITTE

THE GERMAN NINETEENTH century economist Friedrich List famously wrote "*Gedanken sind zollfrei*"—"thoughts are not subject to customs controls". That may be so, but the *expression* of thoughts, ideas and creative action can be affected or hindered by the existence of state borders. This is so for material objects such as books, music recordings and works of art, that can be physically held up at state borders, but also for more intangible expressions of culture, such as television programmes transmitted through the air, that can be affected by restrictive measures taken by the state of reception. International trade liberalisation, as embodied primarily in the WTO Agreement and the work programme of the World Trade Organisation, aims at removing such inter-state barriers to the commercial trade in cultural expressions. This aim is strongly criticised by a number of authors, but also by some interest groups and non-governmental oranisation (NGOs) and, more importantly, by some influential governments. They regret to see the emergence of a "new world order in which national cultural policies may have to give way to the overriding exigencies of the 'free market' "; and they argue that "the objectives of the WTO are incompatible with, even hostile to, the continued development of distinct national cultural identities".[1]

Culture is, in fact, part of the broader "trade linkage" debate,[2] that is concerned with striking a more considerate balance between free trade values and other, opposed or divergent, social values. The special feature of this particular "trade and . . ." area, compared to environmental protection or labour standards, is that the main line of the ideological divide does not run between industrial and developing countries, but within the group of industrialised countries

---

[1] Both quotations are from M.J. Tawfik, "Competing Cultures: Canada and the World Trade Organization—The Lessons from *Sports Illustrated*" (1998) 36 *The Canadian Yearbook of International Law* 279, at 279–280.

[2] See, generally, J.P. Trachtman, "Trade and . . . Problems, Cost-Benefit Analysis and Subsidiarity" (1998) 9 *European Journal of International Law* 32.

itself, namely between the United States on the one hand (this country being, for sound economic reasons, a firm champion of the free flow of cultural goods and services), and Canada and the EU Member States on the other. The governments of the latter group take views that vary from the extreme position of *cultural exclusion* (holding that international trade rules should not apply at all to the cultural sector) to the more moderate position of *cultural specificity* (holding that general trade rules should be adapted to the special characteristics of the cultural sector).

The European Union (more specifically, its main sub-organisation, the European Community) plays a pivotal role in this debate. It has used its considerable global trade negotiation power to limit the impact of free trade on the cultural sector. More particularly, the question whether free trade principles should cover film and broadcasting activities has been a contentious issue for the last 10 to 15 years, first in the bilateral trade relationship between the United States and the European Community, and later within the multilateral framework of the WTO. The question whether, and to what extent, these "cultural industries" (as they are often called) should receive special treatment within the international trade regime was not settled by the WTO Agreement. It is one of the "Marrakesh leftovers" remaining on the agenda of future multilateral trade negotiations.

In this chapter, I will pay some attention to this particular dispute, while putting it in a wider context. In section 1, I will situate international trade law within the wider perspective of international law; cultural activities and cultural concerns have indeed been the object of international legal regulation outside the field of trade law, and the policy objectives pursued in these other arenas are often rather different. Within the context of theWTO itself (section 2), there is a variety of different legal regimes. Alongside the most widely publicised question of the coverage of audiovisual services by the General Agreement on Trade in Services, the culture-and-trade question crops up in other fields of the WTO legal order which have their own, partly distinctive, rules: trade in goods, intellectual property, investment and subsidies. The particular nature of the involvement of the European Community will be considered in section 3. European economic integration has historically been marked by the same tension between free trade objectives and cultural identity concerns that is now emerging at the global level. Inside the EC, this tension has led to the emergence of a constitutional regime regulating the interaction between free trade and national cultural autonomy. As a global trade actor, the EC is led by this constitutional framework to try and mitigate the impact of free trade on culturally sensitive activities. At the same time, the EC may serve as a model for a future international law regime offering a better equilibrium between economic integration and cultural diversity.

CULTURE IN INTERNATIONAL LAW

The concepts of "culture" and "cultural policy" may sound exotic in the US legal tradition and practice, but they are familiar concepts in the domestic law of most Member States of the European Union. In many countries, the constitutional text, as interpreted by their constitutional or supreme courts, formulates fundamental cultural values, and gives direction to the cultural policies which governments must pursue. The same concepts have also acquired a distinct meaning in the language of international law and international relations. One of the UN's specialised agencies, UNESCO, has the word "culture" in its official designation, and the organs of UNESCO commonly use the term for defining the agency's overall scope of activity. In bilateral relations between states, the term "cultural agreement" or "cultural cooperation agreement" is very widely used to designate a specific type of treaty.[3] At the regional European level, the term culture has emerged as a similarly general denominator for the identification of one important sector of the Council of Europe's activity, and a separate title on culture was inserted into the EC Treaty by the Treaty of Maastricht (now Article 151 EC Treaty).

Copyright conventions are the oldest type of multilateral treaty regulating the flow of culture. By giving cross-border protection to the exclusive economic rights of authors, and to some extent also to their moral rights, these conventions help to restrain certain forms of (illegal) culture trade, but at the same time encourage the legal trade in books, music recordings, works of art, film and television productions. The system has been gradually adapted to incorporate new technologies, and is now also, by means of the TRIPS Agreement, embedded within the framework of the World Intellectual Property Organisation.

In *human rights law*, the concept of "cultural rights" is a term of art, although its contours are somewhat vague;[4] in the more specific field of the *law of minority protection and protection of indigenous peoples,* the concept of "cultural identity" occupies a central position.[5] Finally, the protection of *cultural property* or the *cultural heritage* has become a distinct field of international law. In this context, the emphasis is on the limitation rather than on the facilitation of cultural flows, with a view to protecting the cultural identity of the country of origin and, thereby, the world cultural heritage as a whole.[6]

---

[3] T. Oppermann, "Cultural Agreements" (1992) 1 *Encyclopedia of Public International Law*, 885.

[4] For a general discussion of the concept of cultural rights in international human rights law, see A. Eide, "Cultural Rights as Individual Human Rights" in A. Eide, C. Krause and A. Rosas (eds.), *Economic, Social and Cultural Rights—A Textbook* (Dordrecht, Nijhoff, 1995) 229.

[5] Y. Donders, "The Development of the Right to Cultural Identity in International Human Rights Law" in Y. Donders *et al.* (eds.), *Law and Cultural Diversity* (Utrecht, SIM Special No.25, 1999) 65.

[6] There is a very rich literature on this subject. See, among others, K. Siehr, "International Art Trade and the Law" (1993) 243 *RCADI* 9; J. Blake, "On Defining the Cultural Heritage" (2000) 49 *International and Comparative Law Quarterly* 61.

In these various legal contexts, the term "culture" is often used as a general denominator for specific objects or activities that have common characteristics. These characteristics can be summarily identified with reference to sociological theories that define culture as a social (sub)system whose specific function is the symbolic, as opposed to the material, reproduction of society and the creation of meaning in human society. Of course, all human activity participates in shaping the pattern of life and therefore belongs, in the wide definition used by anthropologists, to culture. But one can also single out a number of specialised agencies (like schools, media, art institutions and the cinema and publishing industries) that have been created with this specific object and thereby constitute the cultural system in a narrower sense, the sense in which it is normally used in national and international law.[7]

The domain of culture, so defined, is relevant in the context of *international trade law* because many cultural expressions can move across state borders and become the object of international transactions. The term "culture flows", which is often used to describe such interactions, is perhaps too expressive. It conveys the impression that one can observe a number of material events at the borders of states which, put together, constitute the flow of culture between any two countries. This may be true for cultural goods such as works of arts, records and tapes, films and videotapes, books and periodicals; and for persons exercising cultural activities such as arts performers, students and teachers; but there are also a large number of what could be called invisible operations, namely capital flows (such as the remuneration of copyright holders) and trade in intangible services (such as the transmission of broadcasting programmes) which, though not visibly crossing a state border, can be encapsulated within international trade statistics.

Transnational flows of culture have increased over the years, and this has prompted a lively political and scientific debate on the effects of such flows on the receiving societies. According to the classical views of liberal internationalists, the exchange of ideas and of artistic and literary productions is one of the most promising methods for fostering the development of world understanding and a sense of moral and cultural community among the peoples of the world. Another, contrary view, which had briefly gained institutional prominence in the UNESCO documents of the 1970s and early 1980s, but has reemerged strongly in the last few years, is that unchecked flows of culture turn the world into a global market for cultural commodities which jeopardises the autonomous development of national cultures and also contributes to a more generally undesirable "commodification of culture". According to a third school of thought, both these views focus excessively on the production and diffusion side of culture flows and on the strategies of the "emitters", while considering the final "receivers" as more or less passive objects. In reality, so these authors

---

[7] For a general analysis of the social functions of cultural institutions, see M. Schudson, "Culture and the Integration of National Societies" (1994) 46 *International Social Science Journal* 63.

argue, messages may be reinterpreted or rejected by their receivers; and usually have a rather superficial impact on their cultural values and practices.[8]

Whatever the value of these different views and assumptions, the fact is that they structure the positions adopted by governments, international organisations, and other groups when it comes to formulating legal rules for culture trade. Some of these legal rules seek to encourage culture flows by removing national regulatory obstacles that stand in their way. A traditional example is the Florence Agreement on the Importation of Educational, Scientific and Cultural Material, which was negotiated within the framework of UNESCO shortly after the Second World War.[9] WTO law is firmly within this category, as it purports to expand the flow of goods and services by removing national restrictions, and by creating a framework allowing for the unhindered interaction between private actors. Yet, different priorities are set in the context of other regimes of international law. This is most obviously the case for the trade in art treasures; in this field, international conventions have been adopted with a view to *limiting* international trade so as to protect national cultural identity.[10] Therefore, the statement that "international trade law is about getting rid of the impediments to economic exchange that borders, and nation States impose"[11] may be true if one limits international trade law to instruments such as the WTO Agreement. If, however, international trade law is broadly defined as the set of legal rules dealing "with the movement of goods, services, capital, and in some circumstances, labour, across borders",[12] then its objective is not always to get "rid of impediments", but also, occasionally, to create new impediments to undesirable forms of trade. Maximising free and unhindered trade is, then, not the only value underlying trade law, and the question how far, and in which sense, international trade rules should be coloured by "cultural specificity" is entirely open.

---

[8] For a critical survey of the literature on this question, see C. Roach, "Cultural Imperialism and Resistance in Media Theory and Literary Theory" (1997) 19 *Media, Culture & Society* 47. For a specific analysis of the question of the reception of US television programmes, see D. Biltereyst, "Resisting American Hegemony: A Comparative Analysis of the Reception of Domestic and US Fiction" (1991) 6 *European Journal of Communication* 469.

[9] Agreement concluded on 25 November 1950, 131 UNTS 25.

[10] The two most important such conventions are the 1970 Unesco Convention on the Means of Prohibiting and Preventing the Illicit Import, Export and Transfer of the Ownership of Cultural Property and the 1995 *Unidroit Convention on Stolen or Illegally Exported Cultural Objects*. On the relation between these two instruments, see L. V. Prott, "Unesco and Unidroit: A Partnership against Trafficking in Cultural Objects" [1996] *Uniform Law Review* 59. For a comprehensive analysis of both instruments, see G. Carducci, *La restitution internationale des biens culturels et des objets d'art volés ou illicitement exportés: droit commun, Directive CEE, Conventions de l'UNESCO et d'UNIDROIT* (Paris, LGDJ, 1997).

[11] D.D. McRae, "The Contribution of International Trade Law to the Development of International Law" (1996) 260 *RCADI* 101, at 111.

[12] *Ibid.*, at 110.

Culture Trade in the GATT Prior to the WTO Agreement

The particular nature of trade in cultural goods was clearly recognised in the original text of the GATT. Two cultural exceptions were incorporated in this original text, and are still there today; they correspond to the two types of culture trade which, in the immediate post-war years, were considered to pose special problems for the cultural integrity of nation states. Article XX(f) allows for trade restrictions "imposed for the protection of national treasures of artistic, historic or archaeological value". This provision served as a model for a similar clause in Article 30 (ex Article 36), EC Treaty allowing for restrictions on intra-Community trade justified on grounds of "the protection of national treasures possessing artistic, historic or archaeological value". It was an early announcement of the later developments in international law aiming at the restriction of the trade of certain, particularly valuable, cultural objects. The other cultural clause of GATT is prominently placed in its Article IV, which allows, under specified conditions, screen quotas for films and is, therefore, an exception to the national treatment rule of Article III. At the time the GATT was adopted, culture flows were much more limited than today and the film industry was the only sector of cultural activity that was marked by a clear trade imbalance between industrialised countries, in favour of the United States. Article IV GATT was intended to allow other states, particularly the European states, to carve out a protected domain for their feeble domestic film industries. So, when seen in the light of the time it was adopted, the text of GATT can be said to display some sensitivity to the specific nature of culture trade.[13]

When, some years later, the trade in television programmes grew, the United States government argued that the "exception" of Article IV should be narrowly interpreted to apply to cinema films only, whereas the national treatment principle should fully apply to television programmes. The EEC, for its part, denied the applicability of GATT to the trade in television programmes, arguing that these were services rather than goods.[14] The dispute was never settled, and emerged with full force in the late 1980s, when the European Community adopted common rules affecting the exportation of American TV programmes to the booming European broadcasting markets. By that time, the Uruguay Round offered a new framework for the negotiation of these questions.

---

[13] This point is usefully made by C. Carmody, "When 'Cultural Identity was not at Issue': Thinking about Canada—Certain Measures Concerning Periodicals" (1999) 30 *Law and Policy of International Business* 231, at 254.

[14] The US/EEC dispute on restrictions on the importation of television programmes under the "old" GATT regime prior to the Marrakech Agreement is documented by J. Filipek, "Culture Quotas: the Trade Controversy over the European Community's Broadcasting Directive" (1992) 28 *Stanford Journal of International Law* 323.

The Stalemate on Audiovisual Industries in the Framework of the GATS

During the final years of the Uruguay Round, the United States and the European Community found themselves bitterly opposed on the subject of "audiovisual services" (a term of art comprising both motion pictures and television programmes). The controversy had been started by the intra-EU debates on the enactment of a "European quota" provision intended to limit the predominance of American programmes on European (commercial) television stations. The text of the EC Directive on "Television without Frontiers", as eventually adopted in 1989, contains a provision in its Article 4 that imposes a weakly formulated duty on European television stations to broadcast a majority of European works of fiction.[15] Although the United States are not expressly mentioned in the text of the directive, the US government rightly understood this clause as being primarily directed against exports of US audiovisual material to the European market (although it also affects, for instance, the export of Latin American *telenovelas* to Spain and Portugal). Within the context of the Uruguay Round, the United States government tacitly agreed to deal with this question in the framework of negotiations on the General Agreement on Trade in Services (GATS). Within this framework, the EC and Canada sought to fend off the United States' demand for a full liberalisation of audiovisual services by proposing either a general exception for audiovisual services or a special annex with separate rules.

On this point, the Uruguay Round negotiations ended in a stalemate. Unlike what had happened earlier with the Canada/United States Free Trade Agreement of 1988,[16] no cultural exception was included in the GATS; nor did the US delegation accept the European proposal for a special annex on audiovisual services. The final text of the GATS, unlike some of the working drafts, does not contain the words "culture" or "audiovisual", which means that the general language of the agreement applies to cultural services in exactly the

---

[15] Directive 89/552 of 3 October 1989, [1989] OJ L298/23. For a legal analysis of Art. 4, see B. de Witte, "The European Content Requirement in the EC Television Directive—Five Years After" (1995) 1 *The Yearbook of Media and Entertainment Law* 101. The European content rules are very unevenly applied. Some Member States do not impose compliance with these rules by their commercial television stations, that fail, year after year, to reach the 50% hurdle of European works; see the country reports in Fourth Communication from the Commission to the Council and the European Parliament on the application of Articles 4 and 5 of Directive 89/552/EEC "Television without Frontiers" for the period 1997–98, COM(2000)442 of 17 July 2000.

[16] Art. 2005(1) of the Canada-United States FTA states: "Cultural industries are exempt from the provisions of the Agreement, except as specifically provided in" [there follow four references to specific Articles of the FTA which I do not reproduce here] ((1988) 27 International Legal Materials 281). The price paid for this exemption was that the United States was expressly accorded the right to retaliate if Canada were to adopt cultural policy measures affecting US interests. For discussion of the background and significance of Art. 2005, see I. Bernier, "La dimension culturelle dans le commerce international: quelques réflexions en marge de l'accord de libre-échange Canada/Etats Unis du 2 janvier 1988" (1987) 25 *The Canadian Yearbook of International Law* 243. The clause was later included by reference in the North American Free Trade Agreement (Annex 2106), but was not extended to the relations between Mexico and the other two contracting states of NAFTA.

same way as to other, equally unnamed, services.[17] Yet, the existing European (and Canadian) restrictions on the importation of films and broadcasting programmes were not directly affected by the entry into force of the GATS.[18] The European Community lodged exemptions to the *most-favoured-nation* (MFN) standard, covering the audiovisual coproduction agreements between EU Member States and third states, and the preferential access rules granted in the Television without Frontiers Directive for TV programmes originating from selected European countries (particularly the non-EU states parties to the European Convention on Transfrontier Television). More importantly, the EC failed to accord *national treatment* and *market access* to American audiovisual service providers by not making any specific commitments for the audiovisual sector.[19] The result was a *de facto* exclusion of the audiovisual sector from the GATS regime.

This position has not been modified since. At the internal EC level, the amendments of the Television without Frontiers Directive adopted in 1997[20] did not change the European content rule, despite heated debates between the several Member States, and between the Council and the European Parliament, on this question. The European content requirement is still there and remains, as before, compatible with the GATS.[21] At the international level, nothing has changed either; the WTO agreement on basic telecommunication services, which came into force on 1 January 1998 as the Fourth Protocol to the GATS, again does not apply to the distribution of audiovisual services, thereby leaving untouched the Marrakech stalemate.

So, by the time the Millennium Round of trade negotiations came into view, the positions of the various blocks had not changed compared to what they were during the Uruguay Round. In the preparatory documents drafted by the European Community,[22] and even more clearly in the positions taken by

---

[17] As stated in Arti. I(3)(b) of the GATS, "services includes any service in any sector except services supplied in the exercise of governmental authority".

[18] For a general assessment of the GATS negotiations, and their results, in the audiovisual field, see F. Dehousse and F. Havelange, "Exception culturelle ou spécificité culturelle?" in C. Doutrelepont (ed.), *L'Europe et les enjeux du GATT dans le domaine de l'audiovisuel* (Brussels, Bruylant, 1994) 99; K.F. Falkenberg, "The Audiovisual Sector" in J. Bourgeois, F. Berrod and E. Gippini Fournier (eds.), *The Uruguay Round Results* (Brussels, European Interuniversity Press, 1995) 429.

[19] For the GATS mechanism of schedules of commitments and MFN exemptions, see generally L. Altinger and A. Enders, "The Scope and Depth of GATS Commitments" (1996) 19 *The World Economy* 307; and M.J. Trebilcock and R. Howse, *The Regulation of International Trade* (2nd edn., London and New York, Routledge, 1999) at 283–289.

[20] [1997] OJ L202/60.

[21] B.J. Drijber, "The Revised Television Directive without Frontiers Directive: Is It Fit for the Next Century?" (1999) 36 *Common Market Law Review* 87, at 112.

[22] See particularly the Council Conclusions of 26 October 1999, *WTO: Preparation of the Third Ministerial Conference*, Council Press Release 12121/99, at I: "During the forthcoming WTO negotiations the Union will ensure, as in the Uruguay Round, that the Community and the Member States maintain the possibility to preserve and develop their capacity to define and implement their cultural and audiovisual policies for the purpose of preserving their cultural diversity".

France,[23] the doctrine of cultural specificity was reiterated in strong terms. The actual clash with the United States was delayed due to the Seattle debacle, but a new round of services negotiations had been scheduled for 2000 anyway, as part of the "built-in agenda" of the WTO Agreement, so that the culture-and-trade controversy may soon erupt once more on the WTO agenda. It seems that the United States will not so much try to convince the European Community to make national treatment commitments for audiovisual services as traditionally understood, but rather try to reach agreement on trade liberalisation of electronic commerce transactions while including within this category the programmes offered by the new communication media; many cultural "services" and "goods" are, indeed, already now "exported" and "imported" by means of the internet.

Culture Trade in WTO Law Outside the GATS

The political salience of the audiovisual question in the framework of GATS should not hide the fact that culture-and-trade issues also occur in a number of other contexts of international trade law, namely the trade in goods, the protection of intellectual property, the protection of investment, and the regulation of subsidies, which I will consider briefly. The "agreement to disagree" reached in the Uruguay Round with regard to services does not apply outside the GATS framework, so that the compatibility of national and European cultural policies with trade law rules must be considered separately under the other, non-GATS, headings.

Trade in Goods

It is still not entirely clear why the trade in television programmes should be considered as trade in services. The argument has been made that it should rather be considered as trade in *goods*, so that it is, in fact, covered by the rules of GATT rather than (or in addition to) GATS.[24] However, the negotiations in the Uruguay Round, and later, denote a clear understanding among the states parties that the trade in traditional television programmes is to be dealt with exclusively within the framework of GATS, so that, whatever the original situation

---

[23] See, for instance, the statement by the (then) minister of culture: C. Trautmann, "L'exception culturelle n'est pas négociable", *Le Monde*, 10–11 October 1999, 14; and the *Rapport d'information sur la préparation de la Conférence ministérielle de l'OMC à Seattle*, presented by Mme Béatrice Marre, Assemblée nationale, 30 septembre 1999, www.assemblee-nationale.fr/2/sae/rap-infor/i1824.pdf, at 130 ff.

[24] For a detailed discussion of this question, see J.D. Donaldson, "Television without Frontiers: The Continuing Tension between Liberal Free Trade and European Cultural Integrity" (1996) 20 *Fordham International Law Journal* 90, at 121–129; see also M.J. Hahn, "Eine kulturelle Bereichsausnahme im Recht der WTO?" (1996) 56 *Zeitschrift für ausländisches öffentliches Recht und Völkerrecht* 315, at 326 ff.

might have been, there is now clear subsequent practice of the WTO member states to exclude application of the GATT. However, no such clear exclusion was made for cinematographic *films*, for which the special clause in Article IV of GATT is still in force. Curiously, therefore, it seems that television programmes are now subject to GATS, and cinema films still subject to GATT, together with books, works of art and music recordings.[25] Generally speaking, it seems rather arbitrary "to draw a distinction between television programming and books, magazines, newspapers, and audio recordings, especially since, for all of the above, their real value is their literary or artistic content, which happens to be stored on an 'incidental goods' media, e.g., newsprint, audio tape, or paper";[26] but it is not more arbitrary than the similarly situated distinction between goods and services in internal EC law. Both in EC law and in GATT law, the regulation of the movement of goods received all the emphasis, and the regulation of services was added as an afterthought, without a clear conception of the criteria by which "services" should be distinguished from "goods" and to what extent they should be regulated differently from each other.

The practical importance of the "old" GATT rules has been enhanced by the new dispute settlement regime established by the WTO Agreement. The *Canadian Periodicals* case has shown that the substantive rules of the GATT Agreement can have a direct impact on those cultural industries whose products take the form of "goods" rather than "services". In this case, the Panel and the Appellate Body both found that Canadian regulations seeking to restrict the penetration of US periodicals on the Canadian market by means of quantitative restrictions, differential tax treatment and preferential postage rates were in breach of several GATT rules. [27] Disputes between the USA and the EC, or its Member States, have not emerged so far.

Investment

Although initially the USA sought a comprehensive agreement on investment protection within the framework of the Uruguay Round, this idea was abandoned in view of the opposition of developing states, although the application of GATS to *commercial presence* created an indirect, and sector-wise limited, regime of investment protection. Soon after, efforts were undertaken to elaborate a comprehensive multilateral regime of investment protection within the more congenial atmosphere of the OECD, but public controversy erupted during the negotiations, and the work on the Multilateral Agreement on Investment

---

[25] This is the conclusion drawn by Hahn (*supra* n. 24), at 334.

[26] D Donaldson, *supra* n. 24, at 125.

[27] *Canada—Certain Measures Concerning Periodicals*, complaint by the United States (WT/DS31), Panel report circulated on 14 March 1997, Appellate Body report adopted by the DSB on 30 July 1997. For critical comments on the alleged failure of the WTO bodies to take into account the cultural policy dimension of this case, see Tawfik, *supra* n. 1; Carmody, *supra* n. 13; G. Gagné, "Libéralisation et exception culturelle—le différend canado-américain sur les périodiques" (1999) 30 *Revue Etudes Internationales* 571.

(MAI) was formally abandoned in the autumn of 1998.[28] Again, the vociferous protestations of cultural interest groups had been an important factor in poisoning the negotiation climate and convincing the French (and Canadian) government of the need to scupper the initiative. The fear was that, by facilitating the investment and establishment abroad of multinational cultural industries, the Agreement would damage local cultural identities. However, if the MAI had come into existence, it would most probably have contained some form of exception for cultural industries, because the United States themselves have long-standing restrictions of foreign ownership in the broadcasting sector,[29] so that they could hardly have pushed for full liberalisation.

Copyright

The TRIPS Agreement, though not innovative in substantive terms, has given considerable additional weight to the enforcement of existing substantive rules of copyright protection by making available the WTO compliance mechanism for intellectual property disputes.[30] This has, already after a few years, proved to be an important change in the enforcement of existing international copyright conventions. Indeed, a number of cases submitted to the WTO dispute settlement organs deal with questions of copyright protection.[31] One panel report was adopted recently. In 1997, the Irish Music Rights Organisation had lodged a complaint with the European Commission alleging that a section of the US Copyright Act was in breach of TRIPS. The Commission decided to initiate action under the WTO dispute settlement procedure,[32] and the WTO panel which was eventually set up held, in May 2000, that Section 110(5) of the US Copyright Act, by allowing the playing of "homestyle" radios and televisions in most bars and restaurants without the payment of a royalty fee, was in breach of the United States' obligations under the Berne Copyright Convention and,

---

[28] For discussion of the reasons for the failure of the MAI negotiations, see Trebilcock and Howse, *supra* n. 19, at 36236–5; J. Karl, "Internationaler Investitionsschutz—Quo Vadis? (2000) 99 *Zeitschrift für vergleichende Rechtswissenschaft* 143; "The Sinking of the MAI", *The Economist*, 14 March 1998, at 85.

[29] G. Sacerdoti, "Bilateral Treaties and Multilateral Instruments on Investment Protection" (1997) 269 *RCADI* 251, at 324.

[30] F.M. Abbott, "WTO Dispute Settlement and the Agreement on Trade-Related Aspects of Intellectual Property" in E.-U. Petersmann (ed.), *International Trade Law and the GATT/WTO Dispute Settlement System* (The Hague, Kluwer Law International, 1997) 415.

[31] In addition to the panel report of May 2000 (see the next nn.) the following cases are subject to pending consultations: *European Communities and Greece—Enforcement of Intellectual Property Rights for Motion Pictures and Television Programs*, complaints by the United States (WT/DS124/1 and WT/DS125/1); *Denmark—Measures Affecting the Enforcement of Intellectual Property Rights*, complaint by the United States (WT/DS83/1); *European Communities and Ireland—Measures affecting the Grant of Copyright and Neighbouring Rights*, complaints by the United States (WT/DS82/1 and WT/DS/83/1). Settled was: *Sweden—Measures Affecting the Enforcement of Intellectual Property Rights*, complaint by the United States (WT/DS86/1).

[32] Commission Decision 98/731 of 11 December 1998 [1998] OJ L346/60.

hence, also of their obligations under the TRIPS Agreement.[33] More generally, it seems that the EU states do not find themselves in a defensive position as far as the application of copyright rules is concerned. The alarming view that "the prevailing dictates of free trade in copyright works heighten the potential for the cultural assimilation of a vulnerable nation by a more dominant cultural force"[34] may apply to certain developing countries, where the lack of enforceable copyright protection for foreign authors has acted as a disincentive for the import of cultural products from abroad; but it does not seem to apply to the relations between Europe and the United States. Indeed, the Member States of the EU have agreed, for many years already, to extend equal treatment to foreign copyright holders, and the TRIPS Agreement simply gives additional force to this commitment. It will not, by itself, cause an additional influx of foreign cultural products on European markets

Subsidies

Subsidies are an essential part of the cultural policies of most European states. Many cultural activities, such as film production, public libraries, music performances and public service broadcasting, could not survive without the financial support of local, regional, national and European authorities.[35] The compatibility of cultural subsidies with international trade law is therefore a matter of the highest practical importance. The WTO regime for subsidies is based on a distinction between subsidies for goods and subsidies for services. The normative framework on subsidies for goods consists of some general rules of the GATT, and of specific rules in the Agreement on Subsidies and Countervailing Measures. European subsidies to the film and publishing industries should most probably be considered as "permissible subsidies" in the sense of the latter agreement, that are actionable by other WTO parties only if these subsidies have adverse effects on their economy. In view of the dominant position of US productions on the European film and television markets, it is unlikely that the US government could demonstrate the existence of such adverse effects.[36] As far as services are considered, there is only the commitment, in Article XV GATS, to enter into negotiations on the matter. Pending the outcome of such negotia-

---

[33] *United States—Section 110(5) of the US Copyright Act*, WT/DS160/R, Panel Report of 15 June 2000.

[34] Tawfik, *supra* n. 1, at 288.

[35] The European Community has two main sources of direct funding for cultural activities: the MEDIA programme for the production and distribution of audiovisual works ([1995] OJ L321/25 and L321/33), and the Culture 2000 programme for support to artistic and literary activities ([2000] OJ L63/1). In addition, cultural projects are eligible under the Structural Funds and the EC research programme: see R. Fisher, "Fondi strutturali e spesa culturale: un'anomalia?"]2000] *Economia della Cultura* 33. Even when taken all together, EC subsidies for cultural activities are only a small percentage of the cultural expenditure of its Member States.

[36] T. Cottier, "Die völkerrechtlichen Rahmenbedingungen der Filmförderung in der neuen Welthandelsorganisation WTO-GATT" (1994) 38 *Zeitschrift für Urheber- und Medienrecht* 749, at 754.

tions, a member "which considers that it is adversely affected by a subsidy of another Member may request consultation with that Member on such matters. Such requests shall be accorded sympathetic consideration".[37] For the time being, the compatibility of national and European subsidy schemes with WTO law has not been openly challenged, but it is important to note that the international legal framework on subsidies is subject to further negotiation in the years to come.

TRADE OF CULTURE AND THE CONSTITUTION OF THE EUROPEAN UNION

The Institutional Context: the Division of Powers between the EC and its Member States in the Field of Culture Trade

The first thing to note about the "internal" constitutional framework of the EU is that the first, and still central, policy objective of the European Economic Community was to facilitate economic flows between its member countries by the creation of a common market for goods, persons, services and capital. This is not unlike the aims pursued by the GATT Agreement and, now, by the WTO. It was not obvious, at first, that this market integration goal could have any consequences for the cultural policies of its Member States. Indeed, the EEC Treaty did not even mention the word "culture", nor any of the particular cultural industries such as publishing, cinema or broadcasting. Yet, it gradually became clear, mainly through the case law of the European Court of Justice, that there was no neat separation between economy and culture, and that the economic-sounding concepts used in the EC Treaty could affect cultural goods and activities in so far as these had an economic dimension, which they frequently have. Therefore, the EC Treaty could be said to have had an unstated cultural policy objective right from the start, namely the elimination of national obstacles against the free flow of cultural goods and activities within the territory of the Community.

More particularly, the *free movement of goods* applies, in principle, to "cultural goods" in the same way as to other goods. Article 30 (ex Article 36) EC Treaty allows, it is true, for an exception to free movement for reasons of "protection of national treasures possessing artistic, historic or archaeological value", but the very existence of this provision was seen by the European Court of Justice as proof that, as a rule, free movement rules applied to cultural goods. It held, in its 1968 judgment in the *Italian Art Treasures* case,[38] that all products forming the object of a commercial transaction come within the scope of the rules on free movement of goods whatever their other qualities.

---

[37] GATS, Art. XV(2).
[38] Case 7/68, *Commission* v. *Italy* [1968] ECR 423.

The *freedom to provide services*, in turn, and again according to the European Court of Justice, covers cultural activities; most importantly in the present context, it aims at removing obstacles to the cross-border distribution of television programmes. In pursuing this aim, the European Commission launched, in the 1980s, an ambitious project to (de)regulate cross-border broadcasting which led to the adoption in 1989 of the Television without Frontiers Directive which contains the European content rule mentioned above.

EC legislation impinging on national cultural policy areas, such as this Television without Frontiers Directive, the Directive on the return of cultural objects unlawfully removed from the territory of a Member State,[39] and several EC directives in the field of copyright protection, is justified by the need to facilitate the effective operation of the internal market. Thus, the European Community's powers to harmonise national laws when this appears necessary for the functioning of the internal market, allow it to pursue cultural policy objectives as an ancillary part of measures that are primarily directed at ensuring the smooth functioning of the internal market. However, cultural policy harmonisation pursued for its own sake, that is, without a clear connection with the internal market, is expressly prohibited by the words of Article 151(5) EC Treaty. This internal ancillary competence of the European Community is also reflected in its *external* relations. The EC's competence with regard to a common commercial policy, as granted in Article 133 EC Treaty, covers trade measures dealing with culture. A clear example of such a culturally flavoured trade measure is Regulation 3911/92 on the export of cultural goods,[40] which was adopted in close conjunction with the Directive on the return of cultural objects and works of art (its "internal" counterpart). The aim of the Regulation was to install a uniform system of controls on the export of cultural property at the external borders of the Community, as a corollary of the fact that controls at the internal borders were removed at the end of 1992 which made it illegal to conduct systematic searches for the enforcement of national export controls. It was thought that, without such a common external border control, works of art would first freely be moved from a Member State with strict art export restrictions (say, Italy) to a Member State with a liberal export regime (say, the UK) from where they would leave unhindered the territory of the Community.[41] The legal basis for this Regulation (Article 133) can serve as justification for any, unilateral or conventional, EC measures relating to the trade of cultural goods. In the field defined by Article 133, the European Community even has exclusive competence, so that the Member States are no longer allowed to conclude separate agreements with third states. Therefore, to the extent that international

---

[39] Council Directive 93/7 [1993] OJ L74/74.

[40] [1992] OJ L395/1.

[41] On the connection between the "internal" and the "external" action of the EC in this particular field of protection of the cultural heritage, see B. de Witte, "The Cultural Dimension of Community Law" *Collected Courses of the Academy of European Law*, Volume IV, Book 1 (1995) 229, at 241–245.

agreements regulate the trade in cultural goods, such as works of art, books, periodicals or music recordings, the European Community has exclusive competence, although some of the state practice seems to be inconsistent with this rule.

The status of trade in audiovisual productions is not very clear. Assuming that this is trade in *services* rather than *goods* (a question discussed above), it seems to be a form of "cross-border supply of services" in the sense of the ECJ Opinion 1/94,[42] which means that it is also covered by Article 133 and, hence, falls within the exclusive competence of the European Community. This conclusion is confirmed, with specific regard to the European content requirement for broadcasters, by the "pre-emption doctrine", according to which Member States are precluded from concluding external agreements on matters covered by EC legislation. For these two reasons, it seems that the EC alone has the power to conclude international agreements on the matter. Such agreements are to be based on Article 133 and are, hence, subject to qualified majority decision-making within the Council of Ministers.

Within the WTO framework, this issue has not so far arisen, because audiovisual services were dealt with as part of a global trade package to be concluded, from the European perspective, as a mixed agreement. If, however, a new global trade round failed to take off, and audiovisual services were to become the object of separate negotiations, then the issue of the division of competences between the EC and its Member States would assume practical importance. So far, and particularly in the framework of the Uruguay Round, the mixed-agreement approach effectively granted a veto right to every single member state. This veto right amplifies the international bargaining weight of a minimalist position adopted by single Member States and makes this lowest common denominator position resonate internationally through the combined weight of the whole Community.[43] In the case of the audiovisual services, the member country most opposed to trade liberalisation, France, could therefore ensure the adoption by the EC of its "conservative" position in the international forum. If, however, negotiations on audiovisual services were on some future occasion to be run by the EC alone, internal EC decision-making would follow the qualified majority mode provided by Article 133 EC, and a coalition of liberal states might, just conceivably, outvote France and its allies. For the time being, this is a rather fictional hypothesis, as it assumes the concurrence of too many uncertain factors, namely (a) that separate negotiations on audiovisual services will be started; (b) that the Member State governments, acting through the Council, would politically accept that the EC can conclude a services agreement on its own; (c) that a qualified majority emerges within the Council to meet American demands some way down the road; (d) that this qualified majority

---

[42] [1994] ECR I–5267, paras. 41–47.

[43] J. Jupille, "The European Union and International Outcomes" (1999) 53 *International Organization* 409, at 423; S. Meunier, "What Single Voice? European Institutions and EU–US Trade Negotiations" (2000) 54 *International Organization* 103, at 117.

agrees to outvote France (and possibly other states) in such a highly sensitive matter. Therefore, the conclusion can be drawn that, for the time being, European Community policy-making with regard to audiovisual trade relations remains dominated by the consensus principle, but that this situation could change in the years to come.

The Substantive Constitutional Context: the Duties of the EC Institutions in the Field of Culture Trade

Article 131 EC Treaty declares the abolition of international trade barriers to be an aim of the Community's common commercial policy. There is a striking contrast, though, between the numerous statements in the EC Treaty about the central importance of free trade and market integration *inside* the European Union, and the Treaty's lack of emphasis on free trade values in the relations with third countries. External trade liberalisation rather seems to an objective of the EC like many others, which needs to be balanced against competing values and policy objectives.

One competing policy objective that may, possibly, trump international free trade is that of protecting *cultural diversity*. This objective has been given constitutional recognition in the EC legal order since the entry into force of the Treaty of Maastricht. Article 151(4) of the EC Treaty provides that "[t]he Community shall take cultural aspects into account in its action under other provisions of this Treaty, in particular in order to respect and to promote the diversity of its cultures".[44] This "integration clause" covers all areas of EC policy, including internal measures of harmonisation, but also external trade policy. Therefore, when acting within the framework of the WTO, or any other international economic framework, the European Community must make sure that its action contributes to the preservation and promotion of cultural diversity within Europe.

In *internal* EC policies, the value of cultural diversity is relevant in two ways: it may help to define the *limits of negative integration*, and it may help to shape the content of *positive integration* measures.[45] With regard to negative integration, the value of cultural diversity should be considered by the European Court of Justice when examining whether certain intra-Community restrictions of trade can be justified by an overriding public interest of the Member States;[46] and it should also be taken into account by the Commission when developing its

---

[44] The last part of this phrase was added by the Treaty of Amsterdam, but the value of cultural diversity has been recognised in para. 1 of the same Art. 151 since the Treaty of Maastricht.

[45] On the conceptual pair negative integration/positive integration, and on the institutional conditions in which these two types of integration are embedded, see F. Scharpf, *Governing in Europe: Effective and Democratic?* (Oxford, OUP, 1999), ch. 2.

[46] On the degree to which the ECJ recognises cultural policy values as legitimate public interests in its case law on the common market freedoms: see de Witte, *supra* n. 41, at 255–267.

anti-trust and state aid policies.[47] As far as positive integration is concerned, cultural diversity is a "horizontal" value that the European Union decision-making organs should take into account when elaborating internal market harmonisation measures and regulatory policies. The Television without Frontiers Directive offers an example of this: its primary objective was the abolition of barriers to the distribution of television programmes within Europe (a "negative integration" goal) but at the same time its Article 4, by imposing a European content requirement on all broadcasters, attempts to give protection to cultural diversity within Europe, and towards the outside world. However, the weak wording of Article 4 is a symptomatic reflection of the fact that "interventionist policies, and the interests they could serve, are systematically disadvantaged in the process of European integration", because "the institutional capacity for negative integration is stronger than the capacity for positive integration".[48]

This European content requirement, while enacted within the framework of an internal EC policy instrument, is obviously also a measure of *external trade policy*. In fact, when Article 151 EC imposes a duty on the EU institutions to respect and promote cultural diversity, this duty also extends to possible external threats to cultural diversity. The values entrenched in Article 151 do not directly affect the division of competences between the EC and the Member States in the field of external trade, but they affect the way these competences are to be exercised by the Community. Seen from this angle, the EC's strenuous defence of its audiovisual quota regime, and of other trade restrictions in the field of culture, is not whimsical and unjustifiable protectionism, but a policy line that is consistent with the value judgement expressed in Article 151 EC Treaty. This assumes that it is possible to distinguish beween authentic cultural policies and crude protectionist measures cloaked in lofty cultural language and, more specifically, that the television quota rules, and the state subsidies to cultural activities, effectively contribute to preserve cultural diversity within Europe. These assumptions are not evidently plausible and many trade lawyers may feel sympathy for the statement that "[t]here are surely deeper measures of a society's cultural evolution than how many minutes are occupied by which country's soap operas on local commercial television networks".[49]

In fact, the normative questions underlying the trade-and-culture debate are situated at two different levels. The first level is that of the identification of competing public interest values; the second level is that of the accommodation of these competing values in concrete policy measures. At the first of these two

---

[47] One current "hot topic" in this respect is the way in which the Commission's competition and state aid policies affect the position of public service broadcasters. The Commission should, arguably, take into account the cultural policy functions exercised by public broadcasters. See R. Craufurd Smith, "Getting the Measure of Public Services: Community Competition Rules and Public Service Broadcasting" (1997–98) 3 *Yearbook of Media and Entertainment Law* (1997–98) 147; and R. Craufurd Smith, "State Aid and Public Service Broadcasting: The Position Under European Community Law", (2000) 28(1) *Legal Issues of Economic Integration*, 3.

[48] Scharpf, *supra* n. 45, at 49.

[49] Trebilcock and Howse, *supra* n. 19, at 14.

levels, there is no major disagreement, as all major actors in the European integration process and in the WTO system recognise both the value of free trade and that of cultural diversity (although the meaning of these terms is itself an object of controversy). In many ways, both values are even complementary. The freedom to import and export goods and services with a cultural content contributes to the free exchange of ideas and opinions and to the affirmation of the cultural autonomy of individuals and groups in both the exporting and importing countries. In some situations, however, unrestrained free trade may appear to be a danger for the cultural integrity of states and the cultural rights of their citizens. There is wide agreement on the position of principle that, when such situations arise, a country is entitled to preserve its cultural heritage and to promote the development of cultural activities within its borders. Indeed, the preservation of a national cultural identity is a widely felt concern also in the United States.[50] The peculiar position of the USA, compared to Europe, is that such perceived threats to national cultural identity emerge from *internal* cultural fragmentation, and are certainly not caused by the import of foreign cultural works, the quantity of which is fairly negligible. In some European countries, however, the concern for the preservation of their cultural identity is caused, in large part, by a fear for "*cette extraordinaire machine d'invasion intellectuelle que constituent désormais les Etats-Unis*".[51]

If one accepts, in principle, that the preservation of cultural distinctiveness may justify certain measures that restrict the free flow of commercial trade, the more contentious issue is how such measures should be framed and to what extent they should be allowed to restrict trade. Free trade supporters argue that measures should be chosen that cause the least possible disturbance to trade, so that, for instance, the EC should protect its film and television industry by means of financial subsidies rather than by the more incisive instrument of local content requirements for broadcasters. However, others argue that governments should have the power freely to define their cultural policy priorities without being overly constrained by the need to choose the measures that are "least damaging" to free trade. They posit that the defence of cultural values does not rank lower, in the scale of values, than the promotion of trade.

The political balance between these conflicting views depends on the institutional context in which they are made. The European Community, although it leaves considerable autonomy to its Member States in defining their own cultural policy priorities, has emerged as the common voice of these Member States in the world trade arena. Due to the institutional framework within

---

[50] See, among many others: A. Schlesinger Jr., *The Disuniting of America: Reflections on a Multicultural Society* (New York, Norton, 1992); C. Lindholm and J.A. Hall, "Is the United States Falling Apart?" (1997) 126 *Daedalus* 183; K.L. Karst, "The Bonds of American Nationhood" (2000) 21 *Cardozo Law Review* 1141.

[51] The expression was used by two French cabinet ministers, and is an example of the frequent use of military metaphors in French accounts of the culture trade relations with the USA: C. Allègre and P. Moscovici, "Plaidoyer pour l'Europe des cultures", *Le Monde*, 1 June 1999, 17.

which multilateral trade issues are dealt with in the EC, every single Member State can insist on the need to preserve its cultural policy autonomy when international trade commitments are being proposed; but this same institutional framework makes it very difficult for the EC to develop common policies of its own in this field. In concrete terms: whereas France can effectively constrain some of its reluctant EU partners to adopt its restrictive policy with regard to audiovisual trade in the WTO arena, it does not have sufficient bargaining power to convince them to join its initiative to develop an international regulatory framework for the protection of cultural diversity within the rival framework of Unesco. The role of the European Community, as the intermediary between its Member States' cultural policy preferences and the demands of its international trade partners, will remain a delicate one for many years to come.

11

Is There Any Such Thing As Free or Fair Trade? A Constitutional Analysis of the Impact of International Trade on the European Social Model

MIGUEL POIARES MADURO*

TRADE LIBERALISATION IS often perceived as inevitable. Even those who challenge it attempt to undermine it by, at the same time that they note its ideological consequences and contest its inevitability, using the rhetoric and symbolism of the perceived inevitability to present trade liberalisation and the broader concept of globalisation as a kind of dark, secretive and dangerously inhumane project. As one author puts it: "globalization is universalism minus a conscience".[1] Trade liberalisation is not inevitable, at least not to the extent to which globalisation is normally referred to. States could still reinstate many of their trade protectionism policies effectively. If free trade is assumed to be inevitable it is because, no matter how much one may note some negative consequences of trade liberalisation and globalisation, there is a broader overarching consensus on the overall benefits of trade liberalisation. At the same time, free trade expresses the economic inter-dependence of countries around the globe and a greater awareness of the need to promote and distribute wealth resources at a global level. How that wealth should be promoted and distributed is the key question underlying the debates on how much and what type of free trade should we have. The answer to this question requires us to recognise that there may be different assessments of the economic gains arising from free trade and that there may be different criteria on how they should be distributed. This is the reason for the free trade versus fair trade debate. Furthermore, those different assessments and criteria are normally reflected in different national policies. These policies are, in turn, a reflection of the social self-determination of the different political communities. How can these different balances be

* Faculdade de Direito, Universidade Nova de Lisboa. I would like to thank to Gráinne de Búrca for comments made on an earlier version of this chapter.

[1] P.-M. Dupuy, "International Law: Torn between Coexistence, Cooperation and Globalization—General Conclusions" (1998) 9 *European Journal of International Law* 278, at 282.

made compatible? And, when they cannot, which one should prevail? In this chapter, I argue that the ideological rhetoric which suffuses the free trade versus fair trade debate is embedded in contradictory legitimating criteria and has so far ignored the real question underlying the debate: who should, in different circumstances, determine the balance between free trade and fair trade.

Although each side of the free trade versus fair trade debate proclaims that it promotes the more efficient and/or equitable distribution of resources, the terms in which the propositions are framed do not legitimate such claims. Instead, I will argue that each side simply presupposes a different institutional allocation of the balance between free trade and fair trade. Each side is arguing for a different jurisdiction for social self-determination. As a starting point I will review and reconstruct the arguments on both sides of the debate between free trade and fair trade. I will argue that, in the end, both sides share a single viable and legitimate argument: that either the policies of free trade or the policies of fair trade challenge the social self-determination of their political communities. What differs is the form of that challenge and the political communities upon which the different sides of the debate focus their protective attention. To arrive at this common ground for discourse I will deconstruct much of the traditional rhetoric of the free trade versus fair trade debate in a manner which hopefully will highlight its artificial character and demonstrate its lack of usefulness in addressing the complex questions underlying the debate. It is hoped that once the focus is re-shifted from the ideological rhetoric onto the institutional choices involved in the issue of social self-determination, a viable discourse may take place on where and how best to balance the economic gains of free trade with the social values inherent in the ideals of fair trade.

The overview of the different problems and opportunities brought by free trade will make it possible to understand how the debate on free trade and social rights is related to a constitutional debate on the forms of representation and participation in the different institutional alternatives that are available to the regulation of free trade. I will assume this constitutional dimension in reviewing the impact of the WTO and international trade on European and national social policies. In the second section of the chapter I will highlight the constitutional impact of the challenges brought by free trade to the traditional national jurisdictions for the definition of social policies. In this, it represents a challenge to the constitutional definition of the civic and social values of each political community and undermines some of the foundations for their constitutional social self-determination. My main assumption is that free trade should respect the right to constitutional self-determination of different political communities which includes a right to social self-determination.[2] But, at the same time, I highlight the changes taking place in the forms and forums of such social self-

---

[2] This does not mean that all communities participating in the international trade system are in fact constitutionally or socially self-determining and, as will be clear below, there are important consequences I draw from whether or not a community satisfies the conditions for effective social or constitutional self-determination.

determination and how this requires the creation of a constitutional framework of international trade. My main objective will be to identify how best to protect and promote such social self-determination in a context of free trade and how it can be exercised with regard to the European social model (which is in the hands of both the Member States and the European Union). The third section of the chapter will stress how international trade and the WTO require the European Union to address its own social self-determination and the consequences this will have for the future of the EU social policy and, more broadly, the European Constitution.

The impact of WTO law and, more generally, free trade and globalisation on EU social policy can be approached from different perspectives, all of which require us to rethink both European social policy and its relation with national social policies, while attempting to address the future of the European social model and the social basis of the national political communities and the emerging European political community. All through this chapter I will take into account two different dimensions of the challenge brought by WTO law and globalisation to European social policy. The first dimension regards the general challenge to the European social model, based upon the welfare state, and currently dependent upon EU and state policies. The policies of this social model are developed and promoted at the state and EU level and I will review the challenges brought by free trade and WTO law to those policies and its impact on the constitutional autonomy of the political communities that support them. I will review the different problems and institutional alternatives to the development of the WTO law and their possible impact on social self-determination and, more generally, on the global regulation of social issues. This first dimension of the impact of the WTO on the EU social model will underlie much of the analysis made in sections 1 and 2. The second dimension relates to the possible consequences of the challenges brought by free trade and the WTO law to the EU social policy and its relation with national social policies. I will address how the developments of international trade and globalisation may require an internal reconstruction of EU social policy so that it can take over social functions which international trade law and globalisation no longer allow Member States to pursue. This dimension is present in section 3.

RESHAPING THE "FREE TRADE VERSUS FAIR TRADE" DEBATE

The starting point of the free trade versus fair trade debate is the existence of different domestic social policies. Free trade advocates argue that such social policy differences cannot be used to restrict free trade. Fair trade advocates argue that free trade should take place only if those different social policies do not distort trade competition, therefore guaranteeing that free trade will not restrict the freedom of the different political communities to adopt different social policies. In a context of free trade, the free circulation of companies, capital, products and services generates a process of regulatory competition among different polities: companies will move to where the regulatory environment is more favourable to their objectives (deregulation, lower taxes, financial incentives, etc.); consumers, in turn, can choose among goods and services conforming to different regulations. As a consequence, regulations themselves will also be competing in the market. There are different economic and legal analyses praising or criticising such strategy of trade liberalisation and its accompanying regulatory competition. Some stress the efficiency gains derived from a better allocation of resources and the higher freedom of choice and lower prices available for consumers. Others point to the threat to the welfare state and the risks of a regulatory "race to the bottom": companies will move to states with lower environmental, social, health or consumer standards and still benefit from the free trade in their products and services. The latter perspective usually corresponds to fair trade advocates. They argue that either the different political communities should be authorised to restrict free trade if necessary to protect their social standards or there should be a level playing field whereby all parties participating in free trade will comply with a basic set of social rights. Free trade advocates, in turn, will argue that to authorise some countries to exclude trade from other countries on the basis of non-compliance with the former social policies corresponds, in effect, to authorising that country to impose its social policies on its trading partners and, in many instances, to using those social policies as a cover for economic protectionism. Furthermore, free trade economists normally argue that the best harmonisation of social standards will be that arising *ex post* from the regulatory competition among the different social policies.

This summary of the predominant views of free trade and fair trade advocates already highlights two main types of argument present on both sides of the debate: the first type is based on the restriction imposed by either free trade or fair trade proposals on the freedom of some political communities to choose their own social policies (what I call social self-determination); the second type of argument is based upon the idea of fair competition which each side claims the other undermines. As pointed out by Robert Hudec:

> Differences between domestic social policies can create two kinds of friction in a world of integrated economic relations. At one level, differences between domestic economic policies may appear to distort the international economic exchange that goes on between nations, leading one side to perceive that it is being unfairly disadvantaged. At another level, some countries may feel that their own economic policies are being frustrated by the divergent economic policies of other countries, and these countries may wish to condition further economic exchanges on correction of these policy shortcomings.[3]

In reality both of these levels of friction arising from divergent social policies in a context of free trade can be subsumed under the fear by the different political com-

---

[3] R.E. Hudec, "Introduction to the Legal Studies" in J. Bhagwati and R.E. Hudec (eds.), *Fair Trade and Harmonization: Prerequisites to Free Trade?* Cambridge, Mass., and London, The MIT Press, 1996), ii, 1, at 1.

munities of losing the constitutional autonomy of self-determining their social policies. The argument of unfair competition is either instrumental to the problem of social self-determination or requires, as the basis for the framing and discussion of free trade policy, common global values and a degree of social solidarity which could only exist in the context of a global political community. As things now stand, for reasons I will explain better below, the argument of unfair competition can only legitimately be conceived of as a different representation of the social self-determination problem. Fair traders say that free trade without a common level playing field forces some political communities to lower their social standards in order for their products and services to be competitive in the world market. Free traders will argue that fair traders are simply trying to impose their social standards on other countries by denying these countries access to market competition if they do not conform to those social standards. Both perspectives of unfair competition can therefore be reconstructed as focusing on the challenges to the constitutional autonomy of different political communities to exercise social self-determination and freely choose their domestic social policies. I will develop the nature of those challenges to highlight the core of the dispute between free trade and fair trade. At the same time, I will attempt to prove that no other arguments can, at present, legitimately be put forward by either side of the debate. Therefore, the discussion on the relation between free trade and fair trade must concentrate on developing an appropriate framework to protect and balance the different political communities' claims for constitutional social self-determination.

Critics of free trade usually start by noting how economic and legal integration constrains the social policy-making powers of some states or other polities (such as the EU) and usually endangers the higher social standards of those polities by subjecting them to regulatory competition from countries with lower social standards. It is the challenge of free trade to the welfare state. The WTO provides the legal framework for this challenge. The WTO general legal principles limit the forms and content that national and European regulations may take: first, they prohibit discrimination among trade partners (for example, Article I of the GATT); secondly, they also prohibit discrimination among domestic and foreign products and services once they enter into the national market (for example, Article III of the GATT) ; thirdly, they prohibit restrictions on trade (pecuniary or regulatory, for example, Article XI of the GATT) except where authorised by specific Treaty derogations (authorising customs duties etc. or general exceptions provided for in the Treaty such as (for example, Article XX of the GATT).[4]

The extent to which the prohibition of restrictions on trade included in Article XI precludes *non-discriminatory* regulations affecting trade is a cause of present dispute in the WTO legal debates[5] but it has always been a settled

---

[4] The examples given of the GATT are generally also valid for the GATS.

[5] See, for a recent interpretation and useful comparison with EC free movement law, J.H.H. Weiler, "The Constitution of the Common Market Place" in P. Craig and G. de Búrca (eds.), *The Evolution of EU Law* (Oxford, OUP, 1999), at 355 ff.

interpretation of GATT rules that the contracting parties cannot enact rules restricting the importation of goods which in their process of production may have not conformed with certain social rights and policies, even if those rights and policies are required for the production of the same goods in the country of importation. The starting point for this interpretation is the distinction between incorporated and non-incorporated standards (also known as product rules and process rules). Incorporated standards are those which integrate the product and therefore "accompany" its movement into another market: packaging, composition, labelling etc. In the case of these types of standards, the contracting parties could, in principle, still impose their own non-discriminatory rules on imported products even if these rules would restrict the entry of the latter in the importing market. However, in the case of non-incorporated standards, the same does not occur. Non-incorporated standards do not "travel" with the goods and relate to conditions affecting their production or regulating the company or individual that produces them. It is the case of rules on taxation, in site pollution or labour standards. Most social policies fall into this category. This means that the EU, for example, cannot prevent the importation of goods produced in a state which does not impose the same labour standards (affecting, for example, working time) imposed by the EU and its Member States on companies established in Europe. In other words, the social policies of the EU cannot justify a restriction on the importation of goods which may have been produced according to policies which do not afford the same social protection. As a consequence, European products have to compete with products manufactured in accordance with lower social standards. It is this that is often presented as a form of unfair competition raising risks of a political community being forced to lower its social standards in order to protect the competitive stance of its producers. This is the usual understanding which is encapsulated in the rhetoric of social dumping and race to the bottom and leads to both political and legal arguments favouring some form of protection of a minimum set of social rights and standards in the WTO context of free trade.[6]

It can be asked why, if for so long international trade law has not allowed states and other contracting parties to use their social standards to deny access to their domestic markets, only now are the claims of social deregulation increasingly being heard. The explanation lies in the fact that social deregulation does not come directly from free trade rules but through the competitive process which free trade generates. That means that more so than the direct impact flowing from WTO rules on social regulations, that which raises increased fears of social deregulation is the overall increase in trade arising from the demise of the old trade-controlling mechanisms. Trade liberalisation and the expansion of the global market mean that more and more products and services from more and more states are competing in the same market. That competition indirectly affects

---

[6] See A. Trebilcock, "Social Dimensions of International Trade Liberalization" in P. Demaret, J.F. Bellis, G. García Jiménez (eds.), *Regionalism and Multilateralism After the Uruguay Round—Convergence, Divergence and Interaction* (Brussels, European Interuniversity Press, 1997), 511.

the different regulatory frameworks to which those products are subject in their country of origin. Free trade generates competition between the different political communities' economic and legal systems subject to the goal of efficiency. The extent to which the WTO case law already embodies a notion of free trade rights as protecting the freedom of economic actors to choose among different regulatory systems can be disputed. But, even if legally an obligation is not imposed on countries to lower their social, environmental and consumer standards, economic competition opens their regulatory systems to competition and efficiency criteria, *de facto* subjecting normative ideals to economic competition. This affects their political autonomy in determining their social policies.[7]

Fair trade advocates have been arguing in the academic and political debates in favour of some form of authorisation of non-discriminatory restrictions on trade with respect to social standards or, in the alternative, for the establishment of minimum social standards to be complied with by all contracting parties of the WTO in order to benefit from free trade. However, all proposals favouring the establishment of a social clause in the WTO legal framework have so far proved to be unacceptable for an important number of states, mainly those whose comparative advantages result in great part from their lower social standards. For these contracting parties, the setting of a "level playing field" in the social sphere or the requirement to comply with different non-discriminatory social standards in order to be granted market access is seen as a disguised form of protectionism once it either leads to prohibiting the entrance into a national market of products produced in accordance with different social standards or deprives those products from their competitive advantage. Therefore, those states would be forced to change their domestic social policies in order to gain access to the market of states with different social policies. In this way, fair trade policies can also be accused of affecting the social self-determination of some political communities.

Fair trade advocates are right in noting that free trade challenges the autonomy of their political communities to determine their domestic social policies. The problem is that the solutions they propose also challenge the autonomy of other political communities to determine their social policies. To be truthful, social activists and fair trade advocates present other arguments in favour of the conditionality of free trade upon certain social rights and policies. These are arguments derived from the independent value of social rights, which ought to be universally protected. The most critical views of trade liberalisation and globalisation oppose what is foreseen as the subjection of regulatory ideals and human rights values to the market forces. As one author puts it, "The human rights movement could thus find in market globalization the ultimate victory of the regulatory system that, by nature and operation, cannot properly take into account what the human rights movement holds most dear: that underlying

---

[7] There are also objections which are based on moral and ethical grounds and which I address below.

positive human rights are moral entitlements that ground moral, political and legal claims which must be morally and legally prior to society and the state".[8] The paradox is that a defender of trade liberalisation and globalisation may well be in complete agreement with that notion of human rights and will argue that there is no natural incompatibility between free trade and social rights. On the contrary, the economic growth, freedom and inter-dependence generated by free trade may be the more appropriate ground for the promotion of social rights. In the same way, however, it is possible to argue that international trade law must depart from a set of common social standards corresponding to those human rights. The key to unveiling the reasons for such paradox lies in the fact that the notion of human rights is not enforceable in itself and requires a definition of the content of those rights. Where free trade advocates and free trade opponents disagree is on who should define what those rights are or, in the alternative, on which definition of social rights should prevail.

The social rights rhetoric of fair trade advocates can sustain itself only if fair trade advocates are able to justify why their understanding of social rights should prevail over the different understanding of other political communities. The usual explanation is circular but apparently effective: such social rights are conceived as universal rights which impose themselves on all political communities. Therefore, they do not correspond to the imposition of the values of one political community over another but to values whose claim of legitimacy arises from a universal source, independent of all national and regional political communities. Such values and the rights flowing from them would be found in a trans-national link between the members of the different sub-global political communities. This trans-national solidarity would entail criteria of distributive justice and fairness capable of legitimating uniform social rights and equal conditions of competition.[9] One may even partially accept some form of political relation between the citizens of the different sub-global political communities. However, such a theory of legitimacy faces serious problems when used to justify the conditionality of free trade upon the compliance by all countries with certain social standards. The establishment of global social standards which surpass the judgements of local political communities (state and regional such as the EU) can be properly legitimised only if the independent universal claim of legitimacy upon which they are based satisfies the conditions of a political community with a certain degree of solidarity that can be opposed to that of national or regional political communities. Many of the social rights, mainly positive social rights, advocated by fair traders have costs which would have to be shared by that global political community.[10] If there is no global political community

---

[8] F. Garcia, "Market and Human Rights: Trading Away the Human Rights Principle" (1999) 51 *Brooklyn Journal of International Law* 51, at 52.

[9] For an analysis of this form of fair trade discourse, see: J. Bhagwati, "The Demands to Reduce Domestic Diversity among Trading Nations",in Bhagwati and Hudec (eds.), *supra* n. 3, ii, 9, at 10 ff.

[10] *Ibid.*, at 12–13.

willing to share such costs and to figure out a criterion of distributive justice capable of supporting the application of those global social rights, then there is no reason why one perception of what social rights are should prevail over another. The same reasoning however does not apply to rights which do not imply such costs and which can be constructed as necessary to the protection of constitutional and social self-determination. I will address this difference and its relevance in detail below. At this point, what is clear is that what both sides of the free trade versus fair trade debate assume is that their judgement on the best balance between free trade and social rights ought to prevail. Since each side of the debate does not accept the requirements of a broader political community (including an agreement on a distributive justice criterion) the solution of this conflict cannot be legitimately subject to some form of global criterion or global values (since there is no underlying global political community capable of legitimating it). Instead, the different balances between free trade and social rights are reflected in different social policies of the different political communities, all of which present an *a priori* higher claim of legitimacy than that which can be provided by the rhetoric of either free trade or social rights without an underlying political community. It is on the conflicting judgements and claims to legitimacy of the different political communities that the debate on free trade versus fair trade must focus. Therein lies the real reason for the dispute.

Therefore, the problem of free trade and social policy is not about the rhetoric or the values which ought to dominate globalisation and trade liberalisation. There may actually be a world consensus on the protection of social rights and the promotion of free trade but there is no overarching consensus on the content of those rights and the rules of international trade which ought to control the choice among different conceptions of the social good. The real question to be faced concerns the choice of the process or institution which will balance the legitimate claims of different political communities to have their own judgements on the social good protected and the extent to which this social self-determination of the different political communities ought to and can be protected. It will be more useful if, instead of focusing on a largely inoperative rhetoric of human rights and globalisation, the debate would focus on the normative constitutional criteria that ought to be followed in making those difficult institutional choices.

SOCIAL SELF-DETERMINATION AND THE CONSTITUTIONAL FRAMEWORK OF INTERNATIONAL TRADE

The conclusion to be drawn from the previous pages is that more than the effect it has on different specific social regulations, the contentious nature of free trade comes from the challenges it poses to the social self-determination of some political communities, affecting the foundations of traditional constitutionalism. It challenges the autonomy of different polities to exercise social self-determination and freely choose the social policies to be applicable in their political communities. However, as, hopefully, it has also become clear from the previous analysis, fair trade policies (including conditionality on compliance with certain social standards and/or harmonisation) can also be accused of undermining the social self-determination of other political communities. In this way, both free trade and fair trade affect the constitutional autonomy of the different political communities with regard to social policies.[11] We are therefore left with a conundrum apparently impossible to solve. In effect, whatever solution is found will be an imperfect one. The next part of this chapter is devoted to finding the least imperfect one.

A meaningful debate on the relation between free trade and social rights must depart from a analysis of the way in which the WTO and free trade affect the constitutional definition of our political communities and the extent to which states and other polities (such as the EU) remain the primary way of expressing our individuals interests and participating in both domestic and international decision-making affecting social policies. This analysis will highlight the constitutional character of the challenges brought about by economic integration which, in turn, will determine the criterion of legitimacy and the architecture of the legal framework which will regulate the developments promoted by economic integration and the nature of the relation between trans-national, regional and national decision-making processes. The constitutional relevance of international trade can be seen in the impact it has on the social self-determination of classical political communities (mainly states). But it can also be conceived, in a broader light, as giving rise to a change in the overall patterns of participation and representation in social decision-making. In this sense, it challenges not only the exercise of constitutionalism at the state level but also the conditions of constitutionalism in general.

Free trade gives rise to several constitutional phenomena, all of which affect the traditional mechanisms of representation and participation and the definition of the relevant political communities for social self-determination, giving rise to what we could call a constitutional transformation of social policy:

The New Political Fora of Social Policies

Traditionally, international organisations could not be conceived as affecting the conditions for the domestic political definition of social policies. International organisations were mainly set up to reduce information and transaction costs and to provide the necessary framework for viable co-operation among states since this would be difficult to achieve without the institutionalised processes provided for by those international organisations. The application of this classi-

---

[11] This challenge to the constitutional autonomy of traditional political communities is broader than that simply highlighted in this chapter. See D. Held, *Democracy and the Global Order* (Cambridge and Oxford, Polity Press, 1995), for example, at 16–17.

cal conception of international organisations is highly problematic to organisations such as the WTO or, even, the ILO. The legal norms and political processes which rule over the WTO end up attributing to it an independent normative authority. In this case, the classical paradigm is reversed "with nation-states serving more as agents of the international bodies than as their principles".[12] Once international organisations are perceived by the different social actors as emerging forms of independent power, they will attempt to profit from these organisations to pursue their different agendas. As a result, international organisations will tend to develop political and social goals which may diverge from those of their initial masters (the states and other political entities). There is a circular dynamic between the spill-over of the power initially attributed to the WTO, which raises the interest of social actors for political action in this institution, and the reinforcement of the institution's power precisely by virtue of the political dynamic promoted by the action of those social actors. This cycling dynamic promotes the overall power of the WTO and its role as a global political arena. In the process, the control of social decision-making by traditional political processes (for example, at state and EU level) decreases. The WTO and the ILO are the best examples of international institutions which, more than simply co-ordinating states' policies, promote independent political and social goals which are determined by a constituency of social actors which goes beyond the states and participates in manners different from those occurring in domestic political processes. The consequence, of constitutional relevance for social policy, is that the actors that participate and dominate in this emerging global political arena are not necessarily the same that have participated in the drafting of social policies at the national and European level.

Changing the Domestic Patterns of Representation and Participation in Social Policies

Even if we continue to link the determination of social policies at the global level to an agreement among the more traditional participants in the international community (states and other political entities such as the EU), the fact that the state's social decisions will be decided in the framework of a different state policy sphere means that representation and participation in the drafting of those social policies will change. The co-determination of social policies at the international level means that many of the state determinations of social policy are, at least in part, brought into the realm of foreign or commercial policy. Once we accept that the state (and much less the EU) does not have a homogeneous national interest and that there are different mechanisms and forms of participation involved in different areas of policy-making, one of the consequences of

---

[12] P. Stephan, "The New International Law—Legitimacy, Accountability, Authority and Freedom in the New Global Order" (1999) 70 *University of Colorado Law Review* 1555, at 1557.

the partial transfer of social policy into the realms of foreign and commercial policies is that the relevant participants in the framing of social policy change. The institutions and social actors which participate in the framing of social policies through external and commercial policies are different from those which control social policies as a pure domestic policy of the states or the Union. Furthermore, international trade reduces the power of the political processes in social decision-making by challenging their political monopoly on the definition of the social good. This is so because the emerging decision-making processes of international trade law can be used by a group which lost a domestic political battle to challenge the domestic political outcome.[13] In effect, international trade and economic integration, can be said to offer to some citizens the option of exit with regard to the decisions of their political community and in this sense challenge that political community distribution of representation and participation.

The Transfer of Power to the Market

One of the consequences of the legal and economic processes of regulatory competition arising from international trade is a reduction in the political control over the economic sphere. Liberalisation of trade generates competition among products and services of different polities which, in turns, leads to competition between the different regulatory frameworks to which those products and services are subject . National and other polities (such as the EU) have to determine their policies not only on the basis of their internal preferences but also taking into account the need for their products and services to be competitive in the global market. The consequence is a transfer of power from the political processes to the global market. It is the market that will choose between competing social policies and, in this light, it becomes crucial to assess the "constitutional quality" of representation and participation in the market.

Technocratic Forms of Global Regulation

A similar process of transfer of power will occur if, instead of trusting the regulation of international trade to the market, we decide to subject it to international standards set by international technocratic bodies. Both the markets and these technocratic bodies have an inherent rationality and a set of normative values which is not subject to a traditional form of political discourse or, to put it differently, they "decide" on the basis of a community of participation and representation that is different from that of political processes.

---

[13] In this sense, see D. McRae, "The WTO in International Law", (2000) 3 *Journal of International Economic Law* 27, at 35.

Once we establish that international trade challenges the social self-determination of the traditional political communities and, broadly, impacts on the variables of representation and participation in the framing of social policies, the relation between free trade and social policy acquires a constitutional character. As a consequence, the relevant question becomes the forms of participation and representation now available in the framing of social policies and how to continue to secure the civic solidarity and social self-determination necessary for different political communities to survive. The transfer of power generated by international trade to new forms of decision-making such as the market, international standard-setting institutions and supra-national judicial bodies brings forward new problems of representation and participation which highlight the remaining virtues of the state and other traditional polities and the primordial role that they must continue to play as the default form of representation and participation. Much of the economic debates on regulatory competition and "race to the bottom" are, in reality, about democratic questions. One can speak in this regard of the options of voice and exit which have originally been crafted by Hirschman.[14] In the global market, the mobility granted to companies and capital by free trade enhances their forms of exit in participating and determining the decisions of that market. Companies and capital will move to where the regulatory and economic context is more favourable to their interests (less regulation, lower taxes and social standards, more workforce etc.). When the market is assessed, under a constitutional analysis, in order to balance free trade with social regulation, the possibilities of exit and voice in the market and in the political process should be taken into account for all the different interests affected by the regulation. One of the problems of the current global market is that the participation it grants to certain interests is clearly superior to that of other interests (such as workers, self-employed, unemployed and consumers) as a result of the current available options of exit and voice. Social standards would not necessarily "race to the bottom" if labour had the same mobility as companies and capital. Under the current constrains, the results of the competitive process among regulations subject to market choice is often perceived as reflecting the higher participation (through voice and exit) of large companies and capital.[15]

---

[14] These concepts have been crafted by Hirschman in his well known book *Exit, Voice and Loyalty—Responses to Decline in Firms, Organizations and States* (Cambridge, Mass., Harvard UP, 1970). My use of these concepts in the present context, however, does not fully coincide with the original definition given by Hirschman: voice refers to situations where choices are made or stances taken which express a preference for a certain regulation but do not involve leaving the jurisdiction (this includes voting and lobbying, market transactions within that jurisdiction but also, for example, workers participation and strikes); exit refers to situations where preferences for a certain regulation over another are expressed by moving to a different jurisdiction (and thus the relocation of factors of production but also consumers, taxpayers and unemployed people).

[15] See, e.g., D. Kennedy, "Turning to Market Democracy: A Tale of Two Architectures" 32 *Harvard International Law Journal* 373, at 380: "The dominant players are private traders, and to a far greater extent than in even the most laissez-faire national system, they legislate the rules that govern their trade through contract. And when governments do participate, they operate 'commercially'—as private

All of this corresponds to a change in the patterns of participation and representation already highlighted and raises the question of "how can post-sovereign conditions be fashioned to yield adequate popular participation, open debate, consultation and representation as well as transparency and democratic accountability?".[16] This can also be presented in the form of another constitutional question: once the state can no longer independently determine its own policies, what is the appropriate allocation of power among different levels of decision-making?[17] Both these questions express a change in the framing of social policies which is of constitutional relevance since it affects the conditions of political autonomy that are at the basis of the constitutional regulation of each political community and, at the same time, produce an overall change of the conditions of representation and participation in social decision-making.

This constitutional impact means that the regulation of international trade law and its criterion of legitimacy cannot remain prisoners of the constructs of international law. This simply reflects a major structural difference between the two branches of international norms and institutions:

> The organizing principle for the international trade regime is the economic theory underlying a liberal trade order, that is the principle of comparative advantage; the organizing principle of international law, by comparison, is the concept of the sovereignty of the States. That is to say, international law is built on the fundamental construct of a community of sovereign states whose relation with each other is the substance of the discipline—international trade law runs counter to that construct and in significant ways acts to undermine it.[18]

If one adds to this the impact of international trade and economic integration on the constitutional foundations of the different political communities, one is faced with a broader challenge to rethink the nature of international trade law and its legitimacy with regard to the different political communities. Once the worlds of international law and constitutional law collide, their different legitimacy criteria are bound to raise a complex question: when the powers of international law challenge the conditions of participation and representation at the constitutional level should that challenge not be subject to constitutional regulation?

It is here that the notion of a trans-national political connection emerges. In my view, where international processes interfere in the constitutional self-determination of sub-global political communities they must do so under a claim of legitimacy to be found in constitutionalism itself. This justifies the

---

actors". According to David Kennedy the paradigmatic conception of international trade law (notably WTO law) is devoted to the protection of that dominion from state intervention.

[16] J. Aart, R. O'Brien and M. Williams, "The WTO and Civil Society" (1999) 33 *Journal of World Trade* 107, at 108.

[17] See J. Jackson, "International Economic Law in Times that are Interesting" [2000] *Journal of International Economic Law* 3, at 11.

[18] D. M. McRae "The WTO in International Law: Tradition Continued or New Frontier"? [2000] *Journal of International Economic Law* 27, at 29.

creation of an international constitutional framework to assess the constitutional erosion of the traditional political communities and manage the increased conflicts between those different political communities' constitutional claims. It is this constitutional framework that will provide us with the imperfect solution to our conundrum: how can we protect the social self-determination of competing political communities in the absence of a broader global political community?

The emerging constitutional representations of international trade law attempt to address this problem but they appear to underestimate the value of traditional political communities and to ignore the importance of the constitutional transformations brought by the new forms of participation and representation which are available through the current global processes of social decision-making. There is also a lack of concrete normative proposals to answer some of the more immediate questions raised by the relation between free trade and social policies.

Many argue for the need to subject these global processes to some form of democratic control.[19] In this light, there are those who propose far-reaching models of democratisation of the global community to be undertaken, for example, through profound short- and long-term reforms of the UN system.[20] There are also those which, in a more limited manner, defend the creation of new institutional frameworks for the framing of global social standards which could reintroduce the previous balance of representation and participation in social policies. These are arguments which depart from the need to move beyond local political communities in the framing of social policies. In this view, the only way to re-establish equality of power and representation in the deliberation of those policies is by establishing institutional forms of political dialogue between capital, labour and the political process at the international level.[21] Only this will respect equality of participation in the framing of social policies: "the dialogue about labor law breaks down when capital aquires the unilateral exit option. The idea is to re-establish the conditions of political equality".[22]

There are also those who conceive the process of globalisation itself as an instrument of constitutional development and entrust to principles such as free trade and non-discrimination the leading role in developing such global or international constitutionalism.[23] The World Trade Organisation and the agreements derived from the Uruguay Round would be the primary tool of this perceived global constitutionalism. The role of international trade law is that of guaranteeing the freedom of individuals in the international arena so that they

---

[19] A. Tita, "Globalization: A new Political and Economic Space requiring Supranational Governance" (1998) 32 *Journal of World Trade*, 47, at 51.

[20] Held, *supra* n. 11.

[21] B.A. Langille, "General Reflections on the Relationship of Trade and Labor (Or: Fair Trade is Free Trade's Destiny)" in Bhagwati and Hudec (eds.), *supra* n. 3, 231, at 259.

[22] *Ibid.*, at 260.

[23] See the contribution of Petersmann to this volume and the references below.

can fully enjoy their personal autonomy. For Petersman, global constitutionalism would mean that democracies operate "in a constitutional framework of national and international guarantees of freedom, non-discrimination, rule of law and institutional «checks and balances»".[24] In his view, the way to promote global constitutionalism is by extending the scope and application of international trade law, human rights documents and dispute-settlement mechanisms. These will be the *"avant-garde"* of global constitutionalism. The focus is then on a minimal notion of constitutionalism: non-discrimination, individual rights (mainly economic rights) and dispute-settlement mechanisms. The expectation is that these instances will develop into a set of individual constitutional rights protected from any form of power. The dynamics of international trade will fuel the development of an international rule of law through these economic rights and dispute-settlement mechanisms. Such dynamics will result however in a particular form of constitutionalism. The conception underlying the constitutional construction of WTO law by Petersmann will attribute to the latter the role of protecting economic freedom in the global market and therefore will limit the capacity of the different political processes to interfere with that freedom even when pursuing what is perceived by those political processes as legitimate social goals. Freedom in the global market would be expected generally to be the best instrument for the promotion of social values. It is this that makes it possible for Petersmann to argue that "National and international guarantees of freedom enlarge the 'private sovereignty' of citizens and are fully compatible with their 'collective sovereignty' to decide through national parliaments on the goals and priorities of national social, environmental and other policies".[25] By founding both international trade law and domestic constitutional law on the ideals of freedom and non-discrimination he makes compatible the impact of international trade law on domestic constitutional systems. In a way, international trade law is simply an extension of national constitutional law. As we have seen, however, this compatibility is hard to establish, since it implies a consensual definition of what social rights are and how they are best to be balanced with free trade. It either conflicts with the existence of different constitutional self-determinations by different political communities or requires the global market to be raised to the status of a global political community without an underlying political contract supporting this criterion of legitimacy.

The set of rights which international trade law protects, its emerging Rule of Law, the role which individuals and other non-state actors may be called to play in its development and its impact on the domestic policies of states and other polities such as the EU, all require international trade law to assume constitutional characteristics. Furthermore, they require us to depart from constitutional ideals both in addressing the question of how to make compatible different social self-determinations and the question of representation and

---

[24] *Supra* n. 1, at 447 and 448.
[25] E.-U. Petersmann, "The WTO Constitution and Human Rights" [2000] *Journal of International Economic Law* 19, at 25.

participation in the emerging forms of global social decision-making. In my view, however, it is too early to talk of a global constitution or to assume the existence of a global political community that could justify the definition of social values beyond the independent social self-determinations of different political communities. It is more appropriate to talk of emerging elements of constitutionalism in the international arena that must command the constitutional effects taking place therein. There is no consensus on the social model which ought to result from the development of global constitutionalism. And there is no political community to which one could have recourse to supplement that lack of consensus. At the global level, the aim should be that of securing equality of representation and participation in the exercise of the different political communities' social self-determination. Therefore, in my view, there are no global political conditions capable of legitimising the exercise of such social self-determination at the global level. On the other hand, as we have seen, the exercise of the different political communities' social self-determination is now clearly influenced by the forces of global economic integration. This requires the setting up of constitutional modes of disciplining such forces at the global level but only with the aim of securing the conditions of representation and participation necessary to a legitimate exercise of social self-determination at the level of the local political communities (states or others, such as the EU).

But through what processes should this emerging constitutionalism take place? Should free trade and economic liberalisation be pursued as an end in themselves aimed at promoting competition among states; or does free trade require the setting up of institutions responsible for adopting a "level playing field" and common policies with regard to some public interests? If neither, how can the social self-determination of the original political communities be safeguarded in the context of free trade?

All systems which accept free trade and some degree of regulatory competition in integrated markets generate at least a partial harmonisation of social rights and policies. The difference lies in the institutional framework through which each such harmonisation arises and its impact on the final outcome of harmonisation. As stated by Trubek:

> Once economic interdependence reaches a certain point, and borders no longer serve as major barriers to economic movement, there is a pressure towards uniformity in economic policies. These pressures may come about to ensure fair competition and the smooth functioning of economic enterprises that span national borders ("level playing field"), or they may be the result of "regulatory competition" among sovereignties in a unified space.[26]

What the two processes described by Trubek actually entail is a different institutional choice of the forms of decision-making responsible for balancing free trade and regulation in the global market. One argues for the allocation of

---

[26] "Social Justice 'After' Globalization—The Case of Social Europe", typescript, November 1996, at 5.

such responsibility to the market. The other advocates the setting up of some form of global political process responsible for the regulation of the global market. There is a series of institutional alternatives to the regulation of social standards in relation to free trade.[27] The first option is to entrust the definition of those social standards to the market. The second option is to authorise each political community to condition free trade on the acceptance by other parties of its non-discriminatory social standards (unilateralism). The third option lies in setting common social standards either at the level of the WTO or by demanding ratification of ILO-agreed social rights. However, as we have seen, all of these options present different problems of representation and participation which are aggravated by the lack of an underlying global political community. This only emphasises the need to give up any proposals which focus on a particular idealised institution, be it the global market, an international political process or other institutional alternatives. The more immediate challenge regarding social policy is twofold:

—How can we protect the constitutional social self-determination of different political communities in view of the constitutional transformations in participation and representation within social policies deriving from free trade?

—Once we accept the existence of free trade, how can we improve the representation and participation in the global market by a broader set of social actors?

If we attempt to develop free trade and constrained regulatory competition on the premise that this must safeguard to the fullest extent possible the constitutional self-determination (including social self-determination) of the different political communities, how are we to balance the constitutional conflicts arising from their different social self-determinations? Here also the relationship of free trade with the traditional forms of constitutional participation and representation becomes a crucial element of the delicate balance to be achieved. It is this that ought to determine the immediate agenda of the EU with regard to the WTO and social policy: the ability to preserve the self-determination of its social model while, at the same time, improving the democratic operation of the global market in the process of regulatory competition that free trade necessarily

---

[27] Here I adopt an approach analytically similar to that I developed in the context of the European market in *We The Court, The European Court of Justice and the European Economic Constitution* (Oxford, Hart Publishing, 1998) and which departed from comparative institutional analysis (on this, see: N. Komesar, *Imperfect Alternatives—Choosing Institutions in Law, Economics and Public Policy* (Chicago, Ill., and London, University of Chicago Press, 1994)). A similar approach has recently been applied to the WTO by G. Shaffer, "Comment on Shrimp AB Decision" [1999] *American Journal of International Law*, 507. I must stress, however, that both the institutional alternatives and the criteria to choose among them are substantially altered by the different political, legal and economic contexts of the EU and the WTO. The fact that the same analytical tools are employed does not lead to identical institutional choices as will be shown clearly in the text.

entails. In this sense, there must be a commitment on the part of all contracting parties to respect their different social self-determinations as this is part of the respect owed to their constitutional self-determination in the absence of a prevailing global political community. At the same time, the constitutional nature of this discourse means that a political community can legitimately oppose its social policies to the social policies of another political community only when the former social policies were decided under constitutional conditions allowing the exercise of social self-determination (i.e. balanced representation and participation). In this way, the constitutional concepts of representation and participation are elevated to controlling criteria of the relationship between the social self-determination of different political communities.

How does this constitutional framework operates in practice? An analysis of the current legal debate regarding WTO and social clauses in accordance with this constitutional framework will, hopefully, make clear how that constitutional criterion of legitimacy, based on social self-determination and the concepts of representation and participation, translates into legal solutions. As is well known, there is a current trend which, departing from WTO law as it stands, attempts to "reconstruct socially" the legal norms of the WTO trade agreements. The most powerful alternative in this regard arises from the growing critiques of the traditional distinction between incorporated and non-incorporated standards (also referred to as a distinction between product and process rules). Following some cases in which non-incorporated environmental standards have been considered as violating the WTO rules,[28] some authors have argued in favour of abandoning the traditional distinction between incorporated and non-incorporated standards.[29] This would allow some restrictions on trade arising from non-incorporated standards (including social standards) so long as non-discriminatory and pursuing one of the objectives put forwarded in Article XX of the GATT.

It is true that the distinction between incorporated and non-incorporated standards is highly formalistic. It is based on the perceived extraterritorial effects of the latter and its interference in the sphere of sovereignty of another contracting party. In the case of non-incorporated standards the regulated facts take place outside the jurisdiction of the contracting party, while in the case of incorporated standards, what the contracting party is doing is regulating the effects of those standards (which are part of the products) in their domestic markets. However, both have in common the fact that what the contracting parties want to guarantee is that economic competition will take place in their

---

[28] See the decisions on the *Shrimp-Turtles* case, WTO Doc. WT/DS58/AB/R, and the *Tuna-Dolphin* Reports issued under the old GATT and never adopted.

[29] R. Howse and D. Regan "The Product/Process Distinction—An Illusory Basis for Disciplining 'Unilateralism' in Trade Policy", 11 *European Journal of International Law* 249. See, also, in a more limited and conditional sense (closer to that to be advocated below) V.A. Leary, "Workers Rights and International Trade: The Social Clause (GATT, ILO, NAFTA, U.S. Laws)" in Bhagwati and Hudec (eds.), *supra* n. 3, ii, 177, at 204.

markets only among products which comply with a uniform set of mandatory standards. At the same time, it can be stated that to oblige a contracting party to accept in its own market products manufactured in disregard of that contracting party's social or environmental standards is, in effect, conferring extraterritorial effect on the rules of the state of origin due to the competitive advantage from which its products may benefit. This may require the host contracting party to alter its social policy choices and can be seen as an interference in its domestic sovereignty. From a purely legal point of view the distinction between incorporated and non-incorporated standards appears in this light to be largely a formal one. Substantively, both situations are very similar: in both cases, the objective is to impose on all products and services competing on a certain market the same standards and, by preventing distorted competition, to safeguard the policy autonomy of the regulators. And, in both cases, if free trade is accepted for products not complying with incorporated or non-incorporated standards, it will be the market which will decide on the "winning" rules due to the competition which will take place between products and services complying with different rules. However, there may be good reasons to maintain the distinction between incorporated standards and non-incorporated standards. Those reasons have to do with the different institutional consequences arising from allowing states to regulate trade in regard to non-incorporated standards and the differences between the mechanisms of market competition with regard to incorporated and non-incorporated standards. As I will argue, the market operates differently in the case of competition between incorporated and non-incorporated standards and presents much more serious representative and participation malfunctions in the case of incorporated standards. With regard to the latter, as we will see, the degree of constitutional self-determination of the different political communities is much more deeply affected by regulatory competition.

As stated, the institutional consequence of allowing the free trade and competition in products subject to different incorporated or non-incorporated standards would be the same: the market would become the relevant institution in deciding the appropriate level of regulation.[30] Products and services will compete subject to different standards and the choices of consumers (on which products or services to buy) and companies (on where to produce) will determine the "winning" regulatory standard. But the market which assesses regulatory competition is not just the transactions market but has other forms of participation such as lobbying, voting, and jurisdictional change (moving with the feet). It is this complex set of forms of participation which sometimes justifies the trust placed in the market in cases of regulatory competition. It is argued by some that there would not necessarily be a race to the bottom once the economic growth arising from free trade leads the members of the political communities having lower regulatory standards to exercise political and economic pressure to favour higher standards

---

[30] Whether or not the market will always be an appropriate institution to perform that role is a different question which I address below.

(such as labour protection). This can be subject to a form of constitutional analysis whereby we can review the ability of the market to bring about *ex post* harmonisation in a fair manner by the way in which its regulatory competition takes place in respect of the political autonomy of the different political communities, and in securing the representation and participation of all affected interests. It is by performing this analysis that we can detect the different constitutional ability of the market in the case of incorporated and non-incorporated standards to bring about fair and representative regulatory competition and protect the social self-determination of different political communities.

In cases of incorporated standards the lack of trust in the market to promote regulatory competition has been the understanding which, for long, allowed contracting parties of the WTO to impose restrictions on trade with regard to those standards so long as they were non-discriminatory. There are good reasons to distrust the market in this case, since the group of people affected by the incorporated standards and the jurisdiction of the policy-maker which enacts those standards do not coincide. Representative problems exist here, in that people cannot take into account all the costs and benefits of the regulation. A regulation implies a balance between the production of public and private goods. What happens when the regulation of state A on a certain incorporated standard is subject to regulatory competition with a regulation of state B is that the balance between the production of public and private goods made by the first state is altered by the rules of the other state. For example, if a state has to allow into its market products coming from another state which contain some domestically prohibited additives, the increase, as predicted by that State, in the production of public goods (in terms of consumer and health protection) will not occur (at least, to the extent expected). As a consequence of transaction and information costs, those who stood to benefit most from that regulation will normally not exert *voice* (buying the product or political participation) or *exit* (moving from legal and economic jurisdiction) in favour of the regulation. On the other hand, those regulated and burdened by its costs will find themselves more harmed by the regulation because they will be competing with products not subject to the regulation. They will have ever greater incentives to exert *voice* and *exit* against the regulation. These representative problems are the same as what economists call "externalities" or "information costs". They clearly affect the constitutional conditions necessary for the exercise of social self-determination.

However, the situation is different in the case of non-incorporated standards. Here, the costs and benefits of the regulation are concentrated on the jurisdiction enacting it. The costs involved in a decision to lower labour standards (reducing the production of public goods but increasing the production of private goods) are not transferred to another state by virtue of movement of goods or provisions of services, and we can expect that the constituency burdened by those costs will eventually exert pressure to improve those standards. Products and services will still compete subject to different rules but the different political communities' balance between costs and benefits implicit in those rules remains unaltered and there is no transfer of costs or benefits between those polities. It is this that justifies the argument that a different rationale may be applicable to non-incorporated standards.[31]

Therefore, the distinction between incorporated and non-incorporated standards still makes sense as it is based on the autonomy of different political communities to balance the costs/benefits of social regulations, but only as long as no costs (or no costs of a particular kind) are transferred to other political communities. I argued that in these cases (referring to non-incorporated standards) the market (understood in a broader sense) could be expected to operate better through the inter-play of the different interests at stake in the respective political communities and as long as the costs and benefits are concentrated on those respective political communities. At the same time, the market would provide, in these cases, the best balance between the rights of the different political communities to social self-determination.

But it will be recalled that for the market to operate well in these cases the broader notion of market adopted required an extended notion of participation and representation in the market (which will operate through the different political communities' social self-determination): certain basic human rights, including political rights such as the right to vote and freedom of expression, but also social rights such as freedom of association, collective bargaining and the prohibition of discrimination. These rights should be part of the basic constitutional framework of free trade,[32] required for the legitimacy of the process of regulatory competition generated by globalisation and trade liberalisation. Only such a basic constitutional framework can guarantee the rights of social self-determination of all the political communities which participate in international trade. This proposal coincides with recent suggestions (mainly by ILO officials) to associate free trade with the ratification by all contracting parties of the most basic rights included in the ILO Constitution and conventions.[33] It may even correspond to a political common ground highlighted by Virginia Leary.[34] My argument, however, is broader. It is grounded not simply on pragmatic political reasons but also on constitutional legitimacy: my claim is that only upon acceptance of those rights can a political community legitimately argue its right to social self-determination with regard to the social standards invoked

---

[31] However, this does not mean that there are no problems in leaving it to the market to determine non-incorporated standards. There may still be serious problems. On the other hand, the fact that there are serious problems in leaving to the market the free competition of incorporated standards also does not mean that the available alternatives will always be better.

[32] Other measures may be conceived of, such as the constitutionalisation of global competition law and an extended application of human rights (for example, through their horizontal application to companies holding a dominant market position). Consumers should also see their position reinforced in the global market, through more information and, for example, being given standing with regard to future global competition rules.

[33] See Trebilcock, *supra* n. 6, at 514–515. and Leary, *supra* n. 29, 177, at 202.

[34] *Ibid.*, at 220–221.

from other political communities. If a political community does not fulfil the basic requirements necessary to the exercise of constitutional social self-determination by its citizens, then it cannot legitimately oppose that right to social self-determination to contest the trade and social policies of other political communities which arguably impact on that social self-determination.

THE EU SOCIAL SELF-DETERMINATION

Whatever the policy areas on which one focuses (not only social policy but also exchange rates, monetary and fiscal policies, environmental or consumer protection, public health, justice, crime, human rights, etc.) it is clear that the policy powers of states are increasingly constrained both in practice (by international inter-dependence and competition) and in law (by the growing international law provisions which affect, directly or indirectly, the domestic policies of states).[35] This erosion of the public powers of the state and national political communities (in which international trade law assumes a dominant role) will generate both a challenge to national constitutionalism and a claim for such power to be reintroduced at a different level. The constitutional framework of international trade, I suggested, may serve to bring some form of constitutional legitimacy and control to such processes but will not reverse them. It may also manage the conflicts between the constitutional self-determination of different political communities but it will not restore their absolute sovereignty and constitutional autonomy. The European Union can be seen in part as an attempt to re-introduce a larger degree of political self-determination and accountability at a higher level of decision-making. But, on the other hand, the Union is itself subject to the erosion of powers arising from global competition.

Many have conceived the EU as an attempt to answer to global market competition and reinstate political control over the market in a new forum where common regulatory policies can be agreed. The Union would be the protector of the European welfare state. Others have however conceived the EU as simply a step in the global process aimed at promoting the freedom and economic gains derived from economic integration and see in the limits that such process imposes on public power its great advantage. One of the consequences brought by free trade and globalisation to the EU is precisely the requirement to face the identity of its social policy. This comes about through two consequences of the process of globalisation and free trade: first, the need to reinforce the external and internal powers and decision-making of the Union in order both to reintroduce at the level of the Union forms of political control over the market and to give it the necessary authority and identity to play a stronger role in the framing of international trade law; secondly, the impact that those processes of free trade

---

[35] See, in this sense, e.g., P. Alston, "The Myopia of Handmaidens: International Lawyers and Globalization" [1997] *European Journal of International Law* 8 web version consulted ⟨http://www.ejil.org/journal/Vol8/No3/art4.html⟩.

and globalisation have on the instruments available for states to perform a redistribution function. The EU itself also restricts the capacity of states to answer in individual terms to the social challenges of free trade and globalisation. The question then becomes whether the Union is ready to assume the social functions which Member States can no longer exercise adequately.

Given both the pressures brought by global economic integration and, at the same time, the limits imposed on states' social policy by European economic integration, the European Union becomes the best alternative for the exercise of social self-determination by its Member States. The problem is that the Union may not be prepared to exercise such social self-determination and may also not yet have secured the necessary conditions of participation and representation required for a legitimate exercise of such social self-determination.

The rhetoric of treaties has seen a progressive reinforcement of the social goals of European integration included in the Preambles and initial Articles. This social rhetoric of European integration goes beyond the simple safeguarding of social values in light of the regulatory challenges brought by economic integration. The current rhetoric is even partially linked with a notion of European solidarity whereby the goal of economic and social cohesion is entrusted to the Union. Article 2 EC Treaty states that the Community shall "promote throughout the Community a harmonious, balanced, and sustainable development of the economic activities, a high level of employment and of social protection . . . and economic and social cohesion and solidarity among Member States". This provision is reflected in Title XVII but also in the conception of the Community's social policy as aiming at "the promotion of employment, improved living and working conditions, so as to make possible their harmonisation while the improvement is being maintained, proper social protection, dialogue between management and labour, the development of human resources with a view to a lasting employment and the combating of exclusion" (Article 136(1)). A goal which the Member States recognise will not only ensue from the functioning of the common market but will require direct Community action (Article 136(3)). However, this rhetoric has much of merely symbolic effect without correspondence in the remaining provisions of the Treaties and in the policies of the Union.[36] Hitherto it is clear that Jacques Delors' goal of a European social area has not moved much beyond words, and the real objectives of the EU social policy have remained hidden under this rhetoric. Primarily , it is not clear whether the EU social policy is or ought to be based on a criterion of distributive justice.

So far the dominant idea has been that of Europe's social policy as establishing a common set of social values to be achieved and safeguarded by the different Member States and not as promoting a European ideal of distributive justice expressed in independent political and social goals. In other

---

[36] In this sense, see J. Shaw, "Twin-Track Social Europe—the Inside Track", in D. O'Keeffe and P. Twomey (eds.), *Legal Issues of the Maastricht Treaty* (London, Chancery, 1994), 295.

words, the social constitution of Europe will guarantee a level playing field within Europe and impose on all states a core set of social values to be respected by all but would not entrust to the Union a function of redistribution to be achieved in accordance with a European criterion of distributive justice. The social perspective underlying this limited conception of Europe's social policy identity is that which merges the interests of those who want to guarantee a level playing field in the internal market with regard to social standards with the interests of those who want to use Europe to promote more extensive social rights at the national level. This limited version of the European social policy identity does not really attribute to Europe the right and legitimacy to establish and exercise an independent redistributive function with autonomous social goals. But is this conception compatible with the functions which the Union is expected to take on to defend and protect the European social model in the global arena?

If free trade makes it difficult to guarantee social self-determination at the level of the nation state that will affect the social basis of that political community and an alternative forum must be found to exercise that social self-determination. Recently Habermas has argued that it will not continue to be possible for the nation state to guarantee the mechanisms and instruments of social solidarity on which the welfare state has been founded. The alternative, for Habermas, lies in the project of European integration but for this the reinforcement of its capacity for political action must come hand in hand with the development of a form of civil solidarity among European citizens which will secure and express itself in different redistributive policies.[37] But, for Habermas' project to be viable, the Union must recognise that its project of integration entails in itself a degree of solidarity between its citizens that must, at least, accept a redistribution function to be legitimised by a criterion of distributive justice among all European citizens. The masters of the Union may deny that such civil solidarity is possible within the Union but they may not evade the question any longer.[38]

Entrusting to the European Union the "protection" of the European social model will not be a uncontentious issue. It mixes the question of the balancing power between states and the Union with the question of balancing efficiency *versus* distributive justice. This has never been a peaceful issue and much less will that be the case in the context of a "contested" European political community whose degree of cohesion and solidarity is, at most, weak. The problem is that decisions on those issues are already being taken at the European level. In the absence of an agreed European social contract those decisions simply flow from the functional ideology of market integration. Moreover, European integration has reached a point where its emerging European *demos* and its

---

[37] J. Habermas, *The Postnational Constellation* (London, Polity Press, 2000).
[38] I develop these aspects in more detail in "Europe's Social Self: 'The Sickness Unto Death' " in J. Shaw (ed.), *Social Law and Policy in an Evolving European Union* (Oxford, Hart Publishing, 2000), 325.

redistributive and majoritarian elements can no longer be socially accepted and legitimised without an underlying social contract and a criterion of distributive justice.

If the Union is expected to assume and protect the European social model both by exercising external commercial powers and by reinforcing its internal social identity and cohesion, this will require an extension of the external and internal dimensions of European social policy. This will be viable only with an extension of the scope of competencies effectively exercised by the Union and by relying on a majoritarian model. But this will tend, in turn, to give its policies a broader redistributive impact which cannot be legitimised without an underlying agreement on a criterion of distributive justice for the Union. In fact, the change to a parliamentary and majoritarian system is already taking place and cannot be separated from a debate on the *telos* of the Union and its social self-determination. Those institutional changes have strong redistributive effects and these must be guided by an articulated criterion of distributive justice. In the absence of this, the redistributive effects of the majoritarian system will simply favour the interests of the majority without taking into account the intensity to which different interests are affected by the decisions of the majority. In this way, a majoritarian system needs an underlying social contract based on a criterion of distributive justice to guarantee the social legitimacy of the majority decisions. Such a social contract guarantees the allegiance of all to the polity by stipulating forms of long-term compensation and by protecting the interests of those minorities which may at times be unduly burdened by the redistributive effects of the majoritarian decisions. One of the key elements of such a social contract is the establishment of overall mechanisms and criteria of distributive justice.

The construction of the EU as the adequate level for the best protection of the European social model and social self-determination needs an underpinning social contract which, in its turn, must entail some criterion of distributive justice among the European citizens. In my view, this requires the replacement of the current logic of the European policies of both social harmonisation and redistribution. They must no longer be conceived simply either as securing a "level playing field" or as part of a trade-off among states, but as reflecting independent political and social goals which affirm the EU social identity.

I do not know whether the masters of the Union are ready to take on board the identity debate on Europe's social policy but I believe that the future role of the Union in shaping the constitutional framework of free trade and its impact on the European social model must begin from a discussion on the social identity of Europe itself or, perhaps better still, on a discussion of its underlying social contract. Its role as the ideal forum for the constitutional protection of the social self-determination of Europe depends on that. Do we want the European Union to perform this role?

12

The WTO Impact on Internal Regulations—A Case Study of the Canada–EC Asbestos Dispute

ROBERT HOWSE and ELISABETH TUERK*

INTRODUCTION[1]

THE WTO[2] IS facing increasing criticism. This was highlighted during the third ministerial meeting in Seattle, where massive street protests disrupted the conduct of the conference. Apart from demonstrations, a series of groups used the Seattle ministerial meeting to articulate a range of views on the future of the trading system, in most cases far more subtle than a blanket or dogmatic rejection of globalisation or even the WTO. Non-governmental organisations and public policy-makers from all over the world met to analyse WTO policies

* The authors would like to thank staff of the disputing countries' delegations for making available parts of the written documentation and scientific background on the case. Robert Howse especially thanks Steve Pepa, Petros Mavroidis, Marco Bronckers, Bill Davey, Don Regan, Julie Soloway and Joseph Weiler for challenging discussions on some of these issues over the last couple of years, and Todd Carpunky, Yvan Fauchere, Gaetan Verhoessel and Robert Madelin and his team at DG Trade for more recent exchanges. We also thank Bob Hudec, Merit Janow and Gary Horlick for extremely helpful comments on an early draft (Bob has been enormously generous to us, providing extensive comments on several versions and engaging in multiple email exchanges on the key issues); we also benefited from the reactions of several of the participants at the conference at the European University Institute where the first draft was presented, especially Armin von Bogdandy, Piet Eeckhout, Joanne Scott, Graínne de Búrca, and Ernst-Ulrich Petersmann. The discussion of the case on the Jean Monnet website has also been very helpful to us and we are grateful to Joseph Weiler for providing that forum for discussion. The views expressed in this chap. are the author's personal views and not those of CIEL.

[1] Because of length considerations and in order better to focus on those issues relevant for understanding the implications of WTO disciplines on domestic regulations, the authors decided to not canvass every aspect raised in the *Asbestos* case. Amongst the broad range of issues addressed in this dispute but nevertheless outside the scope of this chap. are questions relating to the panel's obligation under Art. 11 DSU (Dispute Settlement Understanding) the handling of *amicus curiae* briefs or the application of non-violation disputes for measures justified under a general exception. In order to facilitate understanding of the broader implications for internal regulatory autonomy, the authors have also finessed some technical arcania, for example while the panel and the AB (Appellate Body) conducted a separate analysis of fibres and asbestos-containing products under national treatment, we have treated the two analyses as the same because in the end the separation does not make a difference the basic conceptual and doctrinal questions we want to address here.

[2] Marrakesh Agreement Establishing the World Trade Organization (1994) 131 ILM 1125 (hereinafter WTO Agreement).

and their potential impacts. Amongst the most common criticisms was the WTO's alleged role in impeding national governments from granting adequate protection to the environment, or addressing consumer interests and national health and safety concerns.

Different understandings concerning the extent to which WTO rules constrain domestic regulatory autonomy have manifested themselves in recent high profile trade controversies. In the famous *Beef Hormones* case,[3] the USA successfully challenged the EC's ban on beef injected with natural and synthetic growth hormones. The regulatory measure in question had been adopted in a response to European consumers' concerns about potential health effects of such hormones being present in foodstuffs. Similarly, in the case of genetically modified organisms (GMOs), where European consumers' reluctance towards genetically modified foods triggered the European institutions to adopt detailed regulations regarding risk assessment, release authorisation, subsequent monitoring and labelling of GMOs. The WTO consistency of this regulatory framework was repeatedly the subject of controversy in the TBT Committee.[4] So far the European scheme has not been subject to dispute settlement at the WTO. While there have been few cases where domestic regulations on health, safety or the environment have been directly challenged and found in violation of WTO law,[5] the WTO rules may already be having a chilling effect on the strengthening or development of such domestic regulatory schemes in other WTO members, thereby constraining or impeding democratic choices. If the WTO is to regain citizens' confidence, it has to prove its ability to balance the freedom of governments to pursue legitimate domestic objectives with the need to secure the benefits of trade liberalisation.

Given the economic experiences prior to the Second World War, the legal framework created by the founding fathers of the GATT[6] focused on the elimination of discriminatory practices, either explicit border measures such as tariffs and quotas or domestic regulations and policies that discriminate against imports. Thus, the fundamental constraint on domestic regulations in the original GATT was that such regulations must not discriminate either against imports

---

[3] Appellate Body Report, *European Communities—Measures Concerning Meat and Meat Products (Hormones)*, WT/DS26/AB/R and WT/DS48/AB/R, 13 February 1998 (hereinafter *Hormones*). In fact, the Appellate Body decision in this case, unlike that of the panel, was respectful of domestic regulatory autonomy, upholding the panel on very narrow grounds.

[4] Committee on Technical Barriers to Trade, established by Art. 13 of the TBT Agreement (Agreement on Technical Barriers to Trade), Annex 1 A to the WTO Agreement, Multilateral Agreements on Trade in Goods (hereinafter TBT Agreement).

[5] Most of these cases, like the *Hormones* case, *supra* n. 3, have been in the food safety area, pursuant to the WTO SPS Agreement (Agreement on Sanitary and Phytosanitary Measures), Annex 1 A to the WTO Agreement, Multilateral Agreement on Trade in Goods (hereinafter SPS Agreement). For measures which could potentially fall under both the SPS and the TBT, the latter (TBT) defers to the SPS. (Art. 1.5 TBT). Given that the SPS deals predominantly with measures addressing food safety concerns, most other measures would therefore fall under TBT. (Annex A SPS establishes that the SPS covers measures to protect human, animal and plant health, from risks arising form pests and food borne diseases.)

[6] The text of the original GATT 1947 (General Agreement on Tariffs and Trade) is now incorporated as GATT 94 into the WTO Agreement (hereinafter GATT 94).

or between different GATT member states (National Treatment[7] and Most-Favoured Nation Treatment[8] (MFN)). With the increasing success of the GATT in the elimination of discriminatory measures, attention eventually came to focus on non-facially discriminatory policies and regulations thought to have negative impacts on trade. Sometimes, the existence of different regulations in different countries might in itself increase the transaction costs of trade, requiring producers to adapt products to the regulatory environment in different national markets.

Also, and perhaps more importantly, protective discrimination might be hidden or structurally embedded in regulatory schemes that themselves do not explicitly contain nationality-based distinctions. For example, domestic regulations might require a particular technology on safety grounds to which domestic producers had already adapted their production, while a variety of technological approaches might in principle be possible to satisfy the regulatory concern at issue. Because of the possibility that countries might simply shift protectionism from explicit facially discriminatory measures, to regulatory schemes that were covertly or structurally discriminatory, the GATT jurisprudence evolved so as to encompass protective discrimination not reflected in explicit facial classifications on the basis of national origin, and in particularly the test of "like products" in the National Treatment obligation of the GATT, came to be interpreted in such a manner as to provide some scrutiny of non-nationality based regulatory distinctions, to ensure that those distinctions were not merely surrogates for (obviously illegal) nationality-based ones.[9]

Deciding on a case-by-case basis which non-nationality-based regulatory classifications represent *de facto* or hidden discrimination and which represent an innocuous disparate impact on trade, unrelated to protection, is a delicate and complex exercise. Here, casting the net too broadly might transform the WTO dispute settlement organs into a routine reviewing court for ordinary domestic regulations, placing undue limits on non-protectionist regulatory processes.[10] On the other hand, a failure to consider seriously the possibility of *de facto*

---

[7] Art. III GATT. For a superb account of the evolution of the non-discrimination norm in the GATT/WTO regime, see Robert Hudec, "GATT Constraints on National Regulation: Requiem for an 'Aim and Effects' Test" (1998) 32 *The International Lawyer* 623 (hereinafter, "Requiem").

[8] Art. I GATT

[9] Panel Report, *United States—Section 337 of the Tariff Act of 1930*, BISD 36S (1990) (hereinafter *Section 337*); Panel Report, *Canada—Import, Distribution and Sale of Certain Alcoholic Drinks by Provincial Marketing Agencies*, BISD 39S (1992) (hereinafter *Canada Beer*); Panel Report, *EEC—Regime for the Importation, Sale and Distribution of Bananas*; WT/DS/27/ECU/GUA/HON/MEX/USA (hereinafter *Bananas Panel*); Appellate Body Report, *EEC—Regime for the Importation, Sale and Distribution of Bananas*, WT/DS27/AB/R, 25 September 1997 (hereinafter *Bananas AB*).

[10] Of course, in such cases there might still be a possibility to justify the measure under one of the exception provisions of Art. XX, such as Art. XX (b), which refers to measures necessary, *inter alia*, for the protection of human life and health. But as Hudec points out, the kind of justificatory burden imposed in Art. XX assumes that a violation of the GATT has already occurred, and is designed to deal with measures, which are discriminatory, presumptively protective, and therefore which it seems entirely appropriate to expect members to have to justify in dispute settlement as in fact tailored to non-protectionist objectives. Hudec, "Requiem", *supra* n. 7.

discrimination could undermine the integrity of disciplines on discriminatory measures generally, providing a ready means of cheating with impunity on those explicit commitments.

Such considerations resulted in the Uruguay Agreements on Sanitary and Phytosanitary Measures (SPS) and Technical Barriers to Trade (TBT). These Agreements contain a range of disciplines on the regulatory *processes* that generate domestic regulations, requiring the kind of transparency, coherence, and consistency in regulation that provides trading partners with assurances that protectionism is not embedded at some deep level in the regulatory process itself.[11] To the extent that these norms are followed, the need for case-by-case judgments under Article III should be obviated, or at least those judgments should be easier to make with legitimacy. As well, these Agreements seek to reduce gratuitous regulatory diversity, requiring or encouraging (in the case of SPS) the use of international standards as inputs[12] in the domestic regulatory process, where this is consistent with the attainment of the regulatory objectives of the member state. At the same time the SPS and TBT Agreements contain certain substantive criteria or tests, related to "inputs" or "outputs" of the regulatory process, which on some interpretations amount to a second guessing of democratic domestic choices about complex trade-offs between different regulatory objectives, different risks and different regulatory instruments, even in the case of facially non-discriminatory regulations, which have not been shown to be protectionist. Thus, the recent criticisms and worries that we have discussed above concerning the increasing intrusiveness of multilateral trade rules, and trade tribunals, into democratic domestic regulation.

The recent Canadian challenge to France's ban on asbestos in construction materials provides a dramatic example of how WTO rules may be invoked to challenge domestic measures aimed at addressing serious health risks. Asbestos has been long known to be a deadly carcinogen, and France's ban of the substance applied without discrimination to both domestically produced and imported asbestos. Yet Canada argued that the asbestos it exports is a "like

---

[11] At the first glance, such constraints of transparency, coherence, and consistency in regulation could be viewed at posing additional limitations and therefore harming democracy. However, by ensuring openness and transparency, such provisions should actually be able to enhance democratic deliberation, at least as long as they are not applied so as unduly to delay or constrain action in response to democratic will. Therefore a balance needs to be struck between democratic requirements of public justification and democratic requirements of effective action. See generally, R. Howse, "Democracy, Science and Free Trade: Risk Regulation on Trial at the World Trade Organization", (2000) *University of Michigan Law Review*, 2329. On proceduralist understandings of WTO disciplines on domestic regulation see also the chap. by de Búrca and Scott in this volume.

[12] Thus, domestic regulations should be "based on" international standards (SPS 3.1 or TBT 2.4), which does not mean that the outputs of domestic regulation (the substantive regulations actually adopted) must be identical to the international standards, as the Appellate Body emphasised in *Hormones, supra* n. 3, paras. 160ff. Contrast this with the incorporation by reference into WTO law of international standards for international property protection in the Berne and Paris Conventions, where the standards themselves become by incorporation WTO law, binding on WTO members. Cf. TRIPs Agreement, Art. 2 (Agreement on Trade-Related Aspects of Intellectual Property Rights, Annex 1C to the WTO Agreement (hereinafter TRIPS Agreement)).

product" to substitute products used in construction, therefore deserving no less favourable treatment under the National Treatment standard in GATT (Article III:4). Canada also claimed that France has violated the obligation under the TBT Agreement to ensure that its regulations are the least restrictive of trade necessary to attain the legitimate regulatory objective in question, here the protection of human life and health (Article 2.2 TBT). Canada argued that used in a "safe" manner the kind of asbestos (chrysotile) that it exports does not present health risks. But should the complex choice of a simple ban over a regulatory scheme that attempts to control the behaviour of manufacturers and users really be second-guessed by a trade tribunal deciding at a great distance from the domestic regulatory process, and its democratic institutions?

In *Asbestos*, the panel accepted Canada's claim that asbestos and non-asbestos substitutes were "like" products, despite the fact that the former was a proven, deadly carcinogen and the latter were not.[13] This resulted in a finding that France had violated Article III:4 of the GATT, in providing less favourable treatment to asbestos imported from Canada than to like substitute products. However, the panel went on to find that this violation of Article III:4 was justified under Article XX(b) of the GATT as "necessary" for the protection of human health. With regard to Canada's TBT claim, the panel accepted a rather bizarre argument from the EC that because the French measure constituted an outright ban of asbestos it did not fall within the definition of a technical regulation in the TBT Agreement. Therefore, the panel held, the TBT Agreement did not even apply to the measure.

For those concerned with the effects of the WTO on human health and related interests, the panel ruling was hardly a victory, despite the result of upholding the French ban. The notion that health considerations should be irrelevant in determining whether products are "like" for purposes of assessing domestic regulations appeared to speak volumes about the obtuseness of the WTO in regard to basic human interests. However, such a ruling could be understood as the logical outcome, or perhaps *reductio ad absurdum*, of the approach adopted by the Appellate Body to National Treatment in the case of internal tax measures, in cases such as *Japan—Alcohol* and *Canada—Periodicals* and *Chile—Alcohol*. In those cases, the Appellate Body appeared to reject the "aims and effects" approach to Article III, which considered whether the regulatory distinction between products is based on a non-protectionist regulatory purpose (such as protection of human health). Instead, the *Asbestos* panel apparently endorsed the approach of the panel in *Japan—Alcohol*, which was in examining "likeness", to consider only factors that were probative of a competitive relationship between the imported and domestic product in the domestic market-place, including physical similarity, end uses, and consumer tastes and habits.[14] These criteria

---

[13] Panel Report, *European Communities—Measures Affecting Asbestos and Asbestos-Containing Products*, WT/DS/135/R, 18 September 2000 (hereinafter "Panel Report").

[14] See the account of these developments in Hudec, "Requiem", *supra* n. 7. See also Robert Howse and Donald Regan, "The Product/Process Distinction—An Illusory Basis for Disciplining

were as a matter of jurisprudence drawn from the *Border Tax Adjustment* working party,[15] which predated the establishment of the WTO. A fourth criterion was also considered, customs classification, and added to the overall *Border Tax Adjustment* approach.

On such an approach, many legitimate regulatory measures will easily fall foul of Article III, even in the absence of any protectionism. And indeed, the *Asbestos* panel elsewhere in its ruling, actually made a finding that the French ban did not constitute protectionism. Thus, the panel, in developing the market-based approach to Article III apparently adopted by the Appellate Body in the Article III:2 (taxation) cases, interpreted Article III, not as guaranteeing against protectionism in internal regulations, but rather guaranteeing *market access*, subject to the ability of the defending member to provide a non-protectionist *justification* for its measure under one of the heads of Article XX. Indeed, the panel in fact pointed to the existence of Article XX as a reason for taking a market-based approach to Article III: if consideration of regulatory objectives such as health was part and parcel of Article III analysis, would not Article XX be redundant? The effect of such reasoning was to turn Article III into a positive duty on WTO members to justify all regulations that have a negative impact on market access for other WTO members, an outcome at odds with the text and structure of the GATT as it currently stands.

Upon appeal, the Appellate Body[16] reversed the finding of the panel that considerations of health effects could not be taken into account in the analysis of whether two products are "like" under Article III:4. The AB affirmed the basic purpose of Article III as the discipline of protectionist measures, not market access as such. However, the Appellate Body also accepted the appropriateness of applying market-based criteria to likeness in a case such as *Asbestos*, rather than considering regulatory purposes such as protection of health. Thus, the error of the panel was not to have applied such criteria, but to have assumed that in so doing factors such as effects on health could be excluded from the analysis. Hence, in *Asbestos*, the physical differences between products that seemed most relevant to the AB were those that resulted in differential health impacts between asbestos and substitute products. The AB also noted that consumer tastes and habits must be *analysed* as part of the evidence that is relevant to likeness, and that health effects may well be an important basis for consumers to distinguish between products as "unlike". Thus, the approach of the Appellate

---

'Unilateralism' in Trade Policy" (2000) 11 *European Journal of International Law* 249, 262–8, hereinafter "The Product/Process Distinction"; See also Marco Bronckers and Natalie McNelis, "Rethinking the 'Like Product' Definition in GATT 1994: Anti-Dumping and Environmental Protection" in Thomas Cottier and Petros Mavroidis (eds.), *Regulatory Barriers and the Principle of Non-Discrimination in Trade Law* (Ann Arbor, Mich.: University of Michigan Press, 2000), 343–85, hereinafter, "Rethinking the 'Like Product' Definition".

[15] Working Party Report, *Border Tax Adjustments*, 2 December 1970, BISD 18S/97 (hereinafter Working Party Report).

[16] Appellate Body Report, *European Communities—Measures Affecting Asbestos and Asbestos—Containing Products*, WT/DS135/AB/R, 12 March 2001 (hereinafter Appellate Body Report).

Body was to introduce the fundamental human interests at stake not through an examination of regulatory purpose, but rather by making those interests relevant to an analysis of the competitive relationship between products in the market place. This approach did not satisfy one member of the division of the Appellate Body deciding this case, who in a concurring opinion expressed the view that concern by his brethren to preserve an economic approach to likeness analysis had impeded a clear statement of the key human value at stake in this case—the protection of human life and health.

However, the AB made another important statement in this case—it reminded its audience that a mere finding of "likeness" between two products does not oblige the regulating member to treat them identically in regulation. The complaining member must also demonstrate that the differences in regulation amount to "less favourable" treatment as between *domestic* and *imported* like products, each taken as a group. In making this statement, the AB recalled the anti-protectionist purpose of Article III and suggested that "less favourable treatment" is equivalent to protectionism. Thus, a finding of "likeness", on market-based criteria, will not be dispositive of a finding of violation of Article III:4. In future cases, these dicta may have enormous significance—for example, in situations where the regulatory distinction is based on the process of production, even if the "products" (for instance, turtle-friendly and turtle-unfriendly shrimp) are found to be "like", the regulatory distinction may still survive if it does not constitute less favourable treatment of imported than domestic "shrimp". Thus, PPMs that apply equally to imported and domestic like "products", will be consistent with Article III:4.

However, in reversing the panel on the issue of TBT applicability, the AB clearly indicated that in cases such as these, in the future, the interpretation of the TBT Agreement will be critical to the balance the WTO strikes between domestic regulatory autonomy and trade liberalisation. Understandably, the AB did not go on to complete the analysis and apply TBT in this case, since to do so it would not only have had to find additional facts, but also address itself to significant legal issues of first impression. What the AB did do, however, was to address Canada's claims that the panel's Article XX analysis was too lenient or permissive and to reject those claims even though from the perspective of judicial economy it certainly did not need even to consider Article XX (since the finding of an Article III:4 violation was reversed). Here, the AB seemed determined to make new jurisprudence, establishing an especially deferential approach to domestic regulation that addresses vital health interests.

ASBESTOS—THE WTO DISPUTE

It is widely recognised that asbestos is a highly toxic material, which poses a significant threat to human health. For example, exposure to chrysotile asbestos

may increase the risk for asbestosis, lung cancer,[17] mesothelioma or pneumoco-
niosis. These negative effects are also recognised by a recent study of the World
Health Organisation (WHO).[18] However, due to its characteristic features and
intrinsic properties[19] (fire-resistance), asbestos has found wide use in industrial
and other commercial applications. For example, asbestos is used in brake lin-
ings and clutches or in the form of spun fibres for the production of insulating
tissues or cords. Another major commercial application for asbestos is as a reinforcement material for cement, plastic or rubber. Especially before the Second
World War, asbestos was widely used in many countries. Countries that have
already during recent decades imported large quantities of asbestos, now need
to limit to the largest extent possible the negative effect on human health of the
already existing amount of imported asbestos. At the same time, domestic regulators aim towards eliminating this proven and internationally recognised
threat to the health of future generations.[20] In the light of these circumstances
France, which previously had imported lots of asbestos, issued Decree
96–1133[21] which establishes a total ban on asbestos fibres and products containing asbestos fibres.[22] Specifically, the French Decree prohibits the manufac-

---

[17] Asbestos fibres have a very particular texture. The substance consists of bundles of small fibrils, one sticking to another. These fibrils separate very easily lengthways and then can form a cloud
of very fine dust. This dust is often invisible but it can settle everywhere and penetrate very deep into
the lungs. Extremely small fibres are particularly dangerous to health. The smaller the diameter of
these fibrils, the easier it is to inhale such substance and, consequently, the higher the risk of cancer.

[18] See the WHO's International Programme on Chemical Safety (IPCS), *Environmental Health
Criteria 203—Chrysotile Asbestos* (1998) at paras. 144. This study recommends replacing asbestos
by less harmful materials or technologies wherever possible. Already previously, the WHO acknowledged that there existed a link between the characteristics of asbestos and their danger to health. In
1977 the WHO classed asbestos (also chrysotile) as a category I substance, which are proven to be
carcinogens. Little later, in 1986 the International Labour Organisation (ILO) followed the WHO
and adopted Convention No 162, where it referred to the dangers arising from the occupational
exposure to asbestos. See first written submission of the European Communities, to the WTO panel
on *European Communities—Measures Concerning Asbestos and Products Containing Asbestos*,
21 May 1999 (hereinafter EC first submission) at paras. 346 and 351 ff. See also third party written
submission of the United States to the WTO panel on *European Communities—Measures Affecting
Asbestos and Products Containing Asbestos* (hereinafter US written submission) at para. 8 ff.

[19] Asbestos is a mineral with exceptional physical and chemical properties. Specifically, this substance does not burn and is extremely resistant to other chemicals and to mechanical traction. So far
no one has developed a natural or synthetic substitute, which has all these characteristic features of
asbestos fibres. See EC first submission, *supra* n. 18, paras. 343 ff.

[20] See *ibid.*, 1.

[21] Décret No. 96–1133 du 24/12/96 relatif à l'interdiction de l'amiante, pris en application du
code du travail et du code de la consommation. http://www.sante.gouv.fr/amiante/commaitre/
reglementation/reglementation.htm.

[22] It is important to note that France is not the only country responding to these public health
concerns arising out of the use of asbestos fibres. On the contrary, many other countries both within
Europe and abroad have taken action on asbestos. Outside the European Union, such examples are
Switzerland, New Zealand, the Czech Republic and Australia. Also within the European Union, several Member States have introduced national legislation to reduce the negative effects of asbestos.
For example, Denmark and the UK in 1972 or Belgium, Germany, Finland and Italy, which all introduced an almost total ban on asbestos during the 1990s. Finally, since the 1980s there has also been
legislative action on the European level. The most recent directive received a favourable vote on
4 May 1999. The draft version stipulates that a ban on chrysotile asbestos is to be implemented

ture, processing, import, placing on the domestic market, possession for sale, offering, sale or transfer on any ground of all varieties of asbestos fibres and any products containing asbestos fibres.[23]

Article 2 of the Decree establishes an exception for existing products or material containing chrysotile asbestos. This exception is to be applied on a temporary basis, as long as there are no existing substitutes for chrysotile fibres. The use of substitute fibres is tied to two conditions. First, according to the state of art in science, such substitutes must pose smaller health risks to workers exposed to them. Secondly, the substitute has to offer all the technical safety guarantees, which were the original purpose of using asbestos. Decisions on the application of this exception are taken on a case-by-case basis, according to French administrative procedures. Due to the advances of scientific research on asbestos substitute fibres, the number of exceptions has been gradually decreasing. Also, the exceptions are applied on the assumption that, eventually, safer substitutes will be available on the market in virtually all cases, thus obviating the need to use asbestos at all in the longer term.

Already before 1998, Canada repeatedly challenged the French Decree in the TBT Committee and on 28 May 1998 Canada proceeded formally to request consultations with the European Communities.[24] According to Article 4.4 of the DSU[25] Canada alleged that the French ban severely damages Canada's economic interest, and in particular its profits from international trade in chrysotile asbestos. In Canada, asbestos is manufactured exclusively in Quebec. Partly for national unity reasons, but also because of the importance of support from Quebec to any political party in Canada that seeks to form a majority government, Quebec has frequently been the beneficiary of many industrial assistance and protective measures by the Canadian government; this trend has been exacerbated by persistently high unemployment rates in the province, which is home to many of Canada's "sunset" or troubled industries.

ARTICLE III—NATIONAL TREATMENT

Canada claimed that France's asbestos ban violated the National Treatment obligation in Article III:4 of the GATT, because it afforded less favourable

throughout the European Union by 1 January 2005 at the latest. The directive gives each Member State the freedom to choose the pace (and measures), which it deploys to achieve this harmonised position. For further information see EC first submission, *supra* n. 18, paras. 159 ff and paras. 185 ff.

[23] Note that the French Decree does not apply to asbestos as a waste. Therefore there were no issues concerning the Basel Convention on the International Transport of Hazardous Waste, Basel Convention on the Control of Transboundary Movements of Hazardous Wastes and Their Disposal, 22 March 1988 (1988) 27 ILM 859.

[24] Request for Consultations by Canada, *European Communities—Measures Affecting Asbestos and Products Containing Asbestos*, WT/DS135/1, 3 June 1998.

[25] Understanding on Rules and Procedures Governing the Settlement of Disputes, Annex 2 to the WTO Agreement (hereinafter DSU).

treatment to imports of chrysotile fibres and chrysotile-cement products from Canada than to "like products"—substitute fibres and products—some of which are of EC origin.[26] Article III:4 reads as follows: "[t]he products of the territory of any contracting party imported into the territory of any other contracting party shall be accorded treatment no less favorable than that accorded to *like products* of national origin in respect of all laws, regulations and requirements affecting their internal sale, offering for sale, purchase transportation, distribution or use . . ." (emphasis added). It is evident that under Article III:4 discrimination is forbidden only when occurring between imports and "like" domestic products. Consequently, the determination of what constitutes a "like" product, in interrelationship with the interpretation of what constitutes "less favourable treatment", provides the basis for the decision as to whether a domestic regulation is consistent with the National Treatment obligation.[27]

Despite being one of the GATT's core concepts[28] nothing in Article III or any other GATT provision provides any definition for the term "like products". In the 1970s, a GATT Working Party listed the basic factors which should be used when determining similarity of products, with respect to *taxation* measures; such measures are generally supposed to be neutral with respect to consumers' choices in the market-place, given that their purpose is to raise revenue in a manner that does not distort individual market behaviour.[29] These criteria were "the

---

[26] Canada, Premier exposé écrit du Canada, au Groupe Spécial, *Communautés Européennes— Mesures Concernant L'amiante et les produits en contenant*, le 26 avril 1999; Canada, first written submission to the panel in *European Communities—Measures Affecting Asbestos and Products Containing Asbestos*, paras. 280 ff. (hereinafter Canada first submission), Canada, Deuxième exposé écrit du Canada au Groupe Spécial, *Communautés Européennes—Mesures Concernant L'amiante et les produits en contenant*, 30 juin 1999, Canada, second written submission to the panel in *European Communities—Measures Affecting Asbestos and Products Containing Asbestos*, submission paras. 319ff. (hereinafter Canada second submission).

[27] Art. III basically established two types of national treatment obligations. First there are those relating to taxation (Art. III:2) and secondly, there are those relating to various other, non-tax regulations (Art. III:4). With respect to the obligations established for taxation measures, Art. III:2 again distinguishes two situations. Read together with the interpretative note to Art. III:2, one could see two different standards, one applying to like products, another applying to directly competitive or substitutable products. For the latter, difference of treatment alone would not constitute a violation, one would also need proof that internal taxes were applied "so as to afford protection".

[28] The notion of "like" is used some 16 times in the text of the GATT. Also other WTO Agreements, such as the TBT or the GATS, build on the concept of "likeness". GATT panels have stated that this notion of "likeness" is undoubtedly open to quite distinct interpretations. Panel Report, *United States—Measures Affecting Alcoholic and Malt Beverages*, 19 June 1992, BISD 39S/206 (hereinafter *Malt Beverages*).

[29] Thus, where fiscal measures are sometimes used to affect behaviour (pollution taxes for example, where environmental standards are enforced through monetary charges or penalties attaching to the offending conduct) they are generally qualified as behavioural or Pigovian taxes, to distinguish them from typical neutral revenue-raising measures. These kinds of measures would normally not be considered as taxation measures within the meaning of Art. III:2. See Panel Report, *United States—Measures Affecting the Importation, Internal Sale and Use of Tobacco*, DS44/R, (1994) (hereinafter *US—Tobacco*). But for certain specific purposes, i.e. border tax adjustment, an earlier case, *Superfund*, had suggested that neutral fiscal measures and behavioural taxes should be treated the same. See Panel Report, *United States—Taxes on Petroleum and Certain Imported Substances*, BISD 34S, (1988) (hereinafter *Superfund*).

product's end-uses in a given market; consumers' tastes and habits, which change from country to country and the product's properties, nature and quality".[30] In the 1980s a panel on *Japanese liquor taxes*[31] added another criterion, namely uniform classification in tariff nomenclatures. Finally, two WTO panels[32] approached the question of likeness by examining whether there exists some commonality of end-uses and whether the products in question possess essentially the same physical characteristics. In recognition that where measures are being taken for non-fiscal reasons, such as environmental objectives, purely market criteria are inadequate to judge "likeness", panels interpreting Article III:4, as opposed to Article III:2, which deals with neutral fiscal measures, developed an approach termed "aims and effects".[33] This test evaluated whether, on the basis of all the evidence, protectionist intent or impact was evident in the regulatory scheme and its operation.

This approach recognised that the GATT should not be used to subject to scrutiny non-protective regulatory schemes for non-commercial objectives. Its disadvantage related to the difficulties surrounding an inquiry into protectionist "intent", largely replacing an inquiry into the meaning of "likeness" in relation to the objective purposes and structure of the regulatory scheme, with intuitive judgements about motivation. This risked collapsing the inquiry into "likeness" into a general judgement about protective discrimination, and thereby failing to give meaning to the ordinary meaning of the exact words in Article III:4.[34] Moreover, "aims and effects" spilled over into the analysis of fiscal measures under Article III:2, despite the adequacy of market-based criteria to deciding the issue of likeness in the case of measures not aimed at altering market behaviour for some non-commercial purpose.[35] Finally, in the *Japanese Alcohol* case the Appellate Body upheld the panel's focus on the objective market criteria in determining likeness for purposes of applying the national treatment obligations with respect to neutral fiscal measures. The Appellate Body, however, did not elaborate the implications of the rejection of "aims and effects" for Article III:4, merely stressing that the meaning of "likeness" in different provisions of the WTO Agreements would have to be considered in each case separately.[36]

---

[30] Working Party Report, *supra* n. 15, para. 18.

[31] Panel Report, *Japan—Customs Duties, Taxes and Labelling Practices on Imported Wines and Alcoholic Beverages*, 10 November 1987, BISD 34S/83, para. 5.6. (hereinafter *Japanese Alcohol 1988*). Besides the tariff heading criterion, the other two criteria were similar properties and end-uses.

[32] Panel Report, *Japan—Taxes on Alcoholic Beverages*, 1996, WT/DS8/R, WT/DS10/R, WT/DS11/R, para. 6.22 (hereinafter *Japanese Beverages, Panel*). Similar, Panel Report, *Canada—Certain Measures Concerning Periodicals*, 1997, WT/DS31/R, para. 5.25 (hereinafter *Canada Periodicals, Panel*).

[33] See *Japanese Alcohol (1988)*, *supra* n. 31, *Canada Beer*, *supra* n. 9, and *United-States—Taxation of Automobiles*, DS 31/R of 11 October 1994, unadopted (hereinafter *CAFE*).

[34] See Hudec, "Requiem", *supra* n. 7 on the textualist critique of "aims and effects".

[35] *Japanese Alcohol (1988)*, *supra* n. 31.

[36] Appellate Body Report, *Japan—Taxes on Alcoholic Beverages*, WT/DS8/AB/R, WT/DS10/AB/R, WT/DS11/AB/R (hereinafter *Japanese Beverages AB*) 21. In a memorable quotation, the AB

However, in the later *Bananas* case, when interpreting the National Treatment provisions of the General Agreement on Trade in Services (GATS),[37] in respect of non-fiscal measures, the Appellate Body noted that in the *Japanese Alcohol* decision, it had "rejected the "aims and effects" theory with respect to Art. III:2".[38] In dismissing the EC argument that an absence of protective intent in the licensing schemes rendered them consistent with the National Treatment obligation of GATS, the Appellate Body did not explicitly examine the meaning of "likeness".[39] Based on the factual findings of the panel concerning the overwhelming discriminatory impact of the classifications in the scheme in question, the Appellate Body upheld the panel's finding of *de facto* discrimination under GATS. However, the meaning of "likeness", as distinguished from the overall issue of whether the GATS prohibited *de facto* discrimination, was not central to the issues of law appealed in this case, and it is understandable that the decision did not develop the implications of its analysis of the issue of *de facto* discrimination for the meaning of the concept of "likeness" under Article III:4 of the GATT, explicitly noting that in *Japan Alcohol*, its rejection of "aims and effects" was in respect of Article III:2. Thus, it remained an open issue how in light of the rejection of "aims and effects" with respect to Article III:2, likeness should now be understood with respect to Article III:4 of the GATT. One reason it was appropriate that the Appellate Body not expand on this matter in the *Bananas* case was that, whatever the claims of the EC in that case about non-protectionist intent, the scheme in question was a scheme of regulation for commercial or economic purposes, not for purposes external to the management of the market place itself, such as environment, health and safety, and so forth. Thus, this would have been an inappropriate case in which to consider the sensitive issue of how "likeness" should be dealt with in relation to regulatory autonomy as exercised in the service of fundamental non-economic values.[40]

---

specifically notes that "The criteria in Border Tax Adjustments should be examined, but there can be no one precise and absolute definition of what is 'like'. The concept of 'likeness' is a relative one that evokes the image of an accordion. The accordion of 'likeness' stretches and squeezes in different places as different provisions of the WTO Agreements are applied. The width of the accordion in any one of those places must be determined by the particular provision in which the term 'like' is encountered as well as by the context and the circumstances that prevail in any given case to which that provision may apply".

[37] General Agreement on Trade in Services, Annex 1 B to the WTO Agreement (hereinafter GATS).

[38] See *Bananas AB*, *supra* n. 9, para. 241.

[39] Note that the text of Art. XVII.2 GATS reads that National Treatment might be "either formally identical treatment or formally different treatment". It thereby explicitly specifies that *de facto* discrimination is included in Art. XVII GATS. The above remarks of the Appellate Body are therefore strictly speaking *obiter dicta*.

[40] While preferences themselves for bananas could be understood in terms of development purposes as embodied in the Lomé Convention, the licensing schemes found to constitute *de facto* discrimination were rightly understood by the panel and Appellate Body not to be necessary and incidental to those development purposes.

In its submission in *Asbestos*, Canada alleged that asbestos and non-asbestos products were "like",[41] because of having the same product characteristics,[42] end uses, and falling under the same tariff classification.[43] The Europeans countered all of the Canadians' arguments on their own terms, claiming that the properties, nature and quality of asbestos fibres and substitute products and asbestos-containing products and substitute products are different,[44] and pointing also to differences with respect to tariff classification[45] and the end use.

The panel, in following the market-based approach to likeness approved by the AB in *Japan Alcohol* and subsequent cases, considered first of all the physical characteristics of asbestos and the substitute products. While, as the EC argued, there were indisputable physical differences between asbestos fibres and the substitutes, the panel rejected these physical differences as dispositive of *un*likeness.[46] This was based on the notion that the physical differences did not matter to the functionality of the product, i.e. to its end use in construction, etc. Having found that the products had similar physical characteristics and end uses[47] (these two findings as noted being closely related), the panel did not find it necessary to examine consumer tastes and habits.[48] It did turn its mind to the differences in customs classification for the two products, but in light of its findings on physical characteristics and end uses, the panel did not find the difference in customs classification to be "decisive".[49]

---

[41] Note that one of the main points of controversy was which types of substances and products should be compared. Canada suggests comparing (Canadian) chrysotile and chrysotile cement on the one hand with French "like products" such as substitute fibres (PVA fibres, cellulose and glass) and fibre cement on the other. (See Canada first submission, *supra* n. 26, paras. 295 ff , 305ff and 310 ff.) The EC argue that the relevant comparison should be between the following products: first, domestic asbestos fibres and imported asbestos fibres (both prohibited but may be granted a temporary derogation on the same terms); secondly, domestic products containing asbestos fibres and imported products containing asbestos fibres (both prohibited but may be granted a temporary derogation on the same terms); thirdly, substitute domestic products and substitute imported products (both permitted) (see European first submission, *supra* n. 18, paras. 324 ff). The USA used a similar line of argumentation and stated that Canada failed to make the correct product comparison in order to determine whether the relevant products are like products under Art. III. 4. According to the USA the relevant products to compare were the following (1) asbestos must be compared to substitute fibres and (2) products containing asbestos must be compared to products that do not contain asbestos but which perform the same function. (See US written submission, *supra* n. 18, para. 39.)

[42] See Canada first submission, *supra* n. 26, paras. 310 and 317 ff referring to "properties, quality and nature of the product".

[43] For the importance of tariff headings, see first Canadian submission, *supra* n. 26, in paras. 333 ff. Note that in its first submission Canada also refers to consumer tastes and habits (para. 325), whilst in its second submission, it specifically dismisses this point and refers only to the products' end use (paras. 329 ff), tariff heading (para. 336 ff) and properties, nature and qualities (para. 341 ff).

[44] EC first submission, *supra* n. 18, paras. 342 ff.

[45] *Ibid.*, paras. 358 ff.

[46] Panel Report, *supra* n. 13, para. 8.126.

[47] *Ibid.*, para. 8.136.

[48] *Ibid.*, para. 8.140.

[49] *Ibid.*, para. 8.143.

The panel categorically rejected the EC argument that in a case such as that the health risk from the product should be taken into account in the analysis of likeness and should indeed be decisive.[50] The panel suggested that were health considerations to be taken into account in determining whether products were "like" under Article III:4, the exception with respect to health in Article XX(b) of the GATT would be rendered redundant.[51] Here, the panel appeared to be taking to the extreme the implication of the market-based approach to likeness favoured by the AB in *Japan Alcohol* and subsequent cases. In *Japan Alcohol*, the Appellate Body had been careful to qualify its endorsement of the market-based approach in *Border Tax Adjustment* as understood by the *panel* in *Japan Alcohol*—it noted that the market-based criteria in *Border Tax Adjustment* were not *exhaustive* of the factors that, in a given case, might be relevant in assessing "likeness" and it also noted that the approach to "like products" in one legal provision of the GATT might be different from in the case of another legal provision. Thus, the door remained open to the panel in *Asbestos* to consider an additional criterion—the regulatory objective of protecting health—as relevant or indeed decisive in assessing whether the products were "like".

In its cross-appeal, the EC argued that the panel had erred in law in refusing to consider health effects as a separate criterion in determining whether asbestos and the substitute were "like" products.[52]

The disposition by the Appellate Body of the EC cross-appeal on Article III:4 is, to say the least, complex. This disposition has three separate parts to it: (1) an elaboration of the general approach to the interpretation of the treaty language in Article III:4; (2) findings of error of law by the panel; (3) "completing the analysis", where the AB goes on to apply Article III:4 correctly to the facts of the case, picking up at the point where the panel began to err in law.

In outlining the general approach to the interpretation of Article III:4, the AB places fundamental emphasis on Article III:1 as stating the general purpose that animates Article III as a whole. That principle, according to the AB, quoting its own words in *Japan–Alcohol*, "is to avoid protectionism in the application of internal tax and regulatory measures".[53] Thus, the meaning of "like product" must be informed by the anti-protectionism principle of Article III:1. In order for protectionism to be possible, the regulations challenged under Article III:4 must, in the first instance, address imported and domestic products that are in a competitive relationship. Thus, the inquiry into "likeness" in Article III:4 is about whether there is the kind of competitive relationship between the imported product and domestic products that *could* lead to a conclusion of protectionism, *if* the result of the regulatory treatment were that the imported product was treated less favourably. It is, then, not enough that there be *some*

---

[50] EC first submission, *supra* n. 18, paras. 8.127 ff.

[51] *Ibid.*, para. 8.130.

[52] Other Appellant's Submission by the European Communities pursuant to Rule 23 of the Working Procedures for Appellate Review, Geneva, 21 November 2000, paras. 50 ff.

[53] Appellate Body Report, *supra* n. 17, para. 97.

competitive relationship between the imported product and domestic products, rather the issue of likeness is one that includes the "kind" of competitive relationship. Already here, the AB is distinguishing its approach from that of the *panel* in *Japan–Alcohol*, making it clear that what is a stake is a contextual and qualitative judgement about competitive relationships, not merely the economic analysis of cross-elasticity of demand between two groups of products. Such an assessment must be made on a case-by-case basis, informed by the general principle of anti-protectionism, which informs all of Article III.

Once a competitive relationship has been established of the degree and kind relevant to Article III:4, then the second step of the analysis comes into play. Only where the differential treatment of the "like" products amounts to "less favourable treatment" of the group of imported products in relation to the group of like domestic products will there be a violation of Article III:4. In fact, the AB goes out of its way to emphasise that "a Member may draw distinctions between products which have been found to be 'like', without for this reason alone, according to the group of 'like' *imported* products 'less favourable treatment' than that accorded to the group of 'like' *domestic* products".[54] The AB also emphasises that less favourable treatment does not mean just *any* kind of worse treatment—"less favourable treatment" is a concept informed by the anti-protectionist principle in Article III:1. Thus a judgement of "less favourable treatment" implies, "conversely", a conclusion of "protection".

As the AB noted, it did not need to apply the concept of "less favourable treatment" to the facts in *Asbestos*, since it reversed the panel's ruling that the products were "like", therefore obviating the second step of the analysis. However, this statement of the approach to less favourable treatment is a very important one. First of all, the AB has made it clear that even where *products* are in a close enough competitive relationship to be considered "like", members of that class or group of "like" products may still be distinguished in regulation, provided that the result is not less favourable treatment, understood as protection of domestic production. This in effect blunts, without explicitly repudiating, the product/process distinction—the much criticised idea, found in the unadopted *Tuna/Dolphin* panels, that process-based trade restrictions can never be considered as internal regulations consistent with the National Treatment standard of Article III.[55] Even if products that have different process and production

---

[54] *Ibid.*, para. 100. The AB already touched on this point in the *Korea-Beef* case, para 135, see Appellate Body Report, *Korea—Measures Affecting Imports of Fresh, Chilled and Frozen Beef*, WT/DS161/AB/R, 11 December 2000 (hereinafter *Korea-Beef* Appellate Body Report).

[55] See Howse and Regan,"The Product/Process Distinction", *supra* n. 14. Some observers have interpreted the statement in para.100 in a different way, namely as simply restating the proposition of the *Section 337* case, *supra* n. 9, that where there is facially discriminatory treatment of domestic and imported products, nevertheless this may still be consistent with Art. III:4—namely where, although domestic products and imports are governed by different rules or regimes, there is nevertheless no less favourable treatment for imports. If this statement is interpreted this way however the next sentence in para. 100 appears to reverse another proposition of the *Section 337* case, i.e. that in cases where there is differential treatment of imports and domestic products, every instance of the

methods are considered to be "like" under Article III:4 (which, as will be discussed below, they need not always be), regulatory distinctions may be made between them, on *any* grounds, provided the result is *non-protectionist*. Thus, for example, were all "shrimp" considered to be "like" regardless of whether they were turtle-friendly or not, i.e. whether or not caught in a manner that did not result in undue levels of turtle mortality, this would not *necessarily* mean that a regulation that required that all shrimp sold in the USA be turtle-friendly was inconsistent with Article III:4. One would have to consider whether the design and structure of the scheme resulted in less favourable treatment of imported shrimp as a group than domestic shrimp as a group, i.e. did the requirement result in protection of domestic production? The differential impact of such a requirement on imported shrimp *might* alter the competitive relationship between domestic and imported shrimp so as to protect domestic production if, for instance, foreign producers of shrimp faced costs of adapting their fishing practices that domestic shrimp producers did not. However, as the AB emphasises, the comparison is between the group of imports as a whole and the group of domestic products as a whole. Just because one particular foreign producer of shrimp faced a differential burden from the regulation in comparison to one particular domestic producer, a finding of "less favourable treatment" would not be justified.

The AB's emphatic statement about the crucial second step in Article III:4 National Treatment analysis must be borne in mind in considering its approach to the first step of ascertaining whether products are "like"; the AB admits that there is no one approach to likeness that will be appropriate in all cases, and that "likeness" is a matter of judgement—qualitative as well as quantitative. This case-by-case approach may not seem to provide much assurance against a panel casting the net so wide, as it were, that legitimate non-protectionist regulatory distinctions are put into question. But the *second step* of Article III:4 analysis provides a safeguard against that possibility, by requiring the complaining member to establish that the regulatory distinction in question results in

differential treatment must result in treatment no less favourable. This is because the next sentence in para. 100 emphasises that the comparison is between the treatment of the group of like imported products and the group of like domestic products. The AB cannot be reasonably interpreted as intending to overturn such an established jurisprudential principle of the GATT, not even citing or discussing the *Section 337* (*supra* n. 9) panel here. In fact, while in *Section 337* the issue is when facially differential treatment of imports may nevertheless be "no less favourable", in para. 100 the issue is whether a non-national-origin based regulatory distinction between like products nevertheless constitutes less favourable treatment of imports, i.e. protection. From the point of view of discerning protection in respect of origin-neutral regulatory distinctions, the fact that some imported product or other gets worse treated than some domestic product or other is not probative and may be quite misleading. This may be an innocent or purely accidental disparate impact. To determine whether an origin-neutral regulatory distinction is protective, we have to discern whether there is a connection between the design and structure of the scheme itself and less favourable treatment of imports—the issue is systemically less favourable treatment of imports, and therefore the proper framework for assessment is the structure and design of the scheme as it impacts on the treatment of the group of like imported products as a whole relative to the group of like domestic products as a whole.

protection of domestic production. Thus, while, as we shall see, the AB has taken great pains to continue to distance itself from aims and effects analysis with respect to likeness, it has in effect brought "aims and effects" back in at the second stage of considering whether there is "less favourable treatment".[56]

This bring us to the general remarks of the AB concerning likeness of products in Article III:4. The AB first of all recalls the *Border Tax Adjustment* criteria, with the addition of customs classification as the fourth criterion, as one approach that has been developed to likeness under Article III.[57] However, the AB also states that the criteria in question "are neither a treaty-mandated nor a closed list of criteria that will determine the legal characterization of products".[58] Indeed, a panel *must* examine all the "pertinent evidence" of likeness or unlikeness, regardless of whether that evidence goes to the kinds of "potentially shared characteristics" identified in the *Border Tax Adjustment* criteria. This last statement is significantly stronger than the caveat in *Japan—Alcohol* that other criteria may be relevant in certain cases—it actually limits the discretion of the panel, which must weigh all the evidence in *every* case, including evidence that does not go to the potential shared characteristics identified in the *Border Tax Adjustment* criteria. At the same time, the AB notes that because the likeness inquiry is about competitive relationships between products, it is necessary for a panel always *to take into account* evidence that goes to the competitive relationship in its analysis of likeness.

---

[56] This is especially evident when we recall the AB's suggestion in para. 100 of the interchangeability or of equivalence of the notion of "less favourable treatment" with the general notion in Art. III:1 that measures not be applied so as to afford protection to domestic production. In interpreting that concept with respect to National Treatment in taxation under the second sentence of Art. III:2 , into which it is explicitly incorporated by virtue of an Interpretive Note to Art. III, the AB has indicated the primary importance of examining the structure and design of the regulatory scheme in order to make a judgement on objective factors as whether the measure is protective and asserted the irrelevance of protectionist intent to that enterprise, *Japan—Alcohol AB, supra* n. 36. In the subsequent case of *Canada—Periodicals*, however, the AB did not exclude consideration of evidence such as legislative history and ministerial statements, that apparently went to protectionist intent: Appellate Body Report, *Canada—Certain Measures Concerning Periodicals*, 30 June 1997, WT/DS31/AB/R (hereinafter *Canada Periodicals, AB*). Recently, in *Chile—Alcohol*, the AB held it was appropriate to "relate the observable structural features of the measure with its declared purposes": Appellate Body Report, *Chile—Taxes on Alcoholic Beverages*, 13 December 1999, WT/DS87/AB/R, para. 72. These are not inconsistent rulings—an inquiry into the structure and design of the scheme may well be decisive with respect to whether it is protective, obviating the need for making sensitive judgements about intent, but this does not mean that in other cases evidence of intentional protection may well be relevant. Not all findings that a measure is *structurally* protective imply a cryptic judgement of protectionist animus: domestic regulators or legislators may have designed a measure without turning their minds at all to the possibility of a systematically unfavourable effect on imports. This might happen because of un- or under-representation of importer or foreign producer interests, or surrogate domestic interests, in the regulatory process—that could indicate protection at the deeper level of regulatory and political structure. But the measures themselves may lack any direct protectionist animus. Cf. Hudec, "Requiem", *supra* n. 7, 634.

[57] We will refer to all four criteria hereinafter as the *Border Tax Adjustment* criteria.

[58] Appellate Body Report, *supra* n. 16, para. 102.

It is apparent that, here, the AB is engaged in a very subtle balancing act in articulating its approach to "likeness". The AB makes it very clear that a panel cannot simply revert to an "aims and effects"-type analysis as conclusive of "likeness" or "unlikeness"; the panel must *always* examine competitive relationships in the market-place. At the same time, the AB goes out of its way to emphasise that there may be cases where it will be inappropriate to leave matters at that, and raises the possibility that in those cases the evidence that tips the balance may well be evidence that does *not* go into the market-based criteria articulated in *Border Tax Adjustment*. Otherwise, why make it obligatory in all cases to consider such evidence, if it exists?

Now the AB goes on to the second part of its consideration of National Treatment, the correction of the panel's errors of law. The panel erred in not considering and weighing all the evidence, and this error relates to the error of not considering *all* four of the *Border Tax Adjustment* criteria explicitly and separately. First of all, the panel focused exclusively on assumptions about end uses of the products in coming to the conclusion that differences in physical characteristics between asbestos and the substitute products were not of a kind and degree to make these products "unlike". According to the AB, the analysis of physical characteristics should be made separately from an inquiry into end uses. Physical differences between asbestos fibres and substitute products "are "important" because the microscopic particles and filaments of chyrsotile asbestos fibres are carcinogenic to humans, following inhalation".[59] The failure of the panel to find that such differences were "important" stemmed partly from its error of law in conflating analysis of physical characteristics with end uses. But it also stemmed from the panel's error in concluding that health effects are irrelevant in analysing likeness under Article III:4. The panel took the view that, were health considerations to enter into the application of the National Treatment standard in Article III, then the health exception in Article. XX would be redundant. The AB however considered that consideration of health effects under Article. III:4 is a very different kind of inquiry from that under Article XX. Under Article III:4 the issue is how health effects impact on the competitive relationship of products in the market-place, whereas under Article XX the issue is whether a member has a sufficient basis for a adopting or enforcing a WTO-inconsistent measure on grounds of human health.[60]

In addition, the panel committed a further error when it went on to examine end uses as a separate criterion. In concluding that the evidence of end uses sustained a conclusion of "likeness" between asbestos and the substitutes, the panel left matters at pointing out a small number of similar end uses of the two products, while failing to examine evidence of a wide range of dissimilar non-overlapping functions.

---

[59] Appellate Body Report, *supra* n. 16, para. 114.
[60] *Ibid.*, para. 115.

More importantly still, the panel erred in failing to consider at all the evidence of consumer tastes and habits, the third criterion that it was required to consider separately. Here the AB comes closest to taking judicial notice of human health as a fundamental value: "[i]n this case especially, we are also persuaded that evidence relating to consumers' tastes and habits would establish that the health risks associated with chyrsolite asbestos fibres influence consumers' behavior with respect to the different fibres at issue".[61] While acknowledging that the initial consumers of the products are industrial users, the AB notes: "[a] manufacturer cannot, for instance, ignore the preferences of the ultimate consumer of its products. If the risks posed by a particular product are sufficiently great, the ultimate consumer may simply cease to buy that product. This would, undoubtedly, affect a manufacturer's decisions in the marketplace. Moreover, in the case of products posing risks to human health, it is likely that the manufacturer's decisions will be influenced by other factors, such as potential civil liability that might flow from marketing products posing a health risk to the ultimate consumer, or the additional costs associated with safety procedures required to use such products in the manufacturing process".[62]

For the AB then, the test from the perspective of consumer tastes and habits is whether the products would be substitutable and in a competitive relationship in an *idealised* market-place, one where consumers have full information, and where, at least through tort liability, negative externalities have already to some extent been internalised. As the AB emphasises, the fact of an imperfect market-place does not mean that evidence cannot be found that is probative of how consumers *would* behave with respect to the two products in an *idealised* market-place.[63] Indeed, to support the intuitions of the AB here, in the case of asbestos, the evidence of the social costs from the health risks of this substance is such that one would almost certainly expect that, in an idealised market-place where those costs were internalised, asbestos and asbestos products would be very unlikely to be cost competitive. This sort of analysis of consumer tastes and behaviour brings into the picture the kinds of regulatory interests which had under the GATT been taken into account through the "aims and effects" test. It is just that those interests are taken into account here by adopting not the perspective of the regulator as such, but the perspective of consumer behaviour in an idealised market-place. But note that part of the picture of this idealised market-place is a liability rule that makes manufacturers responsible for the health risks posed by their products; such a rule may well be premised not only on

---

[61] *Ibid.*, para. 122.

[62] *Ibid.*, para. 122.

[63] A very similar approach is taken in Bronckers and McNelis, "Rethinking the "Like Product" Definition", *supra* n. 15. According to Bronckers and McNelis, for physically like products to be characterised as "unlike" on the basis of consumer tastes and habits, it would be necessary for "consumers as a whole (rather than specific interest groups)" to distinguish between the products (at 375). We do not understand why this should be the case—competing firms in the market-place often differentiate their products to appeal to sub-groups of consumers, and those differentiations may change competitive relationships substantially.

assumptions about the efficient allocation of risk, but also on judgements about the fair, or just, distribution of risk in a society. It is thus quite possible that this particular conception of the idealised market-place embodies a conception not only of regulation as the "efficient" correction of market failure but also of a just allocation of liability rules and/or property rights.

The final part of the AB's discussion of National Treatment in *Asbestos* consists in completing the analysis—i.e. applying the legal interpretation of Article III:4 as corrected to the facts. Having found that the panel did not err in law in choosing to adopt the *Border Tax Adjustment* approach to likeness, the AB does not undo that choice. The AB first turns to the consideration of physical characteristics. It comes to the conclusion that asbestos and the substitutes are "very different" physically because of the health significance of the differences. Yet the AB does not explain *why* health effects should in this instance be decisive in evaluating whether physical differences are significant enough to point to a conclusion of unlikeness. The AB might have pointed to its speculations about consumer tastes and habits. But if the panel was wrong to conflate an inquiry into physical characteristics with an investigation of end-uses, would not the AB have made a similar error, in evaluating the significance of physical differences through the lenses of the third criterion of consumer tastes and habits? As the AB stated earlier in its examination of Article III:4, one of the questions not answered by any dictionary definition of likeness is "from whose perspective" the significance of differences and similarities is to be evaluated. Of course, one answer is the regulator's perspective, an answer that in some form or other leads back to "aims and effects", an outcome unacceptable to the AB. Another answer is the consumer's perspective. But that leaves it mysterious why an analysis of physical characteristics would be *logically prior* to a consideration of consumer tastes and habits, much less distinct from it.

In any case, the physical properties of the products having been determined to be "very different", on the basis of health considerations, the AB suggests that this amounts to a preliminary or tentative finding of "unlikeness", which Canada has a high burden to bear in reversing, through demonstrating that despite significant physical differences the products are in a sufficiently close competitive relationship, when the other factors are analysed. Here, with respect to end uses, since there was no evidence on the record of the *extent* of non-overlapping, separate end uses for the products relative to similar end uses, the AB concluded that "we cannot determine the significance of the fact that chrysotile asbestos and PCG fibres share a small number of similar end-uses".[64]

Two readings are possible concerning what the AB was saying here. The first reading is that it is saying that it is impossible to apply at all the second criterion of end uses due to a defect in the factual record of the panel. If this is so, then the AB should not be completing the analysis.[65] Because on the AB's own theory of

---

[64] Appellate Body Report, *supra* n. 16, para. 137.
[65] Thus, in *Canada—Periodicals*, *supra* n. 56, where there was inadequate factual analysis in the panel report, the AB held that it could not go ahead and complete the analysis of "likeness".

"likeness" a panel must make a separate and thorough analysis of all four criteria if it adopts the *Border Tax Adjustment* approach. If the factual record as it stood did not permit such an analysis of the second criterion, then the AB could not, on its own terms, go on to apply adequately the *Border Tax Adjustment* approach to "likeness".

The alternative reading of what the AB is doing here is that it uses this criterion to present evidence of the *comparative* importance of similar as opposed to different or non-overlapping end uses. On this reading, the AB would be holding that a member, in order to make a *prima facie* case of likeness, has to provide evidence of likeness (similar end uses) but also evidence of unlikeness (different or non-overlapping end uses) and show at least the preliminary plausibility that the former evidence outweighs or is more probative than the latter. On the one hand, this view of the burden of proof is consistent with the AB's view that the inquiry into likeness is *inherently* a relative or comparative inquiry, entailing an appreciation of kind and degree of similarity; thus even a *prima facie* case of likeness would need to probe degree or extent, which obviously involves comparing the evidence of likeness against all evidence, including that of unlikeness. On the other hand, it seems more intuitively plausible that in an adversarial process, where the complainant provides *some* credible evidence of likeness, it establishes a *prima facie* case, such that one would normally expect that the defending party would now have to muster equal or greater credible evidence of *un*likeness. Thus, this alternative reading raises difficult issues about the burden of proof. But it does exonerate the AB from a straightforward error of completing the analysis on the basis of an inadequate panel factual record.

In the case of consumer tastes and habits, the third criterion, the panel held that since Canada had presented no evidence at all on consumer tastes and habits, it could not overcome the tentative or preliminary characterisation of the products as "like" based on physical characteristics.[66] However, the reason that Canada presented no evidence, the AB noted, was its legal position that the criterion was irrelevant. Here an *error in law*, corrected only upon appeal by the AB, resulted in an inadequate factual record. Was this a reasonable basis on which to conclude that Canada had not met its burden of proof? Or should the AB instead have simply concluded that the factual record was inadequate, and refused to complete the analysis? On balance, we are of the view that the AB acted appropriately. In failing to provide evidence on consumer tastes and habits, Canada was taking an ordinary litigation risk—the risk that if the panel were to disagree with its view that this criterion was irrelevant in the circumstances, it would lose the opportunity to argue in the alternative as it were that consumer tastes and habits did point to a finding of likeness or at least did not detract from such a finding based on physical similarities and end uses.

---

[66] Appellate Body Report, *supra* n. 16, para. 139.

There is, arguably, a more general inconsistency between the way in which the AB completed the analysis and the overall approach to Article III:4 it elaborated in the first part of its discussion of Article III:4. In that part, it suggested that what a panel should do is to consider all the evidence of likeness on the basis of the *Border Tax Adjustment* criteria, and indeed also consider any evidence that does not go *into* the characteristics addressed by those criteria, and then make on overall judgement about whether the products are "like" or not. But, when completing the analysis, the AB appears to privilege the investigation of physical differences as of special and prior importance, such that where that analysis points to a finding of unlikeness, the evidence on the other criteria must be virtually overwhelming to justify an overall, definitive judgement that the products are "like". Given that, in this case, the physical differences are significant in terms of a very fundamental human value, health, the approach does not seem unjustified. But the AB seems to adopt it as a rule of thumb for all cases, regardless of context. Nevertheless, it is important to note the AB does not affirm the converse. That is the AB does *not* say that, where the analysis of physical characteristics points towards *likeness*, the burden of establishing *unlikeness* on the basis of *other* criteria and evidence is especially heavy. Thus, whatever the merits of the AB's prioritisation of physical characteristics, the AB is not deploying that prioritisation in such a way as to reinforce the notion that products cannot normally be unlike once it has been established that they are physically "like".

What then is one to make of the overall ruling of the AB with respect to Article III:4? One way of understanding this ruling is that it navigates between two "constituencies" both of which are important to the legitimacy of the Appellate Body on the WTO rules and institutions more generally.[67] The first constituency is that of the officials (delegates, secretariat employees, etc.) who are the day-to-day guardians of the trading system—these people may be inclined to look for clear, economic guidelines in the application of trade law, and may tend to view "market access" as the main objective of the entire system, subject to certain defined and limited "exceptions". The second constituency is that comprised of the groups and individuals whose interests and values are habitually given short shrift when translated into trade rules and legal interpretation by the middle-level officials. Some of these groups see the only answer to this problem as structural—a roll back of globalisation. Yet there are other groups within the second constituency, such as those who filed applications for leave to submit *amicus* briefs in *Asbestos*, who see change within the system as at least part of the solution, including more sensitive interpretations of WTO law.

---

[67] Here we have been inspired by recent work by Joseph Weiler on the distinction between internal and external legitimacy of the WTO. See Joseph H.H. Weiler, "The Rule of Lawyers and the Ethos of Diplomats: Reflections on the Internal and External Legitimacy of WTO Dispute Settlement", Harvard Jean Monnet Working Paper 9/00, available at www.jeanmonnetprogram. org. Assessing the first 5 years of AB rulings, Weiler observes that the AB has practised a legitimation strategy with "a keen eye on balancing internal and external legitimacy" (at 16).

The *Asbestos* ruling navigates with agility between these two constituencies. It gives to the first constituency an "economic" framework for the application of Article III:4, which is continuous with the recent jurisprudence on National Treatment in taxation. At the same time, it corrects for the narrowness of perspective of the panel, signaling that within the "economic" framework for the analysis of likeness, broader human interests and values such as health must be taken into account. In addition, the AB has maintained two additional safety valves against interpretations of likeness under Article III:4, that threaten the legitimacy of the system by giving inadequate attention to human values and interests of a non-economic nature, in the narrow sense. The first is in the notion that the "economic" framework is not necessarily decisive with regard to likeness in all cases, and evidence that cannot be assimilated to the characteristics important in that framework must be taken into account (even if the AB did not speculate on what such cases might be about). The second safety valve resides in the importance of establishing "less favourable treatment", i.e. protection of domestic production, in order to prove a violation of Article III:4. To the extent that "less favourable treatment" means treatment that is protectionist in aims and effects, this second step in Article III:4 analysis creates the kind of safe harbour for non-protectionist domestic regulations that had been the central intent behind the now repudiated "aims and effects" test. The Member of the AB division who, in his concurring opinion, expressed the view that the AB should have stated outright that carcinogenic asbestos is not "like" non-carcinogenic substitutes clearly, at some point, balked at this balancing act. He could not accept that the concern to preserve the "economic" approach to "likeness" in Article III:4 justifies the failure to make a strong and unambiguous statement that, in a case like this, health effects simply *trump* other considerations or factors that might be in play in assessing "likeness".

Yet, in fairness to the approach of the other two members of the division, the balance they struck is not an unprincipled compromise between interest groups. The WTO system cannot function without the support of the middle-level officials, whether delegates or Secretariat members, who oil its wheels on a daily basis. As recent events have shown, its future development can also be brought to a halt if it has no legitimacy with the broad range of interests that typically feel left out of outcomes produced by the first constituency. There is, at present, no effective political leadership to mediate these constituencies or get them to talk to one another, and the AB is arguably the only functional institution within the multilateral trading system that can articulate the outlines of an overlapping consensus. Given this predicament, the AB's approach to Article III:4 is understandable.

Some may argue that in playing this kind of role the AB has gone to the opposite extreme of its initial approach of sticking to the treaty text. However, the AB is careful to note in its ruling that the treaty text cannot resolve in any kind of straightforward positivistic way the issue of "likeness" in Article III:4. Thus, the Appellate Body has been compelled to find a legitimate solution in the absence of an agreed approach in the treaty text itself. Under such circumstances, it has understandably resorted to techniques of adjudication described by Cass Sunstein in the US domestic context, somewhat misleading perhaps, as "judicial minimalism".[68] These are techniques that Sunstein argues are appropriate in cases where a court must decide a complex matter on which people feel deeply, but also on which the relevant constituencies are deeply divided on the level of principle. The Court must find an outcome in the individual case before it that does not represent a choice between the ultimate values that are contested in any simple or straightforward way. It will thus craft a decision that leaves many things undecided or under-decided; which resolves issues not through reference to high general principles but to narrow factors such as burdens of proof and issues specific to the facts of the case; it will be uninclined to evolve the law in bold steps, by overtly replacing one kind of doctrinal framework with another. This kind of decision people may be able to live with, despite deep divisions among them about the general principles or norms at stake. And based on discussion about the Article III:4 analysis to date among various commentators, the AB may well have succeeded in this respect—for while the first constituency, though puzzled by certain details, sees a further development of the market-based approach,[69] the second constituency sees a greater sensitivity to basic human interests, and the legitimacy of governmental action to protect them.

APPLICATION OF THE TBT AGREEMENT TO THE *ASBESTOS* DISPUTE

In the panel proceedings the EC made the unusual argument that because the French measure was an outright ban it was not a technical regulation within the meaning of the TBT Agreement, and therefore the Agreement did not apply. The definition of a "technical regulation" is: "a Document which lays down product characteristics or their related processes and production methods, including the applicable administrative provisions, with which compliance is mandatory. It may also include or deal exclusively with terminology, symbols, packaging, marking or labeling requirements as they apply to a product, process or production method".[70] The EC argued that a measure banning a product cannot be equated with a measure that specifies the product's characteristics. The panel agreed with the EC's reasoning and held that the TBT Agreement did not apply to the measure in question. In order to characterise the measure as a

---

[68] C. Sunstein, *One Case at a Time: Judicial Minimalism on the Supreme Court* (Cambridge, MA: Harvard University Press, 1999).

[69] See certain of the comments on the ruling posted to the Jean Monnet Discussion Forum, www.jeanmonnet.org, and see the statement by several NGOs reacting to the decision: "NGOs welcome WTO Green Light to French Ban on Asbestos but remain skeptical about the WTO Dispute Settlement Process", Joint Position Statement by Greenpeace International, IBAS (International Ban Asbestos Secretariat), FIELD (Foundation for International Environmental Law and Development) and WWF (World Wide Fund for Nature, International), March 2001, www.field.org.uk.

[70] Annex I:1 TBT Agreement.

straightforward ban, the panel had to accept the EC view that the part of the decree banning asbestos and the part providing for certain limited exceptions were, in essence, two separate measures. The panel's finding that TBT did not apply was also intertwined with its finding that the measure in question was a violation of Article III:4. It regarded Article XX as the appropriate context for considering whether the ban was justified on health grounds.

The Appellate Body reversed the panel's finding that the TBT Agreement did not apply. First of all, it held that the part of the decree establishing a ban and the part providing limited exceptions had to be considered as a unified whole, not two separate measures. The AB rightly observed that the exceptions would have no legal meaning unless they operated in conjunction with a general prohibition. Secondly, the AB rejected the notion that, because the decree banned asbestos as such, it did not describe the characteristics of a product, within the meaning of the TBT Agreement. The AB noted that the French decree did not simply ban asbestos in its natural state—it banned asbestos in products. Thus, the decree did describe a characteristic of products, namely that they be free of asbestos. As the AB clearly understood, one could hardly make the applicability of the TBT Agreement depend on semantic distinctions such as whether a member creates a list of every product and then describes a characteristic of that product as the absence of asbestos rather than simply prohibiting asbestos as a characteristic of any and all products: "there may be perfectly sound administrative reasons for formulating a 'technical regulation' in a way that does *not* expressly identify products by name, but simply makes them identifiable—for instance, through the 'characteristic' that is the subject of regulation".[71] In addition to being based on empty semantics, the EC claim that the TBT Agreement does not apply to a general ban on a toxic substance in products was at odds with one of the basic purposes of the TBT Agreement, stated in the Preamble to the Agreement, namely "to ensure technical regulations and standards, . . . do not create unnecessary obstacles to trade". On the EC reading of TBT, a member could undermine this objective of TBT by simply choosing the most trade restrictive instrument of all—a general ban—and thereby avoiding any scrutiny of whether its policy instrument is an "unnecessary obstacle to trade". By adopting the most restrictive policy instrument one avoids any inquiry about whether less restrictive alternatives might be available! The panel, at least, found the TBT Agreement non-applicable on the assumption that there would be a requirement of Article XX justification; but the EC claim was utterly egregious, since the EC was also of course arguing that there was no violation of Article III:4.

Having found that the TBT Agreement did apply, the AB decided not to "complete the analysis" given that it would have to deal with so many issues of first impression not adjudicated by the panel below, with the very real possibility that applying the relevant TBT provisions would also require a different or

---

[71] Appellate Body Report, *supra* n. 16, para. 70.

more extensive factual record.[72] However, the AB did provide an important clue to how it understood the relationship between the TBT Agreement and GATT, which we will explore in the section of this chapter that follows.

THE RELATIONSHIP BETWEEN TBT AND GATT

There are several possible views concerning the relationship between TBT and GATT. One is that the TBT Agreement should be considered as a *lex specialis* to the general obligations and rights in Articles III and XX of the GATT. This would mean that, if a measure fell within the definition of a technical regulation in the TBT Agreement, its legality would be considered under that Agreement, to the exclusion of Articles III and XX of GATT. A second view is that a complainant may choose to bring a claim under *either* GATT or TBT but not both. A third view is that the obligations and rights in GATT and TBT operate concurrently, and both may apply to a single dispute, provided of course the measure falls within the ambit of some provision or provisions in both Agreements. This third view is basically consistent with the way in which, to date, panels and the Appellate Body have understood the relationship between GATT and other WTO treaties.[73]

Thus, it is not surprising that, in *Asbestos*, the Appellate Body should appear to endorse the third view, remarking that (for those measures that fall within its ambit) the TBT Agreement imposes obligations on members that seem to be *different* from, and *additional* to, the obligations imposed on members under GATT 1994.[74] Although the AB does not expand on why it takes this position on TBT, such a position in our estimation is structurally sound, and an appropriate understanding of both the GATT and the TBT Agreement, and their interrelationship. At first glance, both GATT Articles III/XX and the TBT Agreement appear to deal with the justification of domestic regulatory measures as related to legitimate (non-protectionist) objectives and as the least traderestrictive alternative reasonably available. Thus, it is tempting to conclude that, with respect to technical regulations, the TBT Agreement simply provides a more fine-tuned set of tests or criteria for achieving the same objectives as GATT Articles III/XX.

However, there are fundamental structural differences.[75] The first difference relates to the anti-protection principle, which is central to the manner in which the GATT/WTO system interacts with the domestic regulatory state. The struc-

[72] *Ibid.*, paras. 78–83.

[73] See *Bananas panel*, paras. 7.285.ff; and *Bananas AB, supra* n. 9, paras. 217.ff; see also *Canada—Periodicals AB, supra* n. 56, 19; see also Panel Report, *Indonesia—Certain Measures Affecting the Automobile Industry*, WT/DS54/R, WT/DS55/R, WT/DS64/R, 1998 (hereinafter *Indonesian Autos*). See also Davey and Zdouc, "The Triangle of TRIPs, GATT, and GATS" in *World Trade Forum* (University of Michigan Press).

[74] Appellate Body Report, *supra* n. 16, para. 80, original emphasis.

[75] See Hudec, "Requiem", *supra* n. 7.

ture represented by Articles III/XX preserves a wide field of regulatory autonomy for domestic polities (at least if correctly interpreted), by requiring that a
member has to justify its public policies before the WTO tribunal (i.e. under
XX) only *if* they have been found to be inconsistent with the anti-protection
principle (i.e. under Article III). Thus, as the AB emphasises in *Asbestos*, even if
a measure draws a regulatory distinction between products that have been
determined to be "like", there will still not be a violation of Article III:4, unless
that distinction results in less favourable treatment of the group of like imported
products relative to the group of like domestic products, i.e. unless the regulatory distinction results in *protection* of domestic production.[76] It is the judicious
application of the anti-protection norm that, in important respects, provides
assurances against the WTO Dispute Settlement Body becoming the menacing,
autocratic global government that it is feared to be by many of the system's critics. In the last analysis, if the complaining member cannot prove on balance of
probabilities that my internal regulation protects domestic production, the
WTO dispute settlement organs do not get to second-guess my sovereign regulatory choices under Article XX.[77]

Now, when we turn to the TBT Agreement, we see a quite different juridical
structure. First of all, the obligations in the TBT Agreement apply even to non-
discriminatory technical regulations. Secondly, many of the obligations in the
TBT Agreement are of a "due process" character, ensuring transparency and
integrity in the regulatory process.[78] Indeed, more generally, many features of
the TBT Agreement would appear incomprehensible, but for an appreciation of
its overall focus on regulatory processes. For example, the TBT Agreement contains MFN and National Treatment obligations[79]; these provisions would be
superfluous and inexplicable in the TBT Agreement, if that Agreement were
focused on the substance of regulations themselves, for already in Articles I and
III:4 of the GATT there are essential identical MFN and National Treatment
obligations that apply to "laws, regulations, and requirements". However, as is
indicated in the heading of Article 2 of the TBT Agreement as a whole, the MFN
and National Treatment provisions there, like the other provisions of Article 2,
are with a view to ensuring certain characteristics of the regulatory *process*,
namely the stages of the regulatory process concerning, respectively, the
"Preparation, Adoption, and Application" of technical regulations. Thus,
where the concern about the regulatory process actually entails in the TBT
Agreement some elements of judgement concerning the substance of regulations
themselves, namely, whether a member's measure is the least trade restrictive

[76] Appellate Body Report, *supra* n. 16, para. 100.

[77] A further hedge against this possibility is the sensitive interpretation of Art. XX, which we
explore in the next section of this chap. However, as Hudec notes, Art. XX places a substantial justificatory burden on the defending member, a burden that does not seem to sit well in the case of
measures that have not been found to constitute protective discrimination, but merely have *some*
kind of restrictive impact on trade: Hudec, "Requiem", *supra* n. 7.

[78] E.g. Art. 2.7 of the TBT Agreement establishes transparency requirements.

[79] Art. 2.1 TBT Agreement.

available (Article 2.2), it is the *challenging member* who must prove, on the balance of probabilities, that the regulating state has *failed* to *ensure in the regulatory process* that its measure is the least restrictive of trade. This contrasts with the character of the least restrictive means test applied under those heads of Article XX of the GATT that invoke the notion that a member's measure must be "necessary" for a stated permissible objective, where the substance of regulations must be justified by the defendant, because protection has already been determined to exist (i.e. a violation of Article III or some other provision of the GATT, for example those dealing with discriminatory border measures, for example Article XI). It is true that this burden of proof has been somewhat modified by the notion, prominent in certain cases, that once the complainant has established a "presumption" of violation, the burden shifts to the defending member.[80] However, there is no discovery available in WTO dispute settlement, so where the *complainant* cannot be expected in the first instance to have access to information that would normally allow it to make its claim, for instance detailed information about the internal workings of the defending member's regulatory processes, the burden may be shifted to the defendant once the complainant has gone as far as the tribunal thinks it *can* reasonably be expected to go in establishing its case on balance of probabilities, without being able to compel the production of evidence by the defendant.

Now, if TBT were to *replace* Articles III/XX of the GATT as a comprehensive legal regime in the case of technical regulations, the balance between market access and regulatory autonomy struck by the anti-protection principle would be undermined. On the one hand, the right created, in effect, by Articles III/XX to require that a member provide a justification before the dispute settlement organs for *protective* policies would be lost—once a *prima facie* case of protective discrimination is made out, it seems unreasonable to require the complainant to show that the policies are *not* justified as the least trade restrictive alternative. On the other hand, there is the risk that the balance could easily be tipped the other way, if the panels and Appellate Body were to understand Article 2.2 of the TBT Agreement as playing the kind of role of strict scrutiny of substantive regulatory outcomes that Article XX plays, at least where the applicable paragraph in Article XX indicates a "necessity" test. That is, even nonprotective measures could lead to a strict standard of scrutiny under Article 2.2, thus allowing the WTO dispute settlement organs to second-guess policy outcomes for which there is not even a *prima facie* case of protective discrimination.

If these are the dangers in viewing TBT as a replacement regime for Articles III/XX, how then are we instead to apply the two regimes concurrently, while making sense of both differences and similarities in language and concepts as between the two? The answer lies in some of the complexities and sensitivities involved in applying the anti-protection principle in non-facially discriminatory

---

[80] See also Appellate Body Report, *United States—Measures Affecting Imports of Woven Wool Shirts and Blouses from India*, WT/DS33/AB/R (hereinafter *US Shirts and Blouses*).

measures that nevertheless have a disparate impact on trade. If a panel were only to find a violation of Article III where a protectionist intent could clearly be established behind such measures, many cases of hidden protectionism would not be caught, and this would undermine the durability of the non-discrimination norm as a reasonable balance between market access rights and regulatory autonomy (thus, the rejection of this version of "aims and effects"). If, instead, a panel were to find violation of Article III every time there was an impact or effect on trade from a regulatory distinction not based on market criteria such as those emphasised by the panel in *Japanese Alcohol*,[81] a huge range of non-protectionist regulations would be subject to strict scrutiny under Article XX, opening up a serious threat to regulatory autonomy.

We have already explored how, through its interpretation of "likeness" and "less favourable treatment", the AB has attempted in *Asbestos* to provide a range of safeguards against this latter danger. However, it is clear that determining whether products are "like" and whether there is "less favourable treatment", i.e. protection of domestic products, entails sensitive case-by-case judgements concerning the regulatory scheme, its design, the way that distinctions are drawn within it and the relationship of those distinctions to the operation of the market-place. Such judgements can be made with greater confidence and precision if one can have the window into the regulatory process itself that TBT disciplines should provide. One can have greater confidence that the distinctions in a regulatory scheme are in fact non-protectionist, by requiring certain things about the regulatory process that itself generates those distinctions—transparency, coherence and consistency, use of international standards as "inputs", ensuring at each step of the process that the measures adopted are not more trade restrictive than necessary, given the kind of risk at issue (admittedly in this last case there is some substantive element, as the treaty text suggests that it is appropriate to analyse the results of the process in order to assess whether the obligation to "ensure" has been fulfilled). If a member has fulfilled its obligations under TBT, we can have some assurance that any non-national-origin-based regulatory distinctions that have a trade impact are, nevertheless, non-protectionist. Thus, once the complainant has failed to establish a violation of TBT, it should be well-nigh impossible for it to sustain a claim that Article III:4 is violated. Similarly, a complainant who brings a claim with respect to a technical regulation under Article III, while not making any claim of a TBT violation, will risk the panel being relatively deferential to the defending member's regulatory choices. If the complainant has not sought to impugn the regulatory process itself under TBT, it cannot object to the panel affording considerable deference to non-national-origin-based regulatory distinctions in the scheme, questioned by the complainant The implication of this is that where

[81] It will be recalled that the Appellate Body in *Japanese Alcohol* emphasised that criteria for likeness including these market-based criteria, but that the list was open-ended, with the relevant criteria depending on context, including presumably the regulatory context: AB *Japanese Alcohol*, *supra* n. 36, 21.

a regulatory scheme does not explicitly discriminate against imports, these claims will normally be brought as TBT claims. A related implication is that if, in the case of such a claim, a member happens to invoke both Article III and TBT, the panel should normally proceed in the first instance with the TBT analysis, which gives it an insight into the regulatory process. Only where the scheme provides explicit differential treatment of imports and domestic products, i.e. contains facial distinctions between products on the basis of national origin (domestic or foreign) would the panel commence with Article III:4. If, in the case of non-origin-based regulatory distinctions, there is a violation of TBT, the panel may have a view of the regulatory process that will make it more likely that an Article III:4 violation will be found, i.e. that the distinctions in question result in less favourable treatment or impacts in the sense of protection of domestic production. Of course, for reasons of judicial economy, the panel may decide, having found the measures in violation of the TBT, not to proceed to consider Article III. On the other hand, as already suggested, if the regulatory process *is* in conformity with TBT requirements, it is highly implausible that the non-national-origin regulatory distinctions generated by that process could be impugned under Article III. Of course, there will be cases where claims concerning non-facially-origin-discriminatory measures *will* be litigated under Article III, these being cases where the measure in question is not a technical regulation within the meaning of TBT (and does not fall under SPS either). But because of the broad definition of technical regulation in the TBT Agreement, most claims that are related to regulatory schemes with non-commercial or non-fiscal purposes will not be decided under Article III.

In the case of measures that do contain facial national-origin-based distinctions, a complainant may well wish to make an Article III claim, as such measures are almost certain to constitute violations of Article III, therefore placing the onus of justification on the defendant, if indeed some purpose stated under Article XX can be invoked. (Of course, as the panel stated in the *Section 337* case, it is possible that even a scheme that discriminates facially on the basis of national origin could, in certain circumstances, nevertheless "provide no less favourable" treatment to imports; however, such a facial distinction between domestic and imported products probably should suffice to make a *prima facie* case of "less favourable treatment", which would then have to be rebutted by the *defendant,* who must show that while imports are treated differently there is no protection of domestic production involved in such differentiation. But see the AB ruling in *Korea-Beef*, para. 157.) In the case of facial discrimination, however, the complainant may still wish to bring a TBT claim. Even if the defendant can justify its measures under Article XX, it may still be in violation of some specific provisions of the TBT Agreement. Of course, in the case of Article 2.2, if the defendant has born the burden of proof to show that its measures are the least trade restrictive alternative under Article XX, it is hard to imagine how the complainant could establish a violation of Article 2.2, especially since Article 2.2 requires not that the measures be the least trade restrictive reasonably available, but only the least trade restrictive taking into account the risks that the measure address. Thus, a panel would normally consider the Article 2.2 claim *res judicata* having found that the measure is the least trade restrictive reasonably available for the purpose in question. This would normally suggest the logic of the panel first considering Articles III and XX of GATT before going on to adjudicate the TBT claims. Also, since in order to bear the burden of proof for justification, which it is only reasonable for it to do given that one is dealing with a facially discriminatory measure, the defendant will be bringing forward a great deal of information about its regulatory scheme, this will obviate the difficulty the complainant normally faces under TBT of obtaining the information to prove a violation on a balance of probabilities without the ability to compel disclosure of evidence by the defendant, and thus in turn obviate the need to corrupt or modify burden of proof through the notion of shifting presumptions. Then, after the Article XX analysis, the panel can go on to consider any TBT claims not *res judicata* in consequence of that analysis. Of course, if the defendant is unsuccessful under Article XX, the panel may, on judicial economy grounds, decide not to proceed to the TBT claims, as the measure has already been found in violation of a WTO treaty.

THE *ASBESTOS* DISPUTE AND THE OPERATIVE PROVISIONS OF THE TBT AGREEMENT

We have argued above that, in many respects, the TBT Agreement can be seen as a response to the delicate task of adjudicating claims about *de facto* discrimination in regulations with non-commercial or non-fiscal rationales. The TBT Agreement focuses largely on the regulatory process and its inputs, which involves necessarily *some* examination of the substantive regulatory choices of democratic polities, but avoids WTO tribunals sitting in *de novo* review of non-facially discriminatory policies, against which there is no general presumption in WTO law (unlike facially discriminatory trade restricting measures). The Preamble to the TBT Agreement reflects in a number of its provisions this view of the Agreement. Thus the Members recognise that "no country should be prevented from taking measures necessary to ensure the quality of its exports, or for the protection of human animal or plant life or health, of the environment, or for the prevention of deceptive practices, at the levels it considers appropriate, subject to the requirement that they are not applied in a manner which would constitute a means of arbitrary or unjustifiable discrimination between countries where the same conditions prevail or a disguised restriction on international trade, and are otherwise in accordance with the provisions of this Agreement". This provision can make sense only if nothing *per se* in the TBT Agreement prevents a member from choosing its appropriate level of protection. Otherwise, the provision would have the following, (il)logical structure: no country shall be prevented from doing x, provided it does not do x.

More generally, this crucial provision in the Preamble states the view that the provisions of the TBT Agreement represent a set of specific and limited qualifications to members' general presumed right to regulate as they see fit for the purposes in question—or, to put it the other way round, the Agreement does not set up a general presumption against such regulations as trade barriers, which must then be scrutinised to see if they fit within certain exceptions. The provisions of the TBT Agreement must, then, not be interpreted so broadly as to nullify or fundamentally frustrate the core right to regulate as recognised in the Preamble—they merely place some conditions or qualifications on the exercise of that right.

Article 2.2 is perhaps the provision of the TBT Agreement that most clearly brings into the assessment of a member's regulatory process an element of judgement or scrutiny of its substantive regulatory outcomes. The first sentence of Article 2.2 states an obligation of members with respect to the regulatory process: they must "*ensure* that technical regulations are not prepared, adopted or applied with a view to or with the effect of creating unnecessary obstacles to international trade"(emphasis added). The second sentence indicates that this obligation to "ensure" is to be judged against the substantive results of the regulatory process. It reads: "[f]or this purpose technical regulations shall not be more trade-restrictive than necessary to fulfill a legitimate objective, taking account of the risks non-fulfillment would create". After stating a list of legitimate objectives that is non-exhaustive the provision closes with the following sentence: "[i]n assessing such risks relevant elements of consideration are, *inter alia*, available scientific and technical information, related processing technology or intended end-uses of products". These various qualifications on the substantive criterion that regulations be the least trade restrictive necessary, distinguish the TBT Agreement sharply from the strict scrutiny regime established by Art. XX of the GATT for presumptively discriminatory measures, at least with respect to measures concerned with human life and health (Art. XX (b)).[82] The qualifications remind us that the substantive criterion is with a view, not so much to justifying the measures themselves (being presumptively legitimate, they do not require a justification), but to evaluating the regulatory process that has produced the measures. Thus, the obligation to ensure the least

---

[82] Note that not all of the heads in Art. XX require a "necessity test" as developed by the panel in *Thai Cigarette* for Art. XX (b) which reads, "necessary to protect human, animal or plant life or health": *Thailand—Restrictions on Importation of and Internal Taxes on Cigarettes*, BISD 34S (hereinafter *Thai Cigarette*). Other cases addressed Art. XX (g) which deals with measures "relating to the conservation of exhaustible natural resources". In *Reformulated Gasoline*, the Appellate Body stated for a measure to qualify as "relating to" within the meaning of Art. XX (g), the measures had to exhibit a "substantial relationship" with the conservation of natural resources. See Appellate Body Report in *United States—Standards for Reformulated and Conventional Gasoline*, WT/DS2, 20 May 1996 (hereinafter *Reformulated Gasoline*), 21. In *Shrimp/Turtle*, the Appellate Body stated that the US measure exhibited a "means/ends relationship" with the legitimate policy of conserving an exhaustible and endangered species. See Appellate Body Report, *United States—Import Prohibition of Certain Shrimps and Shrimp Products*, 6 November 1998 (hereinafter *Shrimp/Turtle*) para. 135.

trade-restrictiveness of regulations is relative to the kinds of risks that would arise in the absence of the regulations. Deliberation about the choice of regulatory instrument can be a costly and time-consuming process. How far a member should be expected to go in exhausting all the regulatory alternatives to find the least trade-restrictive alternative is logically related to the kind of risk it is dealing with. Where what is at stake is a well-established risk to human life itself (as we will argue, this is exactly the case with asbestos), a member may be expected to act rapidly, rely on the scientific *acquis* to a large extent, tending towards the more obviously effective and enforceable kinds of regulatory tools, as opposed to the more sophisticated and speculative ones. This suggests the concept of the Precautionary Principle, as articulated by the Appellate Body in *Hormones*: "responsible, representative governments commonly act from perspectives of prudence and precaution where risks of *irreversible, e.g. life-terminating, damage to human health* are concerned"[83] (emphasis added). While, as the AB has noted in *Asbestos,* TBT obligations are "different" from those in GATT,[84] nevertheless it is significant that in its Article XX analysis, not needing to decide the case at bar, the AB considered that the value at stake in the case of *Asbestos* "is both vital and important in the highest degree".[85]

In its submissions to the panel, Canada claimed that France's measure was not rationally related to the objective of protecting health and life, as well as that it is not the least trade restrictive available to fulfill the objective.[86] As the EC suggested in its reply brief, there was, however, no textual basis in Article 2.2 for separately assessing whether a measure is rationally related to its objective. In fact, Canada's arguments about the lack of rational basis for the French ban were essentially identical to its arguments that it is not the least trade-restrictive measure available to fulfill the objective in question.

Canada's first argument was that France had acted on the basis of the historical information about the risks posed by asbestos, and this historical information did not isolate the particular kind of asbestos fibre exported by Canada, chrysotile. According to Canada the health risks that had materialised in the past are in large measure due to the use of asbestos fibres other than chrysotile, which (according to Canada) is in fact safe when used in an appropriate manner.

Given the overwhelming evidence of the serious risks to life and health posed by exposure to asbestos in general, should the TBT Agreement be interpreted as requiring that France, in order to ensure that its measure is the least restrictive of trade available, attempt to undertake new empirical work, which aims to isolate the risks posed by chrysotile, in order to determine whether France could achieve its health objective while not banning this particular form of asbestos? Here, it is important to note that Article 2.2 explicitly lists among the relevant elements of consideration in assessing risk, "*available* scientific and technical

---

[83] See *Hormones* AB, *supra* n. 3, para. 124.
[84] Appellate Body Report, *supra* n. 16, para. 80.
[85] *Ibid.*, para. 172.
[86] Canada, first submission *supra* n. 26, paras. 201 ff.

information" (emphasis added). The TBT Agreement itself appears explicitly to endorse reliance on existing, available information in the assessment of risk. Even in interpreting Article XX, which has no such explicit reference to "available" information, the Appellate Body in *Asbestos* held that France could not be expected to adopt a less trade-restrictive alternative that was as yet unproven in effectiveness.[87]

The *Asbestos* case is a good example of the wisdom of focusing on available information. It is true that the historical evidence of the serious risk to life and health from asbestos reflects data on exposure to many kinds of asbestos, especially those other than chrysotile. However, since the health risks from asbestos have typically taken a long time after exposure to manifest themselves, to do what Canada expects would entail a strategy of waiting until there is inconvertible evidence that chrysotile alone poses the health risks in question, before banning its use. It seems to amount to a nullification of a member's sovereign prerogative to protect the health and life of its citizens (which is also an *obligation* of most WTO states under international human rights law[88]), if it had to wait until a significant number of its citizens became sick or died from exposure to chrysotile in particular, before banning this substance.

In fact, chrysotile as a substance has the same basic properties as other types of asbestos. Canada's argument that it is harmless really reduces to a claim that the way in which, today, chrysotile is encased in building materials and used in accordance with safe procedures renders it harmless.[89] Here, Canada was suggesting that the EC (France) had violated Article 2.2, because it could have attained its objective merely through requiring safe use of chrysotile, a less trade-restrictive alternative.

To what extent does Article 2.2 require a member to adopt a less restrictive alternative regardless of the costs and feasibility of that alternative? Unlike the parallel provision in the SPS Agreement, Article 5.6, and its footnote 3, Article 2.2 does not explicitly state that least restrictive means least restrictive measure "reasonable available taking into account technical and economic feasibility". Yet such an explicit reference in Article 2.2 is not really necessary to capture the notion that regulatory costs of alternative policy alternatives should be taken into account. This is because Article 2.2 contains a much more general qualification on the notion of least restrictive alternative—that the alternative be least restrictive "taking into account the risks non-fulfillment would create". As the Appellate Body clarified in *Hormones*, the notion of risk and risk assessment does not go only to the risks as they emerge under ideal or laboratory conditions, but risks that arise due to limits on the ability to control the way a

[87] Appellate Body Report, *supra* n. 16, para. 174.

[88] See right to life in civil and political covenants and WHO declaration on right to health.

[89] Canada first submission, *supra* n. 26, para. 73 ff: "*Effets sur la santé des principaux types d'exposition à l'amiante*," Institut National de la Santé et de la recherche Médical, Paris, éditions (INSERM: Collection Expertises Collectives, 1997).

product is used.[90] This finding in *Hormones* applies *a fortiori* to the conception of assessing risks under Article 2.2, where the factors to be taken into account have pointedly been left-open-ended, "available scientific and technical information" being only one among them.[91] The European Communities argue, in the *Asbestos* case, that there are significant obstacles to ensuring that chrysotile is "used" in such a way as to obviate serious risks to health and life. "Safe use" as understood by Canada applies only to the installation of components containing chrysotile in the construction process. Even if perfectly enforced, such protocols would not obviate the risks to maintenance workers, much less to do-it-yourself renovators. As the EC argues, devising a regulatory scheme that would protect these potential victims through behavioural protocols would be extremely difficult, at least relative to a straightforward ban on the substance. Here, again, it is worth noting that, for purposes of Art. XX, where the treaty text itself does not have the qualifying language "taking into account the risks non-fulfillment would create", the AB accepted, based upon the facts found by the panel, that in circumstances such as these the alternative measure of controlled use could not be viewed as achieving France's stated level of protection.[92]

Of course, almost any alternative to a ban in most cases will present some significant regulatory challenges and costs. There is a limited number of producers and suppliers of asbestos within Europe and outside. Effectively enforcing the ban would not seem to be very difficult. But, it might be objected, if less-restrictive regulatory options to an outright ban are often going to have higher regulatory costs, would not taking those costs into account under Article 2.2 render the obligation to adopt the least trade-restrictive alternative largely

[90] See *Hormones* AB, *supra* n. 3, para. 187, reading that risks is also "the risk in human societies as they actually exist, in other words, the actual potential for adverse effects on human health in the real world where people live and work and die".

[91] There are some who interpret the language "taking into account the risks non-fulfillment would create" as imposing an additional requirement on the defending Member, namely that the measure not only be the least restrictive of trade, but that it also be proportional, namely that the marginally greater risk of a less trade restrictive measure would need to be balanced against the decree to which the it is less trade restrictive. This is apparently the position of Hudec, "Requiem", *supra* n. 7. However, this interpretation is inconsistent with the structure and purposes of the TBT Agreement. First of all, if a Member had to live with a measure that does not fully realise its policy objective, because that measure is much less trade restrictive than one that realises the objective fully, then a member's fundamental right to determine its appropriate level of protection would be undermined, if not gutted. A member *could* not, in effect, set a level of protection that *required* a very high level of trade restrictiveness for its full realisation. This in turn would make the least restrictive means test in TBT much more intrusive of domestic sovereignty than the test in Art. XX(b), e.g., especially as interpreted by the AB in both *Korea-Beef* and *Asbestos* (see the discussion below at pages 321 ff). That result is obviously perverse, given that the TBT Agreement applies to measures that have not yet been found to be protective, whereas Art. XX will apply in these situations only where protective discrimination, and thus a violation of Art. III:4, has already been established. Our interpretation that the language concerning taking into account the risks non-fulfillment would create provides an additional margin of appreciation to domestic regulators is, by contrast, entirely consistent with the structural differences between the two Agreements, particularly the notion that many measures considered under TBT do not carry the presumption of protective discrimination, unlike Art. XX.

[92] Appellate Body Report, *supra* n. 16, para. 174.

meaningless? Here, however, the language "taking into account the risks non-fulfillment will create" is very important. No risk management scheme will be so perfectly applied and enforced as to reduce risk to zero; thus, if the objective is zero risk then a ban will almost always be the least restrictive alternative (at least assuming relatively few enforcement problems with the ban itself). Thus, at one level, Canada may be justified in suggesting that the TBT Agreement does not allow a member to set its regulations according to the principle of reducing risk to zero,[93] for if so "the least restrictive alternative" obligation could be reduced to something largely meaningless. However, in some cases where risk *management*, at least any available at reasonable cost, is inadequate to prevent the risk materialising, the consequences may not be particularly grave or serious. In those cases, "taking into account the risks that non-fulfillment would create", it might be reasonable for a member to adopt the risk management scheme, despite its imperfections, since those imperfections minimally impair its ability to protect the health and lives of its citizens.[94] In other situations, however, such as that in the *Asbestos* case, where imperfect control of the risk through risk management is likely to result in consequences as serious as life-threatening cancer, not to permit an outright ban as the "least restrictive measure" would impair the very ability of a member to exercise its prerogative (and fulfill its international human rights obligation) to protect the right to life of its citizens. Once interests of this kind of gravity are clearly seen to be at stake, a member need not be required to adopt a less restrictive policy instrument that provides less certain or perfect control of the risk, even by a small margin, despite the possibility that the less restrictive instrument would be *hugely* less restrictive of trade—there is no place for balancing or proportionality analysis. This is consistent with the recognition, in the Preamble to the TBT Agreement, that the provisions of the Agreement do not nullify the basic prerogative to protect the health and life of one's citizens. This being said, a ban on asbestos, while being more restrictive of Canada's trade in asbestos than a measure that banned asbestos only where it was proven that substitutes were less safe than asbestos, might not thereby be less restrictive of trade overall. Substitute fibres are also traded products. To establish trade-restrictiveness in this instance, Canada would have to show that there are barriers to trade in the substitute products, such that any reduction in asbestos trade would not be compensated for by increased trade in substitutes.

A further claim by Canada is that the substitutes for asbestos have not been proven safe—it might turn out that the health and safety objective is actually undermined by a ban on asbestos, if the substituted substances turn out to be harmful or more harmful than chrysotile asbestos itself. In effect, Canada is saying that a less restrictive alternative would be to require that asbestos

[93]   Canada, second submission, *supra* n. 26, paras. 225ff.
[94]   See the observation of the Appellate Body with respect to Art. XX in the *Korea-Beef* case, *infra* n. 99, para. 180

substitutes be used, only when it has been demonstrated that these are safe, or safer than asbestos itself.

The limits of *ex ante* risk prevention through prediction of risks based on testing and experimentation prior to sale in the market-place are, in the case of many risks, quite substantial. This is obviously the case with respect to carcinogenic risks, where it may take years of exposure to a substance before a cancer actually materialises. In the case of ingested substances, one means by which this problem is obviated is the exposure of laboratory animals to levels of the substance that are comparable to that which humans would have over a significant length of time. However, this is of course an imperfect substitute for actual historical epidemiological studies of human populations. Thus, regulation of carcinogenic risks generally displays a strong bias towards those risks that are already known or have materialised in actual use of the substance in the real world. Here, France has weighed the benefit of countering a massively documented risk against the cost of creating a hypothetical and unknown one (whatever risks might be created from the use of substitute fibres). Its decision reflects the heuristics of choice under uncertainty that underlie almost all risk regulation. In rejecting the version of its claim on this issue that Canada made in its Article XX submissions, the AB accepted that members have the right to act on the basis of available information concerning relative riskiness of products: "it seems to us perfectly legitimate for a Member to seek to halt the spread of a highly risky product while allowing the use of a less risky product in its place".[95]

This being said, France has attempted to craft its decree to take account of the possibility that substitute products may not always be less safe than asbestos—thus, there is an exception from the ban in cases where *"l'utlilisation de produit de substitution ne présent pas, en l'état actuel des connaissances scientifiques, un risque moindre pour la santé des travailleurs"*.[96]

Article 2.3 of the TBT Agreement states: "[t]echnical regulations shall not be maintained if the circumstances or objectives giving rise to their adoption no longer exist or if the changed circumstances or objectives can be addressed in a less trade-restrictive manner". This provision reflects in part the realisation that, in regulating, members necessarily make use of the information available at the time they are formulating their regulations. So, if scientific information becomes available that substitute products are as risky or more so than asbestos, and it nevertheless continues to target asbestos only, France may be in violation of Article 2.3. However, the exception in the decree seems well designed to take into account possible developments in the scientific evidence concerning the relative risks posed by asbestos on the one hand and substitute fibres on the other. Taken together, Article 2.2 and 2.3 expresses a finely balanced notion of precaution: a member can base its regulations on the existing, actual evidence of risk, without waiting for a perfect or comprehensive understanding of the risks

---

[95] Appellate Body Report, *supra* n. 16, para. 168.
[96] Decree No 96–1133 of 24 December 1996, Art. 2: see *supra* n. 21.

at issue; on the other hand, when, in the future, there are relevant changes in circumstances, it must revisit its regulatory choices.

ARTICLE 2.4: THE OBLIGATION TO MAKE USE OF INTERNATIONAL
STANDARDS WHERE AVAILABLE

There is a wide range of areas where incompatible technical specifications exist merely by virtue of the historical development of individual national standards systems, and where the differences do not reflect underlying differences in values, attitudes towards risk, or policy priorities. One example that comes to the mind of any frequent traveller between North America and Europe is the size and shape of electrical plugs and phone jacks! One suspects that the persistence of such differences is due either to path dependency, or protectionism, or perhaps a bit of both. Here, as is recognised in the TBT Agreement, international standardisation, in harmonising these gratuitously incompatible requirements, can play an important role in eliminating unnecessary obstacles to trade. Thus Article 2.4 of the TBT Agreement requires the use of international standards "as a basis for" technical regulations, in cases where the use of those standards does not negatively affect the legitimate objectives that a member is seeking to achieve.

In the case of asbestos, there is widespread recognition by international organisations with standards development responsibilities in the areas of occupational health and safety (the International Labour Organisation) and health (the World Health Organisation) that asbestos exposure represents a grave health risk and that governments should take measures to eliminate such exposure. Thus ILO Convention No. 162 recommends, wherever possible, "[the] replacement of asbestos or of certain types of asbestos or products containing asbestos by other materials or products or the use of alternative technology, scientifically evaluated by the competent authority as harmless or less harmful".[97] More specific to the kind of asbestos that Canada exports, the WHO communiqué states that consideration should be given to replacing chrysotile by harmless substitute materials wherever possible.

In banning the use of asbestos, except where there are no safer or technically feasible alternatives, the French decree seems to track very closely the approach to asbestos as a health risk taken by these international standards organisations. However, Canada claimed that the French ban is not consistent with international standards, because there are international standards that specify procedures for the manufacture and use of asbestos in a manner that minimises health risks.[98] But the existence of international standards to make the risk from

---

[97] ILO Convention No. 162 Art. 10 (a).

[98] Canada also claims that France is not following international standards, since the ILO Convention specifies that substitute materials must be scientifically verified as safe. However, France notes in its submission that substitute products must also be tested and their safety verified

asbestos as small as possible is entirely compatible with the basic approach of the international standards bodies that the use of asbestos should be discontinued as soon as possible, except where technically feasible, safer alternatives do not exist. There will remain situations where asbestos is still used, either because of the need for a phase-out period of some length to allow the relevant industries to adjust their practices, find alternatives, etc. or where there are not technically available, safer alternatives. In those situations, standards to make asbestos as safe as possible will play an important role in reducing the remaining health risk.

The EC sought to counter Canada's claim, however, by the argument that the declarations of international standards bodies in this area are merely statements about the risk from asbestos and do not amount to "standards" within the meaning of the TBT Agreement. The definition of "standard" in Annex I to the TBT Agreement is, however, quite broad, including "rules, guidelines, or characteristics for products or related processes and production methods", *inter alia*. It is difficult to understand how a recommendation to replace asbestos with safer materials whenever possible would not amount to a guideline for products, even if there were some question whether it could rise to the status of a "rule", given that there is some flexibility built into the recommendations in question.

ARTICLE XX (B)

In its notice of appeal, Canada also challenged the panel's ruling that, although a violation of Article III:4, the French ban was justified under the GATT's exception for measures to "protect human . . . life or health". Specifically, Canada argued that the panel had committed errors of law in its interpretation of Article XX (b), developing a too deferential and permissive reading of the GATT's general exception. The Appellate Body, having found that the French ban did not violate Article III: 4 GATT, could, for reasons of judicial economy, have decided not to rule on this issue. Nevertheless, it decided to address the Canadian claims, using this as an opportunity to clarify some important issues relating to Article XX (b), establishing a more deferential approach, sensitive to members' regulatory choices and domestic regulations that address vital health interests. In examining the panel's approach to Article XX (b), the AB adopted a two-step approach. In a first step, it addressed the question whether the French ban was indeed directed at the objectives cited in Article XX (b), notably in this case to protect human health. In a second step, it examined whether the measure

by national or international bodies: EC first submission, *supra* n. 18, paras. 249ff, 279 ff. France does not have a unified regulatory regime it appears for testing asbestos substitutes—but nor does the ILO Convention require this—it requires only that the substitute materials themselves be subject to verification for safety, which normally occurs within the standards regime applicable to the industry in question.

at issue was "necessary" to achieve the specific public policy goal, a level of protection against health risk. This approach is in line with previous decisions on measures falling under some of the individual subheadings of Article XX.[99]

In its first step, when analysing whether the panel was right in concluding that the French ban fell within the category of measures embraced by Article XX (b) of the GATT 1994, the AB found that "the panel remained well within the bounds of its discretion in finding that chrysotile-cement products pose a risk to human life or health".[100] For reaching its decision, the panel had to weigh evidence on whether the French ban was designed to *protect* health. It did this in line with *Thai Cigarette*, which had established that "the use of the word 'protection' implies the existence of a risk" and that this consequently meant that a panel had to begin its analysis "by identifying a risk for public health".[101] Thus, if there were no evidence that asbestos posed a risk to human health, then a ban on asbestos would not appear to be designed to protect health. In case of asbestos however, its deadly and carcinogenic characteristics are well and widely recognised, by the consulted scientists and by the relevant international bodies. This more than ample evidence on the dangers of asbestos allowed the panel to conclude that the measure was designed to protect health, and the Appellate Body upheld the panel's finding on that.[102]

However, neither the AB nor the panel said anything about *how much* evidence of health risks is needed to regard a measure as "for the protection of health". Arguably, this risk requirement should be *de minimis*, i.e. the minimum needed to assert with some plausibility that the measure is directed towards the goal of protecting health. With respect to asbestos, the health aspect was, as noted, obvious. In other cases, panels may have to come to grips with measures that respond to less orthodox conceptions of "health"—for instance, conceptions that only "organic" food products are healthy, which are not underpinned by conventional scientific understandings, but reflect more holistic views of human health as implying harmony with natural processes. Here a panel should arguably defer to measures that are taken pursuant to such appreciations of the nature of human health, where the structure and design of the scheme are consistent with it being directed towards such a conception of health, as opposed to some other policy purpose. At the same time, it would obviously be appropri-

---

[99] E.g., in *Korea Beef*, the Appellate Body had stated that "[f]or a measure, otherwise inconsistent with GATT 1994, to be justified provisionally under paragraph (d) of Art. XX, two elements must be shown. First, the measure must be one designed to 'secure compliance' with laws or regulations that are not themselves inconsistent with some provisions of the GATT 1994. Second, the measure must be 'necessary' to secure such compliance": (see Appellate Body Report, *Korea— Measures Affecting Imports of Fresh, Chilled and Frozen Beef*, WT/DS161/AB/R, 11 December 2000 (hereinafter *Korea-Beef* Appellate Body Report) para. 157. The Appellate Body also took a similar approach in *Shrimp/Turtle*, where it first determined that sea turtles were "exhaustible natural resources" and then concluded that the US measure was "related to" the goal of conserving exhaustible natural resources as required by Art. XX (g): see *Shrimp/Turtle*, *supra* n. 82, para. 135.

[100] Appellate Body Report, *supra* n. 16, para. 162.

[101] Panel Report, *supra* n. 13, para. 8.184.

[102] Appellate Body Report, *supra* n. 16, para. 163.

ate, in considering the meaning of health, for the panel, pursuant to Article 31 of the Vienna Convention,[103] to consider definitions of the notion of health, and health risks, in international health law and policy, especially reflected in legal instruments and related policy statements of the World Health Organisation.

Having found that the French ban was a measure that protected human life or health within the meaning of Article XX(b), the panel went on to evaluate the "necessity" of the measure. Canada appealed the panel's "necessity" analysis on four grounds,[104] but here again the AB upheld the panel's findings, concluding that there was no "reasonably available alternative" to the prohibition of the French import ban and, therefore, that the French measure was "necessary to protect human health" within the meaning of Article XX (b). The AB's reasoning is interesting for a series of aspects.

First, the AB made it very clear that it is each WTO member's "right to determine the level of protection of health that [it] consider[s] appropriate in a given situation".[105] France had decided that it wanted to "halt" the spread of asbestos-related health risk, and the AB accepted its goal of reducing these health risks to zero. Here, the AB rejected categorically the notion that a member's right to determine its level of protection should be subject to considerations of proportionality. Thus, a member may choose zero risk as its goal even though, if it had chosen a slightly less ambitious goal, that goal could have been achieved with a vastly less trade-restrictive policy instrument. In effect, as long as it declares its goal as zero risk, a member can be fully justified in its choice of a highly trade-restrictive instrument that achieves 100 per cent reduction in risk, even where the member could achieve a 98 or 99 per cent reduction of risk through a policy instrument that was not trade-restrictive at all. This outcome respects the hierarchy of norms reflected in Article XX— health trumps liberal trade as a value, in the presence of any genuine conflict between the two.[106] However, one must consider this finding in tandem with a related finding, in *Korea-Beef*, that a member will not easily persuade the panel that its objective is zero risk if the policy instrument it chooses is structurally incapable of achieving that objective.[107]

Another significant finding of the AB in addressing Canada's claims on appeal in *Asbestos* is that a member may single out the elimination of one kind of health

[103] Vienna Convention on the Law of Treaties, 23 May 1969, 1155 UNTS 331, 8 ILM 679 (hereinafter Vienna Convention).

[104] Appellate Body Report, *supra* n. 16, para.165.

[105] *Ibid.*, para. 168.

[106] One of the clearest textual indicators of such a hierarchy is the general operative clause of Art. XX, stipulating that "*Nothing* in this Agreement shall prevent" measures for the purposes indicated in the various heads of Art. XX (emphasis added).

[107] "We think it is unlikely that Korea intended to establish a level of protection that *totally eliminates* fraud with respect to the origin of beef (domestic or foreign) sold by retailers. The total elimination of fraud would probably require a total ban of imports. Consequently we assume Korea intended to *reduce considerably* the number of cases of fraud occurring with respect to the origin of beef sold by retailers": *Korea Beef*, *supra* n. 99, para. 178. As this passage indicates, and as the AB reiterates in *Asbestos*, the level of protection need not be articulated in quantitative terms.

risk as its objective, even if it chooses not to take regulatory action against certain other risks. Thus, France can have as an objective zero risk from asbestos, while not necessarily having such an objective with respect to the risks posed by substitute products. This approach accepts that there is a wide range of social, economic and cultural factors that may affect a member's level of protection, other than the gravity of the consequences from materialisation of the risk. The fact that in banning asbestos France is permitting the use of substitute products that may also pose some risk to health does not compromise its choice of zero risk as the level of protection against *asbestos*-related health risks. If France were prevented in those circumstances from making such a choice of level of protection, this would be to compromise what the AB rightly identifies as the entirely acceptable strategy of "seek[ing] to halt the spread of a highly risky product while allowing the use of a less risky product in place".[108] Moreover, France could set its level of protection, and respective approaches to asbestos-containing and substitute products based on *existing* scientific evidence of the relative risks of the two. Before seeking to eliminate the risk from asbestos, it was not required to investigate exhaustively the risks from the use of substitutes.

Having thus established France's chosen level of protection, the AB went on to consider the meaning of "necessary" in Article XX(b). Canada claimed that the ban on chrysotile asbestos was not "necessary", since a less trade-restrictive measure, a "safe use" regime, was available to achieve France's chosen level of protection. In considering Canada's claim, the AB, on the one hand, approved the test in the GATT *acquis* for necessity, namely whether there is a reasonably available alternative less restrictive of trade. On the other hand, the AB referred to its judgment in *Korea-Beef*, where certain refinements were introduced to that test.

In *Korea-Beef*, the AB had observed that while one meaning of "necessary" in ordinary language is "indispensable", this is not the only meaning.[109] One can coherently speak of it having been necessary to do something, without the very strong implication that no other choice was available at all. However, even this less strict notion of necessity is much closer to the idea of the action being indispensable than to the idea that it merely makes a contribution to the goal or objective in question.

The AB thus bifurcates the necessity test. There are situations where the claim may be that a measure is indispensable, i.e the only available measure to achieve a member's chosen level of protection, and there are other situations in which a member may be able to justify its measure as "necessary" within the meaning of Article XX, even if the fit is not *that* close. In these latter situations, determining whether the admittedly not indispensable measure is nevertheless "necessary", "involves in every case a process of weighing and balancing a series of factors which prominently include the contribution made by the compliance

---

[108] Appellate Body Report, *supra* n. 16, para. 168.
[109] *Korea Beef*, *supra* n. 99, para. 161.

measure to the enforcement of the law or regulation at issue, the importance of the common interests or values protected by that law or regulation, and the accompanying impact of the law or regulation on imports or exports".[110] Thus, the AB introduces an alternative, less strict proportionality test into those heads of Article XX, where the word "necessary" is found. What it is crucial to understand, however, is that the AB does not introduce proportionality as an *additional* requirement where the measure is indispensable—a measure that is indispensable for achieving a member's chosen level of protection will be "necessary", regardless of it being vastly more trade-restrictive than the next less trade restrictive alternative,[111] and regardless of whether the next less trade-restrictive alternative comes very close to achieving the member's chosen level of protection. Thus, although it is introducing balancing or proportionality analysis into Article XX, the AB is nevertheless preserving the hierarchy of norms reflected in Article XX. In fact it is introducing balancing so as to provide members with an *additional* "margin of appreciation" in making regulatory choices to achieve the purposes stated in those provisions of Article XX that entail a necessity test.

In *Asbestos*, the AB has further refined the necessity test in Article XX. Since in *Asbestos*, France's claim, logically enough, was that no measure other than a ban could achieve its chosen level of protection, namely zero asbestos-related risk, and the AB accepted that claim, this was a case where the measure was claimed to be, and was found to be, "indispensable". Thus, the AB did not have to go on to engage in the kind of balancing that was discussed in *Korea-Beef*. What the AB did do however was to suggest that there may be differing levels of scrutiny applicable to the analysis of whether a measure is *indispensable*, depending on the importance of the objectives or interests it serves. Thus, it noted that a factor held to be of importance in *Korea-Beef* in conducting a proportionality analysis pursuant to the less strict branch of the necessity test, might be more generally relevant to the ease with which a panel is prepared to find a measure "necessary". In other words, the importance of the values and interests at stake will also operate to determine the level of scrutiny when a panel is considering a claim that the measure is "indispensable" to achieve a member's chosen level of protection.[112] Here, the AB went on to assert: "in this

---

[110] *Ibid.*, para. 164.

[111] Here, it is important to be clear on the precise language in *Korea-Beef*, especially since the AB in para. 172 of *Asbestos* refers to balancing in *Korea-Beef* in a rather loose way that could mislead the reader into thinking it is going to go on to balance in *Asbestos*. The AB said in *Korea-Beef*: "in sum, determination of whether a measure, *which is not 'indispensable'*, may be 'necessary' within the contemplation of Art. XX(d), involves in every case a process of weighing and balancing" (emphasis added).

[112] One frequent criticism of the AB rulings in *Gasoline* and *Shrimp/Turtle*, *supra* n. 82, which held that the language "relating to [exhaustible natural resources]" in Art. XX(g) implied a looser fit than the necessity language in Art. XX (b), was that the AB was actually saying, apparently perversely, that it is easier to justify protecting turtles or dolphins than protecting human lives. One could see the introduction of levels of scrutiny into the analysis of whether a measure is necessary under Art. XX, with especially deferential scrutiny for measures to protect human life from deadly

case, the objective pursued by the measure is the preservation of human life and health through the elimination, or reduction of the well-known, and life-threatening, health risks posed by asbestos fibres. The value pursued is both vital and important in the highest degree".[113]

In judging the relative importance of various objectives contained in Article XX, the AB appears to be altering, or at least supplementing, the hierarchy of norms in the treaty. The intuitive appeal of the notion that health is a vitally important objective, and our annoyance at the way in which the panel was dismissive of health under Article III:4, should not blind us to the ramifications of the interpretive move the AB is making here. One appealing view of Article XX is that it deals with the potential tension between trade liberalisation and other values, through a series of provisions that scrutinise the relation of means to ends, rather than the value of the ends pursued themselves, provided those ends fall within a discrete head of Article XX. Does the AB really have the legitimacy to say to a society that, for instance, the pursuit of religious purity or piety is a less compelling objective than the protection of human health? Does it have the *bona fides* to make a determination that the rights of people count for more than the "rights" of animals? We would suggest that to remain consistent with its role as a treaty interpreter under Article 31 of the *Vienna Convention*, whenever the AB is hierarchising objectives within the heads of Article XX, it must do so following the hierarchies implicit or explicit in international law more generally. In defence of the Appellate Body, it had already cited a statements alluding to international health law and policy materials early in its judgment,[114] which suggested wide international recognition of the gravity of France's objective. This being said, the implications for democratic self-determination of the AB hiearchising objectives are attenuated, if only somewhat, by the fact that it is doing so in order to provide, in certain cases, a greater "margin of appreciation" to members.

How then does this greater "margin of appreciation" figure in the AB's rejection of the Canadian claim that "safe use" is a reasonably available alternative measure? The AB makes several observations about this claim. The first is that "safe use" is not a well-tested alternative, the efficacy of which is already

---

risks, as an indirect answer to this criticism. Of course, the criticism is not in itself very well taken—it ignores that there is additional hurdle under Art. XX(g) that does not exist under Art. XX(b), namely that the measures must be taken in conjunction with restrictions on domestic consumption or production. See *Reformulated Gasoline, supra* n. 82.

[113] An alternative interpretation of what the AB is doing here is that it is saying that there are some interests that are so vital that we simply ignore the distinction between "indispensable" and "necessary" in the looser sense, and simply proceed to the analysis of alternative measures, without balancing, but with a lower or relaxed level of scrutiny. The AB's observation that "France could not reasonably be expected to employ *any* alternative measure if that measure would involve a continuation of the very risk that the Decree seeks to 'halt' " indicates that no balancing or proportionality analysis is being undertaken here, whether because of the importance of the interest at stake or because this is in essence a claim for indispensibility within the meaning of *Korea-Beef, supra* n. 99, para. 174.

[114] Appellate Body Report, *supra* n. 16, para. 114.

demonstrated; this is on the basis of the scientific record before the panel. The second is that there is some actual scientific evidence that available "safe use" procedures still leave some residual risk from asbestos. The third is that "safe use", even if it did effectively protect against these risks in some contexts, would be particularly doubtful in other contexts, those such as do-it-yourself home renovations or the building industry, of the greatest importance to France. Here, the AB makes it clear that a member is under no obligation to attempt to achieve its level of protection using alternatives which lack certainty of effectiveness, before having recourse to a more, and indeed much more, trade-restrictive option. This clearly reverses the tendency, visible in the *Thai Cigarette* case for example, to have a member's measure fail the necessity test if there is some hypothetical less trade-restrictive alternative available, which *may* or *might* be effective in the circumstances. In *Thai Cigarette*, the panel was considering a ban on foreign cigarettes by Thailand, which was concerned about the sophisticated techniques tobacco multinationals use to market such cigarettes among young people in particular, creating new generations of tobacco addicts. The panel determined that various kinds of regulation on the marketing and advertising activities of these multinationals were "reasonably available" less restrictive alternatives, despite evidence on the panel record from the World Health Organisation that it had proved impossible for developing countries, in a number of cases, to achieve their objectives by regulating multinationals in this manner. The corporations tended to find ways of circumventing such regulatory efforts. Applying the "margin of appreciation" in *Asbestos* to these facts, it seems almost certain that the Article XX(b) issue would have been decided the other way by the Appellate Body, as in *Thai Cigarette* the efficacy of the suggested alternatives certainly remained to be demonstrated, especially in the context in which they would be applied.

CONCLUSION

In *Asbestos*, the Appellate Body of the WTO has introduced many important refinements in the interpretation and application of key provisions of the GATT that address the relationship of WTO law to internal regulation. Overall, the consequence is to provide clearer and perhaps more ample assurances to regulators that non-protectionist domestic regulations for important policy purposes will not be significantly constrained by WTO law. This should enhance what Joseph Weiler calls the "external legitimacy" of the WTO.[115] The AB has moved in this direction however in a manner also sensitive to what Weiler terms "internal legitimacy". It has framed its interpretations within the evolving GATT/WTO *acquis*, and has avoided bold colours and strokes, as opposed to subtler tones and finishes. In so doing it has managed to paint a quite different

---

[115] Weiler, *supra* n. 67.

picture from that characteristic of the panels in these matters, while acting with judicial caution. Perhaps, this was in part achievable because the facts of *Asbestos* raised few issues of high normative controversy—it was not a case that suggested or evoked a cultural or intellectual divide about the meaning of health or of science, or for example the appropriate limits of individual member state action to protect the environmental commons, or the balance between human rights as defined in the UN Covenants and trading rights as defined in the WTO. The AB wisely left it to others to speculate about the implications of its interpretive moves in *Asbestos* for such harder cases, giving itself ample room to craft a balance between internal and external legitimacy appropriate to the facts of those cases. At the same time, the overall direction in which it is moving is visible to all who have sharp (and unblinkered) eyes.

Index